T0257670

IET COMPUTING SERIES 30

Personal Knowledge Graphs (PKGs)

Other volumes in this series:

Volume 1   **Knowledge Discovery and Data Mining** M.A. Bramer (Editor)
Volume 3   **Troubled IT Projects: Prevention and turnaround** J.M. Smith
Volume 4   **UML for Systems Engineering: Watching the wheels, 2nd Edition** J. Holt
Volume 5   **Intelligent Distributed Video Surveillance Systems** S.A. Velastin and
             P. Remagnino (Editors)
Volume 6   **Trusted Computing** C. Mitchell (Editor)
Volume 7   **SysML for Systems Engineering** J. Holt and S. Perry
Volume 8   **Modelling Enterprise Architectures** J. Holt and S. Perry
Volume 9   **Model-Based Requirements Engineering** J. Holt, S. Perry, and M. Bownsword
Volume 13   **Trusted Platform Modules: Why, when and how to use them** A. Segall
Volume 14   **Foundations for Model-Based Systems Engineering: From Patterns to Models**
             J. Holt, S. Perry, and M. Bownsword
Volume 15   **Big Data and Software Defined Networks** J. Taheri (Editor)
Volume 18   **Modeling and Simulation of Complex Communication** M.A. Niazi (Editor)
Volume 20   **SysML for Systems Engineering: A model-based approach, 3rd Edition**
             J. Holt and S. Perry
Volume 22   **Virtual Reality and Light Field Immersive Video Technologies for Real-World
             Applications** G. Lafruit and M. Tehrani
Volume 23   **Data as Infrastructure for Smart Cities** L. Suzuki and A. Finkelstein
Volume 24   **Ultrascale Computing Systems** J. Carretero, E. Jeannot, and A. Zomaya
Volume 25   **Big Data-Enabled Internet of Things** M. Khan, S. Khan, and A. Zomaya (Editors)
Volume 26   **Handbook of Mathematical Models for Languages and Computation**
             A. Meduna, P. Horáček, and M. Tomko
Volume 29   **Blockchains for Network Security: Principles, technologies and applications**
             H. Huang, L. Wang, Y. Wu, and K.R. Choo (Editors)
Volume 30   **Trustworthy Autonomic Computing** T. Eza
Volume 32   **Network Classification for Traffic Management: Anomaly detection, feature
             selection, clustering and classification** Z. Tari, A. Fahad, A. Almalawi, and X. Yi
Volume 33   **Edge Computing: Models, technologies and applications** J.Taheri and S. Deng
             (Editors)
Volume 34   **AI for Emerging Verticals: Human-robot computing, sensing and networking**
             M.Z. Shakir and N. Ramzan (Editors)
Volume 35   **Big Data Recommender Systems Vol 1 & 2** O. Khalid, S.U. Khan, and A.Y. Zomaya
             (Editors)
Volume 37   **Handbook of Big Data Analytics Vol 1 & 2** V. Ravi and A.K. Cherukuri (Editors)
Volume 39   **ReRAM-Based Machine Learning** H. Y, L. Ni, and S.M.P. Dinakarrao
Volume 40   **E-Learning Methodologies: Fundamentals, technologies and applications**
             M. Goyal, R. Krishnamurthi, and D. Yadav (Editors)
Volume 44   **Streaming Analytics: Concepts, architectures, platforms, use cases and
             applications** P. Raj, C. Surianarayanan, K. Seerangan, and G. Ghinea (Editors)
Volume 44   **Streaming Analytics: Concepts, architectures, platforms, use cases and
             applications** P. Raj, A. Kumar, V. García Díaz, and N. Muthuraman (Editors)
Volume 54   **Intelligent Network Design Driven by Big Data Analytics, IoT, AI and
             Cloud Computing** S. Kumar, G. Mapp, and K. Cergiz (Editors)
Volume 56   **Earth Observation Data Analytics Using Machine and Deep Learning: Modern
             tools, applications and challenges** S. Garg, S. Jain, N. Dube, and
             N. Varghese (Editors)
Volume 57   **AIoT Technologies and Applications for Smart Environments.** M. Alazab,
             M. Gupta, and S. Ahmed (Editors)
Volume 60   **Intelligent Multimedia Technologies for Financial Risk Management: Trends,
             tools and applications** K. Sood, S. Grima, B. Rawal, B. Balusamy, E. Özen, and
             G.G.G. Gan (Editors)
Volume 115   **Ground Penetrating Radar: Improving sensing and imaging through
             numerical modelling** X.L. Travassos, M.F. Pantoja, and N. Ida

Personal Knowledge Graphs (PKGs)

Methodology, tools and applications

Edited by
Sanju Tiwari, François Scharffe, Fernando
Ortiz-Rodríguez and Manas Gaur

The Institution of Engineering and Technology

Published by The Institution of Engineering and Technology, London, United Kingdom

The Institution of Engineering and Technology is registered as a Charity in England & Wales (no. 211014) and Scotland (no. SC038698).

The Institution of Engineering and Technology
Futures Place
Kings Way, Stevenage
Herts, SG1 2UA, United Kingdom

www.theiet.org

British Library Cataloguing in Publication Data
A catalogue record for this product is available from the British Library

ISBN 978-1-83953-701-1 (hardback)
ISBN 978-1-83953-702-8 (PDF)

Typeset in India by MPS Limited
Printed in the UK by CPI Group (UK) Ltd, Eastbourne

Cover Image: aleksandarvelasevic/DigitalVision Vectors via Getty Images

Contents

About the editors   xiii
Foreword   xv

Section 1: Introduction and Overview   **1**

1   Personal knowledge graphs: an introduction   **3**
Sanju Tiwari, Manas Gaur, Fernando Ortiz-Rodriguez and Francois Scharfi

    1.1   Introduction   3
    1.2   Related work   6
    1.3   Knowledge representation in PKG   8
    1.4   PKG popularity   10
    1.5   PKG construction   11
    1.6   PKG tools and techniques   15
    1.7   PKG, how different from general KGs   16
    1.8   PKG use-cases   17
    1.9   Challenges and issues in PKGs   17
    1.10 Future scope   18
    1.11 Conclusion   18
    References   19

2   Applications of personal knowledge graphs   **23**
Carlos F. Enguix, Sanju Tiwari and Fernando Ortiz-Rodriguez

    2.1   Introduction   23
          2.1.1   PKGs introduction: definition/terminology/synonyms 23
          2.1.2   PKGs related/overlapping/convergent fields   24
          2.1.3   Definition: what is a KG?   24
          2.1.4   Definition: so, what is a PKG? What differentiates a
                  PKG w.r.t. KGs?   26
          2.1.5   PKG types according to underlying models/
                  implementation   26
          2.1.6   Contributions   27
    2.2   PKGs classification according to application type   27
          2.2.1   Generic: PKGs construction from local/remote resources 29
          2.2.2   Personal information managers (PIMs)   29
          2.2.3   E-learning systems   32
          2.2.4   Personal health knowledge graphs (PHKGs)   33

2.2.5	Personal digital assistants (PDAs)	35
2.2.6	Personalized/summarized KGs (*PKG$_2$*)	37
2.2.7	Decentralized web (DW)	40
2.2.8	Neuro-symbolic PKGs	43
2.2.9	Personal Research Knowledge Graphs (PRKGs)	45
2.3	PKGs – a common reference architecture for semantic web-based PKG	46
2.4	PKGs current status and future research	48
2.5	Conclusions	48
References		49

Section 2: Knowledge representation and reasoning   **53**

3 Knowledge representation and reasoning in personal knowledge graphs   **55**
Pierre-Antoine Champin and Rigo Wenning

3.1	The semantic web stack	56
	3.1.1 Representing knowledge	56
	3.1.2 Reasoning	61
	3.1.3 Querying	67
	3.1.4 Validating	68
3.2	PKGs based on RDF	70
	3.2.1 Semantic desktop	70
	3.2.2 From desktop to devices	71
	3.2.3 Re-decentralizing the web	72
3.3	Data sharing and compliance	73
	3.3.1 Policies	74
	3.3.2 Data annotations to connect policies	75
	3.3.3 Data sharing	76
3.4	Conclusion	77
References		77

4 From knowledge to reasoning, a cognitive perspective on personal knowledge graphs   **83**
Dav Raggett

4.1	Motivation	83
4.2	Introduction	83
4.3	Plausible knowledge	85
	4.3.1 The plausible knowledge notation	85
	4.3.2 Statement metadata	87
	4.3.3 Plausible inferences	88
4.4	Computing certainty	90
4.5	Relationship to fuzzy logic	91
4.6	Richer queries and fuzzy quantifiers	92

4.7   Reasoning by analogy   93
4.8   Inferences vs model construction   94
4.9   Metacognition   95
4.10 Non-deductive reasoning and imagined contexts   95
4.11 PKN in relation to RDF and LPG   95
4.12 Scaling and graphs of overlapping graphs   97
4.13 Cognitive architecture for artificial minds   98
      4.13.1 Systems 1 and 2   100
4.14 Modeling the cortico-basal ganglia circuit   100
4.15 Chunks and rules   101
      4.15.1 Chunk rules   101
4.16 Iteration over properties   103
      4.16.1 Operations on comma-separated lists   104
      4.16.2 Named contexts   104
      4.16.3 More complex queries   105
4.17 Natural language   105
      4.17.1 Large language models   105
      4.17.2 Natural language and common sense   106
      4.17.3 Metaphors in everyday language   107
4.18 Continuous learning   107
4.19 Hive minds, knowledge caching and swarm
      intelligence   108
4.20 Complementary role of artificial neural networks   108
4.21 Scalable knowledge engineering   110
4.22 Application to privacy-centered personal assistants   111
4.23 Summary   111
4.24 eBNF grammar for PKN   113
      Further Reading   114

Section 3: Data management and visualization   **115**

5   Named entity resolution in personal knowledge graphs   **117**
     Mayank Kejriwal

5.1   Introduction   117
5.2   Two-step framework for efficient named entity resolution   120
      5.2.1   Blocking step   121
      5.2.2   Similarity/matching step   125
5.3   Evaluating named entity resolution   128
      5.3.1   Evaluating blocking   128
      5.3.2   Evaluating similarity   130
5.4   Evolution of research in named entity resolution   131
5.5   Challenges and opportunities for named entity resolution   132
5.6   Conclusion   135
      References   136

6   Relation extraction techniques for personal knowledge graphs   **149**
Ana B. Rios-Alvarado and Jose L. Martinez-Rodriguez

6.1   Introduction   149
6.2   From knowledge graphs to personal knowledge graphs   151
   6.2.1   Diversity aspects in graphs   152
   6.2.2   A KG of personal nature   152
6.3   Relation extraction for knowledge graphs   153
   6.3.1   Overview of relation extraction techniques   154
   6.3.2   TBox common techniques   155
   6.3.3   ABox common techniques   155
6.4   Relation extraction for PKG   157
   6.4.1   Approaches used in PKG relation extraction   157
   6.4.2   Summary of approaches   158
   6.4.3   Aspects to be considered   160
6.5   Conclusions   162
References   163

7   Visualization tools for personal knowledge graphs   **167**
Allu Niya George and Enayat Rajabi

7.1   Introduction   167
7.2   Graphs   168
7.3   Knowledge graphs   169
   7.3.1   Importance of visualizing knowledge graphs   170
   7.3.2   Applications of knowledge graphs   171
7.4   PKGs   172
   7.4.1   Knowledge graph versus PKG   173
   7.4.2   Applications of PKGs   176
7.5   Importance of visualization   177
7.6   Visualization tools used in PKGs   177
   7.6.1   Obsidian   178
   7.6.2   RemNote   178
   7.6.3   Tiddlyroam   179
   7.6.4   Dendron   179
   7.6.5   Logseq   181
   7.6.6   Foam   182
   7.6.7   Roam Research   182
7.7   Conclusion   185
References   185

Section 4: Natural language processing   **189**

8   Query-answering with text and knowledge graph   **191**
Aravindarajan Subramanian, Sarra Ben Abbes and Rim Hantach

8.1   Introduction   191
8.2   State of the art   192

8.3 Methodology 194
    8.3.1 Approach 1: joint representation approach 195
    8.3.2 Approach 2: joint representation with relational graph
        convolutional network (RGCN) 198
    8.3.3 Approach 3: KG text enrichment 201
    8.3.4 Dataset 204
    8.3.5 Results 205
8.4 Conclusion 206
References 206

9 Extracting personal information from conversations **209**
Anna Tigunova

9.1 Introduction 209
9.2 Conversational datasets 211
    9.2.1 Transcribed dialogue datasets 211
    9.2.2 Social media datasets 213
9.3 Extracting personal attributes 213
    9.3.1 Demographic attributes from transcribed dialogues 213
    9.3.2 Social media profiling 215
    9.3.3 Hierarchical conversational models 216
    9.3.4 Long-tailed personal attribute prediction with CHARM 217
    9.3.5 Conclusion 221
9.4 Extracting interpersonal relationships 222
    9.4.1 Predicting interpersonal relationships 222
    9.4.2 Predicting relationship characteristics 223
    9.4.3 PRIDE: predicting directed, fine-grained interpersonal
        relationships 224
    9.4.4 Discussion 227
9.5 Conclusion 228
    9.5.1 Future research directions 229
References 230

10 Fact summarization for personalized knowledge graphs **239**
Danai Koutra, Davide Mottin and Jing Zhu

10.1 Knowledge graph summarization 240
10.2 Personalized knowledge graph summarization 242
    10.2.1 Personalized KG construction and applications 243
    10.2.2 Personalized graph summarization 247
10.3 Conclusion, future directions and opportunities 250
References 252

11 Personalized recommender systems based on knowledge graphs **255**
Ronald O. Ojino and Fatima N. AL-Aswadi

11.1 Introduction 255
11.2 Background information 256

11.3 Methods of constructing PKG recommendation systems   258
11.4 PKG challenges in recommendation systems   261
11.5 Application domains of PKGs recommendation systems   262
    11.5.1 Personalized commerce and financial
        recommendation systems   263
    11.5.2 PKG recommendation in the Internet of Things   264
    11.5.3 Personalized healthcare knowledge graphs   265
11.6 Sample PKG recommendation application   269
11.7 Conclusion   271
References   272

Section 5: Evaluation and other applications   275

12 Evaluation approaches of personal knowledge graphs   277
Hanieh Khorashadizadeh, Frederic Ieng, Morteza Ezzabady,
Soror Sahri, Sven Groppe and Farah Benamara

12.1 Introduction   277
12.2 Personal knowledge graphs   278
    12.2.1 PKG's creation   279
    12.2.2 PKG's population   280
    12.2.3 PKG's utilization   281
    12.2.4 PKG's challenges   284
12.3 Evaluation methods of KGs   285
12.4 PKG's evaluation approaches   288
    12.4.1 Retrospective evaluation   289
    12.4.2 Performance evaluation   290
    12.4.3 Ground truth evaluation   291
12.5 Conclusion   291
Acknowledgments   291
References   292

13 Personal health knowledge graph construction using Internet of Medical Things   295
Oshani Seneviratne and Manan Shukla

13.1 Introduction   295
    13.1.1 The challenge of data integration in IoMT health
        applications   295
    13.1.2 Personal health data integration   296
    13.1.3 Applications of integrated personal health data   297
13.2 Automated personal health knowledge graph construction   298
13.3 Extract transform load   299
    13.3.1 Extraction of data   300
    13.3.2 Transformation of data to knowledge graph   300
    13.3.3 Loading knowledge graph to patient-specific applications   301
13.4 Applications of IoMT-based personal health knowledge graphs 302

    13.4.1 Chronic disease care   302
    13.4.2 Acute illness treatment   302
    13.4.3 Disease screening   303
  13.5 Future directions   303
  13.6 Conclusion   304
  References   304

14 Integrating personal knowledge graphs into the enterprise   307
  Dan McCreary

  14.1 Introduction of PKGs   307
  14.2 The challenges of integrating PKGs into the enterprise   313
  14.3 Steps in building an integrating personal knowledge
      graphs into the enterprise   319
  14.4 Controlling access to IPKGs   322
  14.5 Conclusion   325

15 Conclusion   327

Index   331

About the editors

Sanju Tiwari (CEO and Founder of ShodhGuru Research Labs, India) is a professor at BVICAM, New Delhi, India and senior researcher at Universidad Autonoma de Tamaulipas. She is DAAD Post-Doc-Net AI Fellow for 2021 and visited different German Universities under the DAAD fellowship. She is a mentor of Google Summer of Code (GSoC 2022-23) at DBpedia and a member of InfAI, Leipzig University, Germany. She is also working as a curator of ORKG Grant Program, at TIB Hannover, Germany. Her current research interests include semantic web, knowledge graphs, linked data, and artificial intelligence. She has to-date published more than 50 research papers and 3 Scopus indexed Books. She is general chair (KGSWC 2020-23, EGETC2022-23, AMLDA 2022-23, AI4S-2023), and program chair, workshop chair, publicity chair, and steering committee and PC member in different renowned international conferences (The Web Conference 2023, SEMANTiCS 2019-23, ESWC2021-23, CIKM2020-22, AICCSA-2021, JOWO-2021, BiDEDE2022-23@ACM SIGMOD, VLIoT@VLDB2022, SIMBIG2022, and ICSC2023). She is working as a guest editor for SCI/Scopus journals (SWJ IoS Press, TEL Emerald, IJWIS Emerald). She is the speaker of IEEE/IETE N2Women and Women's Empowerment and NiWIIT (Nigerian Women In Information Technology).

François Scharffe is an associate professor at the University of Montpellier, France. He is a knowledge scientist with a track record of improving data management in organizations through innovative research. He is also the founder and program chair of the Knowledge Graph Conference. His research interests include knowledge graphs, ontology engineering, data integration, and AI. He holds a PhD degree in "Correspondence Patterns for Ontology Alignment" from the University of Innsbruck, Austria.

Fernando Ortiz-Rodríguez is a full professor and director of the Research Institute at Tamaulipas Autonomous University, Mexico. He is a full professor and the artificial intelligence and innovation lab director, and research advisor for INDEX Mexico. He was a higher education executive director at the International Institute of Studies (IIES); in 2011, he created the First Business School in Tamaulipas, Mexico, and increased academic quality and 30% tuition. Furthermore, he was the information technology manager at Emerson Electric, where he developed more than 40 software, some of them used globally in Emerson, and achieved technology convergence by implementing the first efforts on IoT and Industry 4.0 applied in manufacturing environments back in 2008. As a PhD student, he works at the Ontology Engineering Group at Technical University of Madrid (UPM).

He is a member of Level 1 of National Systems Researchers (SNI) of the National Council of Science and Technology (CONACYT), Mexico's entity promoting scientific and technological activities. He also is a member of Accredited Professor by the National Education Secretary in Mexico, and a member of the Association for Computing Machinery (ACM).

He has edited books for Elsevier, Springer, IGI Global, Taylor and Francis, IET, and IOS press; he has also published journal papers and participated in international conferences. He is the main chair of KGSWC, EGETC, AI4S, and FTSE, and PC and chair from different venues. He received 2021 and 2022 Latin-American awards (U-Gob) for implementing and developing software to help with COVID-19 diagnosis in Mexico.

Manas Gaur is an assistant professor in the Department of Computer Science and Electrical Engineering at the University of Maryland Baltimore County, USA. His research lies at the interface of AI and knowledge graphs to introduce the novel paradigm of knowledge-infused mining and learning (KiML). KiML has been proven to provide explainable and interpretable frameworks for conversational AI, domain adaptation, recommender systems, and rank problems. He is a member of WI-IAT and ISIC. He holds an MTech from Delhi Technical University, Delhi, India, on the topic of "Test Suit Prioritization and Optimization and Meta-Heuristic Algorithms."

Foreword

Knowledge graphs are a popular way of representing information using entities and their relationships. However, traditional knowledge graphs are based on domain-specific corpora and do not include personal information. To address this gap, Personal Knowledge Graphs (PKG) have emerged as a way to represent personal data on top of KGs like DBpedia and Yago. While these KGs are widely used, they lack personal information, which can be encoded in PKGs at an individual level, resulting in variations across users.

The construction of widely used KGs has been a manual process, requiring years of effort. In contrast, PKGs are constructed automatically by processing individual information, often using expert knowledge in clinical questionnaires or ontologies like FIBO. For example, while a KG for asthma may describe a blanket of causes, symptoms, and treatments, a PKG can contain only the relevant information applicable to a specific user or patient.

This book is devoted to giving a basic introduction to PKG and a wide range of applications that could use it. In order to apply natural language processing, the book will delve deeper into methodologies for knowledge representation, reasoning, data management, and PKG visualization. It will also look for new approaches to assessment. To advance PKG research, richer domains of study including the Internet of Things and PKG for Enterprise are offered.

The book is intended to serve as a valuable research guide for graduate students and researchers working in the field of personal knowledge graphs. It covers concepts, tools, and technologies that are relevant to practitioners who want to stay up-to-date with the latest developments in the field.

The book's theme is in line with the latest advancements in personal note-taking applications that can significantly benefit researchers in solving problems in user-specific domains. These advancements can help with entity and relation extraction on personal information.

When we began planning this book in 2021, there were limited research publications available in the field of personal knowledge graphs. Working with Manas Gaur, we decided on the book's theme and invited François Scharffe and Fernando Ortiz-Rodriguez to join us as co-editors.

One of the biggest challenges in editing a book is to identify authors who are genuinely interested in contributing a chapter on the relevant theme while keeping the highest quality standards. After careful consideration, we selected 14 chapters from all proposals, each exploring different major areas of personal knowledge graphs. These include topics such as Named Entity Resolution, Relation Extraction Techniques,

Evaluation and Visualization, Fact Summarization, Knowledge Representation and Reasoning, Personalized Recommender systems, and Query-Answering.

We are really grateful to all authors who have provided outstanding content while having the patience to revise their manuscripts based on the numerous comments made by the editors. We are also thankful to Prof. Amit Sheth for providing his support to accomplish the book project. The editors would finally thank Sanju Tiwari for leading the project, as well as Manas Gaur for his dedication in inviting outstanding authors to complete the book.

April 2023
Sanju Tiwari
Manas Gaur
Francois Scharffe
Fernando Ortiz-Rodriguez

Section 1

Introduction and overview

Chapter 1

Personal knowledge graphs: an introduction

*Sanju Tiwari[a], Manas Gaur[b], Fernando Ortiz-Rodriguez[a]
and Francois Scharfi[c]*

Artificial Intelligence (AI) is receiving significant attention in various domains, such as precision medicine, mental healthcare, manufacturing, education, finance, and many others. Most applications in these domains are concerned with the classification or language generation tasks, wherein confidence in the outcome is measured through traditional metrics and stakeholder agreement. When 91% of companies in these domains started a call for explainability in AI, it propelled the infusion of Knowledge Graphs (KGs) to make AI explainable. Further, the synthesis of AI and KGs added new capabilities in data-driven AI, such as (a) improved performance with minimal training data, (b) user-level explainability, (c) modeling rare events and handling uncertainty, (d) inducing context sensitivity in AI, and (e) better control over the behavior of AI system to ensure safety. Furthermore, with AI and KG together, personalization became possible. The induction of Personal Knowledge Graphs or Personalized Knowledge Graphs (PKGs) began to endure the capabilities of AI that could customize the outcome based on users' persona and enhance user engagement. Moreover, with PKGs, the community of AI could implement trustworthy systems safeguarding user security and ensuring consistency and robustness in outcomes. This chapter allows interdisciplinary researchers and practitioners in AI to contribute their research on methodologies, tools, and applications that discuss PKG's construction, utilization, and inference functionality.

1.1 Introduction

Personal Information Management Systems (PIMSs) were developed to promote user engagement in a variety of applications concerning artificial intelligence (AI), such as movie recommendation, music recommendation, information seeking conversation, summarization, and others [1]. PIMSs store personal information of the users by recording their web-search search activity, personal likes and

[a]Universidad Autonoma de Tamaulipas, Mexico
[b]University of Maryland, USA
[c]Université Montpellier, France

dislikes obtained by repeated interaction with the system, location-specific information, and demographic attributes. The stored information in PIMS could help the system to engage better with the user, be curious in providing asking relevant and good questions, supply apropos response, and satisfy the user's information needs [2].

There are noticeable challenges in PIMS which motivated the construction of PKG: (A) PIMS does not explore the relationship between the entities, thus personalization aspect fails to make an impact. (B) PIMS stores the personal information as distinct instances coming from the interaction of the user with the system. Thus to make it secure, the number of rules to be designed would be exponentially larger than the case when the instances were interlinked with named relationship. (C) It is difficult for the system with PIMS to contextualize an interaction with the user, thus fails to nudge, which information to access, use, and shared.[1] There was no doubt that PIMS can act as personal knowledge base (PKB), but the interlinking of the data instance would yield superior power both in terms of information retrieval and use, and security.

In 2018, Gyrard *et al.* proposed a PKG to organize the patient's personal knowledge and contextualize this knowledge with sensors and web of data. Personalization in healthcare has various benefits, such as (a) patient and clinician matchmaking for good quality care [3], (b) gender-intentional care to improve women health, (c) augmented personalized healthcare which allows patients to self-manage, self-monitor, and provide self-appraisal along with passive monitoring from clinicians, and (d) predict and prevent a rare event involving patient's intention to self-detox, which might lead to severe to chronic healthcare conditions. Sheth *et al.* and Gyrard *et al.* [4] emphasize on the implementation of PKG using the data from multiple contexts: Internet of Things (IoT) Devices, Electronic Medical Records (EMRs), and clinical notes. Montoyo *et al.* proposed a framework for the data integration of a user from heterogeneous sources into a common knowledge base [5]. Yen *et al.* draws attention to other characteristics of PKG which results in new capabilities for AI models: explainability, interpretability, and transferability. Balog and Kenter presented PKG as a unified form of PKB to structure user-centric information [6,7].

PKG differs from general-purpose knowledge graphs (KG) in terms of structure. Balog and Kenter illustrate two key aspects of PKG that separates them from general KGs; The entities in PKG are modeled based on user's personal interest and contains a distinctive shape where user is in the center. Balog and Kenter [6] defined PKG as:

Definition

"A PKG to be a source of structured knowledge about entities and the relation between them, where the entities and the relations between them are of personal, rather than general, importance."

---

[1] https://policyreview.info/glossary/personal-information-management-systems

Ruben Verborgh [8,9] also described PKG in his own words:

Definition

"A PKG is all data that you yourself create combined with all data that others create about you. A PKG can contain any data you create or need online."

An essential utility of PKG can be seen in education, wherein to improve the learning outcomes of a student, their performances need to be compared with other students and the students should receive topic recommendations where they can improve. Embibe, an education platform in India, leverages education KG and develops PKG by introducing an additional node called "competencies"[2]. PKGs can either be constructed from scratch for a specific use case or stacked over general-purpose KGs like DBPedia, Yago, and ConceptNet. There is a need for significant personalization in general-purpose and domain-specific KGs to represent personalized characteristics and connect on the web with Linked Data and KGs [10].

PKG is a valuable resource in the current era of intelligent information systems like Chatbots. Digital personal assistant or chatbots are meant to expand their functionalities beyond responding to questions like "What is the weather outside?" with an answer obtained from "weather.com". A personalized response to this question should utilize personal information of the user gathered by chatbot from previous interactions, identify cues corroborating signs of bad health of the users, and customize the response. An example of personalized response would be, *"Since you just recovered from* **cough and cold***, I suggest taking* **a warm jacket** *as it would be* **cold** *by* **the time you comeback home***"*; the bold-faced phrases in the sentence are created from personalized cues identified by the chatbot. It is important to note that the connection between **cough and cold** and **warm jacket** is a personal concept that is either provided by the user or inferred from large-scale KGs. PKGs support basic functionalities of natural language processing, such as entity linking, NIL-detection, along with PKG population using new information from the user, making it a dynamic structure for engaging and proactive communication between machines and human [11].

Personalized Health Knowledge Graph (PHKG) is a realization of PKG in the health context which is described to be a multi-context KG comprising information from patient healthcare records and physiological sensor (e.g. peak flow meter, Wrist actigraph) data obtained from patient's personal recordings. Ammar *et al.* describe the construction and utility of PHKG through the use of personal health libraries (PHL), which are the source of patient's personal information that are utilized by clinicians to make well-informed decision by taking into account recent events that happened in patient's lives [12]. Such digitized personal profiles can be used by current intelligent information systems to allow self-monitoring, self-appraisal, self-management, and intervention [13].

---

[2]https://www.embibe.com/ai-in-education/articles

With recent advances in AI and personalized information delivery, PKG would be seeing a widespread utility in various domains of social impact. Simultaneously, there would be challenges concerning PKG construction, utilization, and inference, which our deep literature would present. Broadly, this chapter has introduced the basics of personal knowledge graph and presented as a base of all chapters of the proposed book. This book has proposed 14 chapters in 5 sections, to cover multiple aspects of personal knowledge graphs such as *Named Entity Resolution in Personal Knowledge Graphs*: to identify the entities that are referring to the same entity; *Relation Extraction Techniques for Personal Knowledge Graphs*: this chapter explores the relation extraction techniques applied in the construction of PKGs; *Evaluation Approaches of Personal Knowledge Graphs*: this chapter explores the evaluation approaches of PKGs; *Visualization Tools for Personal Knowledge Graphs*: this chapter highlighted the tools for visualization of PKGs; *Applications of Personal Knowledge Graphs*: PKGs are helping to organize user-specific entities and several applications are highlighted in this chapter; *Personal Knowledge Graph Integration Tools and Techniques*: covers the topic of integrating PKGs into a large enterprise; *Fact Summarization for Personal Knowledge Graphs*: fact summarization is playing a significant role in PKGs constructions and this chapter explores about the fact summarization role in PKGs; *From Knowledge to Reasoning, a Cognitive Perspective on Personal Knowledge Graphs*: this chapter will highlight the cognitive perspective of PKGs; *Extracting Personal Facts from Conversations*: extraction of facts is an essential part to construct PKGs; *Knowledge Representation and Reasoning (KRR) in Personal Knowledge Graphs*: this chapter described different projects relying on the standards to build PKGs; *Personalized Recommender Systems based on Knowledge Graphs*: this chapter explores about the personalized recommendation systems to generate the recommendations; *Query Answering in User Specific Knowledge Graphs*: this chapter focused on to combine text and KG for open domain Query Answering; *Automated Personal Health Knowledge Graph Construction Using Internet of Medical Things*: this chapter has explored the technical details of collecting data from wearable devices, creating personal health knowledge graphs, and utilizing them in various health applications.

Rest of the chapter is organized as follows: Section 1.2 highlights the related work, Section 1.3 discusses about the knowledge representation in PKGs, the popularity of PKGs is discussed in Section 1.4 and Section 1.5 discusses about PKG construction. Section 1.6 discusses about the tools and techniques of PKGs and Section 1.7 shows how PKG is different from general KGs and finally concluded the section with use-cases, challenges and future scope.

1.2   Related work

After gaining popularity of Virtual Personal Assistant (VPA) and Digital Personal Assistants systems such as Apple Siri, PKGs are getting more attention to represent the personal data in healthcare domains and other domain-specific areas such as online education, e-learning platforms and many more. This section has presented a

Figure 1.1   PKG comparison

descriptive literature on existing studies of PKGs. A comparison[3] has been conducted by using the ORKG platform with the discussion of PKG existing papers as in Figure 1.1.

Balog and Kenter [6] presented the theory of PKGs as a source of structured information about the personal entities related to the user. They explored the key elements that differ from general knowledge graphs, and also discovered the major issues in developing and using the PKGs by describing a research agenda.

Safavi *et al.* [10] have proposed a new approach of PKG summarization. The primary aim of this approach is to create knowledge graphs and personal summaries in which the facts are closely related to personal interests. These summaries can be saved and available on devices to allow individuals personal information that is closely related with them. They have created summaries as a sparse graph and proposed a summarization framework called GLIMPSE to provide a theoretical background on the summaries utility.

Eleni Ilkou summary's utility [14] has designed PKGs in the educational domain to represent users and learners in e-learning platforms. This novel PKG was based on ontology and linked it with Linked Open Data. The proposed work has focused on two use cases such as collaborative search learning and an e-learning platform. As a result a user-centric data and personalized recommendations have been presented to analyze the e-learning platforms.

Einar [15] has proposed a thesis on PKG to organize personal data from distinct sources. It is presented as a knowledge base to organize different entities such as event, person, locations, and companies interconnected with a user-centric semantic graph structure. Several techniques Knowledge/Information Extraction, Knowledge Representation, and Information Management have been explored to construct the proposed PKG. A framework has been proposed to aggregate the user-centric information and also discover the usage of ontologies to model the personal data.

---

[3] https://orkg.org/comparison/R211826/

Yen *et al.* [7] have proposed an individual's personal knowledge base from text-based Lifelogs. The primary aim of this work is to extract life events from textual data of Twitter and design an individual's personal knowledge base. They have followed a combined learning approach to identify life events in tweets and further transformed to knowledge base facts by extracting the event elements along with subject, object, predicates, and time facts. The lifelogs are collected from 18 twitter users to perform the evaluation and the effective results are shown in life event extraction.

Gentile *et al.* [16] have proposed a PKG specific to the pharmaceutical domain. In health care, information is managed in pdf files, the proposed work mainly focused on building and maintaining the knowledge extracted from pharmaceutical drugs. Users are allowed to continue the knowledge curation task by manually analyzing and reading documents along with semantic enrichment.

Gyrard *et al.* [4] have designed a Personalized Healthcare Knowledge Graph (PHKG) to organize the patient's personal knowledge and contextualize this knowledge with sensors and a web of data. The knowledge has been extracted from different sources with the help of IoT devices, EMRs, and clinical notes.

Sheth *et al.* [13] have proposed augmented personalized health for patients and clinician to make better decisions and take action regularly for augmented personalized health. They have focused on key elements of AI approaches to make augmented personalized health. Augmented Personalized Healthcare aims to strengthen healthcare by personalizing the usage of all significant data collected from sensors, wearables, mobile apps and other IoT devices, social media, and Electronic Medical Records (EMRs).

Montoya *et al.* [5] have proposed a framework for the data integration of a user from heterogeneous sources into a common knowledge base. This framework will help users to deduce their personal information within and across various aspects. The proposed system models data by using RDF and schema.org along with the SPARQL interface.

Schroder *et al.* [17] have proposed an approach to create a PKG with the help of a classification schema. Machine learning models are used to predict statements for non-taxonomic relations and ontology populations.

Yang *et al.* [18] have proposed a model to construct a PKG and generate accurate and reasonable recommendations for users by applying "neural + symbolic" method across multiple services. This model encompasses mainly three parts to acquire the information for constructing PKG and generating recommendations. The proposed model includes three major modules: user information processing, PKG construction, and recommendation module.

1.3   Knowledge representation in PKG

Generally, knowledge graphs empower the representation of entities and their relationships. A user-centric or personal knowledge graph represents the information of a user's parent, children, siblings, etc. along with their additional information such as their birthdays, hobbies, health, school and other personal preferences (languages, education, user address, etc.). According to the literature, it is observed that there are no more specific ontologies to deal with personal information. Some related ontologies can help to represent the knowledge in personal knowledge graphs construction to avoid the repetition of existing related entities. Einar M. Langholm [15] has already discussed some ontologies that can be used for knowledge representation in PKGs. This section has discussed several other ontologies that are significant to represent the knowledge for PKGs in Figure 1.2.

Einar M. Langholm [15] has proposed PKG ontology by formulating competency questions to determine the domain, scope, and requirements of our ontology. The competency questions are categorized into three types: selection, counting, and binary queries. Selection queries represent a subset of entities from the graph, counting queries counts the entities that are returned by selection queries, and binary queries return true or false based on returned results.

A PersonLink ontology has been designed by Herradi *et al.* [19] to define rigorously and precisely family relationships such as child/parents, uncle, and grandparents. This ontology represents interpersonal relationships in a precised way with a generic definition. PersonLink ontology represents and describes the concepts based on the considered culture, and defines them by using an appropriate language.

FOAF ontology [20] is most widely used to define the relationship entities such as agent, person, and object. The major focus of this ontology is to describe personal information and relationships of personal interest for a social network rather than user-centric and it is limited to constructing the PKG.

OntoLife [21] ontology had been designed to describe the biographical events of a person along with personal information. The proposed ontology aims to describe the person's relationships, characteristics, and experiences. Person entity has been considered the backbone of OntoLife ontology. The whole ontology is centered around a person with different properties that relate the person to other entities.

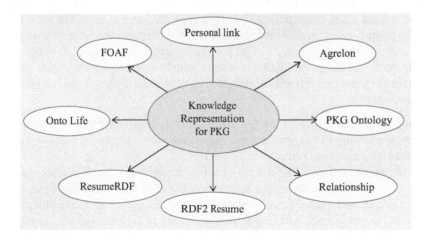

Figure 1.2   Knowledge representation for PKG

Davis and Vitiello have extended the FOAF to create the relationship ontology [22] by including various sub-properties to the property "FOAF: knows" that provide some entities to represent childhood, parenthood, and siblinghood and a very common property "SpouseOf".

ResumeRDF ontology was designed by Bojars and Breslin [23] to describe the information accommodated within a CV or personal resume on the Semantic Web. This ontology allows describing skills, education details, professional work experience, courses, certification attended, and other significant information. There are two namespaces that have been used to express the information:

- http://rdfs.org/resume-rdf/cv.rdfs: Resume ontology
- http://rdfs.org/resume-rdf/base.rdfs: Property value taxonomy

Résumé2RDF has been proposed as an updated and enhanced version of Résumé2RDF by [24]. This ontology is available in five languages: German, English, French, Italian and Albanian. The Résumé2RDF ontology described the structures of classes and relations of a common résumé document by using Web Ontology Language and Resource Description Framework Schema.

Agrelon [25], the agent relationships ontology, describes relations of persons to other organizations and persons. This ontology has modeled different entities such as correspondence, kinship, group affiliation, spiritual contact, occupational contact, and vital contact. AgRelOn encourages uniform cataloging along with semantic search ability of relations among persons and organizations.

1.4   PKG popularity

Dan Mccreary[26] has published a blog to discuss the evolution of PKGs and its popularity in the graph community. Figure 1.3 is proposed to show the phases involved in the evolution of PKG construction. PKG has presented as a class of software for taking notes in the form of non-linear knowledge graphs. Recently PKGs are attracting the graph community and gaining a huge popularity among researchers, developers, authors, students and bloggers. PKG community widely repeated the term "A second brain." There are a few major points highlighted by [26] about the popularity of PKGs in graph community:

Organizing thoughts speedily: PKGs are helpful in organizing the information received by streaming and figure out the important information and making new connection among existing themes.

Reduces the cognitive load: PKGs help to reduce stress during back-to-back work schedules. Our brain can be fixed to a limited number of things, things can be lost if they are not documented timely. Sometimes it is difficult to write down the thoughts during the meetings but PKG can help to take notes during the meetings and connect the notes to the existing knowledge bases. PKG appears as an option to hold the new concept along with their relationship in non-linear graphs.

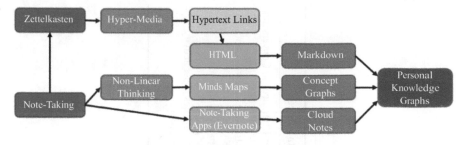

Figure 1.3   PKG evolution [26]

Promoting non-linear thinking: It is always noticed that PKG encourages non-linear thinking.

Long-term persistence: The storage of knowledge has dynamic nature, it is always changed in every few months. When organization changes the tool to store the knowledge, there is a possibility to lose the knowledge. But it is expected to persist for a long time.

1.5   PKG construction

There are several construction approaches that are proposed by different researchers. PKG construction is a promising task to model the graph from different sources. This section will explore all existing work to construct a PKG. Table 1.1 shows the specific studies where PKG construction has been conducted.

Li *et al.* [27] have presented a PKG population with an example as in Figure 1.4. It has been shown that the user-centric knowledge graph explores personal information and relates them with other facts. They represented a five-step framework to construct PKGs from user speech:

User Speech → Personal Assertion Classification → Relation Detection → Slot Filling → Knowledge Graph Population

Three major components are taken into account: Personal Assertion Identification, Relation Detection, and Slot Filling. Personal Assertion Identification concentrates to classify the binary classes from spoken utterances of stated personal facts. Support Vector Machines (SVM) [28] are considered as a solution for binary classification. Personal Assertion Identification phase provides the coarse-grained information to extract the fine-grained personal factual relations from next phases. Relation detection phase identifies the relations in the user utterances to populate the knowledge graph. One utterance can invoke several relations and detecting the relationship is important to construct the backend queries. SVM light package has been applied to classify the utterances in one or more relation classes and created a kSVM model where k depicts the count of relation classes. After relation detection, it is

Table 1.1 PKG Construction Approaches

Ref	Objective	Methods	Data sources
Li et al. [27]	PKG population	Personal Assertion Classification, Relation Detection, Slot Filling	User Utterances in Conversation
Schroder et al. [17]	PKG Construction	Term Extraction, Ontology Population, Relation extraction	Folder structures
Yang et al. [18]	PKG Construction	Pre-processing of data, Information extraction, ontology and KG creation	Unstructured Personal Sources
Langholm [15]	PKG Construction	Information Extraction, Entity Linking, Data Enrichment	Disparate Data Sources
Safavi et al. [10]	PKG Summarization	Sparse Graph	User preferences
Ilkou [14]	PKG Construction	Named Entity Recognition, Natural Language Processing	User Profiles, User activity, User group
Gentile et al. [16]	PKG Construction	Entity and Relation Extraction, Textual Annotation, PDF parsing	

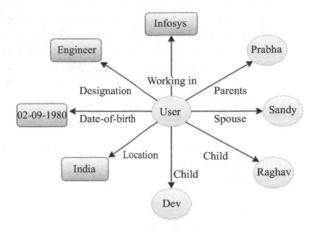

Figure 1.4   PKG example [27]

Table 1.2   An example of utterance, relation and slot

Utterance	Relation	Slot
I am an editor of PKG Book	Editor	Book:PKG

required to extract the specific entities in the next phase of Slot Filling. In this phase, semantic frames are instantiated to consist of different typed components termed as "slots" and represented as a flat list of attribute-value pairs. After detecting relation classes and specific entities, a personal knowledge graph finally created with new extracted user-centered information from personal facts. Table 1.2 has presented an example of utterance, relation and slot.

A recent personal knowledge graph construction approach has been presented by Schröder *et al.* [17]. It is very challenging to extract information from files due to the noisy non-grammatical text snippets nature of files. Schröder and team have proposed a semi-automatic approach to construct PKGs from files. This approach has four significant steps:

domain term extraction → ontology population → taxonomic and non-taxonomic relation learning

In the first step, a heuristic approach has been used to extract the relevant terms and tokenize the basenames from the filenames. After extracting the terms, it is required to organize the named individuals by populating the ontology as a second step. In the case of common individuals with the same context, a unification approach has been applied to unify them into one source. Taxonomy creation is the third step to structure concepts. In this stage, PKG concepts are mapped by the concept labels to the synset of the lexical-semantic net. On the other hand, link prediction has been performed by training a model on positive examples for predicting the non-taxonomic relations. It is assumed that the common non-taxonomic predicate could be recommended between different resources that have a common neighborhood in the classification schema. The proposed approach has been evaluated by implementing a prototype.

A PKG [18] has been constructed to generate the recommendation and categorized in different phases as given in Figure 1.5. The proposed approach has accomplished in three modules:

Modules
– User information processing module
– PKG construction module
– Recommendation module

Data pre-processing task and user intention detection have been done in the user information processing module. Pre-processing is the first step to acquire knowledge for construction of PKG. After preliminary pre-processing of data, they have constructed a PKG ontology O=(C, R) to model the user daily routine data such as intentions, users, events and time. Here, C is represented as a set of classes and R represents the relationship between the classes. This ontology has three layers: granularity layer as the top layer, intention layer as the middle layer and central users as the lower layer. Intention layer is considered as a core class of ontology for organizing and analyzing user information.

After ontology construction, it needs to model the common knowledge of users. The data can be acquired from different websites to construct the common knowledge

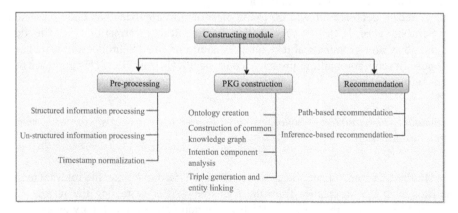

Figure 1.5   PKG construction modules [18]

graph. The acquired data need to clean, fuse and reorganize for constructing the common knowledge graph. The second module is responsible to deeply analyze the user intention such as user emotions, interests, arguments, events, entities and the relationships among them are acquired and extracted in the form of personal knowledge graph.

The last module enhances the personal knowledge graph and the acquiring information to generate a reasonable recommendation. The user information can be extracted from structured or unstructured sources. Structured information is primarily encompasses the adding/deleting/clicking operations in the calendars, contact list, and other apps. It helps to acquire the intention classes, entities and their relationships. On the other side, the unstructured information primarily encompasses the natural language input in voice assistants, search engines, and social apps. They have used BERT [28] for pretraining of user input corpus and SnowBall [29] for relation extraction tasks. Figure 1.3 explains all the phases of PKG construction modules.

A PKG [15] has been constructed from user's resources for generating user data into a common source of personal information to examine the usability and viability of PKG. It is a very challenging task to extract structured knowledge from unstructured personal sources. Inadequacy of significant information and the scarcity of context were encountered as major challenges in information extraction. It is also difficult to interpret the pre-trained models. The proposed framework has aggregated the user's data and existing ontology to construct the PKG. A Digital Personal Assistant can easily leveraged the modeled knowledge in PKG.

1.6 PKG tools and techniques

The PKG assigns the user to describe the detailed relationships, personal views, and opinions about the entities of interest. It associates it with resources such as e-mails and documents. In the era of concept-linking and knowledge graphs, growth has been found in the personal note-taking industry. Several different tools are designed, such as mind-mapping tools, outlining tools, and cross-platform tools like Evernote [26]. These tools allowed users to write and retain notes on various devices (tablets, cell phones, etc.). Several tools are publicly available for Information/Knowledge Extraction, such as scikit–learn,[4] spaCy,[5] StanfordOpenIE,[6] and Natural Language Toolkit (NLTK).[7] Popular tools Protege [30] and WebVOWL [31] are available for ontology authoring and visualization. Langholm [15] has used framework & knowledge structure dataset to develop and evaluate PKG. The Information Extraction dataset is a collection of public datasets that are used to assess and test NLP techniques

---

[4] https://scikit-learn.org/stable/
[5] https://spacy.io/
[6] https://nlp.stanford.edu/software/openie.html
[7] https://www.nltk.org/

in information extraction. PKG tools such as Roam Research[8] and Obsidian[9] are relatively newly introduced as note-taking tools that are adding new features.

Entity linking and relation extractions are the major techniques for constructing PKGs. Entity linking is the task of diagnosing the entities from the text. It is generally categorized into three consecutive sub-tasks: mention detection, candidate selection, and disambiguation [15]. The relation extraction task helps to detect the semantic relationship among entities such as persons, locations, and organizations, referred to in the unstructured text. Relation extraction is generally lessened to a closed domain task by describing the set of relationships and properties to be extracted. Entity resolution (ER) diagnoses when two entities refer to the common underlying entity.

1.7   PKG, how different from general KGs

General KGs, such as DBPedia, Wikidata, and ConceptNet, contain information on different entities and their associated relationships in diverse contexts. For instance, in ConceptNet, {depression is_a hell, depression is_a type_of push, depression is_a type_of sadness} are related to mental health, whereas {depression is_a type_of angular position, depression is_a type_of concave shape, depression is_a type_of concave thing, depression is_a type_of land topographical feature} are related to geographical structure. Identifying such fine-grained context is noticeable in a user query; however, contextualizing the user query with general KG takes a lot of work. As a result, a user's digital trace or personalized data log is required. Converting the personalized data log to PKG using general KG results in contextualized outcomes from AI systems leveraging data augmentation strategies on PKGs and general KGs. Further, in edge computing, where AI systems are required to perform in resource-constrained settings, PKGs are easy to manage and operate compared to general KGs [32]. Moreover, constructing large-scale general-purpose KGs takes time and effort, hence very costly and nontrivial. For example, the cost of building the popular Freebase: KG is estimated at 6.75 billion US dollars [32]. PKGs have a far less complex structure; thus, extracting semantically relevant information is accessible. On the other hand, general KGs have intricate triple patterns for the same knowledge represented in PKG, thus making extracting the required information complex. On the comparison between PKG and domain-specific KG (DKG), there is a trade-off, wherein in some scenarios, DKG would be smaller than PKG (e.g., drug abuse ontology for substance use disorder would be substantially smaller than entities gathered from conversational social data between anonymous users on Reddit's r/Crippling Alcoholism, for instance) and in other scenarios, DKG will be larger than PKG [e.g., Unified Medical Language System (UMLS)]. Concerning the scenario of neural embedding where the utility of KG is best realized in recent AI literature as Knowledge Graph Embeddings, working for PKG yields richer representations compared with general KGs. For instance, while personalizing the response from a conversational agent conditioned upon a user query,

---

[8]https://roamresearch.com/
[9]https://obsidian.md/

PKG-based embedding would yield a much less hallucinated response than General KG Embeddings.[10]

1.8   PKG use-cases

Elleni Ilkou [14] has discussed two use cases: collaborative search and e-learning in PKGs. In collaborative search, PKGs offer semantically enriched features and personalized characteristic that helps applications that do an intelligent search. They have developed a use case "LearnWeb," as a collaborative semantically enhanced search use case for the e-learning platform "LearnWeb" [33]. It linked the input stream data with knowledge graphs to obtain semantic relations among the data and detect the most relevant entities of the collaboration. The proposed approach helps to identify more personalized group project requirements; hence, the inclusion of PKGs benefits promoting personalization, advanced SW features, and better collaboration in general.

In the e-learning use case, they have promoted the use of the knowledge base of the eDoer platform [34] as an open learning recommendation system prototype that links the labor market skills along with available educational resources (OERs). The proposed approach allows users to acquire personalized recommendations based on their accessibility and access, learning preferences and needs, and semantic-based solutions, such as significant to their subject learning content.

PHKG [35] is also presented as a use case for healthcare to represent cumulative multi-modal data that combines all essential personal data for health-related of a patient in the form of a structured graph. The primary concepts, *contextual, personal, and integrated with existing Knowledge Bases*, are used to express the Personal Health Knowledge Graph (PHKG). Mobile Personal Health Knowledge Graphs (mPHKG) [36] has been designed to resolve the issues of data-input problems in Electronic Health Records (EHRs) from the perspective of both clinicians and patients. A context-salient mPHKG supports the recording of health data, and significant context can be automatically connected to health data such as location, time, level of activity, and environmental factors (pollutants, air quality, and humidity).

1.9   Challenges and issues in PKGs

Elleni Ilkou [14] has discussed several challenges in deploying PKGs, such as knowledge acquisition, entity recognition, linking, maintenance and storage of PKGs, and linking with external PKGs. The computation time of searching the entities is also a challenge to tackle in PKGs. Furthermore, PKGs deal with personal user data from personal profiles and store the user activities to manage the collaboration and describe the richer features. Hence privacy is a significant concern in protecting and preventing the user's personal data from unauthorized access.

---

[10] https://mdsoar.org/handle/11603/26600

Balog and Kenter [6] also highlighted the issues and challenges in PKG regarding the evaluation, implementation, and utilization of PKGs. Generally, PKGs are benefited from large-scale and open knowledge graphs such as DBpedia, Wikidata, and Freebase, as these large-scale datasets are not available in the PKG domain. PKG implementation is also an open challenge to deal with the storage of PKG on the cloud, device, or both. It is difficult to predict the PKG interaction with external services during access control and the impact if the user is offline. Link prediction is also an issue in PKG as it requires a massive amount of data.

1.10 Future scope

Despite some of the challenges mentioned above associated with the construction and use of PKGs, PKGs are gaining popularity for being utilized as personal assistants (e.g., intelligent agents). Jang *et al.* developed a new information-seeking-type dataset called **FOCUS**[11] to train conversational agents to generate personalized responses using the persona of the user. Such a dataset can benefit from contextualized and dynamic PKG as the research discussed by Jang *et al.* uses all the persona [37]. Further, PKG can enable conversational agents to select or overlook personalization dynamically based on the user query and the document retrieved by the agent. Thus, allowing agents to be adaptive and engaging. Users do not require personalization in every query. Figure 1.6 presents a conversation scenario where the inclusion of a persona profile improves the quality of response. PKG can significantly impact the response to richer, safer (when needed), adaptive, and reflective (the agent tries to engage more), which is the need in future conversational systems.

Apart from target-oriented conversation, PKG can find better applications in enriching chit-chat conversations by improving state-of-the-art language models trained on Persona Chat, a single largest resource on personalized chit-chat dialogues [38]. Further, the authors of [39] present a demonstration of a chatbot that develops a PKG while in conversation with the user to facilitate reflective and engaging conversations. In addition, it also highlights the utility of PKG in adding constraints to induce safety in conversational systems. Thus, PKG has a crucial role in conversational AI, a tangible resource of advancement in AI and NLP [40].

1.11 Conclusion

The concept of PKGs has gained popularity in the field of representing structured information of entities that are personally related to a user. This chapter has explored the basics of PKGs, such as the evolution of PKGs, representing knowledge, the popularity of PKGs, and the construction of PKGs. Several studies on PKGs have been analyzed in this chapter to explore the methods and data sources for constructing PKGs. It involves some significant phases to build the PKGs; entity classification,

---

[11] https://github.com/pkchat-focus/FoCus

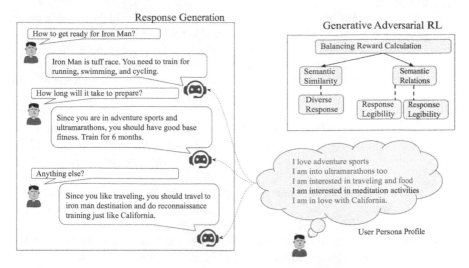

Figure 1.6   An illustration of personalized conversation between a conversational agent and a user. It is important to note the personalized behavior manifested by the agent by taking into account user personal profile. It does so through the use of a generative reinforcement learning approach. PKG can affect the quality of personalization in response by semantically linking the user's persona profile with concepts in PKG.

entity, recognition, entity resolution, slot filling, relation extraction, and link prediction. It is noticed that most of the studies are primarily focused on PKG construction, summarization, and population. PKGs are also presented in the context of conversational systems. The proposed chapter has also covered how PKGs differ from general knowledge graphs. PKGs are in the developing phase and have some issues and challenges to rectify as a future scope. This chapter also highlighted some problems and challenges to overcome in the future.

References

[1]   Bergman O, Boardman R, Gwizdka J, *et al.* Personal information management. In: *Chi'04 Extended Abstracts on Human Factors in Computing Systems*; 2004. p. 1598–1599.

[2]   Al Nasar MR, Mohd M, and Ali NM. Personal information management systems and interfaces: an overview. In: *2011 International Conference on Semantic Technology and Information Retrieval*. IEEE; 2011. p. 197–202.

[3]   Han Q, Ji M, de Troya IMdR, *et al.* A hybrid recommender system for patient-doctor matchmaking in primary care. In: *2018 IEEE 5th International Conference on Data Science and Advanced Analytics (DSAA)*. IEEE; 2018. p. 481–490.

[4]   Gyrard A, Gaur M, Shekarpour S, *et al*. Personalized health knowledge graph. In: *CEUR Workshop Proceedings*, vol. 2317. NIH Public Access; 2018.

[5]   Montoya D, Tanon TP, Abiteboul S, *et al*. A knowledge base for personal information management. In: LDOW@ WWW; 2018.

[6]   Balog K and Kenter T. Personal knowledge graphs: a research agenda. In: *Proceedings of the 2019 ACM SIGIR International Conference on Theory of Information Retrieval*; 2019. p. 217–220.

[7]   Yen AZ, Huang HH, and Chen HH. Personal knowledge base construction from text-based lifelogs. In: *Proceedings of the 42nd International ACM SIGIR Conference on Research and Development in Information Retrieval*; 2019. p. 185–194.

[8]   Verborgh R. What is a personal knowledge graph – with Ruben Verborgh – the graph show. YouTube; 2021. Available from: https://www.youtube.com/watch?v=2EP35HO2HVQ.

[9]   Verborgh R. Personal Knowledge Graphs on the Web. Available from: https://rubenverborgh.github.io/Knowledge-Graph-Conference-2020/#data-pod.

[10]   Safavi T, Belth C, Faber L, *et al*. Personalized knowledge graph summarization: from the cloud to your pocket. In: *2019 IEEE International Conference on Data Mining (ICDM)*. IEEE; 2019. p. 528–537.

[11]   Gao N, Dredze M, and Oard DW. Person entity linking in email with nil detection. *Journal of the Association for Information Science and Technology*. 2017;68(10):2412–2424.

[12]   Ammar N, Bailey JE, Davis RL, *et al*. Using a personal health library-enabled mHealth recommender system for self-management of diabetes among underserved populations: use case for knowledge graphs and linked data. *JMIR Formative Research*. 2021;5(3):e24738.

[13]   Sheth A, Jaimini U, Thirunarayan K, *et al*. Augmented personalized health: How smart data with IoTs and AI is about to change healthcare. In: *2017 IEEE 3rd International Forum on Research and Technologies for Society and Industry (RTSI)*. IEEE; 2017. p. 1–6.

[14]   Ilkou E. *Personal Knowledge Graphs: Use Cases in e-Learning Platforms*; 2022. arXiv preprint arXiv:220308507.

[15]   Langholm E. *Constructing a Personal Knowledge Graph from Disparate Data Sources*. uis; 2021.

[16]   Gentile AL, Gruhl D, Ristoski P, *et al*. Personalized knowledge graphs for the pharmaceutical domain. In: *International Semantic Web Conference*. Springer; 2019. p. 400–417.

[17]   Schröder M, Jilek C, and Dengel A. A human-in-the-loop approach for personal knowledge graph construction from file names. In: *Third International Workshop on Knowledge Graph Construction*; 2022.

[18]   Yang Y, Lin J, Zhang X, *et al*. PKG: a personal knowledge graph for recommendation. In: *Proceedings of the 45th International ACM SIGIR Conference on Research and Development in Information Retrieval*; 2022. p. 3334–3338.

[19]   Herradi N, Hamdi F, Métais E, *et al.* PersonLink: an ontology representing family relationships for the CAPTAIN MEMO memory prosthesis. In: *International Conference on Conceptual Modeling.* Springer; 2015. p. 3–13.

[20]   Brickley D and Miller L. FOAF Vocabulary Specification 0.97, Namespace Document (January 1, 2010); 2010.

[21]   Kargioti E, Kontopoulos E, and Bassiliades N. OntoLife: an ontology for semantically managing personal information. In: *IFIP International Conference on Artificial Intelligence Applications and Innovations.* Springer; 2009. p. 127–133.

[22]   Davis I. *RELATIONSHIP: A Vocabulary for Describing Relationships Between People.* http://vocab org/relationship/. 2004.

[23]   Bojārs U and Breslin JG. ResumeRDF: expressing skill information on the semantic web. In: *1st International Expert Finder Workshop*; 2007.

[24]   Elezi E. *A Seamless Platform to Generate Enriched Semantic Curriculum Vitæ.* Thesis. Universitas Bonn. https://dgraux. github. io/supervision …; 2020.

[25]   Litz B, Löhden A, Hannemann J, *et al.* AgRelOn—an agent relationship ontology. In: *Research Conference on Metadata and Semantic Research.* Springer; 2012. p. 202–213.

[26]   McCreary D. *Personal Knowledge Graphs*; 2022. Available from: https://towardsdatascience.com/personal-knowledge-graphs-9a23a0b099af.

[27]   Li X, Tur G, Hakkani-Tür D, *et al.* Personal knowledge graph population from user utterances in conversational understanding. In: *2014 IEEE Spoken Language Technology Workshop (SLT).* IEEE; 2014. p. 224–229.

[28]   Lee JDMCK and Toutanova K. *Pre-training of Deep Bidirectional Transformers for Language Understanding*; 2018. arXiv preprint arXiv:181004805.

[29]   Agichtein E and Gravano L. Snowball: extracting relations from large plain-text collections. In: *Proceedings of the Fifth ACM Conference on Digital Libraries*; 2000. p. 85–94.

[30]   Musen MA. The protégé project: a look back and a look forward. *AI Matters.* 2015;1(4):4–12.

[31]   Lohmann S, Link V, Marbach E, *et al.* WebVOWL: web-based visualization of ontologies. In: *International Conference on Knowledge Engineering and Knowledge Management.* Springer; 2014. p. 154–158.

[32]   Gunaratna K, Wang Y, and Jin H. *Entity Context Graph: Learning Entity Representations from Semi-Structured Textual Sources on the Web*; 2021. arXiv preprint arXiv:210315950.

[33]   https://learnweb.l3s.uni-hannover.de/lw/; 2021 last accessed on Dec 4, 2022.

[34]   https://labs.tib.eu/edoer/; 2021 last accessed on Dec 4, 2022.

[35]   Rastogi N and Zaki MJ. *Personal Health Knowledge Graphs for Patients*; 2020. arXiv preprint arXiv:200400071.

[36]   Patton E, Seneviratne O, Scioscia F, *et al.* Building mobile personal health knowledge graphs using Punya. In: *The Personal Health Knowledge Graph Workshop 2021*; 2021.

[37]   Jang Y, Lim J, Hur Y, *et al.* Call for customized conversation: customized conversation grounding persona and knowledge. In: *Proceedings of the AAAI Conference on Artificial Intelligence*, vol. 36; 2022. p. 10803–10812.

[38]   Zhang S, Dinan E, Urbanek J, *et al. Personalizing Dialogue Agents: I Have a Dog, Do You Have Pets Too?*; 2018. arXiv preprint arXiv:180107243.

[39]   Roy K, Sheth A, and Gaur M. *ALLEVIATE Chatbot*. UMBC Faculty Collection; 2023.

[40]   Gaur M. *Targeted Knowledge Infusion to Make Conversational AI Explainable and Safe*. UMBC Computer Science and Electrical Engineering Department Collection; 2023.

Chapter 2
Applications of personal knowledge graphs

Carlos F. Enguix^a, Sanju Tiwari^a and Fernando Ortiz-Rodriguez^a

A blog post at Google on 16 May 2012 with the title *"Introducing the Knowledge Graph: things, not strings"* represented one of the first references concerning the current definition of Knowledge Graphs. On the other hand, the article by Krisztian Balog *et al.* *"Personal Knowledge Graphs: A Research Agenda"* represented one of the very first references clearly defining the commonalities of Personal Knowledge Graphs (PKGs) such as presenting a *"Spider-Web"* graph layout having as the user its *"center of gravity."* To date, the literature related to PKGs is currently scarce given that it is still a virgin and promising research field. In this chapter, we present a survey including a classification of different types of applications of PKGs, spanning from E-learning Systems to Personal Information Managers (PIMs), to the Decentralized Web (e.g. the *"Social Linked Data"* (SOLID) stack), and so on. This classification identifies nine overlapping categories given that PKGs may belong to one or more categories. In each classification, we focus/highlight common and outstanding architectural components as reference architectures for each category type. We end-up the chapter by including and suggesting a reference architecture depicting desired main components for a semantic web (SW)-based PKG.

2.1 Introduction

2.1.1 PKGs introduction: definition/terminology/synonyms

The Google's Blog Post on 16 May 2012 presented with the title *"Introducing the Knowledge Graph: things, not strings"* [1] represented one of the first references with respect to the current definition of Knowledge Graphs (KGs). The article by Krisztian Balog *et al.* *"Personal Knowledge Graphs: A Research Agenda"* [2] represented one of the very first references with respect to the definition of Personal Knowledge Graphs (PKGs). So, What is a PKG? We shall define it later in Section 2.1.4. There are several synonyms referencing the same artifact such as Personal Knowledge Base (PKB), Personalized KG, Individualized KG, and Individualized Knowledge Base

^{a}Universidad Autonoma de Tamaulipas, Mexico

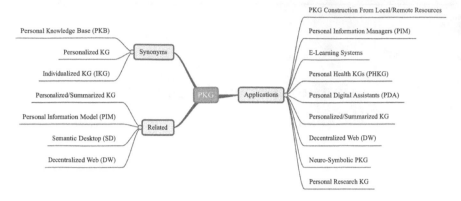

Figure 2.1   Conceptual/mind map of the chapter

(IKG/IKB). Figure 2.1 presents a mind-map depicting synonyms, related fields, and the nine categories of PKG applications identified in this chapter.

2.1.2   PKGs related/overlapping/convergent fields

PKGs are *"mini/down-sized KGs,"* but instead of modeling large general KGs they model user-centric information. Personalized/Summarized Global KGs are views from global/large KGs adapted/constrained to personal user information, we include these in our classification of PKGs according to application types (see Section 2.2 *Personal Knowledge Graphs Classification According to Application Type*). Personal Information Managers (PIMs)[1] consist of all kinds of tools dealing with personal information such as calendar applications, address books, bookmark managers, and e-mail applications. The Semantic Desktop (SD)[2] [3,4] can be considered as a semantic web (SW)-based PIM dealing with machine-readable RDF-based metadata based upon a multi-layered ontology and modularized middleware [5]. We consider the SD as a past reference architecture. Regarding the decentralized web initiative, we shall include as a reference for future research/possible convergence with the *"Social Linked Data"* initiative [6], a proposed tool ecosystem/stack for building decentralized social applications via Linked Data and World Three Consortium (W3C) standards.

2.1.3   Definition: what is a KG?

A KG is a graph-based resource storing structured information about entities, their respective attributes and relationships among entities. From a more formal knowledge representation language, namely descriptions logic (DL) perspective[3] the terminological box (TBox) describes the schema/ontology of the domain in question by defining

---

[1] https://www.wikiwand.com/en/Personal_information_manager
[2] https://www.wikiwand.com/en/Semantic_desktop
[3] https://www.wikiwand.com/en/Description_logic

classes and properties (the ontology part) of the KB/KG, whereas the assertional box (ABox) statements represent facts/instances associated with the TBox's conceptual model/ontology. ABox statements must be TBox compliant, they are assertions that use the vocabulary defined by the TBox. KGs are further sub-divided by Open Knowledge Graphs (OKGs) which are in public domain and publicly available and Enterprise Knowledge Graphs (EKGs) which are of private/closed domain. Representatives of each include, among others:

OKGs

- Common sense: OpenCyc[4]
- Wikimedia-based: DBpedia[5], Wikidata[6], Yago[7]
- General purpose: Freebase[8], ConceptNet[9]
- Scientific publications: the Open Research Knowledge Graph (ORKG)[10]
- World wide news: GDelt Project[11]

EKGs

- Search engine based: Google KG[12], Bing KG[13], Yahoo KG[14]
- Product catalogs: Amazon[15], eBay[16], Walmart[17]
- Social networks: Facebook[18], LinkedIn[19]
- Common sense: Cyc KB[20]
- General purpose: Diffbot[21], IBM Watson[22]
- Scientific publications: Microsoft Academic Knowledge Graph (MAKG)[23]

---

[4] https://github.com/asanchez75/opencyc
[5] https://www.dbpedia.org/resources/ontology/
[6] https://www.wikidata.org/wiki/Wikidata:Main_Page
[7] https://yago-knowledge.org/
[8] https://developers.google.com/freebase
[9] https://conceptnet.io/
[10] https://orkg.org/
[11] https://www.gdeltproject.org/
[12] https://developers.google.com/knowledge-graph
[13] https://blogs.bing.com/search-quality-insights/2017-07/bring-rich-knowledge-of-people-places-things-and-local-businesses-to-your-apps
[14] https://developer.yahoo.com/blogs/616566076523839488/
[15] https://www.aboutamazon.com/news/innovation-at-amazon/making-search-easier
[16] https://tech.ebayinc.com/research/explainable-reasoning-over-knowledge-graphs-for-recommendation/
[17] https://medium.com/walmartglobaltech/retail-graph-walmarts-product-knowledge-graph-6ef7357963bc
[18] https://developers.facebook.com/docs/graph-api/
[19] https://engineering.linkedin.com/blog/2016/10/building-the-linkedin-knowledge-graph
[20] https://www.gdeltproject.org/
[21] https://blog.diffbot.com/introducing-the-diffbot-knowledge-graph/
[22] https://www.ibm.com/topics/knowledge-graph
[23] https://makg.org/

2.1.4   Definition: so, what is a PKG? What differentiates a PKG w.r.t. KGs?

A PKG as compared to KGs differentiates mainly in the focus/perspective of data. KGs focus globally from a general perspective whereas PKGs normally mainly store information related to a particular user's focus/perspective having as the center of the PKG the user itself, and related entities (either directly or indirectly), which are not contemplated in global OKGs/EKGs. The general shape of PKGs is a *"spider web"* layout, as indicated previously, having the user itself as its center. PKGs are integrated with external data sources (local/remote resources). Other characteristics include according to the seminal paper *"Personal Knowledge Graphs: A Research Agenda"* by Balog, Krisztian *et al.* [2]:

PKG general characteristics according to [2]

- Every entity in a PKG is directly or indirectly related to the user
- PKGs may be sparse with respect to entity representation
- Relations may be ephemeral or "short lived"
- Artificial neural network (ANN)-based components may not fit in PKGs given the lack of data availability for the training phase, but typical AI-based machine learning (ML) architectures may do the job. Nevertheless, we include in this survey, a subsection devoted to the applicability of neuro-symbolic approaches w.r.t. PKG application categories (see Section 2.2.8 *Neuro-symbolic Personal Knowledge Graphs (PKG)*)
- Linking in PKGs should include mapping the PKG to external data sources such as external KGs (e.g. linking the user to the Wikidata OKG)
- Entities do not contain an exhaustive list of attributes but just necessary ones, given that PKGs store only the necessary information of user interest requiring possibly Human In The Loop (HITL) intervention

2.1.5   PKG types according to underlying models/implementation

From a modeling/implementation perspective, we identify RDF-based and labeled property graph-based (LPG-based) PKGs. SW RDF-based comprehend PKGs-based upon the SW stack and RDF-based models including resource description framework (RDF) [7], RDF schema (RDFS) [8], web ontology language (OWL) [9], simple knowledge organization system (SKOS) [10], Schema.org[24] [11], and so on. Our research mainly focuses on this type of PKGs, nevertheless we also include some examples of LPG-based PKGs. LPG-based PKGs comprehend non-SW-based property graph systems based upon graph databases such as Neo4j and the great majority of graph databases[25]. SW RDF-based PKGs represent classes, properties, attributes, and instances as RDF graph models via nodes and edges. An RDF graph statement in its simplest form is represented by a node for the subject, an edge for the predicate,

---

[24]https://schema.org/
[25]See list of graph databases at https://www.wikiwand.com/en/Graph_database

and a node for the object (subject–predicate–object) statements. On the other hand, a labeled property graph model is represented by a set of nodes, relationships, properties, and labels. Both nodes and relationships are named and can store properties represented by key/value pairs.

2.1.6 Contributions

The contributions of this chapter, *"Personal Knowledge Graphs Applications,"* are two-fold:

1. To the best of our knowledge, this is the first research paper classifying PKGs types according to application types. Nine overlapping major categories have been included in Table 2.1, spanning from the earliest research prototypes from 2016, to the current year 2023 state-of-the-art (SOTA) PKGs, making use of among others, of SOLID-based decentralized web (DW) architectures and some of them making use of SOTA neuro-symbolic approaches.
2. Despite the fact the scarce research literature presence related to PKG, we have included the great majority, not to mention a quasi-exhaustive list of 23 research papers, of the most representative/important research papers within each of the nine categories, covering conference/workshop papers, patents, master's and Ph.D.s, and SOTA arXiv.org submissions. We foresee that research submissions in the area of PKG become more abundant and somehow more popular, in a similar vein as OKGs and EKGs did.

2.2 PKGs classification according to application type

This classification identifies nine overlapping categories given that PKGs may belong to one or more categories (see Table 2.1 for a summary of the main bibliography included and the respective categories and PKG types, either SW-stack-based or labeled property graph-based (LPG-based)). We start this section with the most common PKG construction pattern *"Generic PKGs Constructed From Local/Remote Resources,"* which in turn may include for instance personal information managers (PIMs), neuro-symbolic PKGs, e-learning systems, and so on. Next we describe PKGs PIMs, followed by E-learning systems, personal health KGs (PHKGs), and the popular personal digital assistants (PDAs). Next we describe personalized/summarized KGs subsection, and mention that they represent user-defined/personalized global/domain-specific KGs views/excerpts and not always include within its architecture the implementation of a PKG. Then we include PKGs compliant with the SOLID-based decentralized web (DW) initiative[26] (see Section 2.2.7.1) and the latest PKG reference architecture making use of deep-learning/transformer-based techniques, namely neuro-symbolic PKGs. We conclude this section with personal research knowledge graphs (PRKGs) which are PKGs devoted/circumscribed to the storage, retrieval and interaction with personal research-related data/information and activities.

---

[26]https://solidproject.org/

Table 2.1   PKG applications categories/types bibliography summary

Reference	CAT	Type	Paper	Pub type	Pub year
[12]	**PKG/PIM**	SW	Constructing a Personal Knowledge Graph from Disparate Data Sources	Master thesis	2021
[13]	**PIM**	SW	Thymeflow, A Personal Knowledge Base with Spatio-Temporal Data	Conference Paper	2016
[14]	**PIM**	SW	A Personal knowledge base integrating user data and activity timeline	Ph.D. thesis	2017
[15]	**PIM**	SW	A knowledge base for personal information management	Workshop Paper	2018
[16]	**PIM**	SW	A Human-in-the-Loop Approach for Personal Knowledge Graph Construction from File Names	Workshop Paper	2022
[17]	**EL**	SW	Personal Knowledge Graphs: Use Cases In E-Learning Platforms	arXiv Preprint	2022
[18]	**PHKG**	SW	Applying personal knowledge graphs to health	arXiv Preprint	2021
[19]	**PHKG/PKG$_2$**	N.A.	Personalized Health Knowledge Graph	Workshop Paper	2018
[20]	**PHKG**	SW	Personal Health Knowledge Graph for Clinically Relevant Diet Recommendations	arXiv Preprint	2021
[21]	**PDA**	N.A.	In-message suggestion by personal Knowledge Graph Constructed From User Email Data	Patent	2017
[22]	**PDA**	N.A.	Personal knowledge graph population from declarative user utterances	Patent	2017
[23]	**PDA**	N.A.	Personal knowledge graph population from user utterances in conversational understanding	Workshop Paper	2014
[24]	**PDA/PKG$_2$**	N.A.	Remembering what you said – semantic personalized memory for personal digital assistants	Conference Paper	2017
[25]	**PKG$_2$**	N.A.	Personalized Knowledge Graph Summarization – From the Cloud to Your Pocket	Conference Paper	2019
[26]	**PKG$_2$/EL**	SW	Personalized Course Recommendation System Fusing with Knowledge Graph And Collaborative Filtering	Journal Paper	2021
[27]	**PKG$_2$**	SW	Personalized Food Recommendation as Constrained Question Answering Over a Large-scale Food Knowledge Graph	Conference Paper	2021
[28]	**PKG$_2$**	N.A.	Personalized Recommendations using Knowledge Graphs – A Probabilistic Logic Programming Approach	Conference Paper	2016
[29]	**PHKG/DW**	SW	Using a Personal Health Library–Enabled mHealth Recommender System for Self-Management of Diabetes Among Underserved Populations: Use Case for Knowledge Graphs and Linked Data	Journal Paper	2021
[30]	**NS**	LPG	PKG: A Personal Knowledge Graph for Recommendation	Conference Paper	2022
[31]	**NS**	N.A.	Building And Using Personal Knowledge Graph To Improve Suicidal Ideation Detection On Social Media	Journal Paper	2020
[32]	**NS/PKG**	N.A.	Personal Knowledge Base Construction From Text-based Lifelogs	Conference Paper	2019
[33]	**NS**	N.A.	Data Augmentation For Personal Knowledge Base Population	arXiv Preprint	2020
[34]	**PRKG/PDA/NS**	LPG/SW	Personal Research Knowledge Graphs	arXiv Preprint	2022

	LEGEND		
	DW	Decentralized Web
	EL	E-Learning System
	NS	Neuro-Symbolic PKG
	PDA	Personal Digital Assistant
	PHKG	Personal Health Knowledge Graph
	PIM	Personal Information Manager
	PKG	Generic Personal Knowledge Graph Constructed From Local/Remote Resources
	PKG$_2$	Personalized/Summarized Knowledge Graph
	PRKG	Personal Research Knowledge Graph
	SW	Semantic Web Stack-based PKG Type
	LPG	Labeled-Property-Graph-based PKG Type
	N.A.	Details of PKG Type Not Available

2.2.1 Generic: PKGs construction from local/remote resources

This is the most generic application type covering all PKGs constructed from local and remote resources. Almost a majority of the PKG covered in the book chapter may belong to this general category and another overlapping more precise categories. As a representative of this generic category we include the works of Langholm, Einar in his Master's *"Constructing a Personal Knowledge Graph from Disparate Data Sources"* [12] where he proposes first a general architecture of his PKG application and also proposes different sub-modules depending on the type of information being dealt with, namely structured, semi-structured, and unstructured data sources with the aid of a customized ontology integrating the Friend of a Friend vocabulary (FOAF)[27], a multilingual and multicultural ontology, PersonLink[28] representing family relationships, the Schema.org[29] vocabulary/ontology and, customized classes and properties. In his, he also mentions the use of Lutra[30], an open source reference implementation of the Reasonable Ontology Templates (OTTRs) language[31]. The OTTR is a language with supporting tools for representing and instantiating RDF graph and OWL ontology modeling patterns. It is designed to improve the efficiency and quality of building, using, and maintaining knowledge bases. The author also includes the Open-Source Apache Jena's Triplestore[32] and the Apache Jena Fuseki[33], SPARQL server with RDF-star[34], and SPARQL-star[35] capabilities.

2.2.2 Personal information managers (PIMs)

As a more specific PKG application category we include in this subsection personal information managers (PIMs) dealing with the management of personal information such as e-mails, calendars, location data, and personal files and folders. As representative systems of this specific category we include the works of the Thymeflow system [13] described below and the semi-automatic PKG construction presented by Markus Schroder *et al.* [16] also described below.

In [13–15] is presented Thymeflow, which presented in 2016 a novel personal knowledge base (PKB) and Ph.D. in the field of PKBs/PKGs. The main architecture of the Thymeflow system is depicted in Figure 2.2. It included spatiotemporal data by integrating location history data, contacts, calendars, and e-mail messages into a single PKB. All of these data sources are transformed into RDF and RDFS extending and making use of the schema.org[36] vocabulary enabling the possibility of submitting complex SPARQL queries. The architecture is based upon

---

[27] https://www.wikiwand.com/en/FOAF
[28] http://cedric.cnam. fr/isid/ontologies/files/PersonLink.html
[29] https://schema.org/
[30] https://ottr.xyz/#Lutra
[31] https://ottr.xyz/
[32] https://jena.apache.org/
[33] https://jena.apache. org/documentation/fuseki2/index.html
[34] https://w3c.github.io/rdf-star/cg- spec/editors_draft.html
[35] https://w3c.github.io/rdf-star/cg- spec/editors_draft.html#sparql-star
[36] https://schema.org/

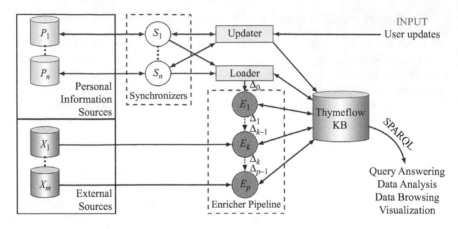

Figure 2.2   This figure depicts the architecture of the Thymeflow PKB system according to [13–15]. This figure is reproduced from the Ph.D. [14] with permission from the authors Montoya and David.

special software modules denominated as *"Loaders/Synchronizers"* and *"Enrichers."* *"Loaders/Synchronizers"* enable access to the aforementioned sources and *"Enrichers"* add/infer new statements in a pipeline manner from data previously loaded by the *"Loaders/Synchronizers"* modules and from external data sources. More specifically, *"Loaders/Synchronizers"* are activated when detecting new updated information, implementing *"Loaders/Synchronizers"* for several protocols namely, CardDav[37] information storing vCard[38] information, CalDav[39] storing iCalendar[40] information, IMAP-based e-mail messages, and location data represented by the Google location history data. On the other hand, *"Enrichers"* are activated when *"Loaders/Synchronizers"* insert/gather new information by taking into account the current state of the PKB, and a series of incremental deltas containing updated information for synchronization. The *"Enrichers"* modules comprehend entity resolution (e.g. personal:Agent), event location history, calendar events, and so on. *"Enrichers"* also use external KGs including Wikidata[41], Yago[42], and the OpenStreetMap[43]. Furthermore, Thymeflow uses named graphs[44] to store provenance data in the TriG RDF serialization format[45]. Last but not least, Thymeflow permits, once the PKB/PKG is populated, the submission of complex SPARQL queries against the PKB/PKG.

---

[37] https://www.wikiwand.com/en/CardDAV
[38] https://www.wikiwand.com/en/VCard
[39] https://www.wikiwand.com/en/CalDAV
[40] https://www.wikiwand.com/en/ICalendar
[41] https://www.wikidata.org/wiki/Wikidata:Main_Page
[42] https://yago-knowledge.org/
[43] OpenStreetMap is a collaborative project to create a free editable geographic database of the world.
[44] https://www.wikiwand.com/en/Named_graph
[45] https://www.wikiwand.com/en/TriG_(syntax)

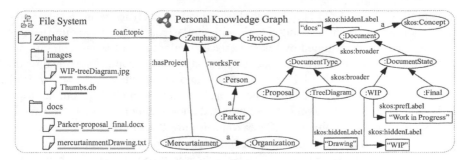

Figure 2.3   File system with folder/file names including both relevant/irrelevant words forming a PKG including SKOS-based taxonomic and non-taxonomic relations. This figure is reproduced from [16] with permission from authors, including Schroder, Markus, via a Creative Commons License Attribution 4.0 International (CC BY 4.0).

In the works of Markus Schroder *et al.* [16] is presented a semi-automatic/Human-in-the-Loop (HITL) PKG construction deployed in four phases, namely domain-term extraction, ontology population, and taxonomic and non-taxonomic relation learning. Their work is based on the hypo that folder/file names contain domain-specific knowledge (e.g. related to project and user and organization names) viable for creating associated PKGs. Folder/file names are related/linked to PKGs via taxonomic and non-taxonomic relations (see Figure 2.3). With the use of foaf:topic, it relates as an association of where the term is mentioned in a given folder/file, whereas named individuals are classified into certain classes and inter-related via properties. The authors also make use of the Simple Knowledge Organization System (SKOS)[46] to define taxonomy hierarchy constructs such as skos:broader, taxonomy class definition skos:Concept, preferable/alternative labels such as skos:prefLabel and skos:hiddenLabel, respectively.

The proof-of-concept prototype implementation makes use of a GUI-based AI/expert system that assists knowledge engineers (KEs) in the construction of taxonomic and non-taxonomic constructs, concept association in folder/file names, and ontology construction based upon classification schemas (CS). The knowledge graph model is RDF-based with subject–predicate–object triples and related provenance metadata such as the agent which generated the triple statement (e.g. KEs or AI-based), timestamp of the statement, and confidence ratio. The domain terminology extraction phase makes use of arbitrary heuristics and rules by tokenizing folder/file names and in some cases tokenized terms are concatenated forming multi-word concepts. Lastly, terms are related to OWL-named individuals stating entities as individuals. The output of this phase is inputted to the management of named individuals phase. If the named individual is new, which is determined by applying the Jaccard similarity coefficient[47], a new named individual is created, and both the SKOS preferred label

[46]https://www.w3.org/2004/02/skos/
[47]https://www.statisticshowto.com/jaccard-index/

(skos:prefLabel) and SKOS hidden label (skos:hiddenLabel) are defined. Next in the unification sub-phase named individuals with similar/equal meaning are unified into a single resource determined by token-based equivalence and Levenshtein distance coefficient[48]. Next, the last sub-phase in the management of named individuals is the ontology population where KEs define classes and name individual types by using a random forest model[49], gazetteer lists[50], and feature vectors[51]. Last but not least, the latest phases include taxonomy creation and non-taxonomic relation learning. In the taxonomy creation phase, SKOS taxonomies are defined on each skos:concept by indicating skos:broader taxonomy definition in a bottom-up approach, given that skos:concepts are considered as leaf nodes in the tree-taxonomy. This is obtained via the use of hypernym[52] and synset[53] relations. Finally, the latest phase consists of the non-taxonomic relation learning phase, by applying link prediction[54] according to the classification schema (CS).

2.2.3   E-learning systems

This subsection deals with PKG applications circumscribed to the definition and construction of E-learning systems. As a representative of this category, we include the system proposed in [17] depicted in Figure 2.4, proposing a PKG adapted for collaborative search and e-learning platforms relying on linked open data (LOD) and the definition of a domain-specific ontology. The author identifies the need for personalization in collaborative e-learning given that EKGs and open knowledge graphs (OKGs), in general terms, do not include personal user-related information. The author emphasizes the use of SW-related infrastructure in order to personalize e-learning platforms and provide explainability to end-user actions. Also, the author clearly remarks on the incremental need for personalized recommendations in the e-learning arena via the use of PKGs. The architecture proposed in this paper, depicted in Figure 2.4, is based on a three-layered architecture, namely the user input stream, the intelligence module, and the back-end module. The user input stream module includes user-related data such as user profile, user activity information, and user groups that the user belongs to. All this user-generated data is inputted into the intelligence module, where it is treated with the natural language processing (NLP) and name-entity recognition (NER) sub-modules, alongside the domain-specific ontology, identifying entities and concepts from external OKGs such as DBpedia. A *"black-box"* recommendation engine filters the most relevant KG entities, which are inputted to the PKG according to user-specific data privacy; here user activity data is linked to external

---

[48] https://www.wikiwand.com/en/Levenshtein_distance

[49] https://www.wikiwand.com/en/Random_forest

[50] https://stackoverflow.com/questions/34995139/nlp-is-gazetteer-a-cheat

[51] https://www.wikiwand.com/en/Feature_(machine_learning)

[52] A word with a broad meaning that more specific words fall under; a superordinate. For example, color is a hypernym of red.

[53] A set of one or more synonyms that are interchangeable in some context without changing the truth value of the proposition in which they are embedded.

[54] https://www.wikiwand.com/en/Link_prediction

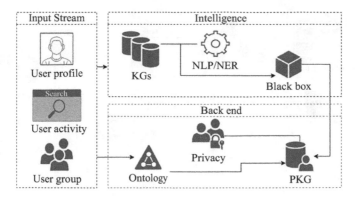

Figure 2.4   This figure depicts the proposed architecture in [17] of the collaborative-search and E-learning PKG system. This figure is reproduced with permission from [17].

KGs and Linked Open Data (LOD). Input stream data is linked to OKGs such as DBpedia, in order to populate the PKG. For the e-learning use case, it makes use of the eDoer personal learning tool[55], which is an open learning recommendation portal connecting educational resources with labor skills, permitting end-user personalized learning recommendations.

2.2.4   Personal health knowledge graphs (PHKGs)

In this subsection, we present three novel systems that represent important break-throughs in the field of Personal Health Knowledge, PKGs, and PHKGs proof-of-concept research prototypes.

In Shirai *et al.* [18], it is stated that knowledge systems in the health-care domain may benefit from the use of PHKGs integrating also health care related domain-specific knowledge graphs (KGs), allowing more complex reasoning engines. They cite what are the major obstacles and challenges in the compilation of PHKG, namely storage of personal health knowledge (PHK) respecting privacy issues, linking to external domain-specific knowledge graphs (KG), and the maintenance/synchronization of PHKGs to external healthcare-related KGs.

Also from the same research team, Seneviratne *et al.* [20] propose a personal health ontology (PHO) agglutinating personal medical-related information and permitting the compilation of a PHKG with personalized diet recommendations. The main architecture of the proposed system is depicted in Figure 2.5. Their PHKG is linked and annotated from a domain-specific KG such as the Food KG[56], enabling reasoning and the submission of personalized diet recommendations. Only the personal health ontology (PHO) and the time series summarization (TSS) component expressing temporal data and based upon synthetic food logs are described in detail. The TSS

---

[55]https://labs.tib.eu/edoer/
[56]https://foodkg.github.io/

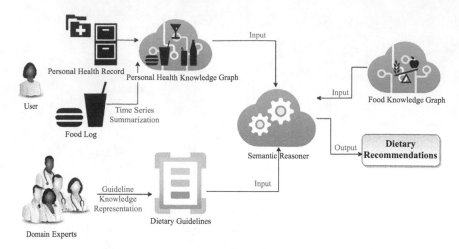

Figure 2.5   This figure depicts the architecture proposed in [20] of a PHKG. This figure is reproduced with permission from [20].

component allows the generation of RDF triples and enables the generation of personal diet recommendations for type 2 diabetes (T2D) patients. The semantic reasoner module allows the generation of personal diet recommendations, which can be queried and translated into SPARQL queries against a SPARQL endpoint. In order to generate personal diet recommendations, the author's workflow includes the built-in reasoner in Protege[57] and the OWLReady2[58] python library permitting transparent access to OWL ontologies, SPARQL queries, and the pFoodReq[59] deep learning-based framework.

The works of Gyrard *et al.* [19] include the creation of personalized health knowledge graphs (*PHKG₂*) (we include this acronym to differentiate from PHKGs) compiled from a series of diverse sources such as environmental sensors/Internet of Things (IoT) devices, and electronic medical records (EMR). This paper criticizes the non-existence of contextual information, the lack of personalization, and the lack of integration of medical knowledge bases (KBs). As a proof-of-concept, they propose the design of a *PHKG₂* (see Figure 2.6), via the use of medical data from the linked open data (LOD) cloud[60], the construction of a domain-specific ontology and the use of rules. The proposed architecture of the *PHKG₂*, integrates information from diverse heterogeneous sources such as IoT sensors, data access to the Kno.e.sis Alchemy API[61] enabling access to the Unified Medical Language System

---

[57] https://protege.stanford.edu/products.php
[58] https://owlready2.readthedocs.io/en/v0.37/
[59] https://github.com/hugochan/PFoodReq
[60] https://lod-cloud.net/
[61] https://www.ncbi.nlm.nih.gov/pmc/articles/PMC8532078/

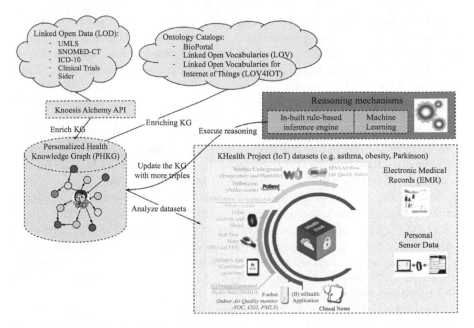

Figure 2.6   This figure depicts the architecture proposed in [19] of a PHKG$_2$. This figure is reproduced with permission from [19].

(UMLS)[62], the Systematized Nomenclature of Medicine Clinical Terms (SNOMED-CT)[63] and so on, and the integration of diverse ontology catalogs such as the Bioportal ontology[64], Linked Open Vocabulary (LOV)[65] and the Linked Open Vocabularies for Internet of Things (LOV4IoT-Health) ontology[66] catering IoT-related information. It also included the KHealth project[67] integrating data from medical records, IoT-related data such as personal health recordings, and making use of the Asthma, FOAF, W3C SOSA ontologies, and so on. The KHealth project also included a rule-based reasoning engine.

2.2.5   Personal digital assistants (PDAs)

Two original and outstanding US patents are presented in this subsection, in addition to a novel *PKG$_2$* research prototype construction. Liu *et al.* [21] in 2017 applied for a US Google patent US9600769B1 entitled *"In-Message Suggestion by Personal*

---

[62] https://www.nlm.nih.gov/research/umls/index.html
[63] https://www.snomed.org/
[64] https://bioportal.bioontology.org/
[65] https://lov.linkeddata.es/dataset/lov/
[66] https://lov4iot.appspot.com/?p=lov4iot-health
[67] http://wiki.aiisc.ai/index.php/KHealth:_Semantic_Multisensory_Mobile_Approach_to_Personalized_Asthma_Care

Knowledge Graph Constructed from User E-Mail Data." To the best of our knowledge, no Google product (e.g. Gmail) currently materializes all the features proposed in this patent. Nevertheless, it can be considered as a reference architecture for deploying a PKG, built from personal e-mail data, adding the generation of an intelligent e-mail suggestion/PDA system. That being said, the PKG includes content-to-content, user-to-content, and user-to-user relations/interactions. The e-mail suggestion engine is activated in the foreground when a user creates an e-mail message, suggesting any of the aforementioned relations with the aid of the PKG. Also, the patent mentions/includes the processing of e-mail messages in background batch mode in order to update the PKG. There is also a human-in-the-loop (HITL) activity when the user provides feedback from the suggestions presented to the user, which in turn updates the state of the PKG. The authors also optionally propose e-mail data extraction via the use of singular value decomposition (SVD)[68] and Latent Dirichlet Allocation (LDA)[69]. The main components of the proposed system include, namely the e-mail service module, the suggestion engine module, including the PKG constructor and the contextual information suggestion sub-modules. Finally, it includes the constructed PKG. The patent does not address the type of PKG being constructed, either LPG-based or SW-stack-based.

In [22], Hakkani-Tur *et al.* submitted a visionary Microsoft US Patent US20170024375A1 entitled *"Personal Knowledge Graph Population from Declarative User Utterances"* filed in 2015 and published in 2017. User utterances refer/include natural language processing (NLP) of speech-to-text statements and the parsing of text in the form of, for instance, e-mail messages, and chat sessions. The *"captured"* statements may include facts representing entities and relations among entities related to a given user and belonging to a predefined set of class classification or a given ontology. These assertions with their respective entities and relations are used to populate a PKG. Once the PKG is automatically constructed and populated, it is used for answering questions via a personal digital assistant (PDA). The PKG refers/contains personal data such as personal and family member's data, including names, addresses, employment details, and so having the user in the center in a typical spider web graph topology as cited in [2], and the rest of entities are either directly or indirectly related to the user. The architecture proposed by the authors, first includes, the *"Utterance-based Knowledge Tool"* that makes use of the *"utterance capture module,"* capturing e-mail messages, chat text sessions, and automatic speech-to-text recognition devices generating declarative user utterances. Next, a *"semantic parser module"* parses the declarative user utterances identifying entities and relationships among entities. It also includes a *"semantic language module"* trained from large sets of training data via either supervised, unsupervised, or combinations of both, machine learning (ML) techniques. The *"semantic parser module"* then outputs a given set of entities and relations, which in turn are processed by the *"graph construction module,"* automatically populating entries in the PKG. Finally, a *"query response module"*

---

[68] https://www.wikiwand.com/en/Singular_value_decomposition
[69] https://www.wikiwand.com/en/Latent_Dirichlet_allocation

returns answers to the given input queries against the PKG. The PKG classes and categories may be constructed based upon triple statements compliant with pre-existing SW-based ontologies and knowledge repositories such as Freebase[70], Schema.org[71], and so on via semantic frames[72], and slot filling[73]. A previous proof-of-concept of the patent is presented in [23] by the same authors, collecting 10 million utterances from Microsoft Cortana query logs. From these, a random sample subset is chosen and is manually annotated totaling almost 13,000 examples of personal assertions some of them containing relations with their respective identified related entities.

Another related paper entitled *"Remembering what you said: semantic personalized memory for personal digital assistants"* [24] represents a PDA that takes into account historical data/logs and via Personalized KGs (PKG_2) lookups improves precision/recall of actions and queries. To achieve such goal, submitted queries take into account similar past actions and queries, by ranking entities and providing semantic enrichment from the PKG_2 in the retrieval stage. In order to build a PKG_2, the following stages should be executed, namely query entity extraction by extracting relevant entities, entity relevance determination, entity attribute and metadata enrichment by augmenting entity information via PKG_2 lookups, feature extraction via n-gram matches[74], the modified best matching BM25F[75] term frequency/inverse document frequency (TF/IDF)[76] ranking function and finally, the last stage, a ranking mechanism is applied based upon support vector machine (SVM)[77], logistic regression[78], Fast-rank[79], and so on. The authors emphasize that entity enrichment with PKG_2 lookups substantially improves query results achieving up to an accuracy of 89.8 with Fast Ranking.

2.2.6 Personalized/summarized KGs (PKG₂)

This subsection is devoted to personalized/summarized KGs (PKG_2) as compared to PKGs. There is a very blur difference among both given that PKG_2 are customized/optimized/constrained views of large general or domain-specific KGs and PKGs are local/specific graph-based KGs with the typical "spider-web" topology, which in turn may make use/access/link-to information from external OKGs and or EKGs.

---

[70]https://www.wikiwand.com/en/Freebase_(database)
[71]https://schema.org/
[72]A semantic frame is sum of the all semantic components in a dialogue segment including the frame starter intent, slots associated to the frame starter intent, the slots that are filled by the user so far, coreferences used and the current outlook of the error paths, source: https://towardsdatascience.com/context-theory-ii-semantic-frames-f96693480779
[73]The goal of Slot Filling is to identify from a running dialog different slots, which correspond to different parameters of the user's query, source: https://paperswithcode.com/task/slot-filling
[74]https://www.wikiwand.com/en/N-gram)
[75]https://www.wikiwand.com/en/Okapi_BM25
[76]https://www.wikiwand.com/en/Tf%E2%80%93idf
[77]https://www.wikiwand.com/en/Support-vector_machine
[78]https://www.capitalone.com/tech/machine-learning/what-is-logistic-regression/
[79]https://github.com/douglasgscofield/fastrank

As main representatives of this subsection, we include four seminal research papers. Safavi *et al.* [25] present an alternative to PKGs entitled *"Personalized Knowledge Graph Summarization from the Cloud to Your Pocket."* In fact, it is a complex PKG_2 providing subsets of huge open knowledge graphs (OKGs) such as DBpedia[80], Yago[81], and Freebase[82], in the order of millions up-to-a billion of triples, summarized to specific personal user interests and topics. These summaries can be accessed and stored on devices with a limited amount of memory/storage such as for instance mobile devices. The depicted system named as *"GLIMPSE"* is an acronym for *"Graph-based Learning Of Personal Summaries"* and consists of the construction of a sparse graph summary maximizing and optimizing a utility function over the aforementioned huge OKGs. The utility function algorithm is linear w.r.t. the number of edges in the OKGs. In order to achieve such goal, GLIMPSE proceeds in a two-stage process by first capturing user KG preferences and secondly constructing personal summaries according to the user's preferences. Personal summaries are obtained via a maximization/optimization utility function constrained to memory/storage of target devices such as mobile devices. GLIMPSE user topic preferences are obtained from past queries. The method applied for obtaining both entity preference and triple preferences is via a unsupervised graph-based model. Summaries are constructed via an objective function optimizing summaries constructed according to user preferences query history and target resource constraints such as memory/storage. In the evaluation stage both real and synthetic queries are evaluated against/comparing "Personalized Page Rank" (PPR) variants [35] and the *"GLIMPSE"* system, achieving up to an average F1-score[83] of about 0.980 depending on what is being evaluated either few topics versus many topics.

Xu *et al.* [26] present in the paper *"Personalized course recommendation system fusing with knowledge graph and collaborative filtering"* the proposal of a hybrid fusion KG and collaborative filtering (CF) algorithm that combines both the use of KGs and CF algorithm increasing precision and recall as compared to solely applying CF. The domain that they tackle is in the area of personalized course recommendation but it may be possible to apply it in different domains such as books movies, and personalized news recommendations, with the use of domain-specific KGs. The authors present a two-staged process, namely first a KG representation learning stage by embedding KG items in a low-dimensional vector space and later applying and fusing with a CF recommendation algorithm. Such two-staged process with the aid of a KG solves somehow the typical cold start problem[84] when new courses and users are included in the system. The authors make use of the TransE [36][85] translation model representing 3-tupled (h.r.t.) KG elements were h(head) and t(tail) represent

---

[80] https://www.dbpedia.org/

[81] https://yago-knowledge.org/

[82] https://www.wikiwand.com/en/Freebase_(database)

[83] https://www.educative.io/answers/what-is-the-f1-score

[84] Cold start is a problem in computer-based information systems which involves a degree of automated data modelling. It concerns the issue that the system cannot draw any inferences for users or items about which it has not yet gathered sufficient information. Source: Wikipedia.

[85] https://paperswithcode.com/method/transe

entities and r(relation) represents the relationship between h and t, which in turn, the TransE model transforms these into embedded vectors (v_h, v_r, v_t). A loss function is applied to determine the existence of a relationship between v_h and v_t via v_r in the KG. Finally, the authors propose a *"Fusion Knowledge Graph Collaborative Filtering"* (FKGCF) algorithm by both fusing KG course semantic similarity with a CF recommendation algorithm. Two similarity functions are joined, namely a semantic similarity function among entities of the KG and an item similarity CF function with an α weighting factor ($0 \leq \alpha \leq 1$). Last but not least, a prediction score for a given user item is calculated and the top-N courses/items recommendations are returned. In the evaluation/experimental phase, they demonstrate that the precision ratio is much higher in the FKGCF algorithm versus the plain user/item CF algorithm.

The paper *"Personalized food recommendation as constrained question answering over a large-scale food knowledge graph"* by Chen *et al.* [27] describes the implementation of a personalized food recommendation system by querying a large food KG, the FoodKG taking into account user eating constraints such as allergies and user preferences/likes/dislikes and also the previous history of simulated food recommendation logs. The system outperforms non-personalized food recommendation systems. More specifically, they propose the system as a personalized constrained question answering (QA) system on top of a huge food knowledge graph named as FoodKG, in the order of a million food items, including recipes, nutritional data, ingredients, and food ontologies. The Knowledge Base Question Answering (KBQA) system receives user input queries and returns personalized food recommendations, by fulfilling and taking into account personal nutrition needs, personal health conditions, and simulated food logs. The acronym of the whole system is entitled PFoodReQ, which stands for *Personalized **Food Re**commendation via **Q**uestion Answering*. PFoodReQ makes use of query expansion, KG augmentation, constraint modeling, and to validate query results they incorporate a novel KBQA benchmark in order to evaluate query results. The proposed PFoodReQ architecture consists of the following modules, namely query expansion (QE), KG augmentation, constraint modeling (CM) and the KBQA module:

- The QE module: this module takes into account the user query in natural language, the dietary preferences such as allergies and personal likes, the nutrient health guidelines as personal constraints appended/expanded to the user query.
- The KG augmentation module: the KG augmentation module receives as input health guidelines and entities from the FoodKG by materializing views of the KG sub-graph determining the belongings of nutrients within ranges of health guidelines.
- The CM module: the CM module includes an embedding-based method where positive, negative and padding (e.g. no constraints) constraints are considered.
- The KBQA module: this module returns the recipes from the FoodKG compliant to personal user constraints applied to the expanded/augmented queries. The KBQA module receives as input queries and KG neighborhood subgraphs (e.g. entities and relations surrounding a main topic entity in the KG).

The last paper in Section 2.2.6 devoted to *"Personalized/Summarized KG"* is entitled *"Personalized Recommendations Using Knowledge Graphs: A probabilistic Logic Programming Approach"* by Catherin and Cohen [28]. This paper describes a personalized recommendation system based on the use of external KGs, the use of a probabilistic logic system named *"ProPPR"* which stands for *"**Programming With Personalized Page Rank**"* and applying three different methods for personalized recommendations, namely EntitySim, TypeSim, and GraphLF which we describe below:

- EntitySim: based upon content user preferences and maximizes the use of the KG link structure in order to make predictions by using a constrained set of prediction rules types.
- TypeSim: it makes use of node types by extending the EntitySim approach and making also the use of prediction rules. More specifically, it is based on the popularity of each node type and obtaining the general predictability of both node types and the entity itself.
- GraphLF: GraphLF stands for *"**Graph Latent Factorization**."* It combines graph based recommendations and latent factorization[86], being agnostic with respect to entity types as compared to the TypeSim method. It is also based on a set of prediction rules.

2.2.7   Decentralized web (DW)

Here we include one of the very first serious and advanced systems deploying/implementing the Social Linked Data (SOLID)-based architecture. We start this subsection by presenting to the reader some background related to the SOLID initiative.

2.2.7.1   SOLID background

In [6] is presented the paper *"SOLID: A Platform For Decentralized Social Web Applications Based On Linked Data"* by Sambra *et al.*, including Sir Tim Berners-Lee the original proposer of the SOLID platform. In this paper, the SOLID ecosystem is presented, a platform for decentralized social Web applications, where data is owned by end-users, decoupled from application data consumers. User's data is accessible through Personal Online Data Stores (PODS), either personally provided (e.g. advanced users) or provided by PODs providers. On the other hand, developers make use of the SOLID ecosystem/stack for creating and accessing user PODs. In SOLID, applications may access user-owned data, which in turn, users may access/interact with these applications. It represents a paradigm shift [37] by switching from centralized social web application architectures with data ownership/control in the hands of huge social web multinational companies, to end-users controlling/accessing data in the form of PODS. The SOLID/POD ecosystem/stack architecture is based upon RDF, Web, and SW recommendations/standards and work-in-progress proposals. As mentioned above PODS can be accessed via the World Wide Web (WWW) and can

---

[86]https://www.wikiwand.com/en/Matrix_factorization_(recommender_systems)

be implemented personally by advanced end-users or can be offered by private/public POD providers. SOLID applications may access and process PODs data as decoupled w.r.t. to data and client web applications. The SOLID/POD architecture includes the use of the following web recommendations/standards and work-in-progress drafts, namely WebID[87] for decentralized/single sign-on authentication, RDF for data representation, SPARQL for complex data querying accessing local user PODs data, and link-following queries for accessing linked user POD's data (data from other user's POD data) and the Linked Data Platform (LDP)[88], which is a W3C recommendation, to provide Representational State Transfer[89] Restful HTTP requests to Linked data.

2.2.7.2 A Social Linked Data SOLID-based PKG Application

The paper *"Using a Personal Health Library–Enabled mHealth Recommender System for Self-Management of Diabetes Among Underserved Populations: Use Case for Knowledge Graphs and Linked Data"* by Ammar, Nariman *et al.* [29] is a paper belonging to both the PHKG and to the decentralized Web (DW) categories and it represents one of the very first/novel implementations/deployments of the SOLID ecosystem in a complex platform, describing the implementation of a decentralized Personal Health Library/Personal Health Knowledge Graph (PHL/PHKG) by using the aforementioned SOLID ecosystem/stack [6]. The main effort of this paper is the generation of a mobile health application dealing with Personal Observations Of Daily Living (ODL) and Social Determinants Of Health (SDoH), via the use of a PHL/PHKG, RDF-based data, and Linked Open Data (LOD), and the use of the SOLID stack alongside the use of Personal Online Data Stores (PODs)[90] in addition to the respective personal electronic health records (EHR). The required/described architecture makes use of W3C Web and Semantic Web (SW) technologies, co-joined with the decentralized SOLID/PODS ecosystem/stack elements. It includes the following main components (see Figure 2.7), namely:

- Semantic-based REST API's and Semantic Web and Linked Open Data (SW/LOD) stack components (e.g. RDF, SPARQL Protocol and RDF Query Language and URIs), such as RDFLib[91], SPARQL, the LDFlex[92] [38] framework, and GraphQL-LD[93] [39].
- An RDF-based PHKG representing specific patient health information.
- RDF-based EHR and global LOD KGs.

---

[87] https://www.wikiwand.com/en/WebID
[88] https://www.w3.org/TR/ldp/
[89] https://www.wikiwand.com/en/Representational_state_transfer
[90] https://solidproject.org/
[91] https://github.com/linkeddata/rdflib.js/
[92] LDflex is a domain-specific language for querying Linked Data on the Web as if you were browsing a local JavaScript graph. Source: https://github.com/LDflex/LDflex.
[93] GraphQL-LD allows linked data to be queried via GraphQL queries and a JSON-LD context. Queries are submitted to SPARQL endpoints and results are converted again into tree format/GraphQL-compliant Source: https://www.npmjs.com/package/graphql-ld.

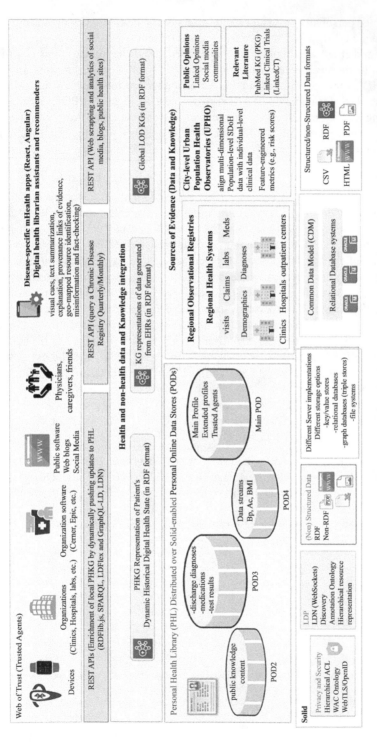

Figure 2.7   This figure depicts the architecture proposed in [29] of a Personal Health Library (PHL) alongside the SOLID stack. This figure is reproduced with permission from [29]. License: https://creativecommons.org/licenses/by/4.0/.

- A set of PODs including the main POD with user profiles and agents trusted, and the rest of the PODs including PHL information such as medications, discharges, and test results.
- SOLID-based/web-IDs decentralized hierarchical Access Control Lists (ACL) and the Web Access Control (WAC) candidate recommendation specification[94] which is a decentralized cross-domain access control system.
- Access to structured and non-structured data in RDF, CSV, HTML, and PDF formats, respectively.

2.2.8   Neuro-symbolic PKGs

This subsection is devoted to the application of latest deep-learning/transformer-based initiatives to PKGs and PKG_2. Given that these are becoming main-stream, we foresee becoming popular such initiatives in spite of the fact that in this seminal paper [2] by Krisztian Balog *et al. "Personal Knowledge Graphs: A Research Agenda,"* it is indicated that neuro-symbolic approaches cannot be applied, from a general perspective, given the lack of training data. Up-to four different complex/advanced proposals are included in this subsection.

In [30] the integration of user data in the form of a personal knowledge graph by using a neural-symbolic strategy is presented. The devised system is entitled *"PKG,"* providing machine-readable data permitting the submission of personal recommendations, based upon a pre-defined ontology. The PKG system is divided into three parts, namely (1) the user information processing module, (2) the PKG construction module, and finally (3) a recommendation module. The user information processing module gathers information from both structured and unstructured sources. The structured information sub-module gathers information from calendars, contact lists, and other structured/semi-structured sources/applications, generating classes, entities, and relationships via static rules. On the other hand, the unstructured information sub-module gathers information from social applications, search engine search input, and voice assistant texts by using a neural-symbolic approach for dealing with deep-learning (e.g. transformer-based) NLP-related tasks. The bidirectional encoder representations from transformers (BERT)[95] [40] is applied for the pre-training of unstructured information alongside the combination of conditional random field (CRF)[96] and bidirectional long-short term memory (Bi-LSTM)[97] and common sense knowledge graph symbolic rules in order to ratify the obtained results from BERT, Bi-LSTM, and CRF [41]. The PKG construction module is enabled after finalizing the user information processing module, including the construction of the PKG ontology subdivided into three concentric layers, namely central-users (e.g. follows the typical spider-web organization of PKGs [2]), the second layer comprised intention level, and finally the third layer the fine-grained level. With the aid of the

---

[94]https://solidproject.org/TR/wac
[95]https://www.wikiwand.com/en/BERT_(language_model)
[96]https://www.wikiwand.com/en/Conditional_random_field
[97]https://analyticsindiamag.com/complete-guide-to-bidirectional-lstm-with-python-codes/

PKG ontology and the processing of the user information module triples are generated, representing relationships between fine-grained entities, and entity linking is produced among certain entities, linking to real entities from the Common Knowledge Graph (CKG). Finally, it is presented the recommendation module, comprising path-based and inference-based recommendations. Path-based recommendations are based upon PKGs paths, considering user information and the respectively associated context, where recommendation items are determined by pre-defined rules. Inference-based recommendations are mainly provided by the CKG, based upon information co-occurrence and knowledge supplement. Although this demo paper included a quite sophisticated reference architecture for a neuro-symbolic-based PKG, each of the architecture components is not properly and thoroughly explained or included a reference to a long/extended version of a previous paper.

In [33], Vannur *et al.* present a hybrid neuro-symbolic system creating/populating a PKB/PKG via the use of graph neural networks (GNNs) for link prediction and rule-based annotators upon the TACRED dataset[98], which is a large-scale relation extraction dataset. The authors proposed the use of data augmentation[99] upon the TACRED dataset including more features for training GNNs without acquiring more data. In their proposal for data augmentation they select 34 personal data entity types (e.g. personal attributes such as first-name, last-name, birthdate, etc.) and for relation extraction, they select a total of 41 relations from the TACRED dataset among other sources. Next, they make use of personal data annotators by assigning entity types to entity mentions provided by a rule-based/pattern-based system. The architecture/pipeline workflow of the PKG population includes personal data annotators, rule-based named entity recognizers (NERs)[100], entity classification and relation extraction modules, and the use of a GNN for link prediction (e.g. for relating entities) as mentioned before. Finally, the PKB/PKG is populated via slot filling[101] and the aforementioned link prediction.

Another related research paper entitled *"Personal Knowledge Base Construction From Text-based Lifelogs"* by Yen *et al.* [32] presents a PKB constructed via a series of steps making use of a neuro-symbolic approach for the PKB population, from a corpus of user tweets representing life events either explicitly or implicitly. Life events are represented as quadruples containing subject-predicate-object-time events. Predicates expressed in natural language (NL) are transformed into PKB relations by using the Chinese FrameNet [42] system, which is a translation into Chinese of the English FrameNet[102] lexical database, which in turn contains a set of more than 200,000 manually annotated sentences linked to 1,200 semantic frames, being both human and machine-readable, used in typical Natural Language Processing (NLP) based applications. Next subject-relation-object triples are timestamped by personal

---

[98] https://nlp.stanford.edu/projects/tacred/
[99] https://www.wikiwand.com/en/Data_augmentation
[100] https://www.wikiwand.com/en/Named-entity_recognition
[101] The goal of Slot Filling is to identify from a running dialog different slots, which correspond to different parameters of the user's query. Source: https://paperswithcode.com/task/slot-filling
[102] https://framenet.icsi.berkeley.edu/fndrupal/about

user tweets timestamp fields, forming in total a quadruple. In their pipelined system, from a general perspective, life event extraction is done in several stages/substages. First, the system classifies tweets as either containing life events or not, then the life events selected describe either explicitly or implicitly life events, also suggesting life events predicates. The next stage in the pipeline is the quadruple generation for each predicate, namely subject-predicate-object-timestamp quadruples. Next quadruple elements are labeled by the Chinese FrameNet-based semantic parser, which represents the final input to the PKB. The authors contemplate the extension of the PKB with knowledge coming from external KGs such as DBpedia and Freebase. The life event corpus construction is based upon a set of more than 25k Chinese user tweets from 18 different users. Three levels of annotations are performed for training and testing by making use of the Chinese FrameNet ontology. The authors also make use, of (1) for feature input and enrichment, of the Stanford part of speech (POS) tagger[103], (2) for sequence labeling, the Multi-task Learning[104], Bi-directional Long-Short-Term-Memory[105], and Conditional Random Field[106] (MTL-BiLSTM-CRF) combined model, (3) for life event detection, a fine-tuned Bidirectional Encoder Representations from Transformers (BERT)[107] system. From the user tweet's corpus, 2/3 of tweets are used for training and 1/3 for testing and validation data. In their experiments, the combined MTL-BiLSTM-CRF model generates roughly the highest F1 score[108] in all stages[109].

We end up this sub-section of Neuro-symbolic PKGs with the paper [31] describing the use of PKGs and analysis of social media microblogs, and deep learning and graph neural networks (GNN) in order to detect individuals with suicidal ideation with a 93% of accuracy and F1-measure[110]. More specifically, the architecture proposed makes use of long short-term memory (LSTM)[111] for extracting textual and visual information, pre-trained Bidirectional Encoder Representations from Transformers (BERT) models[112], and a 34-layer residual neural network (ResNet)[113].

2.2.9   Personal Research Knowledge Graphs (PRKGs)

This is the last of the nine overlapping PKG application types, devoted to PRKGs. Here, we present a proof-of-concept LPG-based research prototype proposed in [34] by Chakraborty *et al.*, materializing the implementation of a PRKG to represent/include information about the research activities and artifacts a given researcher works with or interacts with. The research activities span from personal research

---

[103] https://nlp.stanford.edu/software/tagger.shtml
[104] https://ruder.io/multi-task/
[105] https://analyticsindiamag.com/complete-guide-to-bidirectional-lstm-with-python-codes/
[106] https://www.wikiwand.com/en/Conditional_random_field
[107] https://www.wikiwand.com/en/BERT_(language_model)
[108] https://www.wikiwand.com/en/F-score
[109] The reader may access the experiments section of this paper for further insights.
[110] https://deepai.org/machine-learning-glossary-and-terms/f-score
[111] https://www.wikiwand.com/en/Long_short-term_memory
[112] https://www.wikiwand.com/en/BERT_(language_model)
[113] https://www.wikiwand.com/en/Residual_neural_network

interests, tools and resources used by the user, s/workshops that the user attends, current research projects, students he/she supervises, methods and tasks she implements, to curriculum vitae-related information such as positions held and current position. The system deployed also includes the interaction with external open knowledge graphs (OKGs) such as Wikidata, the Open Research Knowledge Graph (ORKG[114]), and social networks such as Twitter. The PRKG prototype is implemented in the labeled property graph (LPG)-based Neo4j and represents the structured information as RDF graphs. They contemplate the use of the PRKG, an AI-based chatbot that may proactively ask for personal information to populate the PRKG. Also, they include a proactive method for tracking research activities such as the bibliography/research papers downloaded, research papers the user is currently working on, and queries executed against research paper search engines (i.e., Google Scholar, arXiv.org, etc.) providing users relevance feedback[115]; also, e-mail messages sent/received from research groups and so on. They also contemplate the use of neuro-symbolic algorithms for deriving/inferring implicit new facts/information. Finally, they propose sharing PRKG, using role-based access control (RBAC) among members of the user's research groups. In the Appendix, the authors describe the concrete implementation of the PRKG, namely, the use of Neo4j, the transformer-based **Span**-based **E**ntity and **R**elation **T**ransformer SpERT[116] [43] for entity/relation extraction from research papers by training SpERT with the SciERC data set[117] [44].

2.3   PKGs – a common reference architecture for semantic web-based PKG

The details of a typical/lowest common denominator prototype implementation that we include here are from a SW developer/practitioner-based perspective. The system should be based on latest SW recommendations, and draft specifications. The SW-based prototype should follow a SW-stack-based architecture, drawing conclusions from all of the research prototypes and patents presented in this chapter, including the following components/features, namely:

* Ontologies/vocabularies: An ontology, possibly a multi-layered ontology, such as the ones previously proposed in the Semantic Desktop[118]. For instance, we may define a simplified Simple Knowledge Organization System (SKOS)-based ontology[119] or a schema.org[120] based vocabulary/ontology.

---

[114]https://orkg.org/
[115]https://www.wikiwand.com/en/Relevance_feedback
[116]https://github.com/lavis-nlp/spert
[117]SciERC dataset is a collection of 500 scientific abstract annotated with scientific entities, their relations, and coreference clusters. Source: https://paperswithcode.com/dataset/scierc
[118]https://www.wikiwand.com/en/Semantic_desktop
[119]https://www.w3.org/2004/02/skos/
[120]https://schema.org/

- Triplestore/graph database: For storing triple statements such as GraphDB[121], Apache Jena/Fuseki[122], Blazegraph[123], and Virtuoso Open Source[124]. Ideally the chosen triple-store should be compliant with the latest RDF-star/SPARQL-star in-progress specification[125], permitting the definition of *"embedded triples"*, that is, RDF statements including other statements, either in the subject or object of the RDF-star triple statement. The SW-based PKG prototype system should be (1) RDF-star/SPARQL-star compliant, (2) enable virtualized access to relational DBMS (e.g. via the Ontop Virtual SPARQL module[126]), and (3) ideally make uses of fast forward-chaining reasoning/materialization. Other interesting features include the submission of federated SPARQL queries[127], and the availability of several plug-ins (e.g. ranking, keyword-search) and so on. Additionally, ideally support API development with the Python programming language and libraries and related SW-based libraries (e.g. RDFLib[128], pysemtec SW-based Python libraries repository[129]).
- Virtual PKG: Access to relational DBMS via a virtualized access, not materializing, instead performing virtual access to such sources by transforming SPARQL-based queries into SQL on the fly and retrieving results back into RDF [45,46] (e.g. via the Ontop[130] system).
- RDF-izers: For converting structured/semi-structured/unstructured data into RDF with the aid of ontologies, and the use of the Reasonable Ontology Templates[131] [47]:
  1. Structured/semi-structured data: Convert either directly or indirectly structured/semi-structured data into RDF and/or into CSV-based data and from then, into RDF (e.g. Tarql[132]). For instance, convert query results against GMail personal e-mail accounts, into CSV and then convert CSV data into RDF.
  2. Unstructured data: For instance, we purview the use of an NLP pipeline for converting unstructured data into RDF, via a part-of-speech (POS) tagger, a named entity recognition (NER) module, a named entity linking module, and a relation extraction module to finally populate the PKG.
- Access to external OKGs: Enrich the data stored in the PKG by accessing external Open KGs (OKGs) such as Wikidata[133], DBpedia[134], and Yago[135].

---

[121] https://graphdb.ontotext.com/
[122] https://jena.apache.org/documentation/fuseki2/
[123] https://blazegraph.com/
[124] https://github.com/openlink/virtuoso-opensource
[125] https://w3c.github.io/rdf-star/cg-spec/editors_draft.html
[126] https://github.com/ontop/ontop
[127] https://www.w3.org/TR/sparql11-federated-query/
[128] https://github.com/RDFLib/rdflib
[129] https://github.com/pysemtec/semantic-python-overview
[130] https://ontop-vkg.org/guide/
[131] https://ottr.xyz/
[132] https://tarql.github.io/
[133] https://www.wikidata.org/wiki/Wikidata:Main_Page
[134] https://www.dbpedia.org/
[135] https://yago-knowledge.org/

- RDF data validation: Include data validation against RDF graphs either via SHACL[136] or ShEx[137] which is being used by the Wikidata KG initiative under the *"Closed-World"*[138] assumption as compared to typical setup of an Open-World[139] assumption when dealing with SW-related data.
- Recommender system: Include a content-based recommender system (e.g. recommend research papers in the area of the SW as proposed by/in the PRKGs Section 2.2.9).

2.4　PKGs current status and future research

To date, the literature related to PKGs is currently scarce given that it is still a virgin and promising research field. Only PHKGs and PDAs PKG applications have become somehow popular. We foresee an increment in the implementation/deployment of both RDF-based (e.g. Semantic Web Stack) and LPG-based (e.g. OpenCypher/Cypher/Neo4j) PKGs, both in academia and industry. In addition, we also foresee that the SOLID ecosystem/stack including personal PODS or decentralized data stores becoming popular and somehow mainstream, where PKGs may be an important component fitting in the SOLID stack/ecosystem. We also predict the application of state-of-the-art neuro-symbolic approaches regarding the construction of PKGs, to become also quite popular (e.g. in Table 2.1, we already include five representative research papers making use of neuro-symbolic models).

2.5　Conclusions

We have presented an introduction to KGs (see Section 2.1), including both OKGs and EKGs, and presented a small list of representative KGs. We have defined what are PKGs as compared to KGs, and highlighted the differences among them. We also presented a binary taxonomy of PKGs with respect to Modeling/Implementation, including SW-based PKGs and LPG-based PKGs (see Section 2.1.5). We have highlighted the contributions of this chapter, as the first research paper classifying PKGs types according to application types (see Section 2.1.6). We have identified up to nine overlapping PKGs application types and presented a table summarizing PKGs applications types (see Table 2.1 and Section 2.2). In this taxonomy of overlapping PKGs application types, we differentiate PKGs as compared to personalized/summarized KGs (PKG_2) (see Section 2.2.6). Furthermore, we have indicated which subcomponents should be included/be desirable in a typical PKG SW-based reference architecture (see Section 2.3). For LPG-based PKGs, we invite the reader to research links referring OpenCypher/Cypher/Neo4j-based PKG-based implementations as a starting point. We end this chapter by mentioning the current status/future

---

[136] https://www.wikiwand.com/en/SHACL
[137] https://shex.io/
[138] https://www.wikiwand.com/en/Closed-world_assumption
[139] https://www.wikiwand.com/en/Open-world_assumption

research regarding PKGs where we foresee PKG implementations to become more popular that may be a good fit/component within the SOLID stack/ecosystem (see section Social Linked Data (SOLID) Background 2.2.7.1).

References

[1]   Singhal A. Introducing the Knowledge Graph: Things, not Strings; 2012. Available from: https://blog.google/products/search/introducing-knowledge-graph-things-not/.

[2]   Balog K and Kenter T. Personal knowledge graphs: a research agenda. In: *Proceedings of the 2019 ACM SIGIR International Conference on Theory of Information Retrieval*; 2019. p. 217–220.

[3]   In: *Semantic Desktop*. London: Springer; 2007. p. 229–239. Available from: https://doi.org/10.1007/978-1-84628-710-7_12.

[4]   Sauermann L, Bernardi A, and Dengel A. Overview and outlook on the semantic desktop. In: *Semantic Desktop Workshop*. vol. 175. Citeseer; 2005.

[5]   Groza T, Handschuh S, and Moeller K. The NEPOMUK project-on the way to the social semantic desktop. In: *3rd International Conference on Semantic Technologies (ISEMANTICS 2007)*, Graz, Austria; 2007.

[6]   Sambra AV, Mansour E, Hawke S, *et al. Solid: A Platform for Decentralized Social Applications based on Linked Data*. MIT CSAIL & Qatar Computing Research Institute, Tech Rep. 2016.

[7]   Gandon F and Schreiber G. RDF 1.1 XML Syntax W3C Recommendation. W3C; 2014. Available from: https://www.w3.org/TR/rdf-syntax-grammar/.

[8]   Brickley D and Guha RV. RDF schema 1.1 W3C Recommendation. W3C; 2014. Available from: https://www.w3.org/TR/rdf-schema/.

[9]   Consortium WWW, *et al*. OWL 2 web ontology language document overview. 2012; Available from: https://www.w3.org/TR/owl2-overview/.

[10] W3C. Skos Simple Knowledge Organization System – home page. W3C; 2012. Available from: https://www.w3.org/2004/02/skos/.

[11] Guha RV, Brickley D, and Macbeth S. Schema.org: evolution of structured data on the web. *Communications of the ACM*. 2016;59(2):44–51.

[12] Langholm E. *Constructing a Personal Knowledge Graph from Disparate Data Sources*. uis; 2021.

[13] Montoya D, Pellissier Tanon T, Abiteboul S, *et al*. Thymeflow, a personal knowledge base with spatio-temporal data. In: *Proceedings of the 25th ACM International on Conference on Information and Knowledge Management*; 2016. p. 2477–2480.

[14] Montoya D. *A Personal Knowledge Base Integrating User Data and Activity Timeline*, PhD Thesis. Université Paris-Saclay; 2017.

[15] Montoya D, Tanon TP, Abiteboul S, *et al*. A knowledge base for personal information management. In: *LDOW@ WWW*; 2018.

[16] Schröder M, Jilek C, and Dengel A. A human-in-the-loop approach for personal knowledge graph construction from file names. In: *Third International*

Workshop on Knowledge Graph Construction; 2022. Available from: https://github.com/mschroeder-github/kecs.

[17]   Ilkou E. *Personal Knowledge Graphs: Use Cases in e-Learning Platforms*; 2022. arXiv preprint arXiv:220308507.

[18]   Shirai S, Seneviratne O, and McGuinness DL. *Applying Personal Knowledge Graphs to Health*; 2021. arXiv preprint arXiv:210407587.

[19]   Gyrard A, Gaur M, Shekarpour S, *et al.* Personalized health knowledge graph. In: *CEUR Workshop Proceedings.* vol. 2317. NIH Public Access; 2018.

[20]   Seneviratne O, Harris J, Chen CH, *et al. Personal Health Knowledge Graph for Clinically Relevant Diet Recommendations*; 2021. arXiv preprint arXiv:211010131.

[21]   Liu Y and Buehling C. In-message suggestion by personal knowledge graph constructed from user email data. Google Patents; 2017. US Patent 9,600,769.

[22]   Hakkani-Tur D, Tur G, Li X, *et al.* Personal knowledge graph population from declarative user utterances. Google Patents; 2017. US Patent App. 14/809,243.

[23]   Li X, Tur G, Hakkani-Tür D, *et al.* Personal knowledge graph population from user utterances in conversational understanding. In: *2014 IEEE Spoken Language Technology Workshop (SLT).* IEEE; 2014. p. 224–229.

[24]   Agarwal V, Khan OZ, and Sarikaya R. Remembering what you said: semantic personalized memory for personal digital assistants. In: *2017 IEEE International Conference on Acoustics, Speech and Signal Processing (ICASSP).* IEEE; 2017. p. 5835–5839.

[25]   Safavi T, Belth C, Faber L, *et al.* Personalized knowledge graph summarization: from the cloud to your pocket. In: *2019 IEEE International Conference on Data Mining (ICDM).* IEEE; 2019. p. 528–537.

[26]   Xu G, Jia G, Shi L, *et al.* Personalized course recommendation system fusing with knowledge graph and collaborative filtering. *Computational Intelligence and Neuroscience.* 2021;2021.

[27]   Chen Y, Subburathinam A, Chen CH, *et al.* Personalized food recommendation as constrained question answering over a large-scale food knowledge graph. In: *Proceedings of the 14th ACM International Conference on Web Search and Data Mining*; 2021. p. 544–552.

[28]   Catherine R and Cohen W. Personalized recommendations using knowledge graphs: A probabilistic logic programming approach. In: *Proceedings of the 10th ACM Conference on Recommender Systems*; 2016. p. 325–332.

[29]   Ammar N, Bailey JE, Davis RL, *et al.* Using a personal health library-enabled mhealth recommender system for self-management of diabetes among underserved populations: use case for knowledge graphs and linked data. *JMIR Formative Research.* 2021;5(3):e24738. Available from: https://formative.jmir.org/2021/3/e24738/.

[30]   Yang Y, Lin J, Zhang X, *et al.* PKG: a personal knowledge graph for recommendation. In: *Proceedings of the 45th International ACM SIGIR Conference on Research and Development in Information Retrieval*; 2022. p. 3334–3338.

[31]   Cao L, Zhang H, and Feng L. Building and using personal knowledge graph to improve suicidal ideation detection on social media. *IEEE Transactions on Multimedia.* 2020;24:87–102.

[32]   Yen AZ, Huang HH, and Chen HH. Personal knowledge base construction from text-based lifelogs. In: *Proceedings of the 42nd International ACM SIGIR Conference on Research and Development in Information Retrieval*; 2019. p. 185–194.

[33]   Vannur LS, Ganesan B, Nagalapatti L, *et al. Data Augmentation for Personal Knowledge Base Population*; 2020. arXiv preprint arXiv:200210943.

[34]   Chakraborty P, Dutta S, and Sanyal DK. *Personal Research Knowledge Graphs*; 2022. arXiv preprint arXiv:220411428.

[35]   Park S, Lee W, Choe B, *et al.* A survey on personalized PageRank computation algorithms. *IEEE Access*. 2019;7:163049–163062.

[36]   Bordes A, Usunier N, Garcia-Duran A, *et al.* Translating embeddings for modeling multi-relational data. *Advances in Neural Information Processing Systems*. 2013;26.

[37]   Verborgh R. Paradigm Shifts for the Decentralized Web; 2017. Available from: https://ruben.verborgh.org/blog/2017/12/20/paradigm-shifts-for-the-decentralized-web/.

[38]   Verborgh R and Taelman R. LDflex: A read/write linked data abstraction for front-end web developers. In: *International Semantic Web Conference*. Springer; 2020. p. 193–211.

[39]   Taelman R, Vander Sande M, and Verborgh R. GraphQL-LD: linked data querying with GraphQL. In: *ISWC2018, the 17th International Semantic Web Conference*; 2018. p. 1–4.

[40]   Devlin J, Chang MW, Lee K, *et al. Bert: Pre-training of Deep Bidirectional Transformers for Language Understanding*; 2018. arXiv preprint arXiv:181004805.

[41]   Huang Z, Xu W, and Yu K. *Bidirectional LSTM-CRF Models for Sequence Tagging*; 2015. arXiv preprint arXiv:150801991.

[42]   Yang TH, Huang HH, Yen AZ, *et al.* Transfer of frames from English framenet to construct Chinese framenet: a bilingual corpus-based approach. In: *Proceedings of the Eleventh International Conference on Language Resources and Evaluation (LREC 2018)*; 2018.

[43]   Eberts M and Ulges A. *Span-Based Joint Entity and Relation Extraction with Transformer Pre-training*; 2019. arXiv preprint arXiv:190907755.

[44]   Luan Y, He L, Ostendorf M, *et al. Multi-task Identification of Entities, Relations, and Coreference for Scientific Knowledge Graph Construction*; 2018. arXiv preprint arXiv:180809602.

[45]   Xiao G, Ding L, Cogrel B, *et al.* Virtual knowledge graphs: an overview of systems and use cases. *Data Intelligence*. 2019;1(3):201–223.

[46]   Xiao G, Lanti D, Kontchakov R, *et al.* The virtual knowledge graph system ontop. In: *International Semantic Web Conference*. Springer; 2020. p. 259–277.

[47]   Skjæveland MG, Lupp DP, Karlsen LH, *et al.* Practical ontology pattern instantiation, discovery, and maintenance with reasonable ontology templates. In: *International Semantic Web Conference*. Springer; 2018. p. 477–494.

Section 2

Knowledge representation and reasoning

Chapter 3

Knowledge representation and reasoning in personal knowledge graphs

Pierre-Antoine Champin[a] and Rigo Wenning[b]

The difference between a data graph and a knowledge graph lies in the ability of some agent to interpret the data and reason about it and draw some form of insight from it. According to this very general characterization, the "knowledge" quality would not be inherent to the graph but depends on the agent using it. However, when talking about knowledge graph, there is generally the assumption that the semantics of the data is explicitly defined. That way, human agents can avoid ambiguities and misinterpretations, and artificial agents can interpret and reason about the graph in their own way, assisting humans in the task of interpreting it. The techniques to define the explicit semantics of data, in a way that allows machines to conduct meaningful reasoning with the data, have long been studied as a subfield of artificial intelligence and are known as knowledge representation.

As early as the first successes of the web, a graph of documents connected to each other by hyperlinks, its inventor Tim Berners-Lee had the vision that the web could be made even more useful if it also contained pieces of machine-understandable data, also connected to each other as a worldwide graph. This was latter coined as the semantic web [1]. In addition to HTML, the standard language for describing web documents, a number of other standard languages for structured data (RDF, OWL, etc.) where proposed and refined. Those languages draw a lot on the existing literature on knowledge representation, but also have their own specific features to allow them to scale up in the context of an open and unbounded web.

While our topic is *personal* knowledge graphs (PKG), it might therefore be surprising to recommend the use of languages and technologies designed for the web as a whole. There are nevertheless a number of good reasons for doing so. First, these languages are open standards: they are precisely specified, and largely implemented in open-source and commercial products alike. Second, a consequence of the previous point is that recent research on knowledge representation has largely been focused on these languages. Finally, even though PKGs are not intended to be as open or large as the web itself, neither are they expected to work in complete isolation. Some level of

[a]W3C/Inria, Sophia Antipolis, France
[b]W3C/ERCIM, Sophia Antipolis, France

interoperability with other PKGs, and with open data from the web, is also desirable. Standardized languages are therefore required.

In the first section of this chapter, we present the main languages that compose the semantic web stack. In the second section, we present a number of PKG projects using these languages. In the last section, we focus on the social aspects of personal knowledge graphs and describe the standards that support data sharing and compliance.

3.1 The semantic web stack

In this subsection, we will present an overview of the languages that make the semantic web stack, by grouping them in to four dimensions: representing knowledge, reasoning with those representations, querying them, and validating them.

3.1.1 *Representing knowledge*

At the core of the semantic web stack is RDF, the Resource Description Framework [2]. RDF is not a *language* in the classical sense of the term, in that RDF is not primarily defined by the way it is serialized (or "written down"), although serializations are also part of the standard. Instead, RDF's most important feature is its *abstract syntax*, which is a graph data model.

Abstract syntax

As a knowledge representation language, RDF is for making statements about the world, and RDF statements are very simple: they are always made of exactly three parts, called the subject, the predicate, and the object. For this reason, RDF statements are also called triples. For example, an RDF triple could state that "this chapter was authored by Pierre-Antoine" (where "this chapter," "was authored by," and "Pierre-Antoine" are, respectively, the subject, the predicate, and the object). Every RDF triple intuitively states that a relationship, denoted by the predicate, holds between the (things denoted by the) subject and the object.

In order to make a more complex claim, such as "this chapter was authored by Pierre-Antoine and Rigo, who both work for W3C," one has to break it down into atomic triples, in this case:

- "this chapter was authored by Pierre-Antoine"
- "this chapter was authored by Rigo"
- "Pierre-Antoine works for W3C"
- "Rigo works for W3C"

A set of RDF triples is called an *RDF graph*. Indeed, each triple can be seen as an edge, labeled by the predicate, linking two nodes, labeled by the subject and object respectively (see Figure 3.1). This captures well the intuitive meaning of the triple: a named relationship between two objects. When several triples have the same subject (resp. object), they will be represented as outgoing (resp. incoming) edges on the same node (see Figure 3.2).

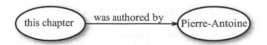

Figure 3.1 One informal RDF triple represented as a simple graph

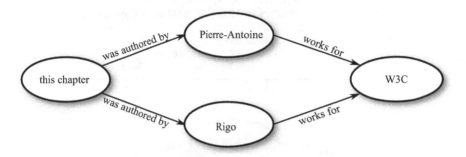

Figure 3.2 Four informal RDF triples making a more complex graph

Identifying objects with IRIs

In the example above, the words "This chapter," "Pierre-Antoine," and "Rigo" are largely ambiguous, as interpreting them correctly depends on the context: which chapter are we talking about? Is there only one person named "Pierre-Antoine" or "Rigo"? Knowledge representation languages aim at eliminating as much as possible this kind of ambiguity. First, because machines are often not as good as humans at using contextual information. Second, because even for humans, the contextual information might not always be available or obvious. Therefore, we need to replace these words with unambiguous identifiers.

To identify the objects of interest, RDF uses International Resource Identifiers (IRIs) [3], which are an extension of the well-known Uniform Resource Locators (URLs) that used to link HTML documents to each other. It is however important to notice here that the use of IRIs in RDF is very different from the use of URLs on the web of documents: contrarily to HTML links, RDF is not, strictly speaking, concerned by the content that can be retrieved through a given IRI – in fact, not all IRIs can be used to retrieve content.[1] RDF considers IRIs as opaque identifiers and makes no assumption about what kind of object they can identify: physical or immaterial, concrete or abstract, real or imaginary, etc.

Because IRIs are very long and hard to read, we will generally not write them in full in our examples, but instead use an abbreviation form called prefixed names [5]. A prefixed name has the form `prefix:suffix`, where the prefix is conventionally associated with an IRI. The prefixed name is to be interpreted as the concatenation of

---

[1] When using RDF to publish data on the open web, it is considered good practice to use IRIs that can be retrieved and to ensure that the retrieved content is a description of the object identified by the URL [4]. But this is not a requirement of RDF itself.

Table 3.1   IRI prefixes used in this chapter

dpv:	https://w3id.org/dpv\#
ex:	http://example.org/
odrl:	http://www.w3.org/ns/odrl/2/
owl:	http://www.w3.org/2002/07/owl\#
rdf:	http://www.w3.org/1999/02/22-rdf-syntax-ns\#
rdfs:	http://www.w3.org/2000/01/rdf-schema\#
s:	http://schema.org/
sh:	http://www.w3.org/ns/shacl\#
xsd:	http://www.w3.org/2001/XMLSchema\#

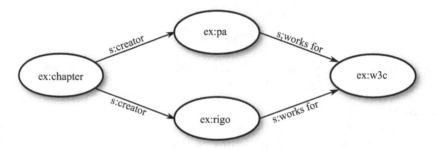

Figure 3.3   Four RDF triples using (abbreviated) IRIs

that IRI with the suffix. In this chapter, we will use the IRI prefixes given in Table 3.1. As an example, **hs:person** corresponds to the IRI http://schema.org/Person. Replacing the informal identifiers from Figure 3.2 with abbreviated IRIs gives us Figure 3.3.

Other kinds of RDF nodes

Besides IRIs, RDF graphs can contain two other kinds of nodes, which are illustrated in Figure 3.4. Literals are nodes used to represent simple values, such as strings, numbers, and dates. They are composed of a lexical form (a string), and an IRI identifying their datatype. The most commonly used datatypes are borrowed from the XML schema specification [6]. The two rectangular nodes on the right of Figure 3.4 represent literals.

Finally, when we need to mention in RDF an entity, but do not know any IRI identifying it, we can use a blank node. Such a node lacks a global identifier and can therefore not be referenced from outside the graph where it occurs. The node at the bottom-center of Figure 3.4 is an example of a blank node.

Concrete syntaxes

RDF graphs can be serialized in a variety of formats, the main ones being:

- RDF/XML [7] was the first proposed syntax, and is based on XML. See Listing 3.1 for an example.

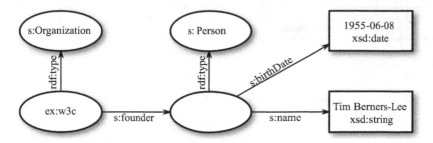

Figure 3.4   An RDF graph involving a blank node and two literals

```
1  <?xml version='1.0' encoding='utf-8' ?>
2  <rdf:RDF xmlns:s='http://schema.org/'
3          xmlns:rdf='http://www.w3.org/1999/02/22-rdf-syntax-ns#'>
4    <s:Organization rdf:about='http://example.org/w3c'>
5      <s:founder>
6        <s:Person>
7          <s:birthDate rdf:datatype='http://www.w3.org/2001/XMLSchema#
           date'>1955-06-08</s:birthDate>
8          <s:name>Tim Berners-Lee</s:name>
9        </s:Person>
10     </s:founder>
11   </s:Organization>
12 </rdf:RDF>
```

Listing 3.1   The graph from Figure 3.4 in RDF/XML

```
1  @prefix xsd:   <http://www.w3.org/2001/XMLSchema#>.
2  @prefix s:     <http://schema.org/>.
3  @prefix ex:    <http://example.org/>.
4
5  ex:w3c a s:Organization ;
6         s:founder [
7             a s:Person ;
8             s:name "Tim Berners-Lee" ;
9             s:birthDate "1955-06-08"^^xsd:date ;
10        ].
```

Listing 3.2   The graph from Figure 3.4 in Turtle

- Turtle [5] is a text-based syntax aiming at terseness. See Listing 3.2 for an example.
- N-Triples [8] is a textual lined-based format. It is a strict subset of Turtle, easier to parse and to process with simple text tools. See Listing 3.3 for an example.
- JSON-LD [9] is a JSON-based format, aiming to allow idiomatic JSON to be interpreted as RDF. See Listing 3.4 for an example.

```
1 <http://example.org/w3c> <http://www.w3.org/1999/02/22-rdf-syntax-ns#
     type> <http://schema.org/Organization> .
2 <http://example.org/w3c> <http://schema.org/founder> _:b1 .
3 _:b1 <http://www.w3.org/1999/02/22-rdf-syntax-ns#type> <http://schema
     .org/Person> .
4 _:b1 <http://schema.org/name> "Tim Berners-Lee"^^<http://www.w3.org
     /2001/XMLSchema#string> .
5 _:b1 <http://schema.org/birthDate> "1955-06-08"^^<http://www.w3.org
     /2001/XMLSchema#date> .
```

Listing 3.3   The graph from Figure 3.4 in N-Triples

```
1  {
2    "@context": {
3      "rdf": "http://www.w3.org/1999/02/22-rdf-syntax-ns#",
4      "xsd": "http://www.w3.org/2001/XMLSchema#",
5      "s": "http://schema.org/",
6      "ex": "http://example.org/"
7    },
8    "@id": "ex:w3c",
9    "@type": "s:Organization",
10   "s:founder": {
11     "@type": "s:Person",
12     "s:name": "Tim Berners-Lee",
13     "s:birthDate": {
14       "@type": "xsd:date",
15       "@value": "1955-06-08"
16     }
17   }
18 }
```

Listing 3.4   The graph from Figure 3.4 in JSON-LD

```
1 ex:w3c rdf:type s:Organization .
2 ex:w3c s:founder _:b1 .
3 _:b1 rdf:type s:Person .
4 _:b1 s:name "Tim Berners-Lee"^^xsd:string .
5 _:b1 s:birthDate "1955-06-08"^^xsd:date .
```

Listing 3.5   The graph from Figure 3.4 in simplified Turtle

In the following, we will use a simple subset of Turtle to provide examples, where:

- all the IRI prefixes of Table 3.1 are considered as implicitly declared;
- IRIs are always represented as prefixed names (e.g. hs:organization);
- literals are always represented with their lexical form in quotes, followed by ^^ and their datatype IRI, e.g. "Tim Berners-Lee"^^xsd:string;
- blank nodes are represented by a local identifier starting with _:, e.g. _:b1;
- every triple is represented on a single line, and terminated with a period (.).

In this simplified turtle, the graph from Figure 3.4 is serialized as Listing 3.5.

3.1.2 Reasoning

RDF is not just a data model. It is a knowledge representation formalism, with a well-defined formal semantics [10]. The role of this semantics is to allow machines to reason with RDF data, i.e. to produce (or *infer*) new data that are necessarily entailed by the data that is already known. RDF semantics alone does not provide for very interesting inferences, but it serves as a basis for more expressive languages, which we present in the following section.

A core feature of RDF's base semantics is however important to point out: the open world assumption (OWA). Under this assumption, only triples that are explicitly stated or inferred can contribute to new inferences. Triples that do not satisfy these conditions are considered unknown and nothing can be derived from their absence. This contrasts to the Closed World Assumption used by some languages (e.g. Prolog [11]), where what is not known to be true is considered false.

Another core feature of RDF's base semantics is that, contrarily to other knowledge representation systems, it does *not* work under the unique name assumption (UNA): two different IRIs may, in RDF, identify the same entity. Both the OWA and the absence of UNA stem from the fact that RDF was designed to work on the open web, where one cannot assume that they have the full knowledge about a particular entity, nor that everyone else is referring to that entity using the same name (IRI).

RDF schema

RDF schema [12] is a language for representing lightweight ontologies in RDF. According to Gruber *et al.* [13], an ontology is "the formal specification of a conceptualization." In other words, it is a precise and, in our case, machine-readable account of a perspective on a given domain of interest. In RDF schema, this conceptualization is described with two categories of concepts: *classes* and *properties*.

Classes represent sets of entities that have something in common. For example, the class of persons, the class of bikes, the class of fruits, the class of apples, the class of red things, etc. As shown in these examples, an entity can belong to several classes at the same time (e.g. an apple, a fruit and a red thing). When the instances of a given class are all instances of another class (as is the case for fruits and apples), we say that the former is a *subclass* of the latter (and the latter a *superclass* of the former).

It is worth pointing out here how classes in RDF schema (and actually, in ontology modeling in general) differ significantly from classes in many object-oriented programming (OOP) languages. We already pointed out that classes in an ontology can overlap, even when one is not a subclass of the other (e.g. bikes and red things). Furthermore, while many OOP languages allow at most one superclass per class, classes in an ontology can have multiple superclasses (e.g. a class of strawberries is a subclass of both fruits and red things). Finally, two classes in an ontology can be subclasses of each other, if they have the exact same set of instances. See Kamburjan *et al.* [14] for an extensive discussion on the gap between ontologies and OOP.

Properties represent binary relationships between entities. For example, the property "mother" relates every person to another person; the property "owner" relates some persons to some bikes. A property is usually described by its domain and its range, which are classes to which the first (respectively the second) entity in the relationship must belong. For example, the property "mother" admits the class of persons as its domain and range. The class of persons is also the domain of the property "owner" (only a person can own something), but the range is probably larger than the class of bikes (persons also own houses, books, etc.). Note that the range of a property can also be a datatype.

A property is a *subproperty* of another if the couple of entities related by the former property are all related by the latter. For example, the property "mother" is a subproperty of "parent," which is itself a subproperty of "ancestor."

Listing 3.6 shows an example ontology, as well as some instance data using it. Of course, any concrete syntax of RDF could have been used instead. We

```
1  ### Ontology
2
3  # defining classes
4
5  ex:Creature rdf:type rdfs:Class .
6
7  ex:Person rdf:type rdfs:Class .
8  ex:Person rdfs:subClassOf ex:Creature .
9
10 ex:Woman  rdf:type rdfs:Class .
11 ex:Woman rdfs:subClassOf ex:Person .
12
13 ex:Man rdf:type rdfs:Class .
14 ex:Man rdfs:subClassOf ex:Person .
15
16 # defining properties
17
18 ex:parent rdf:type rdf:Property .
19 ex:parent rdfs:domain ex:Person .
20 ex:parent rdfs:range ex:Person .
21
22 ex:mother rdf:type rdf:Property .
23 ex:mother rdfs:range ex:Woman .
24 ex:mother rdfs:subPropertyOf ex:parent .
25
26 ex:father rdf:type rdf:Property .
27 ex:father rdfs:range ex:Man .
28 ex:father rdfs:subPropertyOf ex:parent .
29
30 ex:name rdf:type rdf:Property .
31 ex:name rdfs:domain ex:Person .
32 ex:name rdfs:range xsd:string .
33
34
35 ### Instance data
36
37 ex:a rdf:type ex:Person .
38 ex:a ex:name "Archibald"^^xsd:string .
39 ex:a ex:mother ex:b .
40 ex:b ex:name "Brittany"^^xsd:string .
```

Listing 3.6　An example RDF-schema ontology and some instance data

can see from this example that the ontology itself is described using RDF, as follows:

- every class C is declared via a triple C rdf:type rdfs:Class;
- every property P is declared via a triple P rdf:type rdf:Property;
- subclass, domain, range and subproperty are indicated via the respective RDF predicates rdfs:subClassOf, rdfs:domain, rdfs:range and rdfs:subPropertyOf.

Instance data are described in RDF as follows:

- class instances are related to their class via the RDF predicate rdf:type (e.g. line 37);
- properties are used as RDF predicates (e.g. lines 38–40), relating two entities.

Inferences with RDF schema

The semantics of RDF schema [10] extends the semantics of RDF, allowing more inferences to be drawn, based on the specific meaning attributed to predicates such as rdf:type and rdfs:subClassOf. As an illustration, we give below a non-exhaustive list of inferences that can be drawn from the knowledge expressed in Listing 3.6:

- ex:Woman rdfs:subClassOf ex:Creature (by definition, the subclass relationship is transitive)
- ex:mother rdfs:domain ex:Person (ex:mother is a subproperty of ex:parent, so any entity that has a mother also has a parent, and must therefore be an instance of ex:Person, per the domain of ex:parent; more generally, the domain and range of a property are inherited by its subproperties)
- ex:a rdf:type ex:Creature (ex:Creature being a superclass of ex:Person)
- ex:a ex:parent ex:b (ex:parent being a superproperty of ex:mother)
- ex:b rdf:type ex:Woman (per the range of ex:mother)
- Note that ex:a rdf:type ex:Person would be inferred even if it was not asserted in the data (per the domain of ex:mother inferred above, but also per the domain of ex:givenName)

OWL

OWL [15] is a very expressive language for representing ontologies, based on the extensive literature on description logic [16]. It builds on RDF schema and extends it.

In OWL, classes and properties can be defined by combining other classes and properties. One can for example define the class of all bikes that are also red things (intersection), the class of all things that are either bikes or fruits (union), the class of all things that are not bikes (complement), the class that contains exactly a given list of instances (extension). One can define the property "child" as being exactly the inverse relationship of "parent." Classes and properties can be combined to define new classes call *restrictions*. For example, it is possible to define the class of all things that have some "owner" who is in the class "Woman," or all things that have at most two "owner's".

By relating defined classes with subclass axioms, one can express complex knowledge, such as, "all of Alice's bikes are either green or red" becomes:

- the intersection of
  - the class of bikes, and
  - the class (restriction) of things that have some "owner" in
    * the class that contains exactly the instance "Alice" (extension),
- is a subclass of
- the union of
  - the class of all green things, and
  - the class of all red things.

Besides subclass and subproperty axioms, OWL makes it possible to state that two classes (resp. properties) are equivalent (they contain exactly the same instances) or disjoint (they have no instance in common).

Properties can also be assigned with specific characteristics, such as being symmetric or asymmetric, reflexive or irreflexive, functional, transitive. For example, the property "mother" is asymmetric (two persons cannot be mother of each other), irreflexive (one person cannot be their own mother), and functional (any instance as at most one mother). The property "ancestor" is transitive. A property "sibling" would be transitive and symmetric.

Inferences with OWL

Extending Listing 3.6 with the OWL axioms in Listing 3.7, the following inferences (among others) become possible (see also Figure 3.5 for a visual summary of instance data in the listings):

- every ex:Person has exactly one ex:mother, exactly one ex:father, and no other ex:parent, because
  - every ex:Person must have at least one ex:mother (line 5) who must be an instance of ex:Woman (per the range of ex:mother), and who is also their ex:parent (superproperty of ex:mother);
  - every ex:Person must have at least one ex:father (line 10) who must be an instance of ex:Man (per the range of ex:father), and who is also their ex:parent (superproperty of ex:father);
  - ex:Man and ex:Woman are disjoint classes (line 3), these two ex:parents must be two distinct entities; and
  - every ex:Person must have at most two ex:parents (line 15), there can be no other ex:mother, ex:father or, more generally, ex:parent for that ex:Person.
- ex:b ex:mother ex:d (from the reasoning above, an ex:Person has exactly one ex:parent who is an ex:Woman and that has to be their ex:mother)
- ex:b ex:parent ex:c (because ex:child is the inverse of ex:parent)
- ex:b ex:father ex:c (since ex:d is ex:b's ex:mother, her only other ex:parent has to be her ex:father; note that we need to be sure that ex:c and ex:d are not two different names for the *same* person, which is guaranteed by the owl:differentFrom statement between them)

```
 1 ## Class axioms
 2
 3 ex:Man owl:disjointWith ex:Woman .
 4
 5 ex:Person rdfs:subClassOf _:at_least_1_mother .
 6 _:at_least_1_mother rdf:type owl:Restriction .
 7 _:at_least_1_mother owl:onProperty ex:mother .
 8 _:at_least_1_mother owl:cardinality 1 .
 9
10 ex:Person rdfs:subClassOf _:at_least_1_father .
11 _:at_least_1_father rdf:type owl:Restriction .
12 _:at_least_1_father owl:onProperty ex:father .
13 _:at_least_1_father owl:cardinality 1 .
14
15 ex:Person rdfs:subClassOf _:at_most_2_parents .
16 _:at_most_2_parents rdf:type owl:Restriction .
17 _:at_most_2_parents owl:onProperty ex:parent .
18 _:at_most_2_parents owl:maxCardinality 2 .
19
20
21 ## Property axioms
22
23 ex:child owl:inverseOf ex:parent .
24
25 ex:ancestor rdf:type owl:TransitiveProperty .
26 ex:parent rdfs:subPropertyOf ex:ancestor .
27
28
29 ## More instance data
30
31 ex:c ex:child ex:b .
32 ex:c ex:name "Charlie"^^xsd:string .
33
34 ex:b ex:parent ex:d .
35 ex:d rdf:type ex:Woman .
36 ex:d ex:name "Dorothy"^^xsd:string .
37 ex:d owl:differentFrom ex:c.
38
39 ex:a ex:mother ex:e .
```

Listing 3.7   An example OWL ontology extending that of Listing 3.6

- ex:c rdf:type ex:Man (follows from the inference above and the range of the ex:father property)
- ex:a ex:ancestor ex:d (because ex:mother and ex:parent are both subproperties of ex:ancestor, and ex:ancestor is transitive)
- ex:b owl:sameAs ex:e (the owl:sameAs predicate indicates that two IRIs identify the same entity; this is inferred because ex:a can only have one ex:mother; this is not an error nor an inconsistency, as RDF and OWL do not make the unique name assumption)

OWL profiles

As we can see from the examples above, OWL is a very expressive language, which can make reasoning with OWL very complex, or even undecidable. The OWL

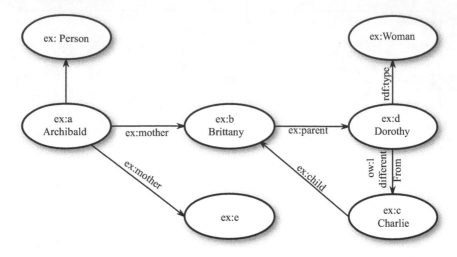

Figure 3.5   A subset of the instance data from Listings 3.6 and 3.7

specification defines a number of subsets of the language called *profiles* [17], with different trade-offs between expressiveness and complexity:

- OWL 2 DL is a very large subset of the language that still guarantees that complete reasoning can be achieved, using well-known Description Logic mechanisms [16].
- OWL 2 EL is targeting ontologies with a large number of classes and/or properties, and providing polynomial time complexity for standard reasoning tasks.
- OWL 2 QL is designed to allow reasoning at query time, by rewriting the query based on the ontology, without having to change the data.
- OWL 2 RL is designed so that reasoning can be implemented using rule-based technologies, such as Prolog [11] or Datalog [18].

Notation 3

Notation 3 (N3) is an extension of RDF that was proposed early on by Tim Berners-Lee [19] and had several implementations, but did not become a standard. However, it has received a lot of attention recently [20–22], and a W3C community group[2] is actively working on updating it, based on implementation experience.

A distinctive feature of N3 is the ability to express rules, as illustrated by Listing 3.8. An N3 rule is made of two subgraphs between curly brackets ({ . . . }), separated by the symbol => , and called respectively the premise and the conclusion of the rule. Identifiers starting with a question mark (?) are variables. For each subgraph in the data that matches the premise of the rule (for some binding of the variables), the triples in the conclusion, replacing the variables by their bound value, can be inferred. Inferred triples can then be used to trigger further rules.

---

[2] https://www.w3.org/community/n3-dev/

```
1  @prefix ex: <http://example.org/>.
2  @prefix rdf: <http://www.w3.org/1999/02/22-rdf-syntax-ns#>.
3
4  {
5      ?x ex:grandparent ?z .
6      ?x rdf:type ex:Person .
7  }
8  =>
9  {
10     ?x ex:parent _:y .
11     _:y ex:parent ?z .
12 } .
```

Listing 3.8   A rule in Notation 3

```
1  PREFIX ex: <http://example.org/>
2
3  SELECT ?n ?pn
4  WHERE {
5      ?x ex:name ?n .
6      ?x ex:parent ?p .
7      ?p ex:name ?pn .
8  }
```

Listing 3.9   A simple SPARQL query

For example, the rule in Listing 3.8 together with the statements **ex:bob ex:grandparent ex:dan** and **ex:bob rdf:type ex:Person**, would generate two new triples **ex:bob ex:parent** X, and X **ex:parent ex:dan**, where X is a fresh blank node. N3 can be used to implement the semantics of RDF schema or OWL 2 QL, and to extend them with business-specific rules.

3.1.3   Querying

SPARQL [23] is the standard language for querying RDF data. A SPARQL query, in its simplest form, is composed of a graph pattern that is expressed in a syntax very similar to Turtle, where some elements are variables (see e.g. Listing 3.9 – variables are identifiers starting with a question mark). When executing a query, a SPARQL engine will look in the data for all subgraphs that match the graph pattern, for some binding of the variables. For each of them, it will return the bindings of the variables appearing in the SELECT clause.

As an illustration, Table 3.2(a) shows the results of our example query on the data from Listings 3.6 and 3.7. The results contain only one binding, as there is only one (explicit) statement with predicate **ex:parent** in this data.

SPARQL can also be used in conjunction with reasoning. A number of different entailment regimes [24] are specifying how different reasoning mechanisms (including those of RDF schema and OWL, presented in Section 3.1.2) impact the results of

Table 3.2   *Result of the query in Listing 1.9 applied to the data in Listings 1.6 and 1.7 with different entailment regimes*

n	pn	n	pn	n	pn
Brittany	Dorothy	Brittany	Dorothy	Brittany	Dorothy
		Archibald	Brittany	Brittany	Charlie
				Archibald	Brittany
(a) Simple entailment		(b) RDFS entailment		(c) OWL entailment	

```
1  PREFIX ex: <http://example.org/>
2  PREFIX rdf: <http://www.w3.org/1999/02/22-rdf-syntax-ns#>
3  PREFIX s: <http://schema.org/>
4
5  CONSTRUCT {
6      ?x rdf:type s:Person .
7      ?x ex:givenName ?n .
8
9      ?p rdf:type s:Person .
10     ?p s:givenName ?pn .
11     ?p s:children ?x .
12 } WHERE {
13     ?x ex:name ?n .
14     ?x ex:parent ?p .
15     ?p ex:name ?pn .
16 }
```

Listing 3.10   A SPARQL CONSTUCT query

a SPARQL query. For example, Tables 3.2(b) and 3.2(c) show the results of the same query on the same data, using the entailment regimes corresponding to RDF schema and OWL, respectively. We see that under RDF schema entailment, statements with the **ex:mother** predicate (a subproperty of **ex:parent**) are taken into account. Under OWL entailment, statements with the **ex:child** predicate (the inverse of **ex:parent**) are also taken into account.

SPARQL is a very expressive language, of which a full description is out of the scope of this chapter. The results of a SELECT query can be filtered, ordered, or aggregated, in a very similar way to what SQL offers for relational databases. SPARQL also offers other types of queries. In particular, CONSTRUCT queries differ from SELECT queries in that their result is not a list of bindings, but a new RDF graph, described by another graph pattern (see an example in Listing 3.10). SPARQL CONSTRUCT queries can be used as a means to express inference rules [25].

3.1.4 Validating

As a data model, RDF is very flexible. This is a strength in some situations, but can also be a hindrance in others. Consider an application using an RDF knowledge graph about

```
1  ex:PersonShape rdf:type sh:NodeShape .
2  ex:PersonShape sh:targetClass ex:Person .
3  ex:PersonShape sh:property _:p1 .
4  ex:PersonShape sh:property _:p2 .
5
6  _:p1 sh:path ex:name .
7  _:p1 sh:maxCount 1 .
8  _:p1 sh:datatype xsd:string .
9
10 _:p2 sh:path ex:mother .
11 _:p2 sh:maxCount 1 .
12 _:p2 sh:node ex:PersonShape .
```

Listing 3.11   A SHACL shape

persons. When querying the knowledge graph and displaying the results, it might be helpful to assume that every person in the graph will have exactly one name. Without this assumption, query results may be unexpected or harder to interpret: for example, in Table 3.2(c), one could not decide whether Brittany has two distinct parents, or one parent with two names. Dealing with the special cases of a person having no name, or of a person having multiple names, might needlessly make applications overly complex.

Note that an OWL ontology is not helpful here, even if it specifies that every person has exactly one name. Under the open world assumption (see Section 3.1.2), such an ontology only guarantees that the name of each person exists in theory, not that it is explicitly present in the knowledge graph. Conversely, even though the ontology in Listing 3.7 states that every person has at most one mother, we saw that the graph in Figure 3.5 is consistent with that ontology, despite **ex:a** having two outgoing arcs with the predicate **ex:mother**. It entails that the two objects **ex:b** and **ex:e** denote one and the same person, but an application still has to deal with this apparent duplication.

Ontologies serve to capture the semantic constraints of the world described by the data. But sometimes we need to syntactically constrain the shape of the data itself. That's the purpose of the Shape Constraint Language SHACL [26]. A SHACL shape is a set of constraints that are checked on some nodes of the graph to be validated. Constraints can be on the nature of the node (IRI, literal, blank node), on its value if it is a literal (minimum and maximum bounds on numbers, regular expressions on strings...), and on its properties.

Listing 1.11 presents a simple example shape. The **sh:targetClass** property (line 2) indicates that this shape must be verified by all nodes with **rdf:type ex:Person**. It has two property constraints (lines 3 and 4), which are further described by blank nodes _:p1 and _:p2. The former states that target nodes must have at most one **ex:name**, and that its value must be a literal with datatype **xsd:string**. The latter states that target nodes must have at most one **ex:mother** and that its value must satisfy the same shape.[3] The graph described in Listing 3.6 complies with this shape: the only target node

---

[3]Such recursive shapes are not required to be supported by compliant SHACL implementations, but a number of implementations support them to some extent.

ex:a has exactly one ex:name and one ex:mother, which satisfy the corresponding constraints (the object of ex:mother, ex:b, satisfies the shape as it has one ex:name and no ex:mother). The graph described by Listings 3.6 and 3.7 together, on the other hand, does not satisfy the shape, as ex:a now has two outgoing arcs with the predicate ex:mother.

Besides SHACL, ShEx [27] is another shape language that is widely used, despite not being an official standard. For an extended comparison of SHACL and ShEx, refer to the book by Labra Gayo *et al.* [28].

While validation is the primary purpose of shape languages, they can be used in other ways. In a separate specification [29], the authors of SHACL propose an extension of the language to express inference rules, where the premise of the rule is expressed in terms of a shape.

3.2   PKGs based on RDF

In this section, we review a number of works that have been using RDF and the semantic web stack of technologies to help build PKGs.

3.2.1   Semantic desktop

The idea of the semantic desktop can be traced back to Leopold Sauermann's master's thesis [30] and the Gnowsis project. This project stems from the observation that, at the turn of the millennium, personal computers were becoming ubiquitous, supporting more and more activities, both for work and leisure. An increasing amount of information was created and gathered through multiple and heterogeneous applications, making it difficult to retrieve, reuse, and combine this information in a useful way. Sauermann developed an RDF ontology for personal information management, and a server for integrating RDF data from existing applications, through ad hoc adapters. Gnowsis also provided dedicated interfaces for linking entities across applications (e.g. a document in the file browser and a person in the address book), and for browsing the PKG thus constructed.

IRIS [31] (an acronym for "Integrate. Relate. Infer. Share".) took a different approach, by providing a set of integrated applications (forked from popular open-source software) tightly coupled to a common underlying RDF knowledge graph. IRIS also emphasized the use of machine learning for automatically linking the entities in the graph: disambiguating contacts in e-mail headers, extracting metadata from common file formats, clustering similar resources into projects.

While previous projects suffered from a reduced user base, the Nepomuk [32] project involved a large consortium of partners,[4] and benefited from being integrated for a number of years to the popular Linux desktop environment KDE,[5] under the name "Semantic Search". Nepomuk's Semantic Middleware played a similar role to

---

[4]https://nepomuk.semanticdesktop.org/Participants.html
[5]https://userbase.kde.org/Nepomuk

Gnowsis' server, but also implemented multiple functionalities to enrich the data in a way similar to IRIS. Nepomuk also put an emphasis on collaborative work and the interconnection of multiple users' semantic desktops, integrating notions of access control and distributed search and storage.

In addition to being connected to existing applications, Nepomuk also supported dedicated applications making full use of the Semantic Middleware. SemNodes [33] was such a tool, allowing users to take nodes and interconnect them with other elements of the semantic desktop, such as e-mails, contacts or calendar events, creating even more relationships in the personal knowledge graph.

In April 2014, KDE switched from Nepomuk to another system (not based on RDF) for its semantic search functionality.[6] The invoked reasons were: ease of use for developers, and stability and performances for end users. Arguably, a decade later, the RDF and semantic web landscape have improved on those front – even though the same arguments are still being used to criticize semantic web technologies, not always backed by quantified evidence.

3.2.2   From desktop to devices

The projects presented in the previous section focused on desktop computers, but in the past decade, the use of digital technologies has moved towards multiple and diverse connected devices. Since 2017, the share of mobile phones in Internet traffic has overtaken that of desktop computers.[7] Building a PKG that accurately captures someone's activity therefore requires to tap all these devices. Furthermore, their ubiquitous nature (our mobile phones follow us everywhere we go), and the wealth of sensors they come equipped with, widen the scope of what such knowledge graphs can contain in an unprecedented way. The trend of capturing and storing detailed information about ones' own digital traces, for future reuse or analysis, has been known as "lifelogging" or "quantified self".

The use of RDF and semantic web technologies for lifelogging has been explored by Packer *et al.* [34]. Data is collected from a user's mobile phone (GPS tracks, nearby devices detected through WiFi and Bluetooth, calendar events and message) as RDF. It is then complemented by external data from public knowledge graphs (like DBPedia[8] or Geonames.[9]) In order for the user to explore the content of this PKG, the authors propose Memorybook, a tool for generating and displaying textual narratives, based on the graph, and enriched with maps, images, and links.

With Thymeflow [35], Montoya *et al.* follow a similar approach, but their primary source of data is a number of online applications. This is a sensible move considering that (1) a user owning multiple devices (smartphone, tablet, laptop) will use such applications to synchronize data across them and (2) some wearable devices cannot be accessed directly, but only through the manufacturer's online service. Enrichment, based on external data sources, is performed incrementally every time a change occurs

---

[6]https://dot.kde.org/2014/02/24/kdes-next-generation-semantic-search
[7]https://gs.statcounter.com/platform-market-share/desktop-mobile-tablet
[8]https://www.dbpedia.org/
[9]https://www.geonames.org/

in the PKG. Despite encouraging results, the authors point out: "the hard truth is that many popular Internet-based services still do not provide an API for conveniently retrieving user data." It means that users cannot fully benefit from the data the create in online applications.

3.2.3 Re-decentralizing the web

While the web was initially designed as a open and decentralized system meant to serve everybody, it has turned into a largely centralized environment, where most of the data is in the hands of a few big companies. Not only does this deprive users of the free use of their own data, but it can have (and has actually had) deep and detrimental societal aspects, such as massive data leaks or the gaming of election results. This realization [36] led the web's inventor, Tim Berners-Lee, to propose what he called a "mid-course correction." The solid protocol aims at re-decentralizing the web, and to give users back control over their data.

Figure 3.6(a) represents the architecture of traditional web applications: every time a user interacts with an application, the data they produce is stored in a database under the control of the application provider. As a result, all that user's data is scattered

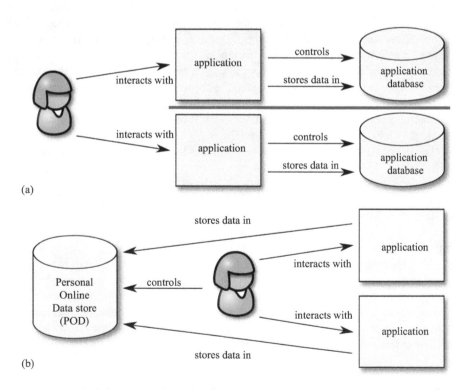

Figure 3.6   *Solid compared to siloed applications. (a) siloed applications, (b) Solid applications.*

in different silos, and each piece of data can only be used within the application that created it. The user cannot benefit from the added value that would result from combining all their data – while the application provider benefits from the combination of multiple users.

Figure 3.6(b) summarizes the paradigm shift proposed by Solid: each user has a Personal Online Data (POD) store over which they have control. The grant each application they use with access to (part of) their POD, so that the data produced while interacting is stored in the POD. Applications may benefit from data created with another application (if the users consents), which allows the user and application providers to get more value from their data. Finally, the data remains accessible to the user even if they stop using the application or the application providers go out of business.

Solid PODs can store any kind of content, but the primary format for data and metadata is RDF. As such, a Solid POD can be seen as a personal knowledge graph. Contrarily to the approaches presented above, this graph is not a secondary source of data, built by converting pre-existing data to RDF but the primary source: applications are expected to consume and produce RDF data directly.

Solid has been developed for several years under the aegis of a W3C Community Group[10] and, at the time of writing, is on its way to become a W3C standard.[11] While we are still in the early days, and the approach illustrated in Figure 3.6(a) is still the dominant one on the web, a number of private and public actors are already staking Solid. In particular, Solid is considered by the European Commission as a relevant building block[12] in the implementation of the Data Governance Act [37]. Local governments are also investing in it, such as the Flemish Community[13].

3.3   Data sharing and compliance

Humans live in society. People have a strong interest in sharing information with others. The digitization of all aspects of our life, fed with massive amounts of data produced by a growing variety of sensors, results in increasingly complex systems, that are ever more difficult to understand for humans. As billions of people live their lives online, knowledge graphs offer a way to tackle this complexity (the velocity, variety, and volume of big data), and to share information more efficiently.

The advertisement industry has constructed huge profiles of individuals by tracking their social networking, browsing habits and other online interactions. Personal data is seen as a high value asset. If a flat profile is already so valuable, putting the information about a person into context, relating it to other people, will create even higher value. The creation of a personal knowledge graph can thus expose the

---

[10]https://www.w3.org/community/solid/
[11]https://lists.w3.org/Archives/Public/public-solid/2022Nov/0001.html
[12]https://joinup.ec.europa.eu/collection/semic-support-centre/personal-data-spaces
[13]https://www.ugent.be/ea/idlab/en/news-events/news/flemish-government-7m-eur-funding-solidlab-vlaanderen.htm

individual to much higher risks, whether the PKG is created by themselves or by others.

At the same time, the development of the data economy is meant to be fueled by the sharing of large amounts of data. Orwell's dystopian vision collides with the high increase in the ability to collect and use data ever more efficiently and intelligently. And because individuals participate in this data economy, they gather information about themselves, but also about others, in their personal knowledge graph. Concerns about privacy and control seem to be in head-to-head conflict with the premises of the data economy. But in fact, things are not so black and white.

This is where policies for data sharing and privacy preservation come into play. As we will show, they make the data economy viable without profoundly harming society. But as societies are complex, those rules are also complex. Computers and networking may have created the problem but they can also help us to resolve it. To do so, we need to establish a balance between interests. This is done by the laws that, in a democratic society, formalize the agreement between all societal actors as resulting from a democratic process.

So if we are to preserve the democratic society and still benefit from the high efficiency of the data economy by making rules, we need to address the following questions: how do we apply laws in a networked society, how does that work in the data economy? From the uncanny story around the use of the so-called cookie-banners to acquiring consent from consumers as required by the European General Data Protection Regulation (GDPR), we know already that many things can go wrong.

Semantic web technologies can make a big contribution here. They allow us to understand and control things in context, and to represent the complex societal systems created by the networked society.

3.3.1   Policies

According to the Cambridge dictionary, a policy is "a set of ideas or a plan of what to do in particular situations that has been agreed to officially by a group of people, a business organization, a government, or a political party." For the purpose of knowledge representation, this can be broken down into two issues. The first one is about what to do in a particular situation, i.e. the expression of rules. The second one is about the social agreement over such rules.

Many ways of representing legal and regulatory rules in a machine-readable form have been explored. Some authors have explored the use of generic rule languages, such as RuleML[14], W3C's Rule Interchange Format RIF [38] or even SHACL [26][15]. Others have proposed dedicated languages, such as

- LegalRuleML [39], an XML-based language specializing RuleML for the legal domain, standardized by OASIS;

---

[14]https://en.wikipedia.org/wiki/RuleML
[15]To the best of our knowledge, Phil Archer was the first one to suggest the use of SHACL for checking regulatory compliance.

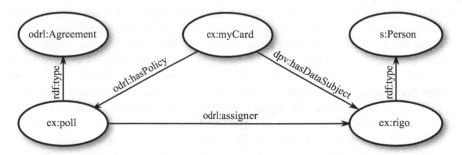

Figure 3.7 An example graph linking a policy, a piece of data, and the data subject

- the Open Digital Rights Language ODRL [40] is an RDF-based language for representing usage policies for contents and services, standardized by W3C;
- Bonatti and Olmedilla [41] have proposed a language to describe policies and reason about them; this language is a subset of OWL and leverages its semantics and reasoning capabilities.

But capturing the structure of rules is only one side of the problem. It is also necessary to accurately represent the commonly agreed concepts (the second part of the Cambridge dictionary definition) that are invoked in rules. In the important domain of policies for data protection, several research projects have worked on expressing the semantics of the GDPR. Among them, the W3C Data Protection Vocabulary Community Group[16] has developed a set of specifications [42,43] that assign IRIs to all the concepts defined in GDPR, so that they can be unambiguously referred to in RDF-based policy languages. This can serve as an example of how to take up the challenge of creating the appropriate semantics for use in intelligent reasoning over personal knowledge graphs that respect the regulatory environment.

While tools are available to represent rules and regulations using semantic web technologies, the creation of legally meaningful machine-readable constraints is an interdisciplinary and complex undertaking. Hence the quest to reuse as much knowledge as possible from already existing use cases. Services like Linked Open Vocabularies [44] and Plow[17] aim to encourage and facilitate the reuse of shared ontologies. However, to the best of our knowledge, no such tool exists yet for the reuse of rules or policies.

3.3.2 Data annotations to connect policies

Within the legal system, rules and expressions are always related to an entity. This entity is subject to these rules. To determine which rules apply to a given entity in

---

[16]https://www.w3.org/community/dpvcg/
[17]https://github.com/field33/plow/

a given context, the relation needs to be either explicitly stated in advance, or computed on demand. Fortunately, the semantic web technologies presented in Section 3.1 offer all the necessary functionalities. Figure 3.7 illustrates how the vocabularies presented above can combine to explicitly link an ODRL policy (a set of rules) to a piece of data, and to the data subject (the person described by the dataset ex:myCard). In other situations, policies can be related to OWL classes instead of specific instances, and the rules applying to a given instance are determined through reasoning [41]. Whether instances or classes are annotated by policies depends entirely on the use case and its additional requirements. But in all cases, all rules applying to a given instance end up being linked to that instance through the appropriate RDF arcs.

It is therefore possible to augment a personal knowledge graph with policy data, expressed as annotation of instances or classes. In the case where a subset of the PKG itself has to be subject to rules or policy, that particular subgraph has to be identified by an IRI, which is related to the policy in a different subgraph. This notion of *named graph* was initially proposed by Caroll *et al.* [45] and has been since integrated into the RDF standard. For example, Solid PODs (see Section 3.2.3) are actually collections of named graphs, where each of them is subject to different access control rules (and could, in theory, be also annotated with, e.g., ODRL policies).

3.3.3   Data sharing

Being able to attach parts of a PKG to the relevant policies is valuable. However, in the data economy, data is expected to be exchanged across organization borders. It is therefore crucial to ensure that not only data but also the rules and constraints they are subjected to, are exchanged in an interoperable way, and complied with by all actors. This way, we can balance between human rights, equity considerations and business needs.

This way of approaching the ethical and legal constraints takes the above systems of policy controlled data handling to the next level. The sticky policy paradigm, introduced in 2002 by Karjoth *et al.* [46], ensures that the rules, limitations, and other constraints, are irrevocably attached to the data all the time. Verifiable credentials [47] offer a way of achieving this, packaging the data with some metadata (possibly including policies) and using a digital signature (or other forms of cryptographic proof) to make the whole tamper-evident. Distributed ledger technologies are another way, allowing for an immutable record of the agreements between the data subjects and someone processing their personal data. Now the fact that someone has the personal data and has processed it for a defined purpose can return as knowledge into the personal knowledge graph, thus growing it.

Many applied research projects have been exploring data-sharing use-cases and developing the necessary semantics to support them. As an example, the SPECIAL project[18] studied data sharing for location-based services. This coincidentally creates

---

[18]https://specialprivacy.ercim.eu/ and especially its deliverables D1.6, D1.7, and D2.1 for the use case on location-based services

a personal knowledge graph of the locations an individual visited, with all the privacy issues that such a graph entails.

3.4   Conclusion

In this chapter, we have described the semantic web stack, a comprehensive list of open standards for representing, reasoning with, querying and validating knowledge graphs. We have described different projects relying on those standards to build personal knowledge graphs, and to allow them to seamlessly interoperate with other knowledge graphs on the web. Finally, we discussed related standards for describing rules and policies, in order to express under which conditions information from personal knowledge graphs can be shared with others, in the advent of the so-called data economy.

The digitization of our lives creates new complex social models. Raymond [48] described how Internet and the web created the conditions without which the open-source ecosystem could not have developed. Creating the conditions of a secure and privacy-preserving data economy in an ever more interconnected world remains an ongoing and challenging endeavor.

References

[1]   Berners-Lee T, Hendler J, Lassila O, *et al*. The semantic web. *Scientific American*. 2001;284(5):28–37. Available from: http://isel2918929391.googlecode. com/svn-history/r347/trunk/RPC/Slides/p01_theSemanticWeb.pdf.

[2]   Cyganiak R, Wood D, and Lanthaler M. RDF 1.1 Concepts and Abstract Syntax. W3C Recommendation; 2014. Available from: https://www.w3.org/TR/ rdf11-concepts/.

[3]   Dürst M and Suignard M. Internationalized Resource Identifiers (IRIs). IETF; 2005. RFC 3987. Available from: https://tools.ietf.org/html/rfc3987.

[4]   Heath T and Bizer C. Linked data: evolving the web into a global data space. In: *Synthesis Lectures on Data, Semantics, and Knowledge*. Springer International Publishing; 2011. Available from: https://link.springer.com/10.1007/ 978-3-031-79432-2.

[5]   Prud'hommeaux E, Carothers G, Beckett D, *et al*. RDF 1.1 Turtle – Terse RDF Triple Language. W3C Recommendation; 2014. Available from: https: //www.w3.org/TR/turtle/.

[6]   Biron PV and Malhotra A. XML Schema Part 2: Datatypes Second Edition. W3C Recommendation; 2004. Available from: http://www.w3.org/TR/ xmlschema-2/.

[7]   Gandon F and Schreiber G. RDF 1.1 XML Syntax. W3C Recommendation; 2014. Available from: https://www.w3.org/TR/rdf-syntax-grammar/.

[8]   Carothers G and Seaborne A. RDF 1.1 N-Triples. W3C Recommendation; 2014. Available from: https://www.w3.org/TR/n-triples/.

[9] Kellogg G, Champin PA, and Longley D. JSON-LD 1.1 – A JSON-based Serialization for Linked Data. W3C Recommendation; 2020. Available from: https://www.w3.org/TR/json-ld11/.

[10] Hayes PJ and Patel-Schneider PF. RDF 1.1 Semantics. W3C Recommendation; 2014. Available from: https://www.w3.org/TR/rdf11-mt/.

[11] Sterling L and Shapiro E. *The Art of Prolog*. 2nd ed. MIT Press; 1994. Available from: http://www.cliplab.org/~logalg/doc/The_Art_of_Prolog.pdf.

[12] Brickley D and Guha RV. RDF Schema 1.1. W3C Recommendation; 2014. Available from: http://www.w3.org/TR/2014/REC-rdf-schema-20140225/.

[13] Gruber T. Towards principles for the design of ontologies used for knowledge sharing. In: *Formal Ontology in Conceptual Analysis and Knowledge Representation*. Kluwer Academic Publishers; 1993. Available from: http://www-ksl.stanford.edu/pub/knowledge-sharing/papers/onto-design.ps.

[14] Kamburjan E, Klungre VN, and Giese M. Never mind the semantic gap: modular, lazy and safe loading of RDF data. In: Groth P, Vidal ME, Suchanek F, *et al.*, editors. *The Semantic Web*. Vol. 13261 of Lecture Notes in Computer Science. Hersonnisos, Greece: Springer International Publishing; 2022. p. 200–216. Available from: https://link.springer.com/10.1007/978-3-031-06981-9_12.

[15] Hitzler P, Krötzsch M, Parsia B, *et al*. OWL 2 Web Ontology Language Primer. W3C Recommendation; 2009. Available from: http://www.w3.org/TR/owl2-primer/.

[16] Baader F, Calvanese D, McGuinness DL, *et al.*, editors. *The Description Logic Handbook: Theory, Implementation, and Applications*. Cambridge University Press; 2003. Available from: http://ksl.stanford.edu/people/dlm/papers/dlhb-contents.pdf.

[17] Motik B, Grau BC, Horrocks I, *et al*. OWL 2 Web Ontology Language Profiles (Second Edition). W3C Recommendation; 2012. Available from: https://www.w3.org/TR/owl2-profiles/.

[18] Ceri S, Gottlob G, and Tanca L. What you always wanted to know about Datalog (and never dared to ask). *IEEE Transactions on Knowledge and Data Engineering*. 1989;1(1):146–166. Available from: https://personal.utdallas.edu/~gupta/courses/acl/2021/other-papers/datalog-paper.pdf.

[19] Berners-Lee T. Notation3 (N3) A readable RDF syntax; 2006. Available from: http://www.w3.org/DesignIssues/Notation3.

[20] Arndt D. Notation3 as the Unifying Logic for the Semantic Web [PhD Thesis]. Ghent University; 2019. Available from: https://biblio.ugent.be/publication/8634507/file/8634516.

[21] Farnbauer-Schmidt M, Charpenay V, and Harth A. N3X: Notation3 with SPARQL expressions. In: Harth A, Presutti V, Troncy R, *et al.*, editors. *The Semantic Web: ESWC 2020 Satellite Events*. Vol. 12124 of Lecture Notes in Computer Science. Springer International Publishing; 2020. p. 79–83. Available from: https://link.springer.com/10.1007/978-3-030-62327-2_14.

[22] Woensel WV, Abidi S, and Abidi SSR. Towards model-driven semantic interfaces for electronic health records on multiple platforms using Notation3.

In: Stefanidis K, Rao P, Kondylakis H, *et al.*, editors. *Proceedings of the Fourth International Workshop on Semantic Web Meets Health Data Management (SWH)*. Vol. 3055 of CEUR Workshop Proceedings. Virtual Conference, October: CEUR; 2021. p. 41–52. ISSN: 1613-0073. Available from: https://ceur-ws.org/Vol-3055/#paper4.

[23] Harris S and Seaborne A. SPARQL 1.1 Query Language. W3C Recommendation; 2013. Available from: http://www.w3.org/TR/sparql11-query/.

[24] Glimm B and Ogbuji C. SPARQL 1.1 Entailment Regimes. W3C Recommendation; 2013. Available from: https://www.w3.org/TR/sparql11-entailment/.

[25] Seye O, Faron Zucker C, Corby O, *et al.* Bridging the Gap between RIF and SPARQL: Implementation of a RIF Dialect with a SPARQL Rule Engine; 2012. Available from: https://hal.inria.fr/hal-00724291.

[26] Knublauch H and Kontokostas D. Shapes Constraint Language (SHACL). W3C Recommendation; 2017. Available from: https://www.w3.org/TR/shacl/.

[27] Prud'hommeaux E, Boneva I, Labra Gayo JE, *et al.* Shape Expressions Language 2.1. W3C Final Community Group Report; 2019. Available from: http://shex.io/shex-semantics/index.html.

[28] Labra Gayo JE, Prud'hommeaux E, Boneva I, *et al. Validating RDF Data*. Vol. 7 of Synthesis Lectures on the Semantic Web: Theory and Technology. Morgan & Claypool Publishers LLC; 2017. Available from: https://book.validatingrdf.com/.

[29] Knublauch H, Allemang D, and Steyskal S. SHACL Advanced Features. W3C Working Group Note; 2017. Available from: https://www.w3.org/TR/shacl-af/.

[30] Sauermann L. The Gnowsis – using semantic web technologies to build a semantic desktop [Master's Thesis]. TU Wien; 2003. Available from: http://www.gnowsis.com/download/2003/sauermann2003.pdf.

[31] Cheyer A, Park J, and Giuli R. IRIS: Integrate. Relate. Infer. Share. In: Semantic Desktop Workshop; 2005. Available from: https://www.semanticscholar.org/paper/IRIS%%3A-Integrate.-Relate.-Infer.-Share-Cheyer-Park/eae1f4a97d160ed7027a663ae6771d83269915cc.

[32] Groza T, Handschuh S, Moeller K, *et al.* The NEPOMUK project – on the way to the social semantic desktop. In: *I-Semantic 2007*. Graz, Austria; 2007. Available from: http://siegfried-handschuh.net/pub/2007/nepomuk_isemantics2007.pdf.

[33] Drăgan L, Handschuh S, and Decker S. The semantic desktop at work: interlinking notes. In: *Proceedings of the 7th International Conference on Semantic Systems*. Graz Austria: ACM; 2011. p. 17–24. Available from: https://dl.acm.org/doi/10.1145/2063518.2063521.

[34] Packer HS, Smith A, and Lewis P. Memorybook: generating narratives from lifelogs. In: *Proceedings of the 2nd Workshop on Narrative and Hypertext*; 2012. p. 7–12. Available from: https://eprints.soton.ac.uk/346890/1/memorybook.pdf.

[35]   Montoya D, Pellissier Tanon T, Abiteboul S, *et al*. A knowledge base for personal information management. In: *LDOW2018-Linked Open Data Workshop at the World Wide Web Conference*. Lyon, France; 2018. Available from: https://pierre.senellart.com/publications/montoya2018knowledge.pdf.

[36]   Nast C. I Was Devastated: The Man Who Created the World Wide Web Has Some Regrets. Vanity Fair. 2018 Jul; Available from: https://www.vanityfair.com/news/2018/07/the-man-who-created-the-world-wide-web-has-some-regrets.

[37]   Regulation (EU)2022/868 of the European Parliament and of the Council of 30May 2022 on European data governance and amending Regulation (EU)2018/1724 (Data Governance Act) (Text with EEA relevance); 2022. Legislative Body: CONSIL, EP. Available from: http://data.europa.eu/eli/reg/2022/868/oj/eng.

[38]   Morgenstern L, Welty C, Boley H, *et al*. RIF Primer (Second Edition). W3C Working Group Note; 2013. Available from: http://www.w3.org/TR/rif-primer.

[39]   Palmirani M, Governatori G, Athan T, *et al*. LegalRuleML Core Specification Version 1.0. OASIS Standard; 2021. Available from: https://docs.oasis-open.org/legalruleml/legalruleml-core-spec/v1.0/os/legalruleml-core-spec-v1.0-os.html.

[40]   Iannella R, Steidl M, McRoberts M, *et al*. ODRL Vocabulary & Expression. W3C Recommendation; 2017. Available from: https://www.w3.org/TR/2017/WD-odrl-vocab-20170223/.

[41]   Bonatti PA and Olmedilla D. Rule-based policy representation and reasoning for the semantic web. In: Antoniou G, Aßmann U, Baroglio C, *et al*., editors. *Reasoning Web, Third International Summer School 2007*, Dresden, Germany, September 3–7, 2007, Tutorial Lectures. Vol. 4636 of Lecture Notes in Computer Science. Springer; 2007. p. 240–268. Available from: http://www.macs.hw.ac.uk/bisel/rewerse/ publications/download/REWERSE-RP-2007-114.pdf.

[42]   Pandit HJ. Data Privacy Vocabulary (DPV). W3C Final Community Group Report; 2022. Available from: https://www.w3.org/community/reports/dpvcg/CG-FINAL-dpv-20221205.

[43]   Pandit HJ. DPV-GDPR: GDPR Extension for DPV. W3C Final Community Group Report; 2022. Available from: https://w3c.github.io/cg-reports/dpvcg/CG-FINAL-dpv-gdpr-20221205/#A6-1-a.

[44]   Vandenbussche PY, Atemezing GA, Poveda-Villalón M, *et al*. Linked Open Vocabularies (LOV): a gateway to reusable semantic vocabularies on the Web. *Semantic Web*. 2017;8(3):437–452. Available from: http://www.semantic-web-journal.net/content/linked-open-vocabularies-lov-gateway-reusable-semantic-vocabularies-web-1.

[45]   Carroll JJ, Bizer C, Hayes P, *et al*. Named graphs. *Journal of Web Semantics*. 2005;3(4):247–267. Available from: https://www.academia.edu/download/46757438/Named_Graphs20160624-9848-1sb9eg6.pdf; https://doi.org/10.1016/j.websem.2005.09.001.

[46] Karjoth G, Schunter M, and Waidner M. Platform for enterprise privacy practices: privacy-enabled management of customer data. In: Dingledine R and Syverson PF, editors. *Privacy Enhancing Technologies, Second International Workshop, PET 2002*, San Francisco, CA, USA, April 14–15, 2002, Revised Papers. Vol. 2482 of Lecture Notes in Computer Science. Springer; 2002. p. 69–84. Available from: http://dud.inf.tu-dresden.de/sirene/publ/KaSW1_02.EP3P4PET.pdf.

[47] Sporny M, Noble G, Longley D, *et al*. Verifiable Credentials Data Model v1.1. W3C Recommendation; 2022. Available from: https://www.w3.org/TR/vc-data-model/.

[48] Raymond E. *The Cathedral and the Bazaar: Musings on Linux and Open Source by an Accidental Revolutionary*. O'Reilly Media; 1999. Available from: https://archive.org/details/CathedralAndTheBazaar.

Chapter 4

From knowledge to reasoning, a cognitive perspective on personal knowledge graphs

Dav Raggett[a]

4.1 Motivation

Work on personal knowledge graphs would greatly benefit from decades of progress in the cognitive sciences. Knowledge is about understanding information based upon past experience, where understanding enables reasoning and decision-making. Today's applications, however, embed limited understanding in application code, as deductive logic is not adequate for human-like reasoning. Humans are always learning and never attain perfect knowledge, and our reasoning out of necessity has to deal with uncertain, incomplete, imprecise, and inconsistent knowledge. This chapter will introduce a cognitive approach to personal knowledge graphs, including plausible reasoning, System 1 for intuitive thinking, including effortlessly and rapidly generating coherent explanations, e.g., for natural language understanding, and System 2 for effortful slower deliberative thought, and how this can enable human-like memory, reasoning and decision-making.

4.2 Introduction

Whilst today's knowledge graphs claim to capture knowledge there is little attention to automated reasoning with the exception of inheritance down class hierarchies. Application logic is instead embedded in application code, making it hard to understand and costly to update. Why should we continue to accept this state of affairs?

A starting point is to consider just what we mean by knowledge and its relationship to information and data. Data is essentially an unstructured collection of values, such as numbers, text strings and truth values. Information is structured data[1], such as tabular data labeled with column names. Knowledge is understanding how to reason

---

[a]European Research Consortium for Informatics and Mathematics (ERCIM)
[1]Unstructured data is often confusingly used as a term for information that does not follow specific data models, for example, text documents, where the structure is formed by characters, words, punctuation and paragraphs.

with information. Knowledge presumes reasoning and without it is just information. As such it is high time to focus on automated reasoning for human–machine cooperative work that boosts productivity and compensates for skill shortages.

Figure 4.1 depicts the evolution of databases from relational databases to graph databases, where the next stage is likely to be the emergence of cognitive databases featuring human-like reasoning. Relational databases are widely used in business, but there is growing interest in the greater flexibility of graph databases based on either RDF or property graphs.

People have studied the principles of plausible arguments since the days of Ancient Greece, e.g., Carneades and his guidelines for effective argumentation. There has been a long line of philosophers working on this since then, including Locke, Bentham, Wigmore, Keynes, Wittgenstein, Pollock, and many others.

Plausible reasoning is *everyday reasoning*, and the basis for legal, ethical and business decisions. Researchers in the 20th century were sidetracked by the seductive purity of mathematical logic, and more recently, by the amazing magic of deep learning. Traditional logic is a sterile dead end, elegant, but ultimately of limited utility! It is now time to exploit human-like plausible reasoning with imperfect knowledge for human–machine cooperative work using distributed knowledge graphs. This will enable computers to analyze, explain, justify, expand upon, and argue in human-like ways.

In the real world, knowledge is distributed, imprecise, and imperfect. We are learning all the time, and revising our beliefs and understanding as we interact with others. Imperfect is used here in the sense of *uncertain, incomplete,* and *inconsistent*. Imprecise concepts are those that lack a crisp definition, and needing to be interpreted in context, e.g., the color *red*, and a *young* person.

Conventional logic fails to cope with this challenge, and the same is true for statistical approaches, e.g., Bayesian inference, due to difficulties with gathering the

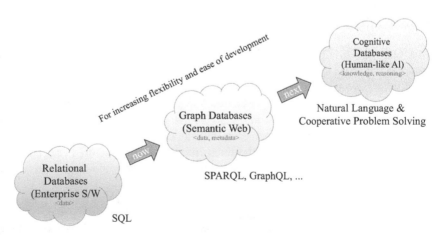

Figure 4.1   Evolution of databases for greater flexibility

required statistics. Evolution has equipped humans with the means to deal with this, though not everyone is rational, and some people lack sound judgment. Moreover, all of us are subject to various kinds of cognitive biases, as highlighted by Daniel Kahneman.

4.3   Plausible knowledge

Consider the logical implication A ⇒ B. This means if A is true then B is true. If A is false then B may be true or false. If B is true, we still cannot be sure that A is true, but if B is false then A must be false. Now consider a more concrete example: *if it is raining then it is cloudy*. This can be used in both directions: rain is more likely if it is cloudy, likewise, if it is not raining, then it might be sunny, so it is less likely that it is cloudy, which makes use of our knowledge of weather.

In essence, plausible reasoning draws upon prior knowledge as well as on the role of analogies, and consideration of examples, including precedents. Mathematical proof is replaced by reasonable arguments, both for and against a premise, along with how these arguments are to be assessed. In court cases, arguments are laid out by the Prosecution and the Defence, the Judge decides which evidence is admissible, and the guilt is assessed by the Jury.

During the 1980s, Alan Collins and co-workers (see further reading) developed a theory of plausible reasoning based on recordings of how people reasoned. They discovered that:

- There are several categories of inference rules that people commonly use to answer questions.
- People weigh the evidence bearing on a question, both for and against, rather like in court proceedings.
- People are more or less certain depending on the certainty of the premises, the certainty of the inferences, and whether different inferences lead to the same or opposite conclusions.
- Facing a question for which there is an absence of directly applicable knowledge, people search for other knowledge that could help give potential inferences.

4.3.1   The plausible knowledge notation

A convenient way to express such knowledge is the **Plausible Knowledge Notation** (PKN). This is at a higher level than RDF, and combines symbolic statements with qualitative metadata used to express certainty and conditional likelihood, etc. PKN supports a variety of statements including properties, relationships, dependencies, implications, and ranges. Metadata can be provided at the end of statements as a comma, separated list of name value pairs enclosed in round brackets.
Property statements declare the values of named properties, e.g.,

flowers of England includes daffodils, roses, tulips (certainty high).

Following the terminology introduced by Collins, *flowers* is the *descriptor*, i.e., the property name. *England* is the *argument*, i.e., the thing the property applies to. *includes* is the *operator*, with *excludes* as its antonym. The values are the *referents*, and either reference things or are literals such as numbers.

PKN statements optionally end with one or metadata parameters, e.g., *certainty* is an example of qualitative metadata, where the value of the parameter is from an enumerated range, e.g., *low, medium*, and *high*.

Some concepts are context dependent, e.g., the meaning of young depends on whether you are referring to a child or an adult. The context can be stated with *for* as in the following examples:

age of young is birth, 12 for child
age of young is birth, 45 for adult

Relationship statements describe relationships between things, e.g.,

robin kind-of songbird
duck similar-to goose for habitat
duck dissimilar-to goose for neck-length
dingy is small for sailing-boat

Where *kind-of* describes the relationship between classes of things. *similar-to* indicates that one class has similar referents for a given descriptor, as named with *for*, whilst *dissimilar-to* has the opposite meaning. The *is* relationship is convenient for properties without descriptors. In this example, *small* is a term for describing the size of something relative to some context.

Relationships take the form *subject, type, object*, so that in the first example above, the subject is *robin*, the relationship type is *kind-of* and the object is *songbird*. **Dependency statements** are relationships that describe a coupling between a pair of properties, e.g.,

climate depends-on latitude
current increases-with voltage
pressure decreases-with altitude

Dependencies can describe a correlation as in the case of *increases-with*, or leave that unspecified, as for *depends-on*. If two locations have similar latitude, then the first statement above implies that they should have similar climates. Dependencies are useful for qualitative reasoning about physical processes[2].

Implication statements are a form of if-then rules with locally scoped variables, for example, *?place*, as in:

climate of ?place includes hot and
rainfall of ?place includes heavy
implies crops of ?place includes rice

---

[2]The model may depend on the state, e.g., the effect of applying heat to water varies according to whether it is in the form of ice, liquid water or steam.

Antecedents and consequents can be properties or relations, as in:

> ?adult is-a adult and age of ?adult less-than 25
> implies age of ?adult is very:young

A simplification is to constrain implications to use conjunctions of antecedents. Disjunctions can then be expressed using multiple implications. Negatives can be expressed using antonyms for relationships, operators, and values. Where knowledge is uncertain, an implication may be held to weakly apply even if not all of its antecedents can be established against the knowledge base. This might be justified if there is a lack of information relating to a specific antecedent so that we do not know whether or not it applies.

Range statements are a form of properties used to describe the domain of scalar values, for example, *temperature*, *age* and *guilt*, in:

> range of temperature includes cold, warm, hot
> range of age includes infant, child, adult for person
> range of guilt includes innocent, guilty (overlap none)

Fuzzy ranges allow values to overlap as needed, e.g., a temperature value that is considered intermediate between cold and warm. This corresponds to Zadeh's fuzzy sets, e.g. (cold 0.8, warm 0.2, hot 0). By specifying *overlap none*, we declare that innocent and guilty are disjoint, so that guilt can be either innocent or guilty, but not both.

Ranges enable the value of different terms in a set to be justified by different lines of argument, for example, using different implication statements, such as:

> temperature of room is cold implies fan-speed is stop
> temperature of room is warm implies fan-speed is slow
> temperature of room is hot implies fan-speed is fast

An explicit temperature measurement can be mapped to a fuzzy set with a certainty value for each qualitative term in the range. Likewise, the inferred fuzzy set for the fan speed can be mapped back to an explicit (i.e., numeric) fan speed.

The mapping can be specified using metadata that declare the lower and upper limits for each term, e.g., for fan speed we might want to map *stop*, *slow*, and *fast* to increasing fan speeds. The shape of the transfer function for each term can be made explicit with additional parameters if so needed, for instance, when using trapezoidal or smoothly changing functions.

> range of fan-speed is stop, slow, fast
> fan-speed of stop is 0
> fan-speed of slow is 0, 1,200
> fan-speed of fast is 1000, 1,800

4.3.2 Statement metadata

Most metadata parameters are qualitative rather than quantitative to reflect their lack of precision, as in many cases we have only a rough idea and are not in a position to give detailed and accurate statistics. These parameters are used to estimate the certainty of each inference. The following parameters are defined:

- **typicality** in respect to other group members, e.g., robins are typical song birds.
- **similarity** to peers, e.g., having a similar climate.
- **strength, inverse** – conditional likelihood for forward and inverse inferences for a given statement, e.g., whether rain predicts cloudy weather and vice versa.
- **frequency** – the proportion of children with a given property, e.g., most species of birds can fly, but not all.
- **dominance** – the relative importance in a given group, e.g., the size of a country's economy.
- **multiplicity** – the number of items in a given range, e.g., how many different kinds of flowers grow in England, remembering that parameters are qualitative not quantitative.
- **certainty** – this can be used to indicate the degree of confidence in a given statement being true.

Statement metadata can also be used in an open-ended way to express qualifiers, as with the following example:

> # Susan told Jenny that she would take the bus to go to the dentist
> Susan tells Jenny (mode phone, time past, that s2)
> Jenny goes-to s3 (id s2, time plus, mode bus)
> s3 is-a dentist

The first statement is a relation Susan tells Jenny. Its metadata indicates this action took place in the indefinite past over the phone and cites a second statement using its identifier (s2).

4.3.3   Plausible inferences

Inferences provide a means to infer a property or relation that is not explicit in the knowledge base. There are two basic approaches:

1. Using implications where all of the rule's consequents are deemed likely if all of the antecedents can be established either directly or indirectly. An example given above implies that the weather is cloudy if it can be established that the weather is rainy.
2. Using relationships to infer that a relationship or property is likely to hold for the object of the relationship, if it can be established to hold directly or indirectly for the subject of that relationship. One example is where it is known that birds have wings, so that if you know that ducks are a kind of bird, then you can reasonably infer that ducks have wings.

Implications and relationships can also be used for inverse inferences with the corresponding likelihood depending on the statement metadata. For implications, you can infer that all of the antecedents are likely to hold if one of the consequents holds, for example, it is somewhat likely to be raining if it is cloudy.

Likewise for relationships, if robins are a typical kind of bird and you know that robins sing, then it is plausible that all birds sing.

When using a relationship for an inference, the likelihood of an inferred property or relationship will depend on the type of relationship used for the inference. Here are a few examples:

Relationship type	Meaning	Reversibility
kind-of	subclass of class	asymmetric
is-a	instance of class	asymmetric
similar-to	similar concepts	symmetric
depends-on	coupled concepts	asymmetric
antonym-for	opposite meaning	symmetric

The reasoner can be given a property or relationship as a premise that we want to find evidence for and against, for instance, here is a premise expressed as a property:

flowers of England includes daffodils

Its inverse would be:

flowers of England excludes daffodils

The reasoner first checks if the premise is a known fact, and if not looks for other ways to gather evidence. One tactic is to *generalize the property referent*, e.g., by replacing it with a variable as in the following:

flowers of England includes ?flower

The knowledge graph provides a matching property statement:

flowers of England includes temperate-flowers

We then look for ways to relate daffodils to temperate flowers, finding the following match:

daffodils kind-of temperate-flowers

So, we have inferred that daffodils grow in England. Another tactic is to *generalize the property argument* as in the following:

flowers of ?place includes daffodils

We can then look for ways to relate England to similar countries, for example:

Netherlands similar-to England for flowers

We find then a match, for example:

flowers of Netherlands includes daffodils, tulips, roses

Thus, providing us with a second way to infer that daffodils grow in England. The certainty depends on the parameters, and the *similarity* parameter with respect to the *similar-to* relation.

The above uses a property as a premise. You can also use relations as premises, for instance:

Peter is young

The reasoner will then look for relevant knowledge on whether Peter is, or is not, young, e.g., Peter's age, and whether that implies he is a child or an adult, based upon pertinent *range* statements and associated definitions for their values.

In a small knowledge graph, it is practical to exhaustively consider all potentially relevant inferences. This becomes increasingly costly as the size of the knowledge graph increases. One way to address this challenge is to prioritize inferences that seem more certain, and to ignore those that are deemed too weak. A useful approach to implementing this is to exploit spreading activation. Further details on this will be given later on in this chapter.

The JavaScript implementation used in the web-based demo works as follows: the starting point is when the reasoner is invoked with a premise, e.g., in the form of a property with the descriptor, argument, operator, and referent. The operator and referent are optional, and can be omitted when you want to find the values.

The reasoner adds the premise as an initial goal, and iteratively looks for direct evidence in the form of property statements or indirect evidence in the form of relations, dependencies, or implications. Inferences may result in queuing new goals for arguments involving multiple steps.

A check is made to see if a goal has been previously considered, in order to avoid indefinite looping behavior. This mimics human recall, in that people generally realize that they have already worked on a goal and hence, there is no point in re-doing that work.

Reasoning works backwards from the premise towards the facts. This is recorded and used in reverse to compute the certainty of inferences by working forward from the facts. Finally, the record is used to generate the explanation.

An open question is when to curtail further search, for instance, immediately after finding direct evidence. A more sophisticated approach is to curtail search based upon diminishing return on effort, analogous to people getting bored and giving up. The web-based demo provides a checkbox that allows users to see the effects of trying harder as it were. It shows that trying harder may just show permutations on what was already discovered, with marginal extra value!

4.4   Computing certainty

The estimated certainty of inferences is computed working forward from the recorded certainty for the facts in the knowledge base. The papers by Collins *et al.* do not define the algorithms, so what follows should be considered as preliminary and meriting work on a more principled analysis grounded in Bayesian statistics.

The use of qualitative parameters for plausible reasoning is due to the lack of detailed statistics, and as such represents best guesses. If certainty is modeled as a number between 0 and 1, we can map qualitative values to numbers, and use algorithms for estimating the numeric certainty, which can later be mapped back to qualitative terms as needed.

One such algorithm is where a goal directly matches multiple properties with non-exclusive values, which can then be combined as a set. The more matches, the greater the certainty of establishing the goal.

If c is the average certainty and n is the number of matches, the combined certainty is $1.0 - (1.0 - c)/n$. If $c = 0.5$ and $n = 1$, we get 0.5. If $n = 2$, we get 0.75. If $n = 4$, we get 0.85. If $n = 256$, we get 0.998.

Collins *et al.* suggest a simplified approach to modeling the effects of the various metadata parameters in which each parameter boosts, weakens, or has no effect on the estimated certainty, and using the same algorithm for all such parameters.

If the original certainty is zero, the parameters should have no effect, and likewise, the effect of a parameter should be smaller as the parameter's value tends to zero.

Treating the effect of a parameter as a multiplier m on the certainty, the number should be in the range 0 to $1/c$, where $c > 0$. If we want to boost c by 25% when $c = 0.5$, $m = 1.25$, but this should shrink to 1 when $c = 1$.

How much should m increase as c tends to 0? One idea is to use linear interpolation, i.e., 1.5 when $c = 0$, 1.25 when $c = 0.5$ and 1 when $c = 1$. This multiplier shrinks to 1 as the value of the parameter tends to 0 and when c tends to 0. Thus, $m = 1 + p/2 - p * c/2$, where m is the multiplier, p is the parameter value (0 to 1), and c is the certainty (0 to 1).

We also need to deal with multiple lines of argument for and against the premise in question. If the arguments agree, we can aggregate their certainties using the first algorithm above. We are then left with a fuzzy set for the different conclusions, e.g. (true 0.8, false 0.2). Note that arguments may present multiple conclusions rather than true or false, as depending on the query posed to the reasoner.

4.5   Relationship to fuzzy logic

Plausible reasoning subsumes fuzzy logic as expounded by Lotfi Zadeh. Fuzzy logic includes four parts: fuzzification, fuzzy rules, fuzzy inference, and defuzzification.

Fuzzification maps a numerical value, e.g., mapping a temperature value into a fuzzy set, where a given temperature could be modeled as 0% cold, 20% warm, and 80% hot. This involves transfer functions for each term and may use a linear ramp or some kind of smooth function for the upper and lower part of the term's range.

Fuzzy rules relate terms from different ranges, e.g., if it is hot, set the fan speed to fast, if it is warm, set the fan speed to slow. The rules can be applied to determine the desired fan speed as a fuzzy set, e.g., 0% stop, 20% slow, and 80% fast. Defuzzification maps this back to a numeric value.

Fuzzy logic works with fuzzy sets in a way that mimics Boolean logic in respect to the values associated with the terms in the fuzzy sets. Logical AND is mapped to selecting the minimum value, logical OR is mapped to selecting the maximum value, and logical NOT to one minus the value, assuming values are between zero and one.

Plausible reasoning expands on fuzzy logic to support a much broader range of inferences, including context-dependent concepts, and the means to express fuzzy quantifiers and modifiers.

4.6   Richer queries and fuzzy quantifiers

Here are some examples of richer queries:

> all ?x where color of ?x includes red from ?x kind-of rose
> few ?x where color of ?x includes yellow from ?x kind-of rose
> which ?x where color of ?x includes yellow from ?x kind-of rose
> most ?x where age of ?x greater-than 20 from ?x is-a person
> any ?x where age of ?x less-than 15 from ?x is-a person
> which ?x where ?x is-a person and age of ?x is very:old
> which ?x where ?x is-a person and age of ?x slightly:younger-than 25

The first example searches the knowledge base to test if all roses are red. The *where* keyword is followed by a filter expressed as a conjunction of properties or relationships. The filter is applied to the set obtained by applying the criteria following the optional *from* keyword, and expressed as conjunction of properties or relationships.

In other words, we first find the set of things that are roses, and then test to see that they are all red. If the query omits *from*, the *where* filter applies to the entire knowledge base.

Traditional logic is limited to two quantifiers: *for all* and *there exists*. Plausible reasoning enables a much richer variety: *none, few most, many, all, which,* and *count.* The meaning of *few, many,* and *most* is interpreted by counting the number of elements obtained from the filter as compared to the size of the set they are drawn from. *which* returns the elements that pass the filter, whilst *count* returns the number of those elements.

The last two example queries involve modifiers that correspond to adverbs or adjectives in natural language. Multiple modifiers can be applied to a given concept, where each modifier is followed by a colon as a delimiter, e.g., *very:slightly:older-than.* This reflects Lotfi Zadeh's conception of fuzzy logic as a means to compute with words: "*small* can be multiplied by *a few* and added to *large*, or *colder* can be added to *warmer* to get something in between."

The meaning of words is often context dependent, e.g., the same person may be considered old by a child, and young by an adult. To determine if someone is very old, we could query their age, and see where this fits in terms used for describing the age of people.

> range of age is infant, child, adult for person
> age of infant is 0, 4 for person
> age of child is 5, 17 for person
> age of adult is 18, age-at-death for person

If John is 63 and Pamela is 82, this implies they are both adults. We can then look at the terms used to describe adults.

range of age is young, middle-age, old, geriatric for adult
age of young is 18, 44 for adult
age of middle-age is 45, 65 for adult
age of old is 66, age-at-death for adult
age of geriatric is 78, age-at-death for adult

This implies that John is middle-aged and Pamela is geriatric. If we then define very old as synonymous with geriatric, we can finally infer that Pamela is very old. A complication is how to compare a numerical age (in years) with the age at death. Essentially, a person's age increases until they die. One way to model that is as follows:

?person is-a person and age of ?person is ?age
implies ?age less-or-equal age-at-death

We also need to define comparative concepts such as *younger than* as equivalent to *less than*, so we can determine if one person is younger than another person by comparing their respective ages. Modifiers such as *slightly* can be interpreted in respect to comparing the difference of ages with a person's age, for example if Mary is 23 and Jenny is 25, the age difference is 2 years so Mary can be considered as slightly younger than Jenny given that 2/25 is 8%.

Many such terms are inherently imprecise concepts that depend on the context and are debatable. Nonetheless, human communication abounds with imprecision, relying on the speaker and listener having roughly the same conceptual model.

4.7 Reasoning by analogy

Analogies involve comparisons between things or objects where similarities in some respects can suggest the likelihood of similarities in other respects, for instance, in their respective properties and relationships, or in ways to solve related problems. Gentner and Markman proposed a basis for modeling analogies in terms of establishing a structural alignment based on common relational structure for two representations, where the stronger the match, the better the analogy.

In some cases, the objects may have the same properties, in other cases, there is a systematic mapping between different properties, e.g., relating electric current to the flow of a liquid in a pipe, and correspondingly, voltage to pressure. If you know that flow increases with pressure, you can infer that current increases with voltage.

Analogical reasoning tests often take the form of A is to B as Y is to —, where students are asked to supply the missing term. This can be readily modeled using PKN, for example, consider the query:

leaf:tree::petal:? # *leaf is to tree as petal is to what?*

when applied to the knowledge:

leaf part-of tree

petal part-of flower

The reasoner finds that *leaf* is related to *tree* via the *part-of* relationship and can then use that to look for a *part-of* relationship involving *petal*, yielding the result *flower*. Now consider

like:love::dislike:?

when applied to the knowledge:

love more-than like
hate more-than dislike

This gives the answer *hate* by matching the object of the relationship rather than the subject. Here is a more complex example showing the output from the reasoner:

Premise: mansion:shack::yacht:?
Found: mansion is large for building
Found: shack is small for building
So contrast is large, small
Found: yacht is large for sailing-boat
Found: dingy is small for sailing-boat

Therefore mansion:shack::yacht:dingy

Analogies involve a form of inductive reasoning and is related to learning from examples, and being able to apply past experience to a new situation based upon noticing the similarities and reasoning about the differences. Such reasoning can be simple as in the above examples or more complicated, for instance, when involving causal modelling.

4.8   Inferences vs model construction

Philip Johnson-Laird (1980, 1983) argues that the best account for human reasoning is not in terms of systematic rules or inference patterns, but rather in terms of the manipulation of mental models. Alan Collins by contrast talks about plausible reasoning in terms of inference patterns. How can both approaches be combined?

One solution is to base model construction on rule execution, where rule actions update working memory with new statements. This would involve an extension of the PKN rule syntax to represent actions as consequents. Such actions can also be used as a means to invoke external behavior, for instance, to direct a robot arm to pick something up, or to communicate with another agent. A cognitive architecture for perception, cognition, and action, is presented in a later section of this chapter, along with a framework for chunks and rules. However, further work is needed to identify a higher level notation for manipulating mental models and for metacognition.

4.9   Metacognition

Metacognition is reasoning about reasoning, including, reasoning about reasoning strategies, for instance, reasoning about how to solve a given problem by comparing it to previous problems and adapting their solutions to match the new context.

Metacognition is applicable to deciding when the current approach is not working well, so that it is time to try a different approach or to give up on the problem, at least for now, and perhaps to consider a different problem relating to the same overall goal.

Metacognition is likewise relevant to managing multiple concurrent goals, when it is necessary to dynamically switch focus between them, and to resource effort on them according to their priorities. Such goals can be at many different levels of abstraction.

4.10   Non-deductive reasoning and imagined contexts

There are many forms of reasoning other than reasoning deductively from facts to conclusions. Inductive reasoning considers similarities and differences across a group of things. Abductive reasoning considers which explanations best suit a set of known facts.

This may involve reasoning with causal models that can be used forwards to predict a potential future, or backwards when seeking plausible explanations or ways to achieve a desired outcome.

A common requirement is the need to represent things that are only true in a given context, whether past, present, or an imagined situation. This is also needed to implement a theory of mind in which a cognitive agent represents and reasons about the likely beliefs of other agents (human or artificial). Story telling is central to human culture, and likewise involves the need to model knowledge specific to a fictional world.

Episodic contexts are those that relate to the passage of time, describing what was happening at different times, and involving the means to support temporal reasoning. This is key to continuous learning and further details are given in a later section.

4.11   PKN in relation to RDF and LPG

The resource description framework (RDF) is a suite of standards from W3C for symbolic graphs, the Semantic Web, and Linked Data. These include SPARQL for querying RDF-based graphs, OWL as an ontology language and SHACL for expressing constraints on sub-graphs as a basis for validation.

RDF is based upon triples, i.e., directed labeled graph edges. RDF has several notations including XML, Turtle, N3[3], and JSON-LD. In RDF, graph vertices are URIs, blank nodes or literals, such as text strings, dates, numbers, and truth values.

---

[3] Notation 3 (N3) is a superset of RDF.

Blank nodes are identifiers scoped to a serialization of a particular graph. URIs are globally unique identifiers, such as HTTP-based universal resource locators (URLs).

Linked data makes use of HTTP as a basis for linking to further information about an RDF identifier, along with the means to download an RDF graph or a text description as appropriate. There is a rapidly growing number of open datasets and many ontologies.

Labeled property graphs (LPG) allow both vertices and edges to be associated with sets of property-values. This is convenient when you want to annotate edges. One example is where the edge represents the relationship between an employer and an employee, where you want to indicate the employee's start date, his/her role, department, and so forth.

PKN is at a higher level than RDF in that each PKN statement corresponds to multiple RDF triples. A PKN relationship corresponds to a single triple, but the statement metadata complicates matters, by requiring the relationship to be reified. Here is an example by a way of explanation:

> # PKN: *John knows Mary (certainty high)*
> @prefix rdf: <http://www.w3.org/1999/02/22-rdf-syntax-ns#> .
> @prefix foaf: <http://xmlns.com/foaf/0.1/> .
> @prefix pkn: <http://example.com/pkn/> .
> _:x rdf:type rdf:Statement .
> _:x rdf:subject <#John> .
> _:x rdf:predicate foaf:knows .
> _:x rdf:object <#Mary> .
> _:x pkn:certainty pkn:high .

Reification replaces an RDF triple by a set of triples for the subject, predicate, and object. This example introduces a blank node (_:x) and an RDF triple that indicates it represents a reified triple. The example uses three RDF namespaces, one for the core RDF syntax, one for FOAF, the friend of a friend vocabulary, and another hypothetical vocabulary for the PKN core terms. The latter is used to annotate the relationship with the qualitative measure of certainty.

A similar approach can be used to represent PKN property statements. The argument is mapped to a subject node, the descriptor to the RDF predicate, and the referent to an object node. The PKN operator, e.g., *includes*, can be declared using another triple with *pkn:operator* as its predicate. One complication is that PKN allows properties to have a comma-separated list of referents. These can be mapped to RDF collections, as in the following example:

> # PKN: *flowers of Netherlands includes daffodils, tulips*
> @prefix rdf: <http://www.w3.org/1999/02/22-rdf-syntax-ns#> .
> @prefix pkn: <http://example.com/pkn/> .
> _:x rdf:type rdf:Statement .
> _:x rdf:subject <#Netherlands> .
> _:x rdf:predicate <#flowers> .
> _:x pkn:operator pkn:includes .

```
_:x rdf:object _:y .
_:y rdf:type rdf:List
_:y rdf:first <#daffodils> .
_:y rdf:rest _:z .
_:z rdf:first <#tulips> .
_:z rdf:rest rdf:nil .
```

In principle, PKN could be easily extended to map referents to RDF identifiers in given namespaces as a basis for automating mapping PKN to RDF. One way to do this would be to borrow the context mechanism from JSON-LD. This would allow the RDF identifiers to be declared in separate files, linked from the PKN knowledge base.

PKN can be mapped to LPGs by mapping PKN properties to LPG node properties, and PKN relationships to LPG relationships. The details depend on the notation for property graphs which vary from one LPG vendor to the next.

4.12   Scaling and graphs of overlapping graphs

Very large knowledge graphs are difficult to deal with. For instance, when visualizing the graph, it is intimidatingly complex when zoomed out and lacks context when zoomed in. The lack of context is also a challenge for automated reasoning. One technique to address this is to transform very large graphs into overlapping smaller graphs that model individual contexts. The transformation can be applied either statically or dynamically according to criteria of interest.

In a large enterprise, subgraphs can be used for different business functions, offering different views for different departments, and dependency tracking for old and new uses given the enduring need to support a mix of new and old applications.

Contexts are also important for temporal reasoning, for handling counterfactuals when reasoning about explanations, and for imagined situations, e.g., when reasoning about plans. Contexts are important for natural language as a basis for grouping things that commonly occur in the same context.

This is further related to Roger Shank's idea of scripts, which describe a stereotyped sequence of events in a given context, such as having a meal in a restaurant. Some events/actions have causal dependencies, whilst others have statistical correlations.

A complementary technique is to associate graph vertices with activations levels that are boosted when accessed or created, and otherwise decay over time, so that the activation level is a measure of how frequently a given vertex is used, mimicking the human forgetting curve. This can be combined with spreading activation as a way of priming related concepts. Each time a vertex is accessed, updated, or added, a wave of activation spreads out along the connected graph edges. The more edges from a given vertex, the weaker the activation boost through each edge. A further weakening occurs at each vertex, to ensure that the wave rapidly decays.

Activation can be combined with stochastic recall to mimic other characteristics of human memory. If two edges have the same activation levels, they will be equally likely to be recalled. A further refinement is to mimic the spacing effect, which progressively reduces the boost when the time interval since the last boost is small compared to a given time window. The effect will be familiar to students in that the benefit of cramming revision into a short time is short lived compared to a more structured approach over a longer period of time.

4.13   Cognitive architecture for artificial minds

Cognitive architecture provides a functional model at a level above that of implementation choices. Consider the human brain as a source of inspiration (Figure 4.2):

This suggests the following functional architecture (Figure 4.3) where the cortex is modeled as a collection of specialized graph databases along with associated algorithms that execute local to the data. The inner part of the brain is mapped to a set of cognitive circuits, analogous to blackboard systems, as each circuit has access to multiple cognitive modules in the cortex. This supports sharing of information along with invocation of cortical functions, including graph algorithms.

In the human brain, different senses are mapped to different cortical lobes. As an example, when we see a lemon, we perceive its shape, size, color, texture and smell. The anterior temporal lobe acts as a hub for relating semantic multimodal models to unimodal models in the different lobes. The same hub and spoke model can be applied to semantic integration across the senses for artificial minds.

The architectural components have the following functions:

Cortex supports memory and parallel computation. Recall is stochastic, reflecting which memories have been found to be useful in past experience. Spreading

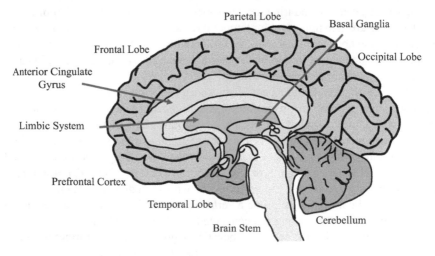

Figure 4.2   Anterior temporal lobe as hub for integration across senses

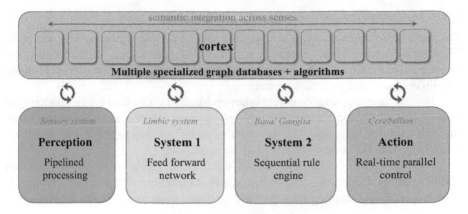

Figure 4.3   Cognitive architecture

activation and activation decay mimics human memory with semantic priming, the forgetting curve and spacing effect.

Perception interprets sensory data and places the resulting models into the cortex. Cognitive rules can set the context for perception, and direct attention as needed. Events are signaled by queuing chunks to cognitive buffers to trigger rules describing the appropriate behavior. A prioritized first-in first-out queue is used to avoid missing closely spaced events.

System 1 covers intuitive/emotional thought, cognitive control and prioritizing what's important. The limbic system provides rapid assessment of past, present, and imagined situations. Emotions are perceived as positive or negative, and associated with passive or active responses, involving actual and perceived threats, goal-directed drives and soothing/nurturing behaviors.

System 2 is slower and more deliberate thought, involving sequential execution of rules to carry out particular tasks, including the means to invoke graph algorithms in the cortex, and to invoke operations involving other cognitive systems. Thought can be expressed at many different levels of abstraction, and is subject to control through metacognition, emotional drives, internal, and external threats.

Action is about carrying out actions initiated under conscious control, leaving the mind free to work on other things. An example is playing a musical instrument where muscle memory is needed to control your finger placements as thinking explicitly about each finger would be far too slow. The cerebellum provides real-time coordination of muscle activation guided by perception. Of note is the fact that the human cerebellum has over three times the number of neurons compared to the cortex, packed into a much smaller space.

4.13.1   Systems 1 and 2

The idea of Systems 1 and 2 was popularized by Daniel Kahneman in his book "Thinking Fast and Slow." System 1 is fast, intuitive, and apparently effortless, yet opaque as we aren't aware how we came to a conclusion. System 1 is subject to many cognitive biases and sometimes wrong.

Natural language understanding is largely handled via System 1, as we understand in real-time what people are saying by constructing a coherent explanation that hides the ambiguity of language. This involves semantic priming together with everyday knowledge that fills in the gaps in what we heard.

Systems 1 and 2 work in cooperation, with System 2's analysis overriding System 1's intuition as needed. System 2 is accessible to introspection and much slower. It also feels effortful, making thinking hard work and quite exhausting!

4.14   Modeling the cortico-basal ganglia circuit

Figure 4.4 illustrates a functional model of the cortico-basal ganglia circuit as an asynchronous sequential rule engine, inspired by John Anderson's work on ACT-R.

The rule engine is connected to different cortical modules via buffers that each hold a single chunk – a collection of name/value pairs. These buffers correspond to a bundle of nerve fibers whose concurrent activation levels can be interpreted as a vector in a noisy high dimension space. Chris Eliasmith uses the term semantic pointers and has shown how chunks can be encoded and decoded using circular convolution.

Perception dynamically updates the chunks to reflect the model of the current state of the world. Events update the chunk buffers to trigger the appropriate behavioral responses.

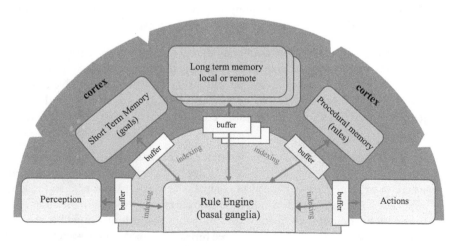

Figure 4.4   Model of cortico-basal ganglia cortical circuit

Procedural knowledge is encoded as collections of rules. The rule engine determines which rules match the current state of the buffers, and stochastically selects a matching rule to execute. Each rule has one or more antecedents and one or more consequents. A consequent may directly update a buffer, or do so indirectly via invoking a cortical operation on a module. These operations are asynchronous and can be loosely compared to the Web's hypertext transfer protocol (HTTP), with methods to retrieve (GET) and update data (PUT), as well as to invoke server-side operations (POST).

4.15   Chunks and rules

The W3C Cognitive AI Community Group has devised a simple notation for chunks and rules, along with a variety of built-in operations, and an open-source implementation with a variety of web-based demos. Each chunk is associated with a chunk identifier, a chunk type and a set of name/value pairs for its properties. The chunk type is a convenient way of grouping chunks, rather than having a predefined meaning.

The chunk notation minimizes the need for punctuation, and you can choose between using a line break or a semicolon as a property separator. Here are examples with both conventions:

```
dog d25 {name molly; breed terrier; gender female; age 6}
dog d26 {
  name butch
  breed bulldog
  gender male
  age 3
}
```

Property values are chunk identifiers, string literals, URLs, ISO8601 dates, numbers, Booleans, and comma-separated sequences thereof. Note that using @ as a prefix is reserved for system identifiers. The chunk identifier (e.g., d25 in the above example) is optional and will be automatically assigned if missing.

4.15.1   Chunk rules

Chunk rules are composed of chunks and have one or more conditions and one or more actions. Conditions and actions are associated with the module they apply to, defaulting to the goal module.

```
count {state start; from ?num1; to ?num2}
=> count {state counting},
increment {@module facts; @do get; number ?num1}
```

This example has one condition and two actions. The condition is matched to the *goal* module buffer. The first action updates that buffer changing the *start* property from *start* to *counting*. The second action applies to the *facts* module and initiates a *get* operation for the given *number*. Rule variables are prefixed with a question mark and scoped to the rule.

Module operations are invoked with *@do*. The above example invokes *get* to asynchronously retrieve a chunk that matches the properties given in the action, excluding the ones prefixed with @. The recalled chunk is put into the named buffer, triggering a fresh round of rule selection.

Both conditions and actions can use *@id* to bind to a chunk identifier and *@type* to bind to the chunk type. The following actions are built-in, with *update* as the default action:

- *@do* **update** to directly update the module's buffer
- *@do* **queue** to push a chunk to the queue for the module
- *@do* **clear** to clear the module's buffer and pop the queue
- *@do* **get** to recall a chunk with matching type and properties
- *@do* **put** to save the buffer as a new chunk in the module's graph
- *@do* **patch** to use the buffer to patch chunk in the module's graph
- *@do* **delete** to forget chunks with matching type and properties
- *@do* **next** to load the next matching chunk in an implementation-dependent order
- *@do* **properties** to iterate over the set of properties in a buffer
- *@***for** to iterate over the items in a comma-separated list

Applications may define additional operations, e.g., for controlling a robot arm. Apart from *clear*, *update*, and *queue*, all actions are asynchronous, and when complete set the buffer status to reflect their outcome. Rules can query the status using *@status*. The value can be *pending*, *okay*, *forbidden*, *nomatch*, and *failed*.

This is loosely analogous to the hypertext transfer protocol (HTTP) and allows rule engines to work with remote cognitive databases. To relate particular request and response pairs, use *@tag* in the action to pass an identifier to the subsequent asynchronous response where it can be accessed via *@tag* in a rule condition.

You can define rules that match a buffer when a module operation has not succeeded. To do this place an exclamation mark before the chunk type of the condition.

Actions can be used in combination with *@id* to specify the chunk identifier, for instance, to recall a chunk with a given identifier. Additional operations are supported for operations over property values that are comma-separated lists of items, see below. The default action is *@do update*, which just updates the properties given in the action, leaving another properties in the buffer unchanged. You can use *@do clear* to clear all properties in the buffer.

While *@do update* allows you to switch to a new goal, sometimes you want rules to propose multiple sub-goals. You can set a sub-goal using *@do queue* which pushes the chunk specified by an action to the queue for the module's buffer.

You can use *@priority* to specify the priority as an integer in the range 1–10 with 10 the highest priority. The default priority is 5. The buffer is automatically cleared (*@do clear*) when none of the buffers matched in a rule have been updated by that rule. This pops the queue if it is not already empty.

Actions that directly update the buffer do so in the order that the action appears in the rule. In other words, if multiple actions update the same property, the property will have the value set by the last such action.

The *@do get* action copies the chunk into the buffer. Changing the values of properties in the buffer would not alter the graph until you use *@do put* or *@do patch* to save the buffer to the graph. Put creates a new chunk, or completely overwrites an existing one with the same identifier as set with *@id*. Patch, by contrast, will just overwrite the properties designated in the action.

Applications can define additional operations when initializing a module. This is used in the example demos, e.g., to allow rules to command a robot to move its arm, by passing it the desired position and direction of the robot's hand. Operations can be defined to allow messages to be spoken aloud or to support complex graph algorithms, e.g., for data analytics and machine learning. Applications cannot replace the built-in actions listed above.

Note if you add to, or remove matching chunks during an iteration, then you are not guaranteed to visit all matching chunks. A further consideration is that chunks are associated with statistical weights reflecting their expected utility based upon past experience. Chunks that are very rarely used may become inaccessible.

4.16   Iteration over properties

You can iterate over each of the properties in a buffer by using *@do properties* in an action for that buffer. The following example first sets the facts buffer to *foo {a 1; c 2}* and then initiates an iteration over all of the buffer's properties that do not begin with "@":

```
run {} =>
   foo {@module facts; a 1; c 2}, # set facts buffer to foo {a 1; c 2}
   bar {@module facts; @do properties; step 8; @to goal} # launch iteration
   # this rule is invoked with the name and value for each property
   # note that 'step 8' is copied over from the initiating chunk
bar {step 8; name ?name; value ?value} =>
   console {@do log; message ?name, is, ?value},
   bar {@do next} # to load the next instance from the iteration
```

Each property is mapped to a new chunk with the same type as the action (in this case *bar*). The action's properties are copied over (in this example *step 8*), and *name* and *value* properties are used to pass the property name and value respectively. The *@more* property is given the value *true* unless this is the final chunk in the iteration, in which case *@more* is given the value *false*.

By default, the iteration is written to the same module's buffer as designated by the action that initiated it. However, you can designate a different module with the *@to* property. In the example, this is used to direct the iteration to the goal buffer. By setting additional properties in the initiating action, you can ensure that the rules used to process the property name and value are distinct from other such iterations.

4.16.1   Operations on comma-separated lists

You can iterate over the values in a comma-separated list with the *@for*. This has the effect of loading the module's buffer with the first item in the list. You can optionally specify the index range with *@from* and *@to*, where the first item in the list has index 0, just like JavaScript.

> # *a chunk in the facts module*
> person {name Wendy; friends Michael, Suzy, Janet, John}
> # *after having recalled the person chunk, the*
> # *following rule iterates over the friends*
> person {@module facts; friends ?friends}
> => item {@module goal; @for ?friends; @from 1; @to 2}

which will iterate over Suzy and Janet, updating the module buffer by setting properties for the item's value and its index, e.g.

> item {value Suzy; @index 1; @more true}

The action's properties are copied over apart from those starting with an "@." The item index in the list is copied into the chunk as *@index*. You can then use *@do next* in an action to load the next item into the buffer. The *@more* property is set to *true* in the buffer if there is more to come, and *false* for the last property in the iteration. Action chunks should use either *@do* or *@for*, but not both. Neither implies *@do update*.

You can append a value to a property using *@push* with the value, and *@to* with the name of the property, e.g.

> person {name Wendy} => person {@push Emma; @to friends}

which will push Emma to the end of the list of friends in the goal buffer.

> person {name Wendy} => person {@pop friends; @to ?friend}

will pop the last item in the list of friends to the variable *?friend*.

Similarly, you can prepend a value to a property using *@unshift* with the value, and *@to* with the name of the property, e.g.

> person {name Wendy} => person {@unshift Emma; @to friends}

will push Emma to the start of the list of friends in the goal buffer.

> person {name Wendy} => person {@shift friends; @to ?friend}

will pop the first item in the list of friends to the variable *?friend*.

4.16.2   Named contexts

It is sometimes necessary to represent knowledge that is only true in a specific context, for example, when modeling another agent's knowledge, or when reasoning about counterfactuals during abductive reasoning. This is supported using *@context*. In its absence, the default context applies. Here is an example adapted from John Sowa.

Tom believes that Mary wants to marry a sailor
believes s1 {@subject Tom; proposition s2}
wants s3 {@context s2; person Mary; situation s4}
married-to s5 {@context s4; @subject Mary; @object s6}
a s6 {@context s4; is a person; profession sailor}

4.16.3   More complex queries

Modules may provide support for more complex queries that are specified as chunks in the module's graph, and either apply an operation to matching chunks, or generate a result set of chunks in the graph and pass this to the module buffer for rules to iterate over. In this manner, chunk rules can have access to complex queries capable of set operations over many chunks, analogous to RDF's SPARQL query language. The specification of such a chunk query language is left to future work, and could build upon existing work on representing SPARQL queries directly in RDF.

A further opportunity would be to explore queries and rules where the conditions are expressed in terms of augmented transition networks (ATNs), which loosely speaking are analogous to RDF's SHACL graph constraint language. ATNs were developed in the 1970s for use with natural language and lend themselves to simple graphical representations. This has potential for rules that apply transformations to sets of sub-graphs rather than individual chunks.

4.17   Natural language

Natural language will be key to enabling flexible dialogs between cognitive agents and humans, including commands, handling questions, providing answers, understanding, and learning from text-based resources. The field of computational linguistics focuses on text processing, but not on representing and reasoning with the meaning of language. Traditional logic is inadequate when it comes to the flexibility of natural language, including uncertainty, imprecision, and context sensitivity. This suggests that different approaches are needed that support plausible reasoning.

4.17.1   Large language models

Large language models such as GPT-3 and BLOOM are based on neural network models trained to predict masked words using a vast corpus of text documents. BLOOM's language model has 176 billion parameters covering 46 human languages. The model maps the user-supplied text to an opaque internal model of the meaning, referred to as the *latent semantics*. This can then be used stochastically to generate text continuations consistent with those semantics.

Large language models are surprisingly good at this and can effectively mimic a wide range of topics and styles of text, e.g., BLOOM generated the italicized text below following the user-supplied prompt shown in regular text:

John picked up his umbrella before stepping out of the door as he had heard the weather forecast on the radio *in the living room that said that heavy rain was forecasted and that there was a high chance of thunderstorms throughout the afternoon. The rain had become a little less torrential as he made his way to his sister's house, so that he didn't feel too drenched when he arrived.*

Large language models show that machine learning can be successfully applied to learning to generate latent representations of the meaning of everyday language and that these representations can be used in reverse to generate plausible text continuations.

Unfortunately, we have yet to discover how to mimic human-like reasoning in terms of operations applied directly to the latent semantics embodied in large language models. Similarly, we cannot yet map the latent semantics to symbolic graphs as another way to implement reasoning. Both challenges are exciting opportunities for research studies.

4.17.2   Natural language and common sense

Another approach to natural language understanding is to combine conventional parsing with symbolic representations of meaning such as the plausible knowledge notation (PKN). Parsing is not particularly difficult, provided that dealing with the ambiguity of natural language is largely delegated to semantic processing.

This involves tasks such as selecting the most appropriate sense of each word according to the context in which it appears, figuring out how to correctly attach prepositional phrases, creating semantic models, and resolving references.

Finding a semantically coherent model of a given text utterance is challenging, despite being apparently effortless for humans. A promising approach is to combine spreading activation with models of everyday knowledge, as a basis for understanding what's implicit in the utterance.

As an example, consider the sentence "John opened the bottle and poured the wine." Human readers know that John is a male adult and that the occasion is likely to be a social event such as a dinner or a party. The wine is a liquid for the guests to drink from their glasses. The bottle needs to be opened before it can be poured into the glasses. Pouring transfers liquid from one container to another, conserving the volume of liquid as it does so.

Human readers are aware of all of this and do not need to spend effort consciously reasoning it out unless that becomes necessary, nonetheless, the background knowledge is key to efficiently finding a coherent model of the utterance.

Further work is now needed to look at how this can be mimicked by cognitive agents. This can start from a small set of examples where the background knowledge and typical inferences can be developed with a modest level of effort.

Natural language generation involves an understanding of the aims of the communication, the knowledge that the listener or reader is likely to already have, and how to minimize what needs to be said. Grice's maxims describe the principles of cooperative dialogue in terms of quantity, quality, relation, and manner.

- Try to be informative and give as much information as needed, but no more.
- Try to be truthful and avoid giving information that is false or not supported by the evidence.

- Try to be relevant and say things pertinent to the discussion.
- Try to be clear and orderly, avoiding obscurity and ambiguity.

How can cognitive agents be designed to implement these maxims? It is likely that cognitive agents can be trained to be effective by using machine learning techniques that pit a generator against an adversary that seeks to distinguish machine generated from human-generated utterances with respect to a large training corpus of short dialogs.

4.17.3   Metaphors in everyday language

Lackoff and Johnson in their book "Metaphors we live by" (1980) showed just how much humans rely on metaphor in everyday thought and language. People will likewise expect cognitive agents to understand and to use metaphors in human-agent dialogs.

One such metaphor is ideas as food, e.g., *raw facts* and *half-baked ideas*. People use many different metaphors, and much of this is culture dependent, i.e., learned from what we read and listen to. In principle, cognitive agents should be able to do likewise, understanding previously unheard metaphors in terms of reasoning about analogies. This is an example of continuous learning.

4.18   Continuous learning

Many AI systems are trained up front and have difficulties in coping when the statistics of the run-time data diverge from that of the training data. Continuous learning is a way to adapt as the data changes and will be essential for resilient operation of cognitive agents.

There are different ways to learn. Syntagmatic learning deals with patterns in co-occurrence statistics. Paradigmatic learning deals with taxonomic abstractions. Skill compilation is the process of speeding reasoning by exploiting experience with previous solutions as a short cut, including the use of analogies. Meta-learning is the process of learning how to learn, including reasoning about strategies and tactics for how to reason.

Learning can be from direct experience by interacting with the world and exploiting a sense of curiosity about how things work. However, there are issues of safety and cost for applying this in practice, e.g., with allowing robots to roam around freely. A work around is to use virtual worlds, but it is challenging to make those a sufficiently faithful representation of the real world.

Another approach is learning from observations and asking questions. Children are incredibly good at this. There is a huge opportunity to learn from large corpora of text documents, images, and videos.

Finally, learning can be arranged in the form of lessons and assessments, i.e., courses designed specifically for AI agents. Enabling AI agents to devise their own knowledge representations as part of machine learning is likely to more scalable than direct hand authoring of knowledge, see the later section on scalable knowledge engineering.

4.19   Hive minds, knowledge caching and swarm intelligence

Cognitive agents can be designed using shared access to remote cognitive databases, analogous to the lobes in the cerebral cortex. By duplicating agents in this way, as each agent learns, the updated knowledge and skills are immediately available to all of the agents, contributing to accelerated communal learning, in what can be thought of as a form of hive mind. Existing knowledge often helps when it comes to learning new knowledge, so it is likely that the speed up will be greater than linear in respect to the number of agents involved.

Resilience in the face of disrupted connectivity to remote cognitive databases can be achieved via mechanisms for selectively duplicating frequently used knowledge to local storage, as a form of knowledge caching. This would come with the need for synching local updates to the cache with the remote cognitive databases when connectivity resumes.

In the face of the unexpected, a diversity of personalities, opinions, knowledge, and skills can be invaluable. Rather than designing a hive of agents with identical clone minds, it makes much more sense to design the hive mind as a collective with shared knowledge and awareness, forming a collective consciousness, whilst allowing a diversity of different skills and perspectives to be deployed as appropriate to the challenges at hand. This would also allow human users to select the personality of the agents they interact with. The collective mind would be engineered to enforce confidentiality in respect to personal privacy.

This can be contrasted with swarm intelligence featuring the collective behavior of decentralized, self-organized agents. Swarm intelligence typically involves identical agents applying relatively simple rules, e.g., to prevent a collection of airborne drones from crashing into each other, and enabling them to fly around obstacles. In principle, the two approaches can be used together, where swarm intelligence is a comparatively low-level solution under the control of the higher-level collective mind.

4.20   Complementary role of artificial neural networks

Deep learning over large corpora has produced very impressive results. Text to image generators such as stable diffusion and DALL-E are trained against many millions of images associated with short text descriptions. Figure 4.5 shows that this approach has captured knowledge about marble, the effects of light and shadow, the human form, and the styles of famous sculptors.

The breadth of the training data is reflected by the ability to generate images in a very wide range of styles. However, there are some obvious limitations.

The woman's hand has too many fingers! This reflects weaker knowledge about hands and fingers compared to that of the human face.

Another example is when the prompt is "one blue ball and two red cubes on a green floor". Stable diffusion clearly lacks an understanding of how to count instances of things, as can be seen in the two examples (Figure 4.6 and Figure 4.7) below generated using that prompt.

Figure 4.5 Marble sculpture of a young woman generated using stable diffusion.

Figure 4.6 Painting of a woman generated with stable diffusion.

The same applies to the BLOOM large language model as can be seen with the following prompt where BLOOM's text is in italics.

There is one blue ball, two green balls and five red balls. How many balls are there in total? *The first possible answer is "7" because there is one blue ball and six other balls. The second possible answer is "4", because the first ball is blue, two of the other six balls are green and the remaining four balls are red.*

Figure 4.7   Images generated with stable diffusion.

Together, this suggests a huge potential for combining deep learning with techniques that support human-like reasoning and learning. Richer semantic knowledge would allow the software to understand text documents and images in the training set at a much deeper level, enabling faster learning from smaller data sets.

It would also enable artists to work collaboratively with AI's to iteratively improve a composition through suggestions on changes to particular aspects. One opportunity would be for generating richer experiences in the virtual reality Metaverse by exploiting learning from a vast corpora of text documents, images and videos.

More generally, AI's should be able to learn everyday knowledge and reasoning from understanding such corpora, just as young children do as they observe the world around them, applying their prior knowledge to reason about possible explanations, and by asking questions.

4.21   Scalable knowledge engineering

Hand-crafted knowledge does not scale and is brittle when it comes to the unexpected, i.e., things that the developers have not anticipated and designed for. Deep learning scales very effectively, but is similarly brittle, and requires vast datasets for training.

Humans are much better at generalizing from a few examples by seeking causal explanations based on prior knowledge. Humans are also good at reasoning using mental models and chains of plausible inferences, supported by metacognition.

We need research focused on extending artificial neural networks to support human-like learning and reasoning. At the same time, we should explore scalability of machine learning for symbolic representations of knowledge as a complementary technology, moreover, hand authoring for small-scale experiments can help illustrate what's needed from more scalable approaches.

An open question is how to apply artificial neural networks to human-like reasoning and learning. It is likely that vector-space representations will prove to be very effective in respect to handling imprecise and context-dependent concepts.

4.22   Application to privacy-centered personal assistants

Today's consumer web is dominated by advertising-based business models that have a strong focus on gathering personal information for metrics and for targeting advertising through live auctions for space on Web pages. Consumers are habituated to clicking away annoying permission requests for enabling tracking.

It is time to make privacy a central part of ecosystems of services. One way to realize this is with personal assistants that act on their user's behalf in respect to providing services using ecosystems of third-party providers. This would support a privacy-centered evolution away from dominance by Web search engines.

Personal assistants acting in this role can be thought of as digital guardian angels and designed to apply and safeguard their user's values as learned from observing their behavior via privacy-protecting federated machine learning. Personal assistants select services matching their user's requests by using service metadata plus independent trust attestations and live auctions.

For this to work, the business models need to align costs and benefits for implementing and operating personal assistants, as well as for attestations based upon aggregating feedback from both users and personal assistants.

Personal assistants share pertinent personal information with the selected services, e.g., their user's travel plans and preferences, when seeking proposals for flights, hotels, local travel, restaurants, museums, etc. Some services are immediate, while others may take significant time to fulfill, and rely on smart notifications to alert users when ready.

Personal information is shared subject to contractual terms and conditions. In principle, this can include the role of personal assistants in downstream checks and permissions. This gets more complicated as data is progressively transformed and merged with other sources of information.

Practical personal assistants will be reliant on advances in human-like reasoning with everyday knowledge, as well as advances in natural language understanding and generation.

4.23   Summary

Plausible reasoning is a major paradigm shift for knowledge graphs, in that it embraces the uncertainty, imprecision, context sensitivity, and inconsistencies in everyday knowledge and use of natural language. This addresses a key challenge for human–agent collaborative work in enabling the use of natural language dialogs.

This chapter has presented two contrasting approaches, one focusing on plausible inferences inspired by Allan Collins, and the other on a procedural approach inspired

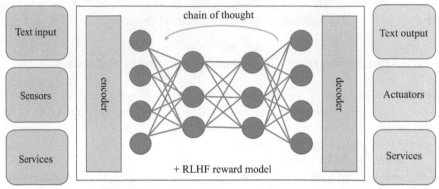

Services include cognitive database and reasoners, along with scripts
and tools to generate tables, charts and other graphics. Actions are
delegated to external real-time control loops.

Figure 4.8   High level neural architecture for cognitive agents

by John Anderson. Further work is needed on how metacognition can be used to combine reasoning with mental models as per Philip Johnson-Laird, and logical reasoning
based upon plausible inferences.

Recent successes with large language models and image generation are very
impressive, and demonstrate the practicality of applying machine learning to latent
semantics, in essence, automating knowledge engineering. This is dramatically more
scalable than hand authoring of knowledge graphs.

Open AI's ChatGPT is a large language model that supports follow-up questions,
and can challenge incorrect premises and reject inappropriate requests. Nonetheless,
it lacks continuous learning and is limited to what was in its training dataset.

Google's Minerva is a large language model that was further trained on technical
datasets. It correctly answers around a third of undergraduate level problems involving
quantitative reasoning. However, it lacks a means to verify the correctness of the
proposed solutions, as it is limited to intuitive reasoning.

New work is needed that operates directly on latent semantics to support plausible
reasoning and model building, combining intuitive reasoning with deliberative ana-
lytic reasoning. In principle, this will enable cognitive agents to learn more efficiently
by understanding training examples at a deeper level. A related challenge is to enable
general purpose agents rather than agents limited to a single domain of competence.

Work is also needed on symbolic graphs as a complementary approach to neural
networks when it comes to scalable knowledge engineering, based upon advances
in machine learning to circumvent the bottleneck of handcrafted knowledge. It is
conceivable that this may offer benefits in respect to avoiding the huge energy costs
involved in applying deep learning to vast corpora. Figure 4.8 depicts a neural architecture that integrates external services such as cognitive databases and inference
engines.

These advances will pave the way for developing digital guardian angels that are better at identifying inappropriate content, including fake news and social media posts that violate the terms of use. Guardian angels have a plenty of other applications including enabling privacy-centric ecosystems of services, managing auctions for service providers and consumers, and orchestrating resources across the computing continuum from the far-edge to the cloud.

More generally, the emergence of cognitive agents that mimic human-reasoning and learning will help to boost productivity and counter the shrinking workforce associated with aging human populations across many countries.

The next generation of AI will probably seem like science fiction and will grow to embrace intellectual and artistic skills better than most humans, based upon learning from vast corpora of text, images and videos, plus foundational courses designed for AIs and interaction with billions of people.

This should enable economies to break free of constraints on growth associated with a limited work force, but at the same time, will necessitate attention to distributing benefits fairly across society and countering the risk of monopolistic control of AI technology and its exploitation.

4.24   eBNF grammar for PKN

Here is an eBNF grammar for PKN:

STATEMENTS ::= statement+

statement ::= (property | relation | implication) ("for" scope)? meta?
    scope ::= name (',' name)*
    meta ::= '(' param (',' param)* ')'
    param ::= name value
property ::= descriptor "of" argument (operator referent)?
    descriptor ::= name | variable
    argument ::= name | variable
    operator ::= "includes" | "excludes " | "is" | name
    value ::= name | number
    referent ::= (value ("," value)*) | variable
relation ::= subject relationship object
    subject ::= name | variable
    relationship ::= name | variable
    object ::= name | variable
implication ::= terms "implies" terms
    terms ::= term ("and" term)*
    term ::= property | relation

QUERY ::= quantifier variable ("where" conditions)? "from" conditions
    quantifier ::= "no" | "all" | "any" | "few" |
               "many" | "most" | "which" | "count"

```
conditions ::= condition ("and" condition)*
condition ::= property | relation

ANALOGY ::= concept ":" concept "::" concept ":" concept
    concept ::= name | variable
variable ::= "?" name?
name ::= letter (letter | digit | "-")* (":" (letter | digit | "-")+)*
number ::= ("-" | "+")? digit+ ("." digit+)?
```

Further reading

Here are some suggestions if you want to read more.

Argument and Argumentation, Stanford Encyclopedia of Philosophy.

Core Theory of Plausible Reasoning, Allan Collins and Ryszard Michalski, *Cognitive Science*, 13(1), 1989.

"Thinking Fast and Slow", Daniel Kahneman, 2011, see excerpt "Of 2 Minds: How Fast and Slow Thinking Shape Perception and Choice", Scientific American, June 15, 2012.

Lotfi Zadeh and the Birth of Fuzzy Logic, *IEEE Spectrum*, June 1995.

John R. Anderson – Biography, American Psychologist, April 1995, see also the ACT-R Website, hosted by CMU.

"Metaphors We Live By", George Lackoff and Mark Johnson, University of Chicago Press, 1980, p. 276.

Structure Mapping in Analogy and Similarity, Dedre Gentner and Arthur Markman, 1997, *American Psychologist*, 52(1), 45–56.

"Mental models or formal rules", Philipp Johnson-Laird and Ruth Byrne, 1993, *Behavioral and Brain Sciences* 16(2), 368–380.

How to Build a Brain: A Neural Architecture for Biological Cognition, Chris Eliasmith, 2013, Oxford University Press.

What We Learn by Doing, Roger Shank, 1995, Institute for the Learning Sciences Northwestern University.

W3C Cognitive AI Community Group, which developed the Chunks & Rules Specification, along with a suite of web-based demos.

Web-Based Demo for Plausible Reasoning and Argumentation, Dave Raggett, 2022.

Stable Diffusion Web-Based Demo by Hugging Face.

BLOOM (BigScience Large Open-science Open-access Multilingual Language Model) hosted by Hugging Face.

Minerva, a large language model pretrained on general natural language data and further trained on technical content, by Google Research.

ChatGPT, a conversational agent by Open AI.

DALL·E 2, image generator by Open AI.

The Semantic Web & Linked Data, Ruben Verborgh, Ghent University.

Metadata and Discovery, University of Pittsburgh.

Section 3

Data management and visualization

Chapter 5

Named entity resolution in personal knowledge graphs

Mayank Kejriwal[a]

Entity resolution (ER) is the problem of determining when two entities refer to the same underlying entity. The problem has been studied for over 50 years, and most recently, has taken on new importance in an era of large, heterogeneous 'knowledge graphs' published on the Web and used widely in domains as wide ranging as social media, e-commerce and search. This chapter will discuss the specific problem of named ER in the context of personal knowledge graphs (PKGs). We begin with a formal definition of the problem, and the components necessary for doing high-quality and efficient ER. We also discuss some challenges that are expected to arise for Web-scale data. Next, we provide a brief literature review, with a special focus on how existing techniques can potentially apply to PKGs. We conclude the chapter by covering some applications, as well as promising directions for future research.

5.1 Introduction

Due to the growth of large amounts of heterogeneous data (especially involving people) on the Web and in enterprise, the problem often arises as to when two pieces of information describing two entities are, in fact, describing the same *underlying* entity. For instance, a company may make an acquisition and attempt to merge the acquired company's database with their own database. It is probable that there is overlap between the two, and that the acquiring company shares some customers with the acquired company. Similarly, a data aggregator may be attempting to merge together profiles from different public websites, or even social media platforms. Such platforms have heavy overlap, leading naturally to the problem of 'resolving' entities.

This problem, called Entity Resolution (ER), has been researched for at least half a century in text, database, and more recently, machine learning, communities, using several methodologies (e.g. rule-based vs. statistical approaches) [1,2]. Figure 5.1 illustrates a prototypical example of such 'duplicate' entities that arise in two personal knowledge graphs (PKGs). An exhaustive treatment of this research is beyond the

[a]University of Southern California, USA

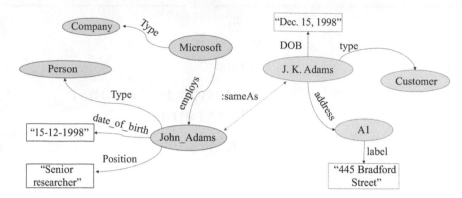

*Figure 5.1   An illustration of the named entity resolution problem between
fragments of two personal knowledge graphs (PKGs)*

scope of this chapter, although a book-level treatment has been provided by various
authors, including [3–6]. Instead, we consider two goals in summarizing the literature
on ER. First, we aim to synthesize common trends that have emerged over the last
half-century. Impressively, despite much independent research across various fields
and applications, there is robust consensus on several issues, including the abstract
workflow of an ER implementation. Second, and in contrast with the first goal, we
aim to discuss the key differences that have also emerged from this body of research.
As will be subsequently discussed, many of these differences tend to be algorithmic,
rather than conceptual, and are a consequence of the natural evolution of the field
over time.

Prior to discussing ER itself, an important prerequisite is deciding the data model
for representing the PKG. Although several options exist, we assume the primary data
model to be the structured Resource Description Framework (RDF) model [7], which
is prominent in the Semantic Web. An alternative model, for datasets that are highly
structured, regular and tabular in nature (which are unlikely for KG applications
and domains) is the Relational Database (RDB) model. This model is important for
historical reasons, given that much of the ER literature has traditionally been within
the database community [2]. Indeed, there are also cases in the literature where
research in the RDB community has been leveraged to solve a compatible problem
(e.g. query optimization) on RDF knowledge graphs [8–10]. Hence, there is good
synergy between the two models, allowing us to limit much of our treatment to the
RDF model (and others similar to it) without necessarily losing generality. For the
sake of completeness, we formally define an RDF graph by first defining an RDF
triple:

Definition 1 (RDF Triple). *Given three disjoint sets of I, B and L, of Internationalized
Resource Identifiers (IRIs), abstract identifiers and literals respectively, a triple in
the Resource Description Framework (RDF) data model is a 3-element tuple (subject,*

property, object), where subject ∈ I ∪ B, property ∈ I and object ∈ I ∪ B ∪ L. The triple is referred to as an RDF triple.

Given this definition, an RDF graph can be defined as a set of triples. Visually, the literals and IRIs represent nodes in the KG (which is a directed, labeled graph by definition), while the triple itself symbolizes an edge. Note that literals cannot have outgoing edges in this model. In practice, due to Semantic Web norms, such as the four Linked Data principles [11], IRIs in RDF KGs are just Uniform Resource Identifiers (URIs), a strict subset of IRIs. This is explicitly required by the first Linked Data principle. Furthermore, abstract identifiers ("blank nodes") are not used in KGs that are intended to be published as Linked Data. Since PKGs, especially those acquired or constructed at large scales, and meant to be linked to other sources, are likely to obey the Linked Data principles (at least approximately), these assumptions almost always hold in practical settings.

While RDF is the dominant data model used for representing KGs in the Semantic Web, it also has other important uses. For example, it is the basis in the full Semantic Web technology stack for representing RDF Schema (RDFS), and the Web Ontology Language (OWL) [12]. These semantic markup languages are important for publishing detailed data schemas and ontologies [13], which serve as the representational metadata for the underlying KGs.

With the assumptions about the data model in place, Named Entity Resolution, henceforth called ER, can be formally defined below:

Definition 2 (Named Entity Resolution). *Given an RDF knowledge graph, Named Entity Resolution is defined as the algorithmic problem of determining the pairs of instances (subjects and URI objects) in the graph that refer to the same underlying entity.*

Entities that need to be resolved but that are not 'named' tend to arise most often in the natural language setting, rather than in KG applications. In the Natural Language Processing (NLP) community, for example, anaphora and co-reference resolution are the related problems of resolving pronouns and non-named entities to their named equivalents [14,15]. Hence, such non-named mentions are not retained in the actual KG that is constructed over the raw text. Therefore, in practice, named ER is virtually identical to ER in the literature.

A critical point to note here is the notion of an *instance* in an RDF PKG. For instance, would we consider both literals and URIs to be instances? In general, the approaches that we consider for practical ER assume that an instance must have a representation using a URI, although many URIs may be disregarded from serving as valid inputs to an ER system. For example, based on the specifics of our domain-specific application, we may decide that we only want to resolve instances of 'customers', rather than 'contractors'. If this is the case, then URLs corresponding to contractor-entities would not be in the named entity sets input to the ER system.

A pragmatic reason for not considering literals explicitly is that, if an entity is represented only as a literal (such as a string or a number) and has no other information or attributes associated with it, domain-specific 'matching' functions would be more appropriate rather than an advanced ER solution. Several such functions are available and widely used for common attributes, such as dates, names, and addresses [16–18]. For example, if the problem was merely restricted to matching people's names, without any other surrounding context or attributes, a string-matching algorithm, some of which rely on phonetics [19], could be used. We subsequently provide more details on such matching functions because, aside from being useful for matching simple literals, they are also useful for converting pairs of entity representations into numeric feature vectors.

5.2   Two-step framework for efficient named entity resolution

Even in early research, the quadratic complexity of pairwise ER was becoming well recognized [1]. Given two RDF graphs D_1 and D_2 that we represent equivalently, with slight abuse of terminology, as sets of named entities (i.e., ignoring edges, literals, and entity-types that are not of interest), a naive ER must evaluate all possible entity pairs, namely the cross-product $D_1 \times D_2$. Even assuming a constant cost per evaluation, which may not always be the case, the run-time complexity is $O(|D_1||D_2|)$.

In the remainder of this section, for two input-sets D_1 and D_2, a named entity pair (e_1, e_2) is denoted as bilateral iff $e_1 \in D_1$ and $e_2 \in D_2$. Given a collection of entities from $D_1 \cup D_2$, two entities e_1 and e_2 are bilaterally paired iff (e_1, e_2) is bilateral.

To alleviate the quadratic complexity of evaluating all possible bilateral pairs, a two-step framework is typically adopted in much of the ER literature [20]. This two-step framework is illustrated in Figure 5.2. The first step, blocking, uses a function called a blocking key to cluster approximately similar entities into (potentially overlapping) blocks [21]. A blocking method then considers which entities share a block to bilaterally pair, with the result that those entity pairs become candidates for further evaluation by a matching or similarity function in the second step [22]. This function, which is also called a link specification function in the literature, may be Boolean or probabilistic and makes a prediction about whether an input entity-pair represents the same underlying entity. Prediction quality metrics, such as precision and recall, can then be used to evaluate the performance of the entire ER system by comparing

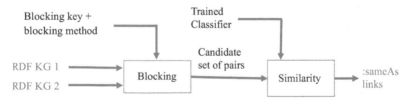

Figure 5.2   A typical two-step ER workflow that is often implemented in practice for solving the problem efficiently and effectively. Although the figure assumes two RDF KGs, a similar workflow would also apply to non-KG datasets, as well as to the deduplication problem (where a single dataset is input).

the predicted matches to those present in an external ground-truth of 'gold-standard' matches.

In most ER systems, D_1 and D_2 are assumed to be structurally homogeneous [2,20], a term introduced in an influential survey [2]. That is, D_1 and D_2 are assumed to contain entities of the same type (e.g., Person), and are described by the same property schema. The latter implies that the same sets of attribute-types are associated with entities in both data sources. An important special application of structural homogeneity is deduplication, whereby matching entities in a single data source must be found. In the rest of this chapter, we assume structural homogeneity as well, except where explicitly indicated. In practice, this assumption is not problematic because, even in the rare case of matching entities between PKGs with drastically different ontologies, an ontology matching solution can be applied as a first step to homogenize the data sources [23–26].

5.2.1 Blocking step

Following the intuitions described earlier, a blocking key can be defined as follows.

Definition 3 (Blocking Key). *Given a set D of entities, a blocking key K is a function that takes an entity from D as input and returns a non-empty set of literals, referred to as the blocking key values (BKVs) of the entity.*

Let $K(e)$ denote the set of BKVs assigned to the entity $e \in D$ by the blocking key K. Given two data sources D_1 and D_2, two blocking keys K_1 and K_2 can be defined using the definition above. Multiple definitions are typically used only when D_1 and D_2 are heterogeneous. Since we are assuming structural homogeneity in this chapter, a single key (namely, $_1 = K_2 = K$), applicable to both D_1 and D_2, is assumed. Without loss of generality, the literals defined above are assumed to be strings although, in principle, any data type could be used.

Example 5.1 (Example of Blocking Key). Earlier, Figure 5.1 had illustrated two RDF PKG fragments describing people. Although the graphs are structurally hetero-geneous, let us assume that an ontology or schema matching step had been applied such that the schema of the second graph is appropriately aligned with that of the first (e.g., DOB is mapped to date_of_birth, and so on). An example of a good block-ing key K applicable to this schema might now be $K = Tokens(\ :\ instance) \cup Year(\ :\ date\_of\_birth)$. We assume that there is a mechanistic function that can extract the year from the date of birth literal, and that ':instance' represents the mnemonic rep-resentation (typically a label in the RDF graph) of the instance. Applied to an entity e from either dataset, K would return a set of BKVs that contains the tokens in an entity's label, as well as a single number for the year of birth, converted to a string. For example, when applied to the instance *John_Adams* from the first KG in Figure 5.1, the output (set of BKVs) returned by the blocking key would be {"John", "Adams", "1998"}. Similarly, when applied to the instance *J. K. Adams* from the second KG, the output returned would be the set {"J", "K", "Adams", "1998"}. Since the two BKV sets have at least one common BKV, the two instances would share at least one block.

Given the single blocking key K, a candidate set C of bilateral entity pairs can be generated by a blocking method using the BKVs of the entities. We briefly describe some prominent blocking methods below.

Example 5.2 (Sorted Neighborhood). Figure 5.3 illustrates the Sorted Neighborhood blocking method on a small relational database describing people. A single BKV is first generated (in this case, we concatenate the initials of first and last-name tokens, and the first two digits of the zipcode) for each instance in the table. Next, the BKVs are used as 'sorting keys'. Finally, a sliding window is slid over the table and all records within the window are paired and added to the candidate set of pairs that is input to the similarity step. For example, assuming a sliding window of 4, record pairs (1,2), (1,3), (1,4), (2,4), (3,4) and (2,3) are added to the candidate set C in the first sliding iteration, because the records with IDs 1, 2, 3 and 4 fall within the first window. The window slides forward by one record, and in the second iteration, new record pairs (2,5), (3,5) and (4,5) are added to C. The method terminates when the window cannot slide any further.

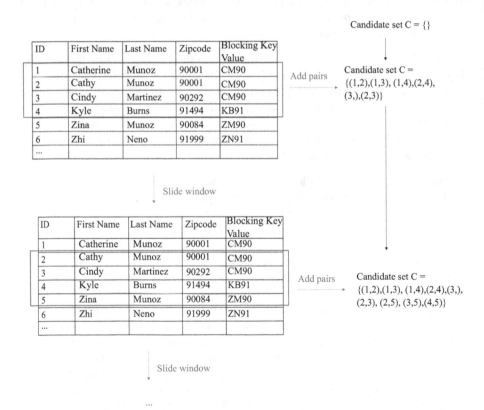

Figure 5.3   An illustration of the sorted Neighborhood blocking method

Besides Sorted Neighborhood and simpler blocking methods, such as simple indexing (called 'traditional blocking') clustering methods, such as Canopies, have also been successfully used for blocking [27,28]. The basic algorithm takes a distance function and two threshold parameters tight ≥ 0 and *loose* $\geq$ *tight*. It operates in the following way for deduplication (where duplicate entities must be detected in a single data source):

1. A 'seed' entity is chosen randomly from the set of all entities in the PKG. Let us denote this entity as *e*.
2. A linear-time distance-based search is conducted in the feature-representation space and all other entities in the PKG that have a distance less than *loose* to *e* are placed into a 'canopy' represented by *e*.
3. Using the results from the above search, entities with a distance less than *tight* to *e* are removed from further consideration.
4. The three steps above are repeated until each entity in the PKG has been assigned to at least one canopy.

In the worst case, there could be entities that represent a singleton-canopy, i.e., no other entities have been assigned to them. An important point to note in the above steps is that entities that have a distance less than *tight* to *e* also* have distance less than *loose* by definition. Thus, before being removed from further consideration, they are guaranteed to have been assigned to at least one canopy (represented by *e*). Indeed, not including the extreme (and usually, rare) case of singleton canopies, the standard behavior for most entities is that they will be assigned to at least one canopy.

Furthermore, it is easy to extend the method to the two-PKG (or even multi-PKG) case by using the entities from the smallest PKG (or some other such well-defined selection rule) exclusively as seed entities. This extension has the added advantage of rendering the algorithm deterministic, since the randomization inherent in the original version above (which determines both the set and order of seed entities ultimately considered) is no longer present. We note that the theoretical or empirical properties of the Canopies algorithm, similar to other blocking algorithms, has not been well explored in the multi-PKG case where more than two PKGs have to be resolved. Indeed, proper algorithmic architectures for multi-PKG ER remains an under-addressed problem in the AI and database literature.

Unlike an algorithm such as Sorted Neighborhood, the Canopies method is not actually dependent on an 'explicit' blocking key or scheme. However, that does not mean it is assumption-free. The choice of the feature space, and the distance function used, are both important decisions that serve as proxies for the blocking key required by more traditional approaches preceding Canopies. Hence, at least one paper in the literature [29] has referred to methods like Canopies as *instance-based blocking* as opposed to *feature-based blocking*, of which both Sorted Neighborhood and traditional blocking are paradigmatic examples.

However, this is not to imply that Canopies and Sorted Neighborhood do not share complementary features, both in their usage and in their developmental history. Both have been enormously popular in the ER community, and variants and versions of both, each professing to be beneficial for different use cases and datasets, have been described over the decades. That being said, the original version continues to be heavily used [21], and is a popular choice when the distance function is well defined (which is often the case for text data, since functions such as Jaccard or Cosine can be efficiently used [28]) or when it is very efficient to execute (such as certain distance functions in Euclidean space).

One example of a variant is the use of a nearest-neighbors approach, rather than a thresholding approach, for determining which entities to assign to a canopy and to remove from further consideration. Another variant, which shares characteristics of a feature-based blocking method, is to use an explicit blocking key to first generate BKVs for each entity. Canopies is then applied, not to the entities themselves, but to the BKVs of the entities [21]. If more than one BKV is possible per entity, a set-based function is required. Thus, this method is considerably more complex than the original method, but may have advantages in specific use cases.

What is the relationship between canopies and blocks? As might be evident from the terminology itself, a canopy itself can be thought of as a block. Because canopy 'blocks' can be overlapping, the blocks are different from those found in traditional blocking where it is common to assume that blocks are not overlapping (i.e., that nodes can be assigned to at most one block, or that BKV sets always have at most size one).

Some techniques have been proposed in both the ER literature (but also beyond) that could potentially be considered as 'alternatives' to blocking. A method that is especially noteworthy in this regard is *Locality Sensitive Hashing (LSH)*. In recent times, LSH has become popular in the Big Data community for presenting an efficient (albeit, approximate) solution to the important problem of nearest-neighbors search in spaces that have high dimensionality [30]. Specifically, given a an LSH family of hash functions may be defined using five parameters: (i) a distance measure d, (ii) two 'radii' denoted as r and s, with $r < s$, (iii) two probabilities (p_r, p_s with $p_r > p_s$) associated with r and s as suggested by the terminology.

An LSH family is considered to be (r, s, p_r, p_s)-sensitive if it is the case that any point u falling inside a sphere with radius r centered at point v (note that the computation of this obviously depends on the feature space and d) necessarily has the same hash as v with a minimum probability of p_r, dependent on a probability distribution defined on the hash family. Furthermore, it is also required that if u does not fall within a similarly defined sphere, but with radius s, the probability that u and v have the same hash is at most p_s [30]. Such (r, s, p_r, p_s)-sensitive families are widely used in practice, and a number of them have been defined in recent papers, because highly efficient algorithms can be designed to hash big datasets and determine (with some probability) when two points are very close to (or far from) each other.

One can see the application of this algorithm to blocking under the right conditions, as the goal of blocking is very similar to that of LSH. Indeed, an LSH-like algorithm is directly applicable to instance-based blocking methods like Canopies that rely explicitly on distance functions rather than blocking keys. However, it must be borne in mind that the requirements of LSH are stricter, whereas Canopies can be used with any well-defined distance measure. A good example of a distance function which is amenable to LSH is the Jaccard function, which can be approximated through the MinHash function (which has the requisite properties and sensitivity defined earlier).

Certainly, despite its rigid assumptions, LSH should be considered as a viable baseline for more complex blocking methods. Beyond ER, it has also been applied to problems such as ontology alignment [31], and on occasion, it has also been applied to the similarity step of ER.

5.2.2 Similarity/matching step

Although the expectation is that the candidate set generated by blocking contains most (and in the ideal situation, all) of the true positives (duplicate entity pairs) present in the PKGs being resolved, its approximate and efficient nature also leads to many true negatives being present[1]. Additionally, a few false negatives may get 'excluded' from the candidate set. In a subsequent section, we discuss the evaluation of blocking to measure the extent to which this is taking place. Note that, once excluded, there is no hope of recovering 'false negatives' (except to re-execute a different blocking algorithm or two-step workflow on the entire dataset) in the similarity step. However, a 'good' similarity function can distinguish between true positives and true negatives effectively, leading to better results in the overall two-step workflow. Indeed, it is easy to see that the similarity function must be finer-grained, compared to blocking, as it needs to make that distinction, which blocking proved incapable of doing due to its focus on efficiency rather than effectiveness [2].

While the similarity function is referred to differently in different communities, within the Semantic Web, it is often referred to as a *link specification* function [22]. We adopt similar terminology here due to the chapter's focus on PKGs rather than relational databases or other similar data models.

Definition 4 (Link Specification Function). *Given two data sources D_1 and D_2, a link specification function is a Boolean function that takes as input a bilateral pair of entities, and returns True if the input entity pair refers to the same underlying entity (i.e., is a duplicate pair) and returns False otherwise.*

Because the underlying real-world link specification function, if it even exists analytically, is not known or discoverable given small sets of duplicate examples, it has to be inferred or learned. In some cases, domain knowledge is used to devise sets of rules as a viable link specification function. In all but the most trivial cases, the function is approximate and unlikely to be perfect. In the treatment below, we assume the 'link specification function' to mean the approximated version of the function rather than the unknown underlying function. Note that the function can be real-valued i.e., given a pair of entities, it may return a value in [0,1], which can be properly interpreted as a score or the model's belief that the pair represents a duplicate.

---

[1] Interestingly, the issue of false positives does not arise, because the similarity step has to make the final decision on what constitutes a positive. Hence, it does not make sense to determine which pairs are 'false' positives since one similarity function may falsely declare a pair to be a duplicate (hence, false positive) while another may not. True positives are a subset of the pairs in the ground-truth set of duplicates and must be included in blocking for *any* similarity function to make that determination.

| Bob's pizza place | 1223 W. 290 St. | 4.97 / 5 stars | Parking available |
| Bob's pizza | 290th & Normandie | 4.96 / 5 stars | Parking available but limited |

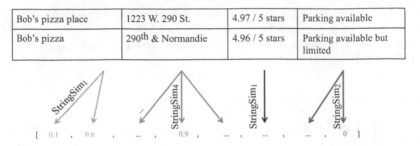

[0.1   ,   0.6   ,   ...   ,   0.9 ,   ...   ,   ...   ,   ...   ,   0   ]

Figure 5.4   Conversion of an entity pair to a feature vector that could then be used in ordinary classification systems (e.g., deep neural networks)

It is also not uncommon to have 'hardened' link specification functions that would just return 0 or 1.

With the preliminaries above, the similarity step in the two-step workflow can be thought of as the application of L to each pair in the candidate set [2,20]. If L is real-valued, further assumptions are required to make the distinction between duplicates and non-duplicates. A simple approach is to use a threshold (determined heuristically, or through a set of 'development set' duplicates and non-duplicates set aside for exactly this purpose): pairs in the candidate set for which L returns a score greater than the threshold are classified as duplicates and similarly for non-duplicates. In theory, one can even have two thresholds (denoted as *lower* and *upper*), not dissimilar to blocking methods like Canopies. Pairs with scores that fall between the thresholds are usually considered to be indeterminate and flagged for manual review, or (in more complex systems) undergo processing by a more expensive, and separately trained, link specification function.

Many link specification functions have been explored by researchers through the decades, including in the expert systems community, machine learning, natural language processing, Semantic Web, and databases. For a good survey of such techniques in databases (primarily), we refer the reader to [2], as well as a book on data matching [20]. Below, we provide more details on a machine learning-centric approach to the problem.

If using machine learning to derive the function L, the most important step is to determine how to extract a feature vector (whether real-valued or discrete) given a *pair* of entities. The procedure is illustrated schematically in Figure 5.4, for the case where both entities (represented as records) share the same schema or ontology. Recall that we referred to this common case as one exhibiting *structural homogeneity*. As the figure illustrates, a library of feature functions is assumed. The feature function is like a 'primitive': it takes a pair of primitive data types (such as strings or dates) as input and returns a numeric feature. Without loss of generality, let us assume that the output is always real-valued. Given such a library of feature functions, a pair in the candidate set can be converted to a well-defined and fixed-length feature functions.

Indeed, if we assume m feature functions, and n such 'fields' representing the schema of the entity, the feature vector would have mn dimensions[2].

Fortunately, many feature functions are available to practitioners. Some have been known for almost a century, while others are more recent. Primitive data types processed by these functions include strings, tokens, and even numbers. In some cases, the semantics of the field can play a role. For instance, *phonetic* feature functions are an excellent fit for strings that represent names. Good descriptions may be found in a variety of sources, including [2,20]. Domain-specific feature functions have also been proposed in the literature, but may be more difficult to locate or implement. Interestingly, neural networks have been used frequently in recent years to bypass the application of hand-picked feature functions. For example, the work in [32] considers the use of such representation learning for extracting features from geographically situated entities represented using latitudes and longitudes, rather than strings or other descriptive information.

An alternative way of extracting features is by generating hashes using several well-known LSH families [33]. According to this model of feature generation, the underlying link specification function can be modeled through a functional combination of various distance measures for which LSH-sensitive families exist. A validation of this model would be consequential as it significantly eases the burden of scalability, both in the blocking and similarity steps. In the most general case, the hashes could be used as features, and an appropriate learner would be used for discovering an explicit functional combination (or rules) for class separation. The process and evaluation are described in more detail in Chapter 7 of Kejriwal (2016).

A machine learning classifier is trained on positively and negatively labeled training samples, and is used to classify vectors in the candidate set. Several classifiers have been explored in the literature, with random forest, multilayer perceptron and Support Vector Machine classifiers all found to perform reasonably well [33–35]. In more recent years, neural networks have also been applied [36].

Independence of the Blocking and Similarity Steps

The two-step workflow, and our description of blocking and similarity, seems to suggest that the two steps are largely independent. Historically, and even in actual practice, this has been the case, and it is even possible to 'swap' out different blocking algorithms while keeping the similarity step constant (and similarly for swapping the similarity modules while keeping blocking constant). However, it behooves us to mention that nothing *prevents* blocking and similarity from being interlocked. Namely, the two steps can be set up such that they 'interact' in a real system i.e., we do not need the candidate set to be completely generated prior to

---

[2]Note that this could also be the case when an entity is missing a value for a given field, or if the feature function fails for some reason. Such cases could be encoded by using a special value (such as −1) in its position in the feature vector. Such preprocessing is important, and largely a function of robust engineering, and ensure that the (ordered) feature vector always has mn well-defined values. Variable length feature vectors are typically very difficult for the majority of machine learning algorithms to handle.

executing the similarity step. A simple example of this is a system that tries to conserve space by not storing the candidate set explicitly, but piping pairs to the similarity step *as* they are generated by blocking. The system still maintains the assumption, however, that decisions made in the similarity step have no impact on blocking (i.e., there is no backward feedback). Furthermore, depending on the blocking method used, there may be a loss in overall efficiency, since the same pair may be classified several times by the similarity step (as we are not maintaining a set-based data structure). Even in this simple example, the tradeoffs between time and space efficiency must be carefully negotiated.

A small, but growing, number of applications in recent years have also been challenging the backward-feedback assumption we mentioned above, example references being [37,38]. An example of a blocking method that takes backward feedback into account is *comparisons propagation*, which tries to use decisions made in the similarity step to *estimate*, in real time, the *utility* of a block [39]. Intuitively, if a block is yielding too many non-duplicates (according to the similarity function), then it may be best to cut losses and stop processing the block rather than continue processing it and generating more 'useless' pairs for the similarity step to classify as non-duplicates. In a rational decision-making setting, the expected gain from processing the block any further is outweighed by the loss in efficiency, making it appropriate to discard it.

While such techniques are promising, their implementations have mostly been limited to serial architectures, owing to the need for continuous data-sharing between the similarity and block generating components [37,39]. Experimentally, the benefits of such techniques over independent techniques like Sorted Neighborhood or traditional blocking (with skew-eliminating measures such as block purging) have not been established extensively enough to warrant widespread adoption. Therefore, the two-step workflow, with both steps relatively independent, continues to be predominant in much of the ER research [40].

5.3   Evaluating named entity resolution

The independence of blocking and similarity suggests that the performance of each can be controlled for the other in experiments [2]. In the last decade both blocking and similarity have become increasingly sophisticated. It is now the rule, rather than the exception, to publish either on blocking or on similarity within an individual publication [21]. Despite some potential disadvantages, this methodology has yielded the adoption of well-defined evaluation metrics and standards for both steps.

5.3.1   Evaluating blocking

The primary aim of blocking is to scale the naïve similarity-only ER system that bilaterally pairs all entities with one another. Blocking serves this goal by generating a smaller candidate set than this 'exhaustive set'. However, if time-complexity reduction were the only goal, optimal blocking would simply yield the empty set as the candidate set. Such a system would ultimately be without utility because it would generate a candidate set with zero duplicates coverage.

In other words, duplicates coverage and candidate set reduction are two competing goals that every blocking technique (blocking key and blocking method) aims to trade off between [41]. This tradeoff can also be formalized. As a first step, let us denote Ω as the set $D_1 \times D_2$; in other words, the exhaustive set of all bilateral pairs. Let Ω_M denote the subset of Ω that contains all (and only) matching entity pairs. Ω_M is designated as the ground-truth (equivalently, gold standard). Finally, we use C to denote the candidate set generated by applying the blocking method. Using this notation, Reduction Ratio (RR) can be defined using the formula below:

$$RR = 1 - \frac{|C|}{|\Omega|} \qquad (5.1)$$

A higher RR implies greater time-complexity reduction (and depending on the infrastructure, space-complexity reduction) achieved by the blocking method, compared to generating the exhaustive set [21]. Although less commonly used for this purpose, RR can also be evaluated relative to the candidate set of a baseline blocking method [38]. The only change required in the formula above is to replace Ω with the candidate set of the baseline method. In its relative usage, such an RR would have positive value if the blocking method resulted in greater savings compared to the baseline method; otherwise, the relative RR would be negative.

Importantly, even minor differences in RR can have an enormous impact in terms of run-time because of its quadratic nature. For instance, consider the case where Ω contains 10 million pairs (a not unreasonable number that could be achieved if the two data sources only had around 1,000–2,000 instances each). An improvement of even 0.1% on the RR metric would imply savings of thousands of pairs. The same percentage could represent millions of pairs on even larger datasets.

While RR is a good way of measuring the complexity reduction goal of blocking, the Pairs Completeness (PC) metric, defined below, quantifies the method's duplicates coverage:

$$PC = \frac{|C \cap \Omega_M|}{|\Omega_M|} \qquad (5.2)$$

Interestingly, the PC serves as an upper bound on the recall metric that is used for evaluating overall duplicates coverage in the ER system (i.e., after the similarity step has been applied on the candidate set). For example, if PC is only 70%, meaning that 30% of the duplicate pairs did not get included in the candidate set, then the ER system's overall recall can never exceed 70%.

While not theoretically necessary, in practice, there is a tradeoff between achieving both high PC and RR. In most blocking architectures, the tradeoff is negotiated by tuning one or more relevant parameters. For example, the sliding window parameter w in Sorted Neighborhood (illustrated earlier through an example) can be increased to achieve higher PC, at the cost of lower RR [41].

Although we can always plot PC–RR curves to visually demonstrate the tradeoff in a blocking system, a single number is desired in practical settings. In the literature, this number is usually just the F-Measure, or harmonic mean, between the PC and RR:

$$F - Measure = \frac{2.PC.RR}{PC + RR} \tag{5.3}$$

A second tradeoff metric, Pairs Quality (PQ), is less commonly known than the F-Measure of PC and RR in the wider community, but can be illuminating for comparing different blocking architectures:

$$PQ = \frac{|C \cap \Omega_M|}{|C|} \tag{5.4}$$

Theoretically, PQ may be a better measure of the tradeoff between PC and RR than the F-Measure estimate, which weighs RR and PC equally, despite the quadratic dependence of the former. For this reason, PQ has sometimes been described as a precision metric for blocking [21], although the terminology is superficial at best. The intuitive interpretation of a high PQ is that the generated blocks (and by virtue, the candidate set C) are dense in duplicate pairs. A blocking method with high PQ is therefore expected to have greater utility, although it may not necessarily lead to high precision or recall from the overall ER architecture.

PQ can sometimes give estimates that are difficult to interpret. For example, suppose there were 1,000 duplicates in the ground-truth, and the candidate set C only contained ten pairs, of which eight represent duplicates. In this example, PQ would be 80%. Assuming that the exhaustive set is large enough, such that RR is near-perfect, the F-Measure would still be less than 2% (since PC is less than 1%). The F-Measure result would be correctly interpreted as an indication that, for practical purposes, the blocking process has failed. The result indicated by PQ alone is clearly misleading, suggesting that, as a tradeoff measure, PQ should not be substituted for the F-Measure of PC and RR. An alternative, proposed by at least one author but not used widely, is to compute and report the F-Measure of PQ and PC, instead of PC and RR [21].

5.3.2   Evaluating similarity

As similarity is most similar to a machine learning classification problem (such as sentiment analysis), the best way to evaluate it given the real-world requirements of ER is to compute precision and recall. Specifically, once a candidate set C is output by blocking and processed by similarity, the final expected output is a *partition* of C into sets C_D and C_{ND} of pairs of resolved ('duplicated') and non-resolved ('non-duplicates') entities.

Given a ground-truth set Ω_M (using the terminology of the previous section) of actual duplicate entity-pairs, the true positives (TPs), false negatives (FNs), and false positives (FPs) can be computed in the usual way. Precision is just the ratio of TPs to the sum of TPs and FPs, while recall is the ratio of TPs to the ratio of TPs and FNs. Like most machine learning problems, optimizing precision in an ER application can come at the cost of optimizing recall. One way to measure the tradeoff is by plotting a Receiver Operating Characteristic (ROC), which plots true positives against false positives [42]. However, it is simpler to obtain a single-point estimate of this tradeoff by computing the harmonic mean (F-Measure) of precision and recall. Note that if F-Measure is used to evaluate similarity, as well as blocking (along the lines discussed in the previous section), a clear distinction must be noted between the two when reporting the results, as they are measuring tradeoffs between different quantities. An alternative to a single-point estimate is a precision-recall curve that, although related in a complex way to the ROC curve, expresses the tradeoff much more directly at different (precision, recall) points. Historically, and currently, precision-recall curves dominate ROC curves in the ER community [40,43,44].

We emphasize that computing a measure such as accuracy is usually not a good idea. The reason is that the vast majority of pairs are expected to be non-duplicates, meaning that if a system were to predict every pair in the candidate set to be a non-duplicate pair, the resulting accuracy would be very high! Such a measure is clearly without utility. Precision and recall preempt this problem because neither takes true negatives into account in the computation.

5.4   Evolution of research in named entity resolution

Owing to its 50-year history, many systems and research methods have been proposed for ER. Figure 5.5 shows how different streams of thought have emerged over the decades. While necessarily simplified (e.g., many of these classes of approaches have overlapped, and some are still widely used), the figure largely tracks what has happened in the broader AI community and its many applications. For the more technical reader, we recommend books on both ER and knowledge graphs (which tend to contain chapters on ER) [3–5,45].

In the Semantic Web community, rule-based systems were considered state-of-the-art [22] and are still widely used, in the immediate aftermath of Linked Open Data (which opened up ER as an important problem in that community). However, due to their many advantages, machine learning approaches have gained in popularity over the last decade. Such approaches, primarily supervised in nature, take training pairs of duplicates and non-duplicates and learn optimize parameters in a given hypothesis

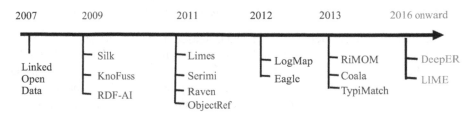

Figure 5.5   A timeline of approaches (primarily for the similarity step) that have evolved to address ER

space to achieve high performance on an unseen test set. However, we note that rule-based and machine learning approaches are not necessarily exclusive or independent of one another. Indeed, a number of interesting hybrid approaches have been proposed, some of which are named in Figure 5.5. Also of interest are 'low supervision' approaches that rely on techniques such as active learning [46–48]. Deep learning has also been applied with some success to ER [36].

Beyond the similarity step, where machine learning has been applied and studied much more extensively, methods have been proposed in the last two decades to learn blocking keys given training data of duplicates and non-duplicates [49–52]. More recently, such approaches have also been tried for heterogeneous data collections [53]. This was quite a departure from the traditional approach, which was to manually specify blocking keys that seemed 'intuitive'. As multiple approaches have now showed, a systematic approach to learning blocking keys can lead to non-trivial savings in complexity reduction, or in improved PC and PQ. The technique for learning blocking keys is less straightforward than training classifiers for similarity, but theoretically similar to problems such as set covering [54]. Along with blocking scheme learning, research also continues on developing new blocking methods (or variants of existing methods, like Sorted Neighborhood) for novel ecosystems such as Linked Open Data [55].

5.5   Challenges and opportunities for named entity resolution

Despite being a 50-year-old problem, and improvements in Artificial Intelligence and deep learning technology, ER remains a challenging problem due to the rapid growth of large and heterogeneous datasets published on the Web. In the previous section, a critical challenge that was described is the non-obvious ability of existing systems to simultaneously address challenges such as domain-independence, scalability and heterogeneity. At the same time, in the existing AI literature, there are theoretical and applied mechanisms to address some of these challenges. A machine learning paradigm such as transfer learning, for example, could potentially be used to handle the domain-independence requirement by first bootstrapping an ER system in a few 'anchor' domains, and then using transfer learning to adapt the system to other domains. In theory, such an approach seems feasible, but in practice, it is very difficult to execute. Some other challenges, which were also expounded upon in [56] are:

1.   **Schema-free approaches to ER:** The increased diversity and heterogeneity of PKGs published on the Web indicates that the present time is a good one for further investigating so-called *schema-free approaches* to ER. We note that the traditional approaches have been primarily inspired by the Relational Database community, which tends to assume some form of schema or ontology matching in order to 'align' the types of instances before processing them further (e.g., through the two-step workflow). Conventionally, many algorithms considered such a homogeneous type-structure as a given, for both qualitative and computation reasons. We already saw in the previous sections that many algorithms

only seem to apply if the structural homogeneity condition is met. However, more recently, there has been much literature calling this assumption into question and seeking to extend methods to work without it. In some of our own papers, we suggested a schema-free implementation of the classic Sorted Neighborhood algorithm that is specifically designed for RDF KGs, and empirical results showed that the method compares favorably to the more established baseline [57,58]. However, schema-free approaches to ER remain relatively novel in the community, and many conceptual and methodological questions remain. For example, how can we tell which schema-free features are of 'good' quality, and construct such feature functions effectively? Can deep learning play an important role to automate such construction? Finally, could such approaches allow us to bypass ontology matching altogether prior to ER? And how do we apply such approaches to domains that are not completely structured, but contain a mix of structured data and free text (of which social media applications, augmented with user meta-data, are good examples [59–62])?

2. **Improving Linked Data Quality**: We discussed earlier that an important prior step, often treated as an assumption in core ER research, to conducting Named Entity Resolution is to first determine which types of nodes between two KGs should be aligned. In the deduplication scenario (as opposed to resolving entities in two or more PKGs), this problem can also arise. For example, if an individual is both an author and professor, and these are two types in the KG, then it is plausible that two instances of the individual are present in the PKG. Only executing an ER algorithm on the set of *professor* instances, or on the set of *author* instances (independently) is unlikely to yield high-quality results. Hence, proper type alignment is generally necessary to find the balance between running the two-step ER workflow on the full set(s) of nodes [63,64], even with blocking, and being too restrictive in which pairs of types should be considered as 'aligned' for the purposes of being eligible for such processing.

On the Web, the problem of type alignment is exacerbated because of the quality of Linked Data. Many different types of entities are present, and it is not always evident whether one type should be aligned with another. A related problem is property alignment. Because this problem particularly arises with 'cross-domain' or encyclopedic KGs, such as DBpedia (which contains over 400 types), improving the quality of Linked Data published online, as well as re-using existing ontological types, is an important future direction. One reason why this continues to be challenging is that there is also ambiguity surrounding the construction of good ground truths for highly complex types. In a preliminary experimental work that we published [64], we found that there may be at least three different ways (both inductive and deductive) of constructing reasonable ground truths, which are not always consistent. This can cause an extra layer of noise when evaluating type alignment (and following that, ER) systems. There is reason to believe that such noise is not merely hypothetical but actually exists in real Linked Open Datasets currently on the Web [56]. On the positive front, because there are far fewer types than entities and properties, improving their quality and enforcing better publishing standards can lead to outsize progress in addressing these issues. In turn, adoption of Linked Data improves and more ambitious data integration applications at Web scale become feasible.

3. **Transfer Learning:** Transfer learning, surveyed in [65] (among many other papers), is a valuable avenue to pursue for resolving entities in large Linked Open datasets without requiring enormous amounts of training data. Although transfer learning (even for ER) is not a completely novel line of research [66], it has not found widespread utility yet in ER due to several technical challenges, and relatively low quality compared to fully supervised approaches. Even in other machine learning research, its progress is not completely evident, although it bears saying that it has continued to be researched actively in several mainstream applications [67]. However, recent advent of large language models like BERT and ChatGPT suggest that feasible transfer learning solutions may be around the corner. 'Pre-trained' versions of such models, which can be downloaded off-the-shelf and fine-tuned on specific datasets at relatively low cost [68], contain much background knowledge that could boost performance on ER datasets. At the same time, these models also have some problems (such as lack of explainability but also others [69–72]) that may pose problems in domains where a high degree of confidence is needed. Beyond classic transfer learning, other novel learning approaches, such as zero-shot and few-shot learning, also continue to be investigated for difficult machine learning problems [73,74]. Such techniques could prove to be essential for ER, especially with the advent of neural language models [68].

4. **ER in PKGs versus Personal Knowledge Networks (PKNs)**: Although KGs have witnessed increased adoption in multiple domains over the last ten years, there has been a similar (and largely independent) rise in the field of *network science*. Network science has proven to be particularly powerful in understanding complex systems [75], especially those where relational structure plays an important role. A classic example is social networks, which bears close resemblance to PKGs. In recent years, it has also been applied to understanding other interesting and high-impact social domains, such as illicit finance [76], economics [77], international geopolitics and humanitarian applications [78,79], e-commerce [80–82], social media analytics [83–86], crisis informatics [87], misinformation and sensationalism detection [88], and human trafficking [89–91]. ER in the network domain is far less studied, as has its connections to ER in KG-centric communities like Semantic Web. Visualization of outputs, designing of better interfaces, and efficient human-in-the-loop tooling, both in network science and Semantic Web, remains under-studied as well [92–96]. At the same time, there is clearly a vital connection, and not just because PKGs and networks can both be represented as graphs. To take the human trafficking domain as an example, KGs have also been applied to the problem with significant success [97–100]. Another example is e-commerce [101,102].

5. **Theoretical Progress in ER as an 'AI-Complete' Problem**: Named Entity Resolution is an inherently practical problem, but a theoretical understanding of the problem could open up new algorithmic directions. An example of such a treatment is the Swoosh family of algorithms [103]. More recently, with an increased

focus on Artificial General Intelligence (AGI), there is an open question as to whether ER can be viewed as an 'AI-complete' problem i.e., solving ER with sufficient accuracy and robustness may provide concrete evidence that we have made definitive progress on AGI. Examples of AI-complete problems include commonsense reasoning [104] and knowledge representation [105], open-world learning (including reinforcement learning techniques for open-world learning [106,107]). These problems, if solved, could revolutionize the applications of AI in a variety of domains, and become the underlying basis for industries of the future [108]. However, much theoretical work needs to be done before any of these claims can be validated with certainty.

Beyond developing better theoretical foundations, one must also bear in mind that ER does not exist in isolation, but that noise in real-world ER systems may have close connections to noise in other steps of the KG construction and refinement pipeline, such as information extraction, data acquisition [109–111] and general knowledge capture [112]. Scalable ER, especially in massive distributed ecosystems like schema.org [113–115] or other Web-scale and 'Big Data' applications [116–118], also remains an important under-addressed problem in the research community. This problem is only likely to get worse as advanced extensions to Linked Open Data [119] and other such ecosystems are proposed in the years to come (in part, due to the advent of large language models). In the network science community, there has also been increased focus on algorithmic scalability [120].

6. **Other Applied Directions**: As PKGs are used in different ways in different domains and use-cases, the issue of properly building domain-specific PKGs (of which ER is an important component) remains critical and is an important application of the general research direction of domain-specific KG construction [121]. Semantic search, especially in domain-specific applications [122], is another important direction as it will likely require advances in domain-specific search [123,124]. Because of the rise of large language models, and deep learning more generally, we believe that an ER approach that melds the best of traditional approaches to the problem with deep learning could lead to significant advances in upcoming years [125]. This is true for KG research, more generally [126]. An example of such an application is hypothesis generation and geopolitical forecasting using (for example) multi-modal KGs rather than directly using raw text or video sources [127]. Finally, many applications require processing and conducting ER on datasets that are structurally heterogeneous. Even today, structural homogeneity remains a strong assumption in the ER community. Removing this assumption from future approaches is a promising direction [128], but is not without challenges [52,129].

5.6   Conclusion

Named Entity Resolution is an important application that has been researcher for almost half a century. While the early applications of ER were limited to patient records and census data, they have proliferated in an era of Big Data and open knowledge. It is likely to continue playing an important role in Artificial Intelligence efforts in both government and industry in the near- and long-term future, especially in data-intensive text applications. As a recent book discussed, industry is now starting to invest intensively in AI systems to grow or maintain a competitive advantage, and open assets such as Linked Data and off-the-shelf large language models are important drivers in such implementations. Because of the open nature of these assets, there is a more level playing field than was historically the case. Properly implementing, scaling, and evaluating advanced algorithms, and ensuring that the data is 'clean', may well provide the edge in many cases. For most datasets, achieving such quality requires concerted effort in ER. 'Properly' in this context also implies gaining a better understanding of bias in training or evaluating an ER model [130], and other weak spots of the model.

This chapter provided a background on ER essentials. Particularly important is the two-step workflow, comprising blocking and similarity, and their respective evaluation methodologies and metrics, which has emerged as a standard for ER. However, many important research questions and opportunities still remain, several of which we covered in the previous section. Another important research area that is particularly important to ER but that we did not mention in the previous section is the efficient generation of unbiased training sets. While this may not prove to be a problem if zero-shot learning and few-shot learning techniques are adapted to address ER, at present, only supervised learning techniques currently have the quality necessary for high-stakes applications. Hence, generation of high-quality training sets remains an important problem. Unlike regular machine learning applications, random sampling and labeling does not work very well because most pairs of nodes in the KG are not duplicates.

References

[1]   Newcombe HB, Kennedy JM, Axford S, *et al.* Automatic linkage of vital records: computers can be used to extract "follow-up" statistics of families from files of routine records. *Science*. 1959;130(3381):954–959.

[2]   Ipeirotis PG, Verykios VS, and Elmagarmid AK. Duplicate record detection: a survey. *IEEE Transactions on Knowledge and Data Engineering*. 2007;19(1):1–16.

[3]   Kejriwal M. *Domain-Specific Knowledge Graph Construction*. Springer; 2019.

[4]   Tiddi I, Lécué F, and Hitzler P. *Knowledge Graphs for Explainable Artificial Intelligence: Foundations, Applications and Challenges*. IOS Press; 2020.

[5]   Kejriwal M, Knoblock CA, and Szekely P. *Knowledge Graphs: Fundamentals, Techniques, and Applications*. MIT Press; 2021.

[6]   Qi G, Chen H, Liu K, *et al. Knowledge Graph*. To appear; 2020.

[7]   Klyne G and Carroll J. Resource Description Framework (RDF): Concepts and Abstract Syntax-W3C Recommendation. 2006.

[8]   Angles R and Gutierrez C. Querying RDF data from a graph database perspective. In: *European Semantic Web Conference*. Springer; 2005. p. 346–360.

[9]   Sequeda JF and Miranker DP. Ultrawrap: SPARQL execution on relational data. *Journal of Web Semantics*. 2013;22:19–39.

[10] Sahoo SS, Halb W, Hellmann S, *et al*. A survey of current approaches for mapping of relational databases to RDF. *W3C RDB2RDF Incubator Group Report*. 2009;1:113–130.

[11] Bizer C, Heath T, and Berners-Lee T. *Linked Data—The Story So Far*. University of Southampton, ePrints Soton; 2009.

[12] Allemang D and Hendler J. *Semantic Web for the Working Ontologist: Effective Modeling in RDFS and OWL*. Elsevier; 2011.

[13] McGuinness DL, and Van Harmelen F. OWL web ontology language overview. *W3C Recommendation*. 2004;10(10):2004.

[14] Elango P. *Coreference Resolution: A Survey*. University of Wisconsin, Madison, WI; 2005. p. 12.

[15] Sukthanker R, Poria S, Cambria E, *et al*. Anaphora and coreference resolution: a review. *Information Fusion*. 2020;59:139–162.

[16] Koudas N, Marathe A, and Srivastava D. Flexible string matching against large databases in practice. In: *Proceedings of the Thirtieth International Conference on Very Large Data Bases*, Vol. 30; 2004. p. 1078–1086.

[17] Hall PA and Dowling GR. Approximate string matching. *ACM Computing Surveys (CSUR)*. 1980;12(4):381–402.

[18] Aho AV and Corasick MJ. Efficient string matching: an aid to bibliographic search. *Communications of the ACM*. 1975;18(6):333–340.

[19] Pinto D, Vilariño D, Alemán Y, *et al*. The Soundex phonetic algorithm revisited for SMS text representation. In: *International Conference on Text, Speech and Dialogue*. Springer; 2012. p. 47–55.

[20] Christen P. The data matching process. In: *Data Matching*. Springer; 2012. p. 23–35.

[21] Christen P. A survey of indexing techniques for scalable record linkage and deduplication. *IEEE Transactions on Knowledge and Data Engineering*. 2011;24(9):1537–1555.

[22] Volz J, Bizer C, Gaedke M, *et al*. Discovering and maintaining links on the web of data. In: *International Semantic Web Conference*. Springer; 2009. p. 650–665.

[23] Otero-Cerdeira L, Rodríguez-Martínez FJ, and Gómez-Rodríguez A. Ontology matching: a literature review. *Expert Systems with Applications*. 2015;42(2):949–971.

[24] Shvaiko P and Euzenat J. Ontology matching: state of the art and future challenges. *IEEE Transactions on Knowledge and Data Engineering*. 2011;25(1):158–176.

[25] Kejriwal M and Szekely P. Supervised typing of big graphs using semantic embeddings. In: *Proceedings of the International Workshop on Semantic Big Data*; 2017. p. 1–6.

[26]   Tian A, Kejriwal M, and Miranker DP. Schema matching over relations, attributes, and data values. In: *Proceedings of the 26th International Conference on Scientific and Statistical Database Management*; 2014. p. 1–12.

[27]   McCallum A, Nigam K, and Ungar LH. Efficient clustering of high-dimensional data sets with application to reference matching. In: *Proceedings of the Sixth ACM SIGKDD International Conference on Knowledge Discovery and Data Mining*; 2000. p. 169–178.

[28]   Baxter R, Christen P, and Churches T. A comparison of fast blocking methods for record linkage. In: *Proceedings of the Workshop on Data Cleaning, Record Linkage and Object Consolidation at the Ninth ACM SIGKDD International Conference on Knowledge Discovery and Data Mining*. Washington, DC. 2003.

[29]   Ma Y and Tran T. TYPiMatch: type-specific unsupervised learning of keys and key values for heterogeneous web data integration. In: *Proceedings of the Sixth ACM International Conference on Web Search and Data Mining*; 2013. p. 325–334.

[30]   Datar M, Immorlica N, Indyk P, *et al.* Locality-sensitive hashing scheme based on p-stable distributions. In: *Proceedings of the Twentieth Annual Symposium on Computational Geometry*; 2004. p. 253–262.

[31]   Duan S, Fokoue A, Hassanzadeh O, *et al.* Instance-based matching of large ontologies using locality-sensitive hashing. In: *International Semantic Web Conference*. Springer; 2012. p. 49–64.

[32]   Kejriwal M and Szekely P. Neural embeddings for populated GeoNames locations. In: *International Semantic Web Conference*. Springer; 2017. p. 139–146.

[33]   Kejriwal M and Miranker DP. An unsupervised instance matcher for schema-free RDF data. *Journal of Web Semantics*. 2015;35:102–123.

[34]   Rong S, Niu X, Xiang EW, *et al.* A machine learning approach for instance matching based on similarity metrics. In: *International Semantic Web Conference*. Springer; 2012. p. 460–475.

[35]   Soru T and Ngomo ACN. A comparison of supervised learning classifiers for link discovery. In: *Proceedings of the 10th International Conference on Semantic Systems*; 2014. p. 41–44.

[36]   Gottapu RD, Dagli C, and Ali B. Entity resolution using convolutional neural network. *Procedia Computer Science*. 2016;95:153–158.

[37]   Whang SE, Menestrina D, Koutrika G, *et al.* Entity resolution with iterative blocking. In: *Proceedings of the 2009 ACM SIGMOD International Conference on Management of Data*; 2009. p. 219–232.

[38]   Papadakis G, Koutrika G, Palpanas T, *et al.* Meta-blocking: taking entity resolution to the next level. *IEEE Transactions on Knowledge and Data Engineering*. 2013;26(8):1946–1960.

[39]   Papadakis G, Ioannou E, Palpanas T, *et al.* A blocking framework for entity resolution in highly heterogeneous information spaces. *IEEE Transactions on Knowledge and Data Engineering*. 2012;25(12):2665–2682.

[40] Köpcke H and Rahm E. Frameworks for entity matching: a comparison. *Data & Knowledge Engineering*. 2010;69(2):197–210.

[41] Hernández S, Hernández MA, and Stolfo SJ. Real-world data is dirty: data cleansing and the merge/purge problem. *Data Mining and Knowledge Discovery*. 1998;2(1):9–37.

[42] Hanley JA and McNeil BJ. The meaning and use of the area under a receiver operating characteristic (ROC) curve. *Radiology*. 1982;143(1):29–36.

[43] Köpcke H, Thor A, and Rahm E. Evaluation of entity resolution approaches on real-world match problems. *Proceedings of the VLDB Endowment*. 2010; 3(1-2):484–493.

[44] Menestrina D, Whang SE, and Garcia-Molina H. Evaluating entity resolution results. *Proceedings of the VLDB Endowment*. 2010;3(1-2):208–219.

[45] Christophides V, Efthymiou V, and Stefanidis K. Entity resolution in the web of data. *Synthesis Lectures on the Semantic Web*. 2015;5(3):1–122.

[46] Ngomo ACN, Lyko K, and Christen V. Coala–correlation-aware active learning of link specifications. In: *Extended Semantic Web Conference*. Springer; 2013. p. 442–456.

[47] Kejriwal M and Miranker DP. Semi-supervised instance matching using boosted classifiers. In: Gandon F, Sabou M, Sack H, *et al.*, editors. The Semantic Web. Latest Advances and New Domains – 12th European Semantic Web Conference, ESWC 2015, Portoroz, Slovenia, May 31–June 4, 2015. Proceedings. vol. 9088 of Lecture Notes in Computer Science. Springer; 2015. p. 388–402. Available from: https://doi.org/10.1007/978-3-319-18818-8_24.

[48] Kejriwal M and Miranker DP. Minimally supervised instance matching: an alternate approach. In: Gandon F, Guéret C, Villata S, *et al.*, editors. *The Semantic Web: ESWC 2015 Satellite Events – ESWC 2015 Satellite Events*, Portorož, Slovenia, May 31–June 4, 2015, Revised Selected Papers. vol. 9341 of Lecture Notes in Computer Science. Springer; 2015. p. 72–76. Available from: https://doi.org/10.1007/978-3-319-25639-9_14.

[49] Kejriwal M and Miranker DP. An unsupervised algorithm for learning blocking schemes. In: *2013 IEEE 13th International Conference on Data Mining*. IEEE; 2013. p. 340–349.

[50] Kejriwal M and Miranker DP. A two-step blocking scheme learner for scalable link discovery. *OM*. 2014;14:49–60.

[51] Kejriwal M. Unsupervised DNF blocking for efficient linking of knowledge graphs and tables. *Information*. 2021;12(3):134.

[52] Kejriwal M. Disjunctive normal form schemes for heterogeneous attributed graphs. CoRR. 2016;abs/1605.00686. Available from: http://arxiv.org/abs/1605.00686.

[53] Kejriwal M and Miranker DP. A DNF blocking scheme learner for heterogeneous datasets. CoRR. 2015;abs/1501.01694. Available from: http://arxiv.org/abs/1501.01694.

[54] Caprara A, Toth P, and Fischetti M. Algorithms for the set covering problem. *Annals of Operations Research*. 2000;98(1):353–371.

[55]   Kejriwal M and Miranker DP. Sorted Neighborhood for schema-free RDF data. In: Gandon F, Guéret C, Villata S, *et al.*, editors. *The Semantic Web: ESWC 2015 Satellite Events – ESWC 2015 Satellite Events*, Portorož, Slovenia, May 31–June 4, 2015, Revised Selected Papers. vol. 9341 of Lecture Notes in Computer Science. Springer; 2015. p. 217–229. Available from: https://doi.org/10.1007/978-3-319-25639-9_38.

[56]   Kejriwal M. *Populating a Linked Data Entity Name System: A Big Data Solution to Unsupervised Instance Matching*, vol. 27. IOS Press; 2016.

[57]   Kejriwal M and Miranker DP. Sorted Neighborhood for schema-free RDF data. In: *European Semantic Web Conference*. Springer; 2015. p. 217–229.

[58]   Kejriwal M and Miranker DP. On the complexity of sorted neighborhood. arXiv preprint arXiv:150101696. 2015.

[59]   Hu M, Rao A, Kejriwal M, *et al.* Socioeconomic correlates of antiscience attitudes in the US. *Future Internet.* 2021;13(6):160. Available from: https://doi.org/10.3390/fi13060160.

[60]   Kejriwal M, Fang G, and Zhou Y. A feasibility study of open-source sentiment analysis and text classification systems on disaster-specific social media data. In: *IEEE Symposium Series on Computational Intelligence, SSCI 2021*, Orlando, FL, December 5–7, 2021. IEEE; 2021. p. 1–8. Available from: https://doi.org/10.1109/SSCI50451.2021.9660089.

[61]   Kejriwal M, Wang Q, Li H, *et al.* An empirical study of emoji usage on Twitter in linguistic and national contexts. *Online Social Networks Media.* 2021;24:100149. Available from: https://doi.org/10.1016/j.osnem.2021.100149.

[62]   Kejriwal M and Zhou P. On detecting urgency in short crisis messages using minimal supervision and transfer learning. *Social Network Analysis and Mining.* 2020;10(1):58. Available from: https://doi.org/10.1007/s13278-020-00670-7.

[63]   Kejriwal M and Szekely PA. Supervised typing of big graphs using semantic embeddings. CoRR. 2017;abs/1703.07805. Available from: http://arxiv.org/abs/1703.07805.

[64]   Kejriwal M and Miranker DP. Experience: type alignment on DBpedia and Freebase. arXiv preprint arXiv:160804442. 2016.

[65]   Cao B, Pan SJ, Zhang Y, *et al.* Adaptive transfer learning. In: *Proceedings of the AAAI Conference on Artificial Intelligence.* vol. 24; 2010. p. 407–412.

[66]   Baxter J. Theoretical models of learning to learn. In: *Learning to Learn.* Springer; 1998. p. 71–94.

[67]   Mesnil G, Dauphin Y, Glorot X, *et al.* Unsupervised and transfer learning challenge: a deep learning approach. In: *Proceedings of ICML Workshop on Unsupervised and Transfer Learning. JMLR Workshop and Conference Proceedings*; 2012. p. 97–110.

[68]   Devlin J, Chang MW, Lee K, *et al.* Bert: pre-training of deep bidirectional transformers for language understanding. arXiv preprint arXiv:181004805. 2018.

[69]   Shen K and Kejriwal M. Understanding prior bias and choice paralysis in transformer-based language representation models through four experimental probes. CoRR. 2022;abs/2210.01258. Available from: https://doi.org/10.48550/arXiv.2210.01258.

[70]   Tang Z and Kejriwal M. Can language representation models think in bets? CoRR. 2022;abs/2210.07519. Available from: https://doi.org/10.48550/arXiv.2210.07519.

[71]   Shen K and Kejriwal M. On the generalization abilities of fine-tuned commonsense language representation models. In: Bramer M and Ellis R, editors. *Artificial Intelligence XXXVIII – 41st SGAI International Conference on Artificial Intelligence, AI 2021*, Cambridge, UK, December 14-16, 2021, Proceedings. vol. 13101 of Lecture Notes in Computer Science. Springer; 2021. p. 3–16. Available from: https://doi.org/10.1007/978-3-030-91100-3_1.

[72]   Kejriwal M and Shen K. Do fine-tuned commonsense language models really generalize? CoRR. 2020;abs/2011.09159. Available from: https://arxiv.org/abs/2011.09159.

[73]   Xian Y, Schiele B, and Akata Z. Zero-shot learning-the good, the bad and the ugly. In: *Proceedings of the IEEE Conference on Computer Vision and Pattern Recognition*; 2017. p. 4582–4591.

[74]   Ravi S and Larochelle H. Optimization as a model for few-shot learning. In: *International Conference on Learning Representations*; 2016.

[75]   Kejriwal M and Shen K. Can scale-free network growth with triad formation capture simplicial complex distributions in real communication networks? CoRR. 2022;abs/2203.06491. Available from: https://doi.org/10.48550/arXiv.2203.06491.

[76]   Kejriwal M and Dang A. Structural studies of the global networks exposed in the Panama papers. *Applied Network Science*. 2020;5(1):63. Available from: https://doi.org/10.1007/s41109-020-00313-y.

[77]   Kejriwal M and Luo Y. On the empirical association between trade network complexity and global gross domestic product. CoRR. 2022;abs/2211.13117. Available from: https://doi.org/10.48550/arXiv.2211.13117.

[78]   Kejriwal M. Link prediction between structured geopolitical events: models and experiments. *Frontiers Big Data*. 2021;4:779792. Available from: https://doi.org/10.3389/fdata.2021.779792.

[79]   Kejriwal M, Peng J, Zhang H, *et al*. Structured event entity resolution in humanitarian domains. In: Vrandecic D, Bontcheva K, Suárez-Figueroa MC, *et al*., editors. *The Semantic Web – ISWC 2018 – 17th International Semantic Web Conference*, Monterey, CA, USA, October 8–12, 2018, Proceedings, Part I. vol. 11136 of Lecture Notes in Computer Science. Springer; 2018. p. 233–249. Available from: https://doi.org/10.1007/978-3-030-00671-6_14.

[80]   Kejriwal M, Shen K, Ni C, *et al*. Transfer-based taxonomy induction over concept labels. *Engineering Applications of Artificial Intelligence*. 2022;108:104548. Available from: https://doi.org/10.1016/j.engappai.2021.104548.

[81]   Kejriwal M, Shen K, Ni C, *et al*. An evaluation and annotation method-ology for product category matching in e-commerce. *Computers in Indus-try*. 2021;131:103497. Available from: https://doi.org/10.1016/j.compind. 2021.103497.

[82]   Kejriwal M, Selvam RK, Ni C, *et al*. Locally constructing product taxonomies from scratch using representation learning. In: Atzmüller M, Coscia M, and Missaoui R, editors. *IEEE/ACM International Conference on Advances in Social Networks Analysis and Mining, ASONAM 2020*, The Hague, Nether-lands, December 7–10, 2020. IEEE; 2020. p. 507–514. Available from: https://doi.org/10.1109/ASONAM49781.2020.9381320.

[83]   Luo Y and Kejriwal M. Understanding COVID-19 vaccine reaction through comparative analysis on Twitter. In: Arai K, editor. *Intelligent Computing – Proceedings of the 2022 Computing Conference*, Volume 1, SAI 2022, Virtual Event, July 14–15, 2022. vol. 506 of Lecture Notes in Networks and Systems. Springer; 2022. p. 846–864. Available from: https://doi.org/10.1007/978-3-031-10461-9_58.

[84]   Melotte S and Kejriwal M. A geo-tagged COVID-19 Twitter dataset for 10 North American Metropolitan areas over a 255-day period. *Data*. 2021;6(6):64. Available from: https://doi.org/10.3390/data6060064.

[85]   Melotte S and Kejriwal M. Predicting zip code-level vaccine hesitancy in US Metropolitan areas using machine learning models on public tweets. CoRR. 2021;abs/2108.01699. Available from: https://arxiv.org/abs/2108.01699.

[86]   Luo Y and Kejriwal M. Understanding COVID-19 vaccine reaction through comparative analysis on Twitter. CoRR. 2021;abs/2111.05823. Available from: https://arxiv.org/abs/2111.05823.

[87]   Kejriwal M and Zhou P. Low-supervision urgency detection and transfer in short crisis messages. In: Spezzano F, Chen W, and Xiao X, editors. *ASONAM '19: International Conference on Advances in Social Networks Analysis and Mining*, Vancouver, British Columbia, Canada, August 27–30, 2019. ACM; 2019. p. 353–356. Available from: https://doi.org/10.1145/3341161. 3342936.

[88]   Zhang S and Kejriwal M. Concept drift in bias and sensationalism detection: an experimental study. In: Spezzano F, Chen W, and Xiao X, editors. *ASONAM '19: International Conference on Advances in Social Networks Analysis and Mining*, Vancouver, British Columbia, Canada, August 27–30, 2019. ACM; 2019. p. 601–604. Available from: https://doi.org/10.1145/3341161. 3343690.

[89]   Kejriwal M and Gu Y. Network-theoretic modeling of complex activity using UK online sex advertisements. *Applied Network Science*. 2020;5(1):30. Available from: https://doi.org/10.1007/s41109-020-00275-1.

[90]   Kejriwal M and Kapoor R. Network-theoretic information extraction qual-ity assessment in the human trafficking domain. *Applied Network Science*. 2019;4(1):44:1–44:26. Available from: https://doi.org/10.1007/s41109-019-0154-z.

[91]　Hundman K, Gowda T, Kejriwal M, *et al.* Always lurking: understanding and mitigating bias in online human trafficking detection. In: Furman J, Marchant GE, Price H, *et al.*, editors. *Proceedings of the 2018 AAAI/ACM Conference on AI, Ethics, and Society, AIES 2018*, New Orleans, LA, USA, February 2–3, 2018. ACM; 2018. p. 137–143. Available from: https://doi.org/10.1145/3278721.3278782.

[92]　Kejriwal M and Zhou P. SAVIZ: interactive exploration and visualization of situation labeling classifiers over crisis social media data. In: Spezzano F, Chen W, and Xiao X, editors. *ASONAM '19: International Conference on Advances in Social Networks Analysis and Mining*, Vancouver, British Columbia, Canada, August 27–30, 2019. ACM; 2019. p. 705–708. Available from: https://doi.org/10.1145/3341161.3343703.

[93]　Kejriwal M, Shao R, and Szekely PA. Expert-guided entity extraction using expressive rules. In: Piwowarski B, Chevalier M, Gaussier É, *et al.*, editors. *Proceedings of the 42nd International ACM SIGIR Conference on Research and Development in Information Retrieval, SIGIR 2019*, Paris, France, July 21–25, 2019. ACM; 2019. p. 1353–1356. Available from: https://doi.org/10.1145/3331184.3331392.

[94]　Kejriwal M and Szekely PA. Constructing domain-specific search engines with no programming. In: McIlraith SA and Weinberger KQ, editors. *Proceedings of the Thirty-Second AAAI Conference on Artificial Intelligence, (AAAI-18), the 30th innovative Applications of Artificial Intelligence (IAAI-18), and the 8th AAAI Symposium on Educational Advances in Artificial Intelligence (EAAI-18)*, New Orleans, LO, February 2–7, 2018. AAAI Press; 2018. p. 8204–8205. Available from: https://www.aaai.org/ocs/index.php/AAAI/AAAI18/paper/view/16990.

[95]　Kejriwal M and Szekely PA. Technology-assisted investigative search: a case study from an illicit domain. In: Mandryk RL, Hancock M, Perry M, *et al.*, editors. *Extended Abstracts of the 2018 CHI Conference on Human Factors in Computing Systems, CHI 2018*, Montreal, QC, Canada, April 21–26, 2018. ACM; 2018. Available from: https://doi.org/10.1145/3170427.3174364.

[96]　Kejriwal M, Gilley D, Szekely PA, *et al.* THOR: text-enabled analytics for humanitarian operations. In: Champin P, Gandon F, Lalmas M, *et al.*, editors. *Companion of the The Web Conference 2018 on The Web Conference 2018, WWW 2018*, Lyon, France, April 23–27, 2018. ACM; 2018. p. 147–150. Available from: https://doi.org/10.1145/3184558.3186965.

[97]　Kejriwal M and Szekely PA. Knowledge graphs for social good: an entity-centric search engine for the human trafficking domain. *IEEE Transactions on Big Data*. 2022;8(3):592–606. Available from: https://doi.org/10.1109/TBDATA.2017.2763164.

[98]　Kejriwal M. A meta-engine for building domain-specific search engines. *Software Impacts*. 2021;7:100052. Available from: https://doi.org/10.1016/j.simpa.2020.100052.

[99]   Kejriwal M and Szekely PA. myDIG: personalized illicit domain-specific knowledge discovery with no programming. *Future Internet*. 2019;11(3):59. Available from: https://doi.org/10.3390/fi11030059.

[100]   Kejriwal M, Szekely PA, and Knoblock CA. Investigative knowledge discovery for combating illicit activities. *IEEE Intelligent Systems*. 2018;33(1):53–63. Available from: https://doi.org/10.1109/MIS.2018.111144556.

[101]   Gheini M and Kejriwal M. Unsupervised product entity resolution using graph representation learning. In: Degenhardt J, Kallumadi S, Porwal U, *et al*., editors. *Proceedings of the SIGIR 2019 Workshop on eCommerce, co-located with the 42st International ACM SIGIR Conference on Research and Development in Information Retrieval, eCom@SIGIR 2019*, Paris, France, July 25, 2019. vol. 2410 of CEUR Workshop Proceedings. CEUR-WS.org; 2019. Available from: http://ceur-ws.org/Vol-2410/paper26.pdf.

[102]   Balaji J, Javed F, Kejriwal M, *et al*. An ensemble blocking scheme for entity resolution of large and sparse datasets. CoRR. 2016;abs/1609.06265. Available from: http://arxiv.org/abs/1609.06265.

[103]   Benjelloun O, Garcia-Molina H, Menestrina D, *et al*. Swoosh: a generic approach to entity resolution. *The VLDB Journal*. 2009;18:255–276.

[104]   Kejriwal M, Santos H, Mulvehill AM, *et al*. Designing a strong test for measuring true common-sense reasoning. *Nature Machine Intelligence*. 2022;4(4):318–322. Available from: https://doi.org/10.1038/s42256-022-00478-4.

[105]   Shen K and Kejriwal M. Understanding substructures in commonsense relations in ConceptNet. CoRR. 2022;abs/2210.01263. Available from: https://doi.org/10.48550/arXiv.2210.01263.

[106]   Kejriwal M and Thomas S. A multi-agent simulator for generating novelty in monopoly. *Simulation Modelling Practice and Theory*. 2021;112:102364. Available from: https://doi.org/10.1016/j.simpat.2021.102364.

[107]   Haliem M, Bonjour T, Alsalem AO, *et al*. Learning monopoly gameplay: a hybrid model-free deep reinforcement learning and imitation learning approach. CoRR. 2021;abs/2103.00683. Available from: https://arxiv.org/abs/2103.00683.

[108]   Kejriwal M. *Artificial Intelligence for Industries of the Future – Beyond Facebook, Amazon, Microsoft and Google*. Springer; 2023. Available from: https://doi.org/10.1007/978-3-031-19039-1.

[109]   Kejriwal M, Sequeda JF, and Lopez V. Knowledge graphs: construction, management and querying. *Semantic Web*. 2019;10(6):961–962. Available from: https://doi.org/10.3233/SW-190370.

[110]   Kejriwal M. Knowledge graphs: a practical review of the research landscape. *Information*. 2022;13(4):161. Available from: https://doi.org/10.3390/info13040161.

[111]   Tiwari S, Mihindukulasooriya N, Osborne F, *et al*., editors. *Proceedings of the 1st International Workshop on Knowledge Graph Generation from Text and the 1st International Workshop on Modular Knowledge Co-located with 19th Extended Semantic Conference (ESWC 2022)*, Hersonissos, Greece, May 30,

2022. vol. 3184 of CEUR Workshop Proceedings. CEUR-WS.org; 2022. Available from: http://ceur-ws.org/Vol-3184.

[112] Kejriwal M, Szekely PA, and Troncy R, editors. *Proceedings of the 10th International Conference on Knowledge Capture*, K-CAP 2019, Marina Del Rey, CA, November 19–21, 2019. ACM; 2019. Available from: https://doi.org/10.1145/3360901.

[113] Kejriwal M, Selvam RK, Ni C, *et al.* Empirical best practices on using product-specific Schema.org. In: *Thirty-Fifth AAAI Conference on Artificial Intelligence, AAAI 2021, Thirty-Third Conference on Innovative Applications of Artificial Intelligence, IAAI 2021, The Eleventh Symposium on Educational Advances in Artificial Intelligence, EAAI 2021*, Virtual Event, February 2–9, 2021. AAAI Press; 2021. p. 15452–15457. Available from: https://ojs.aaai.org/index.php/AAAI/article/view/17816.

[114] Selvam RK and Kejriwal M. On using product-specific Schema.org from web data commons: an empirical set of best practices. CoRR. 2020;abs/2007.13829. Available from: https://arxiv.org/abs/2007.13829.

[115] Nam D and Kejriwal M. How do organizations publish semantic markup? Three case studies using public Schema.org Crawls. *Computer*. 2018;51(6):42–51. Available from: https://doi.org/10.1109/MC.2018. 2701635.

[116] Kejriwal M. Populating a linked data entity name system. *AI Matters*. 2017;3(2):22–23. Available from: https://doi.org/10.1145/3098888.3098897.

[117] Kejriwal M. Entity resolution in a big data framework. In: Bonet B and Koenig S, editors. *Proceedings of the Twenty-Ninth AAAI Conference on Artificial Intelligence*, Austin, TX, USA. January 25–30, 2015. AAAI Press; 2015. p. 4243–4244. Available from: http://www.aaai.org/ocs/index. php/AAAI/AAAI15/paper/view/9294.

[118] Kejriwal M. Populating entity name systems for big data integration. In: Mika P, Tudorache T, Bernstein A, *et al.*, editors. *The Semantic Web – ISWC 2014 – 13th International Semantic Web Conference*, Riva del Garda, Italy, October 19–23, 2014. Proceedings, Part II. vol. 8797 of Lecture Notes in Computer Science. Springer; 2014. p. 521–528. Available from: https://doi.org/10.1007/978-3-319-11915-1_34.

[119] Kejriwal M and Szekely PA. Co-LOD: continuous space linked open data. In: Suárez-Figueroa MC, Cheng G, Gentile AL, *et al.*, editors. *Proceedings of the ISWC 2019 Satellite Tracks (Posters & Demonstrations, Industry, and Outrageous Ideas) co-located with 18th International Semantic Web Conference (ISWC 2019)*, Auckland, New Zealand, October 26–30, 2019. vol. 2456 of CEUR Workshop Proceedings. CEUR-WS.org; 2019. p. 333–337. Available from: http://ceur-ws.org/Vol-2456/paper94.pdf.

[120] Tang J, Vazirgiannis M, Dong Y, *et al.* BigNet 2018 Chairs' Welcome & Organization. In: Champin P, Gandon F, Lalmas M, *et al.*, editors. *Companion of the Web Conference 2018 on the Web Conference 2018, WWW 2018*, Lyon, France, April 23–27, 2018. ACM; 2018. p. 943–944. Available from: https://doi.org/10.1145/3184558.3192293.

[121] Szekely PA and Kejriwal M. Domain-specific insight graphs (DIG). In: Champin P, Gandon F, Lalmas M, *et al.*, editors. *Companion of The Web Conference 2018 on The Web Conference 2018, WWW 2018*, Lyon, France, April 23–27, 2018. ACM; 2018. p. 433–434. Available from: https://doi.org/10.1145/3184558.3186203.

[122] Kejriwal M, Liu Q, Jacob F, *et al.* A pipeline for extracting and deduplicating domain-specific knowledge bases. In: *2015 IEEE International Conference on Big Data (IEEE BigData 2015)*, Santa Clara, CA, October 29–November 1, 2015. IEEE Computer Society; 2015. p. 1144–1153. Available from: https://doi.org/10.1109/BigData.2015.7363868.

[123] Kejriwal M, Schellenberg T, and Szekely PA. A semantic search engine for investigating human trafficking. In: Nikitina N, Song D, Fokoue A, *et al.*, editors. *Proceedings of the ISWC 2017 Posters & Demonstrations and Industry Tracks co-located with 16th International Semantic Web Conference (ISWC 2017)*, Vienna, Austria, October 23–25, 2017. vol. 1963 of CEUR Workshop Proceedings. CEUR-WS.org; 2017. Available from: http://ceur-ws.org/Vol-1963/paper613.pdf.

[124] Kejriwal M and Szekely PA. An investigative search engine for the human trafficking domain. In: d'Amato C, Fernández M, Tamma VAM, *et al.*, editors. *The Semantic Web – ISWC 2017 – 16th International Semantic Web Conference*, Vienna, Austria, October 21–25, 2017, Proceedings, Part II. vol. 10588 of Lecture Notes in Computer Science. Springer; 2017. p. 247–262. Available from: https://doi.org/10.1007/978-3-319-68204-4_25.

[125] Kejriwal M and Szekely PA. Scalable generation of type embeddings using the ABox. *Open Journal of Semantic Web*. 2017;4(1):20–34. Available from: https://www.ronpub.com/ojsw/OJSW_2017v4i1n02_Kejriwal.html.

[126] Cochez M, Declerck T, de Melo G, *et al.*, editors. *Proceedings of the First Workshop on Deep Learning for Knowledge Graphs and Semantic Technologies (DL4KGS) co-located with the 15th Extended Semantic Web Conference (ESWC 2018)*, Heraklion, Crete, Greece, June 4, 2018. vol. 2106 of CEUR Workshop Proceedings. CEUR-WS.org; 2018. Available from: http://ceur-ws.org/Vol-2106.

[127] Zhang T, Subburathinam A, Shi G, *et al.* GAIA – a multi-media multi-lingual knowledge extraction and hypothesis generation system. In: *Proceedings of the 2018 Text Analysis Conference, TAC 2018*, Gaithersburg, Maryland, USA, November 13–14, 2018. NIST; 2018. Available from: https://tac.nist.gov/publications/2018/participant.papers/TAC2018.GAIA.proceedings.pdf.

[128] Kejriwal M. Sorted Neighborhood for the semantic web. In: Bonet B and Koenig S, editors. *Proceedings of the Twenty-Ninth AAAI Conference on Artificial Intelligence*, Austin, TX, January 25–30, 2015. AAAI Press; 2015. p. 4174–4175. Available from: http://www.aaai.org/ocs/index.php/AAAI/AAAI15/paper/view/9295.

[129] Kejriwal M and Miranker DP. On linking heterogeneous dataset collections. In: Horridge M, Rospocher M, and van Ossenbruggen J, editors. *Proceedings of the ISWC 2014 Posters & Demonstrations Track a Track Within the 13th International Semantic Web Conference, ISWC 2014*, Riva del Garda, Italy, October 21, 2014. vol. 1272 of CEUR Workshop Proceedings. CEUR-WS.org; 2014. p. 217–220. Available from: http://ceur-ws.org/Vol-1272/paper_17.pdf.

[130] Kejriwal M and Miranker DP. Decision-making bias in instance matching model selection. In: Arenas M, Corcho Ó, Simperl E, *et al.*, editors. *The Semantic Web – ISWC 2015 – 14th International Semantic Web Conference*, Bethlehem, PA, October 11–15, 2015, Proceedings, Part I. vol. 9366 of Lecture Notes in Computer Science. Springer; 2015. p. 392–407. Available from: https://doi.org/10.1007/978-3-319-25007-6_23.

Chapter 6

Relation extraction techniques for personal knowledge graphs

Ana B. Rios-Alvarado[a] and Jose L. Martinez-Rodriguez[b]

Personal knowledge graphs (PKGs) refer to knowledge graphs (KGs) that contain information about personal descriptions. Thus, PKGs contain definitions and/or descriptions of information concerning a person or user. The development of PKGs is an essential aspect of decision-making applications where it may be necessary to involve user information such as preferences (tastes, styles, colors), physical characteristics (health, ergonomic), and historical (academic, legal), to mention a few. One of the main aspects of constructing such structures lies in the information components connected to form a graph. These components, called triples, are composed of Subject–Predicate–Object elements, where the Subject is oriented to be a real-world entity about a person, the Object is an entity or value that is said of the Subject, and the Predicate is the relationship that exists between these two things. However, the construction of PKGs is often a challenge, whether performed manually (by an expert) or automatically (computationally). On the one hand, their definition has not been widely studied, so the construction of PKGs is time-consuming even if performed manually. On the other hand, their computational construction is a process that, according to the source of information (and its structure), can implicate various language challenges to obtain the necessary triple elements accurately (to extract the relations that will be used in the construction and connection of triples). This chapter presents an overview of techniques for extracting relations applied in the construction of PKGs. The idea is to provide conceptual aspects on the extraction of relations for the construction of KGs and then to review the most common techniques applied to PKGs. Finally, some considerations in the extraction of relations and the construction of PKGs are presented.

6.1 Introduction

The Web of Data provides a data model that enables the exchange and dissemination of information by computers (and humans) using a structured format provided by

[a]Universidad Autónoma de Tamaulipas, Facultad de Ingeniería y Ciencias, Mexico
[b]Universidad Autónoma de Tamaulipas, Unidad Académica Multidisciplinaria Reynosa Rodhe, Mexico

knowledge graphs (KG). It is assumed that the data represented through KG requires less human intervention to be ready for consumption (querying, transmission) and for configuring and executing algorithms for data integration or factual inference (not explicitly defined statements). KGs are usually constructed following the Resource Description Framework (RDF) model, defining the *triple* as a basic unit of information with the form <Subject, Predicate, Object>. Subject and Object represent real-world entities that act as nodes and are joined through the Predicate or semantic relationship (edge). Thus, combining multiple RDF triples supported by an ontology (for defining classes, subclasses, and properties, among other semantic components) forms a KG. Some examples of KGs are YAGO, Wikidata, and DBpedia [1], which are built from Wikipedia, but there are other KGs within domains such as medical [2], and industry 4.0 [3], to mention a few.

In recent years, information about a person has become essential for personalizing different configurations from the business point of view. For example, it helps customize advertising campaigns, chatbot responses, and content recommendations, to mention a few. Information about a person may contain data showing private and public aspects regarding their preferences, relationships, demographic, and historical information, among others. Therefore, the information that corresponds to each person is varied and is usually composed of different characteristics according to the available data, which could make it difficult to represent with traditional databases that have a defined schema. For this reason, KGs are structures that support the formal representation of information to model a person's information flexibly so that it is possible to create a *personal knowledge graph (PKG)*.

According to Balog and Kenter [4], a PKG is a resource of structured information about entities personally related to its user, their attributes, and relations. In this way, it is possible to model the information related to a person by following a schema or ontology that defines potential descriptions to be used in the triples. Such a schema contains various properties according to the domain at hand; for example, a person within the academic environment can indicate information regarding taught subjects, instructions on evaluating students, thesis, research areas, collaborators, and so on. Following the RDF model, a PKG can link personal items to external resources such as Wikidata or DBPedia such that it is possible to enrich the information. It has been shown that PKGs can be helpful for recommender systems [5] or to structure personal medical information [6] linked to health repositories such as UMLS and SNOMED-CT for disease monitoring and control.

Although the benefits of KGs for information representation, integration, and consumption have been demonstrated, their construction is often a challenge involving conceptual analysis of an information domain and the precise construction of the information triple elements. The construction of KGs can be performed manually by an expert in an information domain, which entails a cost with respect to time invested, availability, and adequate handling of the required representation schemes. On the other hand, if the construction of the KG is performed automatically, it is necessary to involve areas such as NLP and/or machine learning to deal with aspects of the language that help to detect precisely (and unambiguously) the language elements that will be part of each RDF triple component. In this sense, a crucial task for constructing

KGs is the extraction of semantic relations, which is in charge of obtaining named entities and their relation. In other words, it is required to obtain things from the real world that are mentioned in a text and the way they are associated with each other. For example, from the sentence *"Tenzin Gyatso was born in Tibet in 1934,"* we can obtain the relations **wasBorn** (Tenzin Gyatso, Tibet) and **wasBorn** (Tenzin Gyatso, 1934). This process involves challenges in recognizing, on the one hand, unambiguous named entities and, on the other hand, semantic relations, which, although regularly represented by an action (verb), can also act as other language elements such as word qualifiers (e.g., prepositions, or conjunctions), nouns, or phrases.

The construction of PKGs follows the same challenges presented above for constructing general KGs regarding the RDF triple components identification. However, as PKGs are inherent to a specific topic, additional challenges are involved in the representation process, such as selecting and creating schemas or ontologies to define the type of available user descriptions. This task is complex because there needs to be a widely accepted definition of a PKG and what it should cover, making it challenging to define the scope of what could be defined to extract the semantic relationships that will later form the graphs. Therefore, this chapter reviews the techniques some approaches use for extracting semantic relations applied in the construction of PKGs. In this regard, some basic concepts are first presented to support the process of extracting semantic relations used to construct KGs and PKGs. Next, a review of the most common techniques for extracting semantic relations from general domain data is presented to analyze how these techniques are used (or reused) for extracting semantic relations focused on personal data. Likewise, some aspects that should be considered for identifying relationships oriented to the construction of PKGs are presented.

The outline of the chapter is as follows. Section 6.2 provides preliminaries for RDF, KGs, and PKGs. Section 6.3 presents an overview of the relation extraction task, involved subtasks, and common techniques used in the construction of KGs. A review of techniques for relation extraction focused on constructing PKGs is presented in Section 6.4. Section 6.5 presents the conclusions.

6.2 From knowledge graphs to personal knowledge graphs

A KG refers to a data structure for representing knowledge in terms of concepts and their relationships (facts/statements) modeled as a graph. In other words, a KG is composed of real-world entities (nodes) associated with predicates or properties (edges) that define what is to be mentioned or described about them. Ontologies are fundamental components of a KG that define taxonomies, classes, properties, and rules, which allow humans and machines to understand and reason about its content. From the Semantic Web perspective, each KG component must be uniquely identified (e.g., by an IRI) to look up its associated content. Then by linking diverse components, it is possible to navigate/discover more things (as done on the Web). Therefore, as the RDF triple is the central unit of a KG, we can make the following definition. Given a set of IRI elements (I), a set of blank nodes B, and a set of literals (L), an RDF triple (t) takes the form:

$$t := (s, p, o) \in (I \cup B) \times I \times (I \cup B \cup L).$$

In other words, the subject can contain an IRI or a blank node, the property is composed of an IRI, and the object can contain an IRI, a blank node, or a literal value. Thus, a set of interconnected RDF triples forms a KG.

6.2.1 Diversity aspects in graphs

KGs are assembled from numerous data sources containing different domains of information. Therefore, KGs can be very diverse in terms of structure and granularity. For example, there can be triples of a particular person, mentioning their name, where they live, and who they know, but you could also mention more specific things such as their height, eye color, and age, among others. To address this diversity, three aspects of representation are considered:

1. *Schema*: A schema (in particular, a semantic one) allows for defining the meaning of the high-level terms used in the graph, which facilitates reasoning about networks using those terms. A standard for defining schemas in RDF is RDF Schema (RDFS), which mainly provides options for defining subclasses, subproperties, domains, and ranges. However, a more specialized way to indicate schemas is through Web Ontology Language (OWL), which allows the creation of ontologies. Thus, with an ontology, you can define axiomatic aspects that support the definition of statements, with aspects to declare negations, equivalences, and differences, among other logical rules.
2. *Identity*: Identity indicates which nodes in the graph (or from external sources) refer to the same real-world entity. As mentioned above, one way to achieve this is by assigning IRIs to each triple component. However, this can be taken further by defining data types and labels interpretable by both computers and humans.
3. *Context*: The context can indicate a specific environment in which a knowledge unit is maintained. This can be indicated with different forms of triple representation, adding descriptive information, which will be discussed later in this chapter.

It can also be mentioned that KGs can be queried through a query language such as SPARQL, using a navigation rule, or by defining complex patterns. A more detailed description of KGs can be consulted at [7].

6.2.2 A KG of personal nature

On the other hand, a PKG is actually a KG that focuses on a specific Subject, a person's data. From the definition of KG (and the RDF triple), we can take into account that a PKG has, as the focus of attention, triples derived from a resource of type person, particularly on the subject component **<s, rdf:type, :Person>**, where **:Person** is a class (owl:Class) that represents a person (human) and may be defined in various ontologies or vocabularies (e.g., foaf:Person, schema:Person, dul:NaturalPerson,

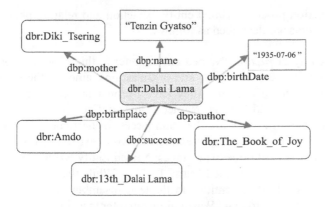

Figure 6.1 Example of PKG

wikidata:Q215627, wikidata:Q5). Therefore, mainly those properties whose domain (class of the subject in the triple) is of type Person can be used in the PKG. Figure 6.1 shows a PKG with information corresponding to the "Dalai Lama."

As stated by Balog and Kenter [4], it is possible to add triples to the PKG that are not directly linked to the central node (the user) as long as they are related to the user in some way. Although a PKG is a user (or person)-centered structure, it can be integrated with external data sources to enrich the graph or provide a way to find additional and useful data. Moreover, it is worth mentioning that there may be a small line of separation between what is taken as a "pure" PKG or what is achieved with the KG summarization task, whose goal is to obtain a sample of a general KG restricted to only information of a user [8]. For example, obtaining from DBpedia those triples linked to a particular person (as subject). While such data might be within the scope of a PKG, the idea is to include more personalized data not included in any general KG, for example, belongings (e.g., a guitar, a car), appointments, life events, temporality data, medical data, and also private data. In this sense, although both styles focus on mentioning details of the person, in a strict PKG, the information may become more tailored, i.e., with particular aspects of the person. For this paper, both approach styles are considered as PKGs.

6.3 Relation extraction for knowledge graphs

Information extraction is an area that allows obtaining structured information from unstructured or semi-structured data sources. This is an important area because it is required to analyze text and obtain the main components for constructing KGs, particularly the semantic relation extraction task. Specifically, a semantic relation expresses a connection between two words in relation to their meaning. In other words, a semantic relation [9] is a tuple whose elements (entities, things, concepts) are joined through a semantic fragment that acts as a predicate (e.g., noun, verb, preposition, conjunction). Semantic relations are essential to constructing KGs as they help establish what is being discussed in a text. Two parts are involved in the relation extraction process: named entity extraction and relation phrase extraction. These components are described as follows:

1. *Named entity extraction*: Named entities refer to things or concepts of the real world, such as people, places, and organizations, among others [10]. They are said to be "named" because they have a proper name, for example, Mexico City, New York, and Obama. Named entities define relevant things mentioned in a text; therefore, they are the main pieces for defining a KG. However, the complete process for an entity extracted from a text to be conformed as a KG resource consists of three main stages: Named Entity Extraction, Named Entity Disambiguation, and Named Entity Linking. While the first stage is in charge of finding mentions of entities in the text, disambiguation determines which mention is referred to (e.g., Washington can refer to a city, a former president, or a type of apple). Finally, the linking stage defines an IRI for the extracted element so that it can be uniquely identified. Although the purpose of this chapter is not to focus on named entity extraction, this task has been approached in several ways, as presented by Al-Moslmi *et al.* [11], based on dictionaries, different types of patterns (lexical, syntactic, and semantic), graphs, machine learning, among others.

2. *Extraction of relation phrases*: Once the entities are obtained, the next step is to find how they are related. In other words, this stage aims to find the predicates or relation phrases that link the named entities (e.g., bornIn, birthPlace). The number of elements (concepts or entities) involved in a relationship is greater than zero, where a relationship can be unary (one element), binary (two elements), or n-ary ($n>2$ elements). In the case of a binary relation, structures of the form $\mathbf{p}(s,o)$ indicate that a predicate relates the subject and object. On the other hand, in the case of n-ary relations, several participants are playing different roles and generally describing an "event" or situation; for example, the sentence "Tenzin Gyatso wrote The Book of Joy in 2016" indicates a relation involving an action and the temporality in which it occurred.

6.3.1   Overview of relation extraction techniques

As mentioned above, the extraction of relations considers several concepts/entities; therefore, several techniques or strategies exist to obtain such components. In any case, Natural Language Processing is usually applied to obtain language elements that are subsequently analyzed to determine the function that the words represent. Even though the main goal of the chapter is to check the different techniques applied to relation extraction for PKGs, it is important to present those techniques used in a general information domain and discuss what is reused and proposed from such techniques in the construction of KGs.

Facts, events, and data contained within statements (oral or written declarations or communications) are particularly helpful sources that contain relations used to build KGs. According to their purpose, these relations can be categorized into two main types: terminology components (TBox) and assertion components (ABox).

Thus, techniques for extracting the two kinds of relations involved in constructing KGs are mentioned. However, our main focus is on the extraction of ABox components.

6.3.2 TBox common techniques

TBox comprises a set of components that define concepts and structure relationships to indicate class hierarchy, disjoint classes or equivalent classes, and data properties. Some techniques start from scratch for identifying TBox structure relations, and others reuse information from additional resources such as knowledge bases published on the web. In the case of extracting TBox relations from scratch, the main techniques focus on linguistic and lexical patterns [12], machine learning algorithms [13], deep learning [14] [15], and inductive logic programming [16]. On the other hand, some works start from the taxonomic structure contained in WordNet [17], which is considered a source of lexical information containing hyperonymy, hyponymy, and synonymy relations, among others, that have been reviewed and accepted by a linguistic community. This structure enriches several specialized domains since its main content is of the general domain.

6.3.3 ABox common techniques

ABox refers to assertions about individuals (instances) that indicate facts and descriptions belonging to a vocabulary. ABox statements must use the vocabulary defined by the TBox. There are several challenges for populating the instances (entities) corresponding to ABox, such as recognizing entities mentioned in the text, disambiguation of entities, and linking (association) entities to a class or a concept, among others. Therefore, considering the main technique used, the approaches for relationship extraction can be organized as follows:

- *Syntactic patterns*: This type of technique is based on the analysis of lexical components of the text to subsequently apply rules to obtain the syntactic structure of the words (parse tree) [18]. Then, such structure is used to build patterns or templates that define relations. This technique is based on defining and searching (matching) patterns in the text. A well-known relation extraction approach is Open Information Extraction (OpenIE) [19], whose idea is to define generic patterns to obtain semantic relations regardless of the information domain. For example, to define a relation composed of nouns (NN) joined by a verb (VB) to form triple structures such as NN-VB-NN. Some approaches within this type of technique are [18], [20], [21]:
- *Discourse representation structures* (*DRSs*): DRS provides appropriate representations for constructing taxonomies and elaborating connections between propositions mentioned in the text. It is based on first-order logic representations (FOL) over statements to enable representations such as implication, negation, and disjunction, among others. Therefore, DRS offers an argument-style articulation of ideas that can be validated through the conjunction of all implied propositions in the exploited text containing statements. Boxer [22] is a tool that offers the

analysis and representation of DRS components from plain text. Boxer can represent events in an *n*-ary relationship style by defining the components involved in a situation, such as participants (who generate and receive action), actions involved, and dates, among others. Approaches such as LODifier [23] and FRED [24] perform DRS representations for the Semantic Web.

- *Dependency parser*: Approaches in this category obtain an ordered tree that denotes the sentence structure with relationships called dependencies, where verbs are the dominant words and other words are dependent or subordinate (e.g., adjectives, nouns, and noun phrases). Stanford PCFG parser allows obtaining a dependency tree from plain text [25]. In this case, examples of deep parsing-based approaches are those proposed by Exner *et al.* [26], Mintz *et al.* [27], and Niu *et al.* [28], to mention a few.

- *Frame semantics*: It is based on the idea of having a context of the words or concepts to acquire a more comprehensive understanding. For example, the word "educate" involves several components such as education, teacher, student, books, knowledge, and the relationships between them. These components are organized into "frames," which are accompanied by the meaning of the terms and constituents. A major project that defines several frames is FrameNet [29], with which it is possible to extract *n*-ary relations from the text, as in the works proposed by Corcoglioniti *et al.* [30], Exner and Nugues [26], and Fossati [31].

- *Machine/deep learning*: This approach aims to provide the computer with the ability to identify patterns from large amounts of data to produce relationship predictions from unlabeled data. The idea is to create a training dataset from labeled statements containing entities and binary relationships associated with existing data from knowledge graphs (such as Freebase or DBpedia) and then train a supervised classification algorithm to create a model to predict (typically) binary relationships. The training sentences are commonly enriched in multiple ways (e.g., POS tags, lexical and/or syntactic data, contextual information, and external sources, to mention a few) to create generalizations useful to obtain new relations. A well-known approach of this type is the so-called Distant Supervision [32], [33], which uses different types of algorithms, such as logistic regression and SVM [34]. Some approaches use deep learning and word embeddings [35], such as those based on piecewise convolutional neural networks (PCNN) [36] or those based on long short term memory (LSTM) networks [37].

Several logical reasoning tasks can be applied to the TBox and ABox notation to indicate coherence, eliminate redundancy, and deduce facts about individuals. While pattern-based approaches tend to provide more accurate extractions, they are limited to only certain types of relations depending on the number and type of patterns defined. Although the accuracy of relation extraction techniques has been increasing in recent years, it still needs to be improved due to the large number of components that can be identified involving different language features and aspects mentioned later in the following subsections.

6.4   Relation extraction for PKG

As previously presented, extracting semantic relations is a challenging task that involves identifying components and their representation according to the type of relationship to be built (e.g., binary, *n*-ary). On the other hand, an approach for extracting relations for PKGs is expected to consider two aspects: that the relationships are associated with a user or person and that they are of interest to the user. Additionally, it is possible to add indirect relations (those at a distance >1 from the user) as long as they are of interest to the user. Therefore, regardless of whether any of the techniques mentioned above are used to extract relationships, the two previous aspects must be fulfilled.

6.4.1   Approaches used in PKG relation extraction

This subsection presents a review of works for extracting relations focused on the construction of PKGs. The purpose of each approach is highlighted as well as whether it reuses any traditional relation extraction technique. To the best of our knowledge, no proposals have been published to extract TBox relations related to the development of PKG ontologies. Therefore, works focused on ABox components are mainly discussed.

It is possible to define several categories to organize the proposed approaches. For example, according to how to extract or parse the relations, the approaches usually employ matching techniques based on the definition of patterns or rules, using lexical, semantic, and contextual information.

Schröder *et al.* [38] presented a semi-automatic approach for building PKGs from a file system (names of files and directories) and expert feedback. The approach consists of four stages: domain term extraction, ontology population, and taxonomic/non-taxonomic relation learning. First, they use heuristics to obtain relevant terms from the user's domain. Then they identify individuals (entities), considering if they have already been mentioned in the context or if they are new appearances; this process is supported by a random forest model trained with positive examples from feedback. In the next stage, taxonomic and non-taxonomic relationships are detected, the former through mappings with a lexical-semantic network and the hierarchy of the files, and non-taxonomic relationships are extracted through a supervised model. Examples for training the models are prepared through a GUI that collects feedback from expert domain users.

Following the definition of rules and matching, Langholm [39] proposed a strategy to build a KG from various data sources such as emails, blog posts, and public discussion sites such as Reddit. To do so, they follow a pipeline of operations that combine grammatical tagging, NER tools, word embedding, lexical-syntactic patterns and rules, and entity resolution. The strategy is enhanced by an ontology that they build with the grounds of aspects that solve questions of Selection (Where did I buy my car?), Binary (Do I know an electrician?), and Counting (How many students do I know?), which they do by combining existing ontologies and vocabularies such as FOAF, schema.org, Person Link Ontology, among others.

Within the matching techniques, we can highlight those proposals for relation extraction that are in charge of generating PKGs in the healthcare domain.

Gyrard *et al.* [6] depend on rules and annotations to develop a Personal Healthcare Knowledge Graph (PHKG) that includes patient data and is enriched by contextual knowledge given by environmental sensors and data from the Web of Data (symptoms and treatments for diseases). The PHKGs they generate are used to support the design of applications for managing chronic diseases such as asthma, obesity, and Parkinson's. The authors add that building a PHKG requires information from heterogeneous resources such as sensors (IoT), clinical notes, and electronic medical records. On the other hand, Seneviratne *et al.* [40] propose a data model to capture diet preferences and the personal context of patients with Type 2 Diabetes to provide personalized diet information. The authors developed a personal health ontology that combines patient medical information, social aspects of their health, and lifestyle observations. A personal healthcare knowledge graph is generated based on frequent pattern mining and categorical clustering methods.

In addition to applying pattern-matching techniques, other approaches perform a semantic relation extraction based on a combination of techniques involving supervised models (such as deep learning) to support the process. Yang *et al.* [5] presented a system to build PKGs from structured and unstructured data from sources such as News, NUS SMS, and Social Apps, to mention a few. While entities and relations are extracted with a slot-filling strategy (from structured sources), they use a supervised model based on BERT and Bi-LSTM to obtain relations according to user intent, event data, sentiment analysis, and communication (e.g., personal data).

Vannur *et al.* [41] use a combination of neural network models and rule-based annotators and dictionaries to obtain a personal knowledge base from the TACRED dataset. The authors define generic patterns that allow identifying each element of the relationship (S-P-O), with which they produce data augmentation used to train a graph neural network model to predict person-to-person relationships.

Cao *et al.* [42] build a knowledge graph with suicide-oriented data, which is used to detect suicidal ideation in social networks. For this purpose, they define an ontology with six main blocks of data obtained from social networks: Personal Information, Personality, Experience, Post Behavior, Emotion Expression, and Social Interaction. The data is obtained through mappings of information the user indicates in their social network, machine learning algorithms, and measures based on word frequency.

Xiang Li *et al.* [43] present a framework for extracting relations and knowledge graphs from spoken language utterances contained in conversational dialogues. They exploit Freebase information to obtain snippets composed of pairs of entities to create training data for their framework. The proposal includes three components: Personal Assertion Classification, to identify utterances relevant to personal facts; Relation Detection, to classify utterances into one of the predefined relation classes; and Slot Filling, to label relation arguments.

6.4.2 Summary of approaches

Table 6.1 presents a review of relationship extraction approaches for PKGs. The approach and its publication year are presented. In a relation extraction process, it is necessary to obtain the named entities. Thus, the main technique that each approach uses for this purpose is presented, where the codes refer to M (Matching),

Table 6.1 Relation extraction approaches for PKG

Approach	Year	Entity recognition	Relation parsing	Technique	Rep.	Vocabulary	Input Domain	Data source	Evaluation data	Evaluation metrics
Li *et al.*	2014	M	ML	Snippets, SVM	Graph	Freebase (18 types)	Conversational dialogue	U	NIST KBP Slot Filling task	P,R,F1
Gyrard *et al.*	2018	M	M	Annotation	RDF	UMLS, SNOMED	Chronic diseases	U, SS, S	–	–
Cao *et al.*	2020	MP	MP, DL	Pretrained models	–	Suicide ontology	Suicide	SS	Reddit, Sina Weibo Dataset	A,PR,F1
Vannur *et al.*	2021	DL	DL	Patterns, Graph neural networks	RDF	PKG ontology	News	U	TACRED	AUC
Seneviratne *et al.*	2021	M	M	Pattern mining, categorical clustering	RDF	Personal Health Ontology	Diet, Diabetes	S	Competency Questions	–
Langholm	2021	NER	M	NLP, OpenIE	RDF	PKG ontology	Personal assistant	SS, U	Reddit, own data	Quantitative
Schröder *et al.*	2022	M, ML	M, LP	Lexical-semantic mapping	RDF	Taxonomic, non-taxonomic	Industrial, File system names	U	own data	A
Yang *et al.*	2022	M, ML	M, ML	Bert, snow data, LSTM	RDF	PKG ontology	News, voice assistant, social	S,U	Manual feedback, NUS SMS	A

ML (Machine Learning), MP (Mapping), LP (Link prediction), NER (Named Entity Recognition Tool), and DL (Deep Learning). Likewise, the technique used to obtain the relation phrase is mentioned (following the same codes indicated in the entity extraction). In this regard, the next column presents additional details of the main strategy for obtaining such a relation. Except for a couple of approaches, the extracted information is jointly represented through RDF triples using diverse vocabularies and input data. In this sense, three types of data are processed according to their structure: U (unstructured), SS (semi-structured), and S (structured). For example, structured data contain formatting tags, such as text in XML files, tables, and databases. Finally, the codes of the main evaluation metrics refer to A (accuracy), P (precision), R (recall), and AUC (Area Under Curve).

6.4.3 Aspects to be considered

As presented in the previous section, extracting semantic relations for PKGs is possible through diverse techniques and strategies that take different types of data and structures as input. There is a tendency to use matching and supervised/deep learning techniques. In addition, it can be noted that several methods proposed in traditional relation extraction approaches (such as those based on frames and discourse representation structures) have not been exploited for this scenario. Such techniques would complement (rather than replace) the actually used methods, allowing more rich component extractions. Therefore, to adapt traditional relation extraction techniques (and new ones) for PKGs, it is necessary to take into account some aspects and challenges as mentioned below:

1. *Content*: The input text should contain facts related to the user. However, the amount of information available with such facts is scarce, and this information may include ambiguous terms, making it difficult to get a correct interpretation. There might be cases where the extracted relationships are focused on only one user in particular, so new relations or those including a different user may not be considered. The idea is to create a PKG discussing a specific user and their interests (or related information) rather than a general KG with other people mentioned on it. Some sources of information regularly used as input are based on social media (e.g., Reddit), conversations, personal assistants, and news, to mention a few.

2. *Domain*: Certain domain and schema types could be exploited depending on who the content is addressed to or where it will be used. It is possible to extract general relationships based on actions/verbs (e.g., "Tenzin Gyatso addressed a message to his followers") or under an information domain ("The Dalai Lama was the political leader of Tibet"). In any case, the information must adhere to vocabularies or ontologies. Thus, the information that can be mentioned about a user could vary concerning tastes, preferences, possessions, curriculum, work aspects, personal relationships, and contexts (medical, security, education, and so on). Therefore, in addition to being able to have content that provides valuable information to exploit relations, it is necessary to know where it should be attached to know what limits the PKG will contain.

3. *Importance*: One of the keys to representing personal information is that such information must be of interest to the user. In other words, the information must be relevant and related to the user or person according to the domain. However, deciding whether the information is relevant is a complicated task. It depends on what the user is looking for and whether what is indirectly related to it is actually useful. Therefore, this task may require manual intervention by the user.

4. *Type of structure*: Another aspect to take into account has to do with the structure of the text. Various data sources that serve as an input for the extraction techniques handle the information of a particular user through a different data representation (unstructured/structured/semi-structured), for example, as organized by Wikipedia. The selection of the most suitable technique depends on the structure, which implies that the less structured the text is, the more difficult it becomes to extract components due to the lack of features describing the information.

5. *Representation*: According to the details you want to indicate about an event, the relations can typically be represented as binary or *n*-ary. On the one hand, binary relations help display direct things, such as user descriptions. On the other hand, *n*-ary relationships are helpful for giving details of a situation, either to describe additional data from a binary relationship or to include the roles of participants in an event. Figure 6.2 presents four distinct types of relation representations: binary (a), RDF* (b), reified (c), and *n*-ary (d). In the latter three, an event

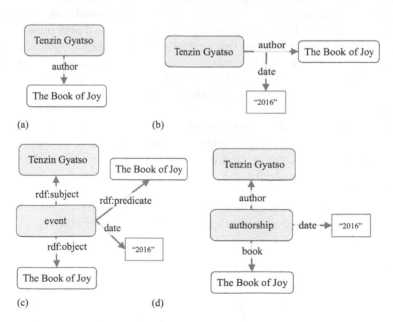

Figure 6.2   Examples of binary, RDF*, reified and n-ary relations

(authorship) is declared over which the participants (author, book, and date) are added. However, a different number of triples is required to specify the members of the statement.

6. *Privacy*: One of the aspects that still needs to be taken into account is privacy. Since the documents from which the information is extracted may be sensitive, it is necessary to manage security schemes that guarantee the integrity of the data while ensuring the privacy, consistency and validity of the information.

7. *Temporality*: Some aspects of information are only valid for a particular period indicated during the representation, for example, the term of office of a president. Another case is related to users' tastes or interests, which may change or evolve. It is, therefore, a challenge to update or modify this dynamic part of the information. It is worth mentioning that an *n*-ary representation is indispensable to indicate aspects of temporality.

8. *TBox relations*: Although strategies for obtaining subsumption relations have been proposed, it is still challenging to obtain TBox relations. In other words, to obtain those relations that allow the automatic construction of ontologies in the PKG domain. Since immediate results are required, TBox structures of general domains have been used and adapted manually, so there are no specific proposals for handling more particular user needs. In order to automatically create an ontology in the PKG domain, a large amount of information is required (consistent, integrated, valid, novel) from which the main elements such as classes, subclasses, properties, instances, axioms, rules, among others, can be automatically identified. Therefore, it is a difficult task that has yet to be tackled.

9. *Ensembles*: Combinations of techniques have been proposed in order to complement each other at different stages of a text mining process. For example, applying techniques to extract snippets that then serve as input for training machine learning strategies. However, the combination of techniques is done at the data level. It is challenging to make a combination at the algorithm level, where a complete understanding of the processes and the correct integration of components might take a lot of work.

10. *Evaluation*: In the evaluation and construction of PKGs, experts are required to validate the information represented. This kind of evaluation is costly from the point of view of the time invested, the availability of people, and also the existence of such experts. Although some proposals are based on machine learning with training datasets obtained from social networks and other data sources, it is still necessary to have gold-standard datasets that are defined for specific user data in various contexts, domains, representations, structures, and so on.

6.5 Conclusions

This chapter presented a review of semantic relation extraction techniques for PKGs. Some general concepts of knowledge graphs and what personal knowledge graphs cover are shown. Semantic relations are fundamental for creating KGs, so a description of the task of semantic relations and the most common approaches and techniques to perform this task in a general domain are presented. Subsequently, some strategies for creating PKGs are presented, in which the techniques used to extract the semantic relations are reviewed.

Even though PKGs are fundamental pieces for organizing user information, the techniques for their construction have been scarcely studied, where most techniques reuse strategies and schemes proposed for general domains (or adapted from such a domain). One of the reasons is that performing relation extraction for PKGs faces several challenges in addition to the inherent aspects of text analysis and natural language processing (e.g., segmentation, tokenization, parsing, and disambiguation, to mention a few). A PKG is supposed to only contain statements relevant (or interesting) to a particular user. However, it is challenging to know whether the information is relevant or not where several factors are involved, such as the domain and data context or the information purpose.

Given the advent of data science in the industry, companies tend to analyze large volumes of information to extract specific data from potential customers to generate customized products for particular consumers. Similarly, the trend in applications and software products is the intelligent personalization of stored data in order to provide the user with a tailored user experience. This can be achieved by incorporating PKG techniques into data processing.

As more applications appear, such as personal assistants, medical, human resources, or others that require flexible and easy-to-integrate information, then there will be proposals and strategies of different complexities that support the development of PKGs, where schemas and ontologies can be defined and consolidated to assist in the extraction of statements. Moreover, the development of PKG strategies would increase with the proposal of new benchmarks with different degrees of granularity for evaluating results and even methodologies for extracting relationships for PKGs.

References

[1] Färber, M., Bartscherer, F., Menne, C., and Rettinger, A. (2018). Linked data quality of DBpedia, Freebase, Opencyc, Wikidata, and Yago. *Semantic Web, 9*(1), 77–129.

[2] Schriml, L. M., Munro, J. B., Schor, M., *et al.* (2022). The human disease ontology 2022 update. *Nucleic Acids Research, 50*(D1), D1255–D1261.

[3] Bader, S. R., Grangel-Gonzalez, I., Nanjappa, P., Vidal, M.-E., and Maleshkova, M. (2020). A knowledge graph for industry 4.0. *European Semantic Web Conference* (pp. 465–480). Springer.

[4] Balog, K. and Kenter, T. (2019). Personal knowledge graphs: a research agenda. In *Proceedings of the 2019 ACM SIGIR International Conference on Theory of Information Retrieval* (pp. 217–220). ACM.

[5] Yang, Y., Lin, J., Zhang, X., and Wang, M. (2022). PKG: a personal knowledge graph for recommendation. In *Proceedings of the 45th International ACM SIGIR Conference on Research and Development in Information Retrieval*.

[6] Gyrard, A., Gaur, M., Thirunarayan, K., Sheth, A. P., and Shekarpour, S. (2018). Personalized health knowledge graph. In *Joint Proceedings of the International Workshops on Contextualized Knowledge Graphs, and Semantic Statistics*.

[7] Hogan, A., Blomqvist, E., Cochez, M., *et al.* (2021). Knowledge graphs. *ACM Computing Surveys (CSUR), 54*(4), 1–37.

[8] Safavi, T., Belth, C., Faber, L., Mottin, D., Müller, E., and Koutra, D. (2019). Personalized knowledge graph summarization: from the cloud to your pocket. In *IEEE International Conference on Data Mining (ICDM)*, (pp. 528–537).

[9] Bach, N. and Badaskar, S. (2007). A review of relation extraction. *Literature Review for Language and Statistics II, 2*, 1–15.

[10] Yadav, V., and Bethard, S. (2018). A survey on recent advances in named entity recognition from deep learning models. In *Proceedings of the 27th International Conference on Computational Linguistics, COLING 2018, Santa Fe, New Mexico, USA* (pp. 2145–2158). ACL.

[11] Al-Moslmi, T., Ocaña, M. G., Opdahl, A. L., and Veres, C. (2020). Named entity extraction for knowledge graphs: a literature overview. *IEEE Access, 8*, 32862–32881.

[12] Panchenko, A., Faralli, S., Ruppert, E., *et al.* (2016). Taxi at semeval-2016 task 13: a taxonomy induction method based on lexico-syntactic patterns, substrings and focused crawling. In *Proceedings of the 10th International Workshop on Semantic Evaluation (SemEval-2016)* (pp. 1320–1327). ACL.

[13] Martel, F. and Zouaq, A. (2021). Taxonomy extraction using knowledge graph embeddings and hierarchical clustering. In *Proceedings of the 36th Annual ACM Symposium on Applied Computing* (pp. 836–844). ACM.

[14] Al-Aswadi, F. N., Chan, H. Y., and Gan, K. H. (2020). Automatic ontology construction from text: a review from shallow to deep learning trend. *Artificial Intelligence Review, 53*(6), 3901–3928.

[15] Navarro-Almanza, R., Juárez-Ramírez, R., Licea, G., and Castro, J. R. (2020). Automated ontology extraction from unstructured texts using deep learning. In *Intuitionistic and Type-2 Fuzzy Logic Enhancements in Neural and Optimization Algorithms: Theory and Applications* (pp. 727–755). Springer.

[16] Lima, R., Espinasse, B., and Freitas, F. (2018). Ontoilper: an ontology-and inductive logic programming-based system to extract entities and relations from text. *Knowledge and Information Systems, 56*(1), 223–255.

[17] Jurgens, D. and Pilehvar, M. T. (2016). Semeval-2016 task 14: semantic taxonomy enrichment. In *Proceedings of the 10th International Workshop on Semantic Evaluation (SemEval-2016)* (pp. 1092–1102). ACL.

[18] Rios-Alvarado, A. B., Martinez-Rodriguez, J. L., Garcia-Perez, A. G., Guerrero-Melendez, T. Y., Lopez-Arevalo, I., and Gonzalez-Compean, J. L. (2022). Exploiting lexical patterns for knowledge graph construction from unstructured text in Spanish. *Complex & Intelligent Systems*, 1–17.

[19] Etzioni, O., Banko, M., Soderland, S., and Weld, D. S. (2008). Open information extraction from the web. *Communications of the ACM, 51*(12), 68–74.

[20] Martinez-Rodriguez, J. L., Lopez-Arevalo, I., and Rios-Alvarado, A. B. (2018). OpenIE-based approach for Knowledge Graph construction from text. *Expert Systems with Applications, 113,* 339–355.

[21] Zagorulko, Y. A., Sidorova, E., Akhmadeeva, I., and Sery, A. (2021). Approach to automatic population of ontologies of scientific subject domain using lexico-syntactic patterns. *Journal of Physics: Conference Series.* IOP Publishing.

[22] Bos, J. (2008). Wide-coverage semantic analysis with boxer. In *Semantics in Text Processing. Step 2008,* (pp. 277–286).

[23] Augenstein, I., Maynard, D., and Ciravegna, F. (2016). Distantly supervised web relation extraction for knowledge base population. *Semantic Web, 7*(4), 335–349.

[24] Gangemi, A., Presutti, V., Reforgiato Recupero, D., Nuzzolese, A. G., Draicchio, F., and Mongiovì, M. (2017). Semantic web machine reading with FRED. *Semantic Web, 8*(6), 873–893.

[25] Klein, D. and Manning, C. D. (2003). Accurate unlexicalized parsing. In *Proceedings of the 41st Annual Meeting of the Association for Computational Linguistics* (pp. 423–430). ACL.

[26] Exner, P. and Nugues, P. (2014). REFRACTIVE: an open source tool to extract knowledge from syntactic and semantic relations. In *Proceedings of the Ninth International Conference on Language Resources and Evaluation (LREC'14),* (pp. 2584–2589).

[27] Mintz, M., Bills, S., Snow, R., and Jurafsky, D. (2009). Distant supervision for relation extraction without labeled data. In *Proceedings of the Joint Conference of the 47th Annual Meeting of the ACL and the 4th International Joint Conference on Natural Language Processing of the AFNLP* (pp. 1003-1011). ACL.

[28] Niu, F., Zhang, C., Ré, C., and Shavlik, J. W. (2012). DeepDive: web-scale knowledge-base construction using statistical learning and inference. *VLDS, 12,* 25–28.

[29] Baker, C. F., Fillmore, C. J., and Lowe, J. B. (1998). The Berkeley FrameNet Project. In *COLING 1998 Volume 1: The 17th International Conference on Computational Linguistics.*

[30] Corcoglioniti, F., Rospocher, M., and Aprosio, A. P. (2016). Frame-based ontology population with PIKES. *IEEE Transactions on Knowledge and Data Engineering, 28*(12), 3261–3275.

[31] Fossati, M., Dorigatti, E., and Giuliano, C. (2018). N-ary relation extraction for simultaneous T-Box and A-Box knowledge base augmentation. *Semantic Web, 9*(4), 413–439.

[32] Augenstein, I., Maynard, D., and Ciravegna, F. (2016). Distantly supervised web relation extraction for knowledge base population. *Semantic Web, 7*(4), 335–349.

[33] Gerber, D. and Ngomo, A.-C. N. (2012). Extracting multilingual natural-language patterns for RDF predicates. In *International Conference on Knowledge Engineering and Knowledge Management* (pp. 87–96). Springer.

[34] Xu, W., Hoffmann, R., Zhao, L., and Grishman, R. (2013). Filling knowledge base gaps for distant supervision of relation extraction. In *Proceedings of*

the *51st Annual Meeting of the Association for Computational Linguistics (Volume 2: Short Papers)* (pp. 665–670). ACL.

[35] Sanagavarapu, L. M., Iyer, V., and Reddy, Y. R. (2021). OntoEnricher: a deep learning approach for ontology enrichment from unstructured text. In: *Cybersecurity and High-Performance Computing Environments* (pp. 261–284). Chapman and Hall/CRC.

[36] Zeng, D., Liu, K., Chen, Y., and Zhao, J. (2015). Distant supervision for relation extraction via piecewise convolutional neural networks. In *Proceedings of the 2015 Conference on Empirical Methods in Natural Language Processing* (pp. 1753–1762). ACL.

[37] Peng, N., Poon, H., Quirk, C., Toutanova, K., and Yih, W.-t. (2017). Cross-sentence n-ary relation extraction with graph LSTMs. *Transactions of the Association for Computational Linguistics, 5*, 101–115.

[38] Schröder, M., Jilek, C., and Dengel, A. (2022). A human-in-the-loop approach for personal knowledge graph construction from file names. In *Third International Workshop on Knowledge Graph Construction.*

[39] Langholm, E. (2021). *Constructing a Personal Knowledge Graph from Disparate Data Sources.* Master Thesis, University of Stavanger. Retrieved from https://hdl.handle.net/11250/2787142

[40] Seneviratne, O., Harris, J., Chen, C.-H., and McGuinness, D. L. (2021). Personal health knowledge graph for clinically relevant diet recommendations. *ArXiv.*

[41] Vannur, L. S., Ganesan, B., Nagalapatti, L., Patel, H., and Tippeswamy, M. N. (2021). Data augmentation for fairness in personal knowledge base population. In *Pacific-Asia Conference on Knowledge Discovery and Data Mining* (pp. 143–152). Springer.

[42] Cao, L., Zhang, H., and Feng, L. (2020). Building and using personal knowledge graph to improve suicidal ideation detection on social media. *IEEE Transactions on Multimedia, 24*, 87–102.

[43] Li, X., Tur, G., Hakkani-Tür, D., and Li, Q. (2014). Personal knowledge graph population from user utterances in conversational understanding. *IEEE Spoken Language Technology Workshop (SLT)* (pp. 224–229). IEEE.

Chapter 7
Visualization tools for personal knowledge graphs

Allu Niya George[a] and Enayat Rajabi[b]

Personal knowledge graphs (PKGs) deal with user-centric information and focus on personalizing data from various sources of interest to the user. They help to organize information deliberately and improve the competencies of both the individual and the organization. Visualizing knowledge graphs also enhances the users' understanding of the data and expands users' decision-making capabilities. This chapter presents the concept of PKGs and their visualization tools. We will discuss the benefits of knowledge graphs and compare knowledge graphs with PKGs. The main advantages and applications of PKGs are also illustrated in this chapter. Moreover, various personal knowledge management and visualization tools like Obsidian, RemNote, TiddlyRoam, Dendron, Logseq, Foam, and Roam Research are also presented here.

7.1 Introduction

Knowledge graphs are one of the most enthralling concepts in data science. They store facts about various entities, their attributes, and relationships [1]. They are generally characterized by using a predefined ontology [2] which includes explicit formal specification of classes and relationships among them. The domain experts usually design the ontology for a knowledge graph. The entities in knowledge graphs have global importance and can help organizations face information silos across their organizational units. The application of knowledge graphs is vast and they can be used in many industries. They are not limited only to healthcare, finance, fraud detection, chatbots, recommendation systems, and intelligent systems but can be used across multiple sectors [3,4,5].

This chapter presents the concept of PKG and its visualization tools. PKGs usually consist of entities and their relationships that contain information that is up-to-date, personal, and contextual to users [2]. PKGs also support integration with external knowledge repositories and contain personalized information aggregated from different heterogeneous sources that interest users [1].

Nowadays, it has been observed that the productivity of individuals increases using personal knowledge management tools drastically. Personal knowledge management tools improve individuals' decision-making capability and problem-solving

[a]Cape Breton University, Canada
[b]Department of Business Analytics, Cape Breton University, Canada

abilities [6]. These tools integrate new information into the individual knowledge database through the continuous and interactive framework [7] and help improve individual and corporate effectiveness.

This chapter explains the PKGs and their visualization tools. Section 7.2 explains directed and undirected graphical models. Section 7.3 describes knowledge graphs, the importance of visualizing them, and their applications in various fields. Section 7.4 elaborates on PKGs, their advantages, and their application in various sectors like the medical industry, e-learning platforms, research fields, and conversational systems. Section 7.5 explains the importance of graph visualization in effectively comprehending the massive amount of data. Section 7.6 explains the concept of personal knowledge management, and Section 7.7 deals with the various related visualization tools like Obsidian, Remnote, Tiddlyroam, Dendron, Logseq, Foam, and Roam Research. Finally, we conclude this chapter in Section 7.8.

7.2 Graphs

Graphs consist of nodes (vertices) that are interconnected by relationships (edges). They are sometimes quoted as networks, which are very simple, yet highly powerful in elucidating how different things are connected. The two types of graphical models are directed graphical model and undirected graphical model. The relationships in the former are directed and explicitly contain a start node and an end node, whereas relationships in the latter are undirected and can have several interpretations. Figure 7.1 presents a directed graphical model and Figure 7.2 presents an undirected graphical model [8].

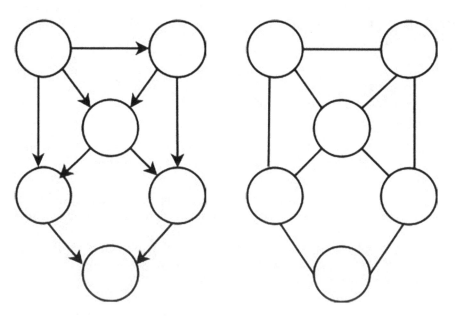

Figure 7.1   Directed graphical model   *Figure 7.2 Undirected graphical model*

Figure 7.3   Property graph

Directed graphical models, also referred to as Bayesian networks or causal models, are more prevalent within artificial intelligence, and machine learning segments, whereas undirected graphics, also called Markov networks, are more popular within physics and vision communities [8].

The property graph model is considered the most popular in modern graph databases. The nodes and relationships in a property graph model contain a key and a value. The label on each node represents its role in the graph. For instance, in Figure 7.3, node A is labeled as an employee, and node B is labeled as a project. The values stored inside the node are its properties. Therefore, node A contains the properties of *emp_id:101*, *emp_name: Bob*, and *emp_gender:male*. Similarly, node B contains the properties of *name:analytics*, *project_id:2345*, and *Hours_spent:58*. Also, both nodes are connected via a "*works_in*" relationship with associated properties. The relation between the two nodes can be read as: *Bob has worked on the analytics project since 2022.*

In the property graph model, there are no limits on the number of nodes and the relationships that connect them. Some nodes have plenty of properties, while others might have very few. Similarly, some relationships have many properties, but in most cases, it is fewer. Property graphs are described as much more straightforward and a potential first step for adopting knowledge graphs.

7.3   Knowledge graphs

Graph technology has accelerated and has become a celebrated topic recently. As a result, knowledge graphs have been the focal point in research since 2012 and have become so popular in the current world [5]. Knowledge graphs (KG) are a directed heterogeneous multigraph in which both the edges and nodes have labels. Nodes represent entities, ranging from everyday objects such as people, organizations, and locations to highly domain-specific entities like proteins and viruses (if the domain represents a biological one) [9]. On the other hand, edges specify the attributes of an entity or depict the relationship between the entities [10]. Generally, knowledge graphs retrieve information about an entity from various sources and encode it into structured information by clearly depicting their relations with each other [2].

Knowledge graphs emerged as an attractive aspect and a valuable asset for extensive search, recommendations, and mining scenarios [11]. They focus on the prominent or globally important entities rather than the insignificant ones we interact with daily [1]. The knowledge graphs use an organizing principle to organize various

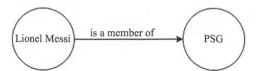

Figure 7.4   Single relation between nodes

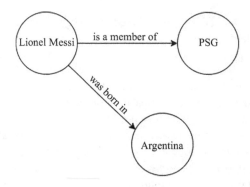

Figure 7.5   Multiple relations between nodes

nodes, thereby giving more contextual understanding [12]. For instance, if Node A is *"Lionel Messi"* and Node B is *"Paris Saint-Germain"* Football Club (PSG), then it is likely that the edge would be "is a member of" as presented in Figure 7.4.

Knowledge graphs can have multilevel relationships [8]. For instance, we know that *Lionel Messi* was born in *Argentina*, as Figure 7.5 shows. In this case, we add one more node labeled *Argentina* to the existing knowledge. However, as the volume of data increases, the nodes and relationships within a knowledge graph will also increase, as each node is linked with multiple other nodes through several relationships. This makes a knowledge graph more complex.

7.3.1   *Importance of visualizing knowledge graphs*

Each node in a knowledge graph represents the domain entity and the arcs between the nodes depict the semantic relationships between the entities. By visualizing the knowledge graph, a user can interactively surf the domain concept and select one of the concepts to do further exploration [13].

Nowadays, organizations depend heavily on knowledge graphs due to the massive increase in data. Visualizing a knowledge graph brings life to data and makes it more tangible and useful [14]. Moreover, it helps to understand the dynamic forces of different phenomena and how the various entities are connected well. Knowledge graphs visualization can provide insights into various relationships and dependencies that exist. This is very useful in making better decisions. For instance, supply chain management is a complicated system with many dependencies. Knowing those dependencies and visualizing them will help make faster decisions with higher confidence. Moreover, an optimized knowledge graph visualization can provide more efficient and target-oriented results in real-time [15]. Furthermore, visualization provides an inner structure of the connected complex data which provides an intuitive way of understanding it more effectively than any other automated or manual process [16].

7.3.2   Applications of knowledge graphs

7.3.2.1   Knowledge retrieval

Knowledge graphs are extensively useful in retrieval systems, hypothesis generation systems, question–answering systems, etc. [17]. Based on users' input, a retrieval system can identify all related entities and their relationships to a given entity and present complete knowledge about it [18]. The human knowledge about the various real-world entities in knowledge graphs improves the search engines' ability to interpret queries and documents. Nowadays, entity data from KGs is being used by various commercial web-based search engines to enhance their search results. For instance, Facebook uses Graph Search, and Google depends more on the data from the Google Knowledge Graph for better search results.

7.3.2.2   Question–answering systems

The question–answering systems leverage knowledge graphs as their principal component [4]. Nowadays, chatbots answer human queries by referring to large-scale knowledge graphs. These chatbots can derive rules and provide faster and more efficient results to human queries by learning the stored relationships between various entities in the knowledge graph [19].

The role of question–answering systems is to find answers to the natural language questions from the knowledge graph [20]. Generally, in the neural machine translation method, question–answering over knowledge graphs converts the natural language into a structured query language. However, the major shortcoming of this approach is its out-of-vocabulary problem. Simpler natural language questions can have decent performance [21]. For instance, a simple question such as "where was Lionel Messi born?", in the graph mentioned in Figure 7.5 can be answered flawlessly with the help of a single edge in a knowledge graph. However, the result generation would be quite challenging if the question becomes more complex.

7.3.2.3   Unified data access

Knowledge graphs provide integrated access to multiple data domains within an organization (known as data fabric) and to third-party data or global data seamlessly [22]. They can connect data across numerous domains and disclose interesting relationships within the data. They can combine siloed data sources into a single central view, providing a more precise picture of the data.

7.3.2.4   Provides recommendations

Knowledge graphs can be leveraged effectively to provide recommendations in various domains [13]. The recommender systems deliver user recommendations based on their preferences by utilizing the expressive power of knowledge graphs [23]. For instance, imagine two hypothetical users, Alice and Bob, who are great fans of Science Fiction movies and both like the movie *Inception*. Bob also likes *Jurassic World*

Dominion, but Alice has not watched it. In this case, the recommender system would recommend Jurassic World Dominion to Alice, as their likings are similar.

Recommender systems aim to retain customers, improve sales, and provide a more personalized customer experience. The main approaches in building recommender systems are collaborative filtering and content-based filtering. In collaborative filtering, new recommendations are provided solely based on the historical interactions between users and items. This method uses the nearest neighborhood algorithm to group users into clusters of similar types, determine what recommendations similar users would want, and then recommend each user per the preferences of its cluster. The content-based filtering strategy will make use of supplementary user or item information. This filtering technique makes recommendations for more things based on the user's preferences, the item's features, and the user's past record or explicit comments [23].

7.4 PKGs

PKGs confer the personalization of the existing knowledge graphs. It provides structured information about the entities and their relationships, which are personally related to a user [1]. Even though general-purpose knowledge graphs such as DBpedia, YAGO, and Freebase are well established [1], none of them directly represent users' personal information [24]. Given that information personalization has gained momentum in today's world, the emerging concept of PKGs will fill the gap by offering pocket-sized knowledge graphs specific to the user's interest [24]. "Spider-web" layout is the highlight for PKG, in which all other nodes are connected to a single central node – the user; Figure 7.6 pictures a simple illustration of the PKG. The

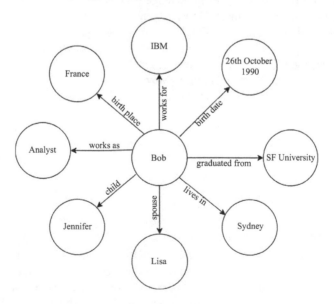

Figure 7.6   PKG illustration

illustration shows that *Bob* is a French national, born on 26 October 1990, graduated from *SF University*, and works for *IBM* as an Analyst. He lives in *Sydney*; his spouse is *Lisa*, and his child is *Jennifer*. This paradigm of customizing personal knowledge about the users can improve one's experience in PKGs [25].

7.4.1   Knowledge graph versus PKG

7.4.1.1   Representation of knowledge

Knowledge graphs contain structured information which is organized based on a predefined ontology [26]. In a movie ontology, for instance, Movie, Director, Year_of_Release, and Actor are the four classes (unique items in data) that might have the following relationships:

- Movie → has director → Director
- Movie → was released on → Year_of_Release
- Movie → has Actor → Actor

Apart from the relationships mentioned above, there are many other properties that can be included. For this example, we represent only three relationships, and their ontology can be viewed in a graph format in Figure 7.7.

Ontology is a general framework on which we can add specific real data instances to each ontological relationship. For example, the ontological relationship Movie -> has director ->Director can be translated into a knowledge graph as Avatar -> has director -> James Cameron is depicted in Figure 7.8. Apart from the relationships mentioned above, there are many other properties that can be included. For this

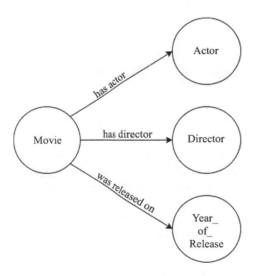

Figure 7.7   Ontology representation

Figure 7.8   An instance of knowledge graph

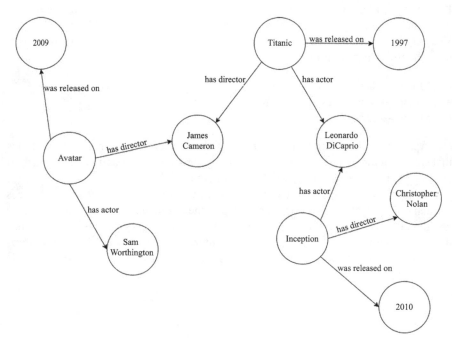

Figure 7.9   Knowledge graph illustration

example, we represent only three relationships, and their ontology can be viewed in a graph format in Figure 7.7.

Similarly, by adding all our individual information about the different movies, we can start to see the commencement of our knowledge graph that contains the data encoded using our ontology. Figure 7.9 shows the illustration of the knowledge graph.

On the other hand, the PKG contains only the entities and relationships of personal interest to the user, which is organized based on a global schema [1].

7.4.1.2   Knowledge recommendation

A publicly accessible knowledge graph can provide generic recommendations, whereas a PKG generates personalized recommendations for a user [2]. For instance,

Table 7.1   Knowledge graph versus PKG

Criteria	Knowledge graph	PKG
Representation of knowledge	Focus on prominent and globally important entities.	Focus on entities and relationships that are of personal interest to the user.
Knowledge organization	Have structured information organized based on a predefined ontology.	Organized based on a global schema.
Knowledge recommendation	Provides general recommendations.	Provides personalized recommendations.

if one patient makes a query for food recipes, then a knowledge graph provides more general responses that contain any food recipes. In contrast, a PKG can provide recommendations based on the patient's health conditions. Table 7.1 summarizes all the points mentioned above.

7.4.1.3   Advantages of PKGs

A PKG may contain entities of daily tasks and interactions which are more personal to the user [2]. Since it emphasizes the personal interactions and tasks of a user, the entities and relations, its contents can change over time. The major advantages of PKG are:

- *Provides contextual information*: While a knowledge graph captures only structured generic knowledge about commonly known entities [1], a PKG provides more liquefied, contextual, and dynamically changing information about the user [2]. For instance, a vegan querying an online restaurant platform is recommended by appropriate vegetarian restaurants in this case.
- *Evolves with time:* Unlike the general-purpose knowledge graph, a PKG offers an increasing significance for individual preferences and interests that evolves [2,27]. For instance, in the medical domain, the recommendation system enabled by a PKG can provide more personalized responses to a patient, taking into account his current health conditions, health goals, food habits, etc. It provides responses based on the current circumstances (which can change over time) of the patient [2].
- *Provides tailored recommendations:* PKGs are small-sized user-centric knowledge graphs which can better understand the interests and interactions of the users, thereby providing more tailored recommendations to them. For instance, they can be leveraged to personalize different online learning platforms and online collaborative learnings to better respond to their user learning preferences and interests [24].

7.4.2　Applications of PKGs

7.4.2.1　Healthcare

A knowledge graph in healthcare contains all the relevant information widely used in a medical domain (not particularly patient-specific information). For example, it can contain all the causes, symptoms, and treatments available for asthma. However, a personal health knowledge graph (PHKG), as a subgraph of the aforementioned knowledge graph, consists of the causes, symptoms, and treatments a specific patient undergoes [2]. Since the PHKG is familiar with the patient's health conditions [28], it can provide tailored recommendations for the queries made by the patient.

7.4.2.2　e-Learning

During the COVID-19 pandemic, the number of e-learners increased massively. Personalization in e-learning platforms aims to create an adaptive environment for the learners by recommending relevant content to the user based on their curriculum, area of interest, learning path, and learning preferences. It provides information about users, groups, and queries by giving much importance to their privacy [24]. Along with e-learning platforms, online collaborative learning and collaborative work have become more popular. However, web search applications can benefit from using PKGs, which offer semantically improved features and personalization capabilities [24].

7.4.2.3　Research

While doing research, maintaining all the research activities of a researcher in an organized manner is a tedious task. Chakraborty *et al.* [3] envision that personal research knowledge graphs can be used to represent all researchers' research activities in a structured manner. Although academic search engines and recommendation systems can provide recommendations for the researcher, PKGs can be leveraged to personalize different scholarly applications, recommendation systems, and conversational chat-bots, which can assist a researcher in their daily chores. The more personal information about the researcher is available, the better the tools' performance.

7.4.2.4　Human/machine conversational systems

Li *et al.* [25] introduced a statistical language understanding approach for automatically constructing a user-centric knowledge graph from the spoken dialogues by the user. With automatic speech recognition (ASR) advancement, virtual personal assistants (VPA) like Apple Siri and Microsoft Cortana have started prominently populating. However, the paradigm of constructing a PKG from the personal assertion sentences by the user (e.g., "My daughter is getting married" or "Today is my birthday") can improve the VPAs experience. For instance, "show me the direction to my friend's home" – a VPA may not respond accurately to this command previously, but once it has a user-centric knowledge graph, then the responses made by it would be more accurate. Hence, by customizing the knowledge about the user, the performance of the VPA systems improves drastically and can make more accurate responses once it knows much about the user's behaviors and interests.

7.4.2.5 Social media analytics

Nowadays, social media can be considered one of the platforms for sharing a person's emotions. Social media are becoming integral to daily life for information acquisition, emotion release, personal communication, and self-expression. This emotional expression can be used to detect suicidal thoughts in an early phase, thus there is a good chance of preventing it. In a study [29], the researchers built a structured personal suicide-oriented knowledge graph that can detect one's suicidal thoughts through the posts that one puts on social media. Moreover, dynamic maintenance of the user-centric knowledge graph is essential for accurate results.

7.5 Importance of visualization

In general, data exploration is a vital step in data analysis. It is considered the first step, which involves using various data visualization tools and statistical methods to reveal the dataset characteristics and patterns within the data [14]. Data visualization can provide meaningful insights across multiple application domains such as business, research, social media, healthcare, etc. Furthermore, converting the input data into an effective visualization will increase decision-making power [30].

In data analysis, visualization tools and techniques are not only used in the beginning stage of data exploration but also in the end stage, which is the presentation of the final result. In the initial stages of data analysis, the know-how of the source data is very little, and the analysis goals are ambiguous. In this stage, visual data exploration plays a key role in understanding the data [21] and thereby validating or rejecting the hypothesis regarding the data [31]. The data scientist can validate their assumptions and findings through visual data exploration. They can redesign or repeat the process or even conclude the entire process if needed [14].

Even though visualization offers more accessible communication to a layman by providing meaningful insights and thereby enhancing decision-making capability, the challenge sprawls in learning these visualization tools [32]. Most existing tools require the user to have programming knowledge and proficiency in handling numerous syntaxes for producing visualization, which is a tedious and time-consuming task [30].

Today's data world is increasing in terms of volume, veracity, and the velocity at which it accumulates on various sources. The world around us is filled with rich relationships between multiple entities. Graph visualization helps to comprehend these massive amounts of data at a glance and better. For instance, the different departments within an organization may use various technologies. This often creates information silos within the organization and isolates each department from sharing their information with others. With the advent of no-code knowledge graphs, the connections between the departments are made easier by eliminating the information silos and enhancing decision-making capability.

7.6 Visualization tools used in PKGs

Different techniques can be used to visualize PKGs for classifying, storing and organizing individual information they encounter daily. Doing so will improve individual effectiveness [6] leading to various effective collaborations, which improves corporate effectiveness. Below given are some of the tools used for visualization:

7.6.1   Obsidian

Obsidian[1] is a native application that can be accessed on mobile and desktop. It offers paid versions for professionals as well as free basic versions. It works well in Android/IOS devices and operating systems like Windows/Mac/Linux. Obsidian can work entirely offline too. It is a powerful tool for organizing information in a structured manner. Obsidian uses the lightweight markup language markdown, which is the language used by sites like GitHub and Reddit. It can be used both as a markdown editor and as a knowledge base application. Figure 7.10 depicts an obsidian way of organizing information, on which the graph view helps to visualize the relationship between the notes in the vault.

7.6.2   RemNote

RemNote[2] is an all-in-one tool that empowers students, researchers, and professionals. It is a free web-based application but offers extra paid features too. It works well on Android mobile devices and with a native desktop app in Windows/Mac/Linux. The advantages of RemNote are that it supports smart flashcards and provides license

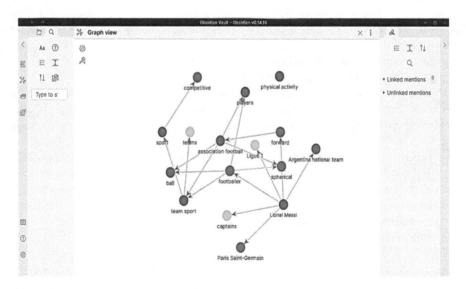

Figure 7.10   Screenshot of Obsidian graph view

---

[1] https://obsidian.md/
[2] https://www.remnote.io/

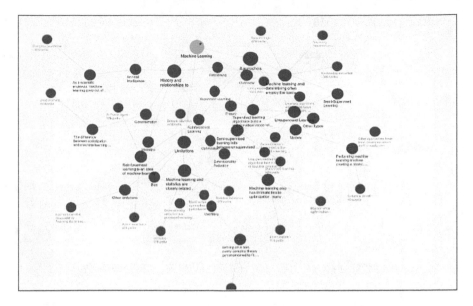

Figure 7.11   Screenshot of RemNote graph view

discounts for classrooms and educational institutions. The disadvantages are limited collaboration opportunities and a lack of advanced administration. Figure 7.11 depicts how RemNote organizes information, and the graph view helps to visualize the relationship between the nodes.

7.6.3   Tiddlyroam

Tiddlyroam[3] is free, open-source software built on a highly customizable framework. It helps to create our wiki by making connections between various nodes. It is a cross-platform tool that works well on Windows/Mac/Linux OS. It provides a visual graph with bidirectional linking. The main advantages noted are it uses a single HTML file which can be accessible even after many years.

Moreover, it is highly adaptable, so people can change it to fit their application needs. Another advantage is that even a non-IT professional can easily use this tool. Figures 7.12 and 7.13 demonstrate the Tiddlyroam representation at "1-step distance" and "4-step distance".

7.6.4   Dendron

Dendro[4] is free, open-source software. It is a markdown-based personal knowledge management solution that can be used to create, organize and collaborate on a

---

[3] https://tiddlyroam.org/
[4] https://www.dendron.so/

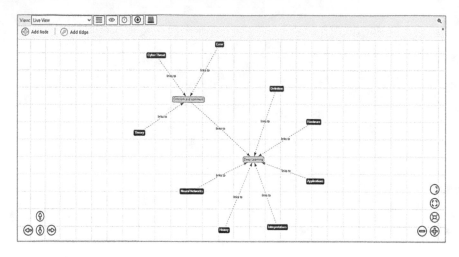

Figure 7.12   Tiddlyroam "1 step distance" representation

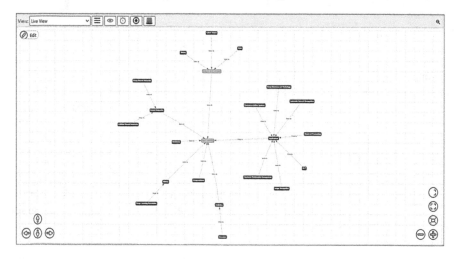

Figure 7.13   Tiddlyroam "4 step distance" representation

knowledge-base of any size. It offers various features like backlinks, tagging, graphical views, etc. Apart from a PKG, it can be used for customer relationship management, blogging, documentation purposes, tasks and to-dos, and organizing meeting notes. The main advantage of Dendron is that it is built into VS Code which would be easy for those working in the same environment, as the switching costs would be reduced in this case. Figure 7.14 shows a local note graph in Dendron, which provides the current node and its immediate neighbors. Figure 7.15 also depicts a full note graph view in Dendron.

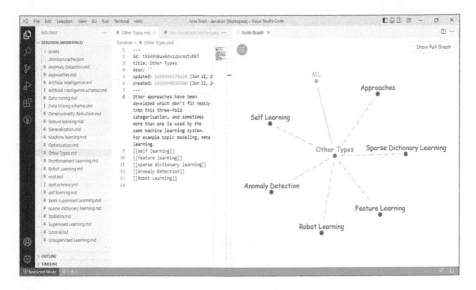

Figure 7.14   Local note graph view in Dendron

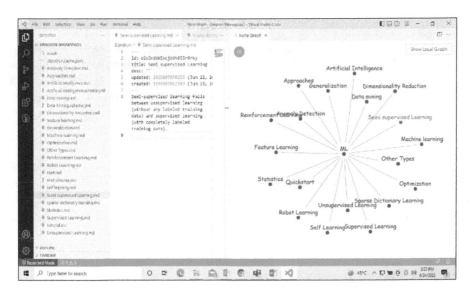

Figure 7.15   Full note graph view in Dendron

7.6.5   Logseq

Logseq[5] is free, open-source software. It is highly beneficial for academic writing, organizing to-do lists, and recording one's unique life. In Logseq, the storage is

[5]https://logseq.com/

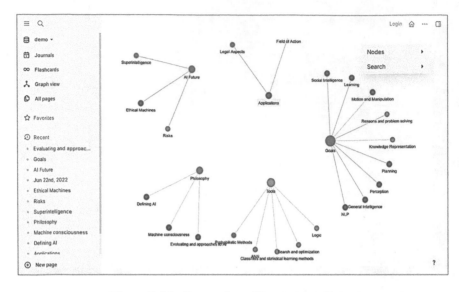

Figure 7.16   Screenshot of Logseq graph view

completely done locally. It provides a visual graph with bidirectional linking. Logseq is highly influenced by other PKG tools like Roam Research, Tiddlywiki, Workflowy, and OrgMode. It is considered a platform for knowledge sharing and management and gives high priority to privacy, longevity, and user control. Logseq integrates with the whiteboard tool Excalidraw and works on top of the lightweight markup language Markdown and Org-mode files (Figure 7.16).

7.6.6   Foam

Foam[6] is free and open-source software. It is considered personal knowledge management and sharing system built on VSCode, and it pairs well with GitHub. In Foam, the storage is completely done locally. It supports visual graphs with bidirectional linking. The primary benefit of using Foam is that since it is built on top of the VSCode, numerous amounts of extensions available in the ecosystem can be used. Figure 7.17 depicts the Foam graph view.

7.6.7   Roam Research

Roam Research[7] is a commercial web-based application. It helps a flat structure with powerful tagging abilities. Roam can have either local or web storage and supports a graphical view with bidirectional linking. The major benefit of using Roam is that it is swift and easy to create a new page in Roam just by using the '[[]]' command, unlike

---

[6]https://foambubble.github.io/foam/
[7]https://roamresearch.com/

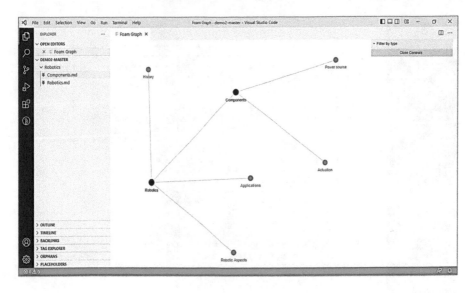

Figure 7.17   Screenshot of Foam graph view

Table 7.2   Personal knowledge management tools

Tool	Open-Source software	Free	Paid	Native App	Web App	Mobile OS		Desktop OS		
						Android	IOS	Windows	Mac	Linux
Obsidian		☑	☑	☑		☑	☑	☑	☑	☑
RemNote		☑	☑		☑	☑		☑	☑	☑
Tiddlyroam	☑	☑		☑				☑	☑	☑
Dendron	☑	☑		☑				☑	☑	☑
Logseq	☑	☑			☑			☑	☑	☑
Foam	☑	☑			☑			☑	☑	☑
Roam Research			☑		☑		☑	☑	☑	☑	

tools like Notion. The new page can be created anywhere without thinking much about the hierarchy. Moreover, Roam uses plain text and acts as a simple interface for taking and connecting atomic notes. Figure 7.18 shows the Roam research graph view.

Table 7.2 summarizes all the personal knowledge management tools discussed above.

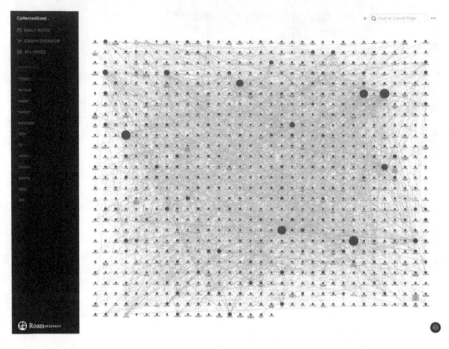

Figure 7.18   Image of Roam Research graph view[8]

Using the numerous techniques for PKGs covered in this chapter, one can efficiently manage information by gathering, organizing, and accessing it. Although the aforementioned tools appear comparable on the surface, each differs fundamentally from the others and hence is distinct.

As Table 7.2 depicts, Obsidian is a native app that can be used on desktop and mobile devices. It provides both free basic versions and variants that cost money for professionals. RemNote is a multipurpose tool to help professionals, researchers, and students. Although it is a web-based application, it also offers additional premium features. It functions well with a native desktop program in Windows, Mac, or Linux, as well as on Android mobile devices.

Tiddlyroam is a kind of open-source, free software that can be easily customized. By connecting different nodes, the users can build their own wiki. It is a cross-platform program that functions well with Windows, Mac OS, and Linux. It offers a visual graph with bidirectional linking. Dendron is another personal knowledge management tool based on markdown and can be used to create, arrange, and collaborate on knowledge of any size. It has several capabilities, including tagging, graphical views, and backlinks.

It is beneficial for keeping track of one's personal life, managing to-do lists, and composing academic papers. In Logseq, all the storage is done locally. It offers

---

[8]Image source: © https://thesweetsetup.com/obsidian-vs-roam/

a visual graph with bidirectional linking. Foam is a system based on Visual Studio Code for managing and sharing personal knowledge. Storage is done entirely locally in Foam. Moreover, it also supports bidirectional linking. On the other hand, Roam Research is a commercial web-based application. It offers both web and local storage. It also provides a graphic view with a two-way connection.

7.7   Conclusion

This chapter defined the concepts of PKGs, their visualization tools, and how it varies from knowledge graphs. We discussed knowledge graphs, which contain labeled nodes and edges that encode the retrieved information from various sources in a structured manner. PKGs focus on the personalization of the existing knowledge graphs. It provides organized information about entities and relationships which are more personal to the user. We have also seen that we can leverage PKGs in various fields, including recommendation systems, healthcare, extensive searches, etc. We also discussed a predefined ontology for organizing information in a knowledge graph and discussed information organization based on a global schema in PKGs. Additionally, we introduced different PKG visualization tools like Obsidian, Remnote, Tiddlyroam, Dendron, Logseq, Foam, and Roam. These digital tools can be used to gather, organize and access one's knowledge, thereby improving individual effectiveness. We compared these tools with one another and highlighted their advantages and disadvantages.

References

[1]   Balog, K. and Kenter, T. (2019). Personal knowledge graphs: a research agenda. In *Proceedings of the 2019 ACM SIGIR International Conference on Theory of Information Retrieval*, pp. 217–220. https://doi.org/10.1145/3341981. 3344241

[2]   Rastogi, N. and Zaki, M. J. (2020). Personal Health Knowledge Graphs for Patients (arXiv:2004.00071). arXiv. https://doi.org/10.48550/arXiv.2004. 00071

[3]   Chakraborty, P., Dutta, S., and Sanyal, D. K. (2022). *Personal Research Knowledge Graphs* (arXiv:2204.11428). arXiv. https://doi.org/10.48550/ arXiv.2204.11428

[4]   Huang, X., Zhang, J., Li, D., and Li, P. (2019). Knowledge graph embedding based question answering. In *Proceedings of the Twelfth ACM International Conference on Web Search and Data Mining*, pp. 105–113. https://doi.org/ 10.1145/3289600.3290956

[5]   Faerber, M., Bartscherer, F., Menne, C., and Rettinger, A. (2017). Linked data quality of DBpedia, Freebase, OpenCyc, Wikidata, and YAGO. *Semantic Web*, *9*, 1–53. https://doi.org/10.3233/SW-170275

[6]   Jefferson, T. L. (2006). Taking it personally: personal knowledge management. *VINE*, *36*(1), 35–37. https://doi.org/10.1108/03055720610667345

[7]   Cheong, R. and Tsui, E. (2010). The roles and values of personal knowledge management: an exploratory study. *VINE, 40.* https://doi.org/10.1108/03055721011050686

[8]   Nickel, M., Murphy, K., Tresp, V., and Gabrilovich, E. (2016). A review of relational machine learning for knowledge graphs. *Proceedings of the IEEE, 104*(1), 11–33. https://doi.org/10.1109/JPROC.2015.2483592

[9]   Kejriwal, M. (2022). Knowledge graphs: a practical review of the research landscape. *Information, 13*(4), 161. https://doi.org/10.3390/info13040161

[10] Sheth, A., Padhee, S., and Gyrard, A. (2019). Knowledge graphs and knowledge networks: the story in brief. *IEEE Internet Computing, 23*(4), 67–75. https://doi.org/10.1109/MIC.2019.2928449

[11] Zou, X. (2020). A survey on application of knowledge graph. *Journal of Physics: Conference Series, 1487*(1), 012016. https://doi.org/10.1088/1742-6596/1487/1/012016

[12] Dörpinghaus, J., Stefan, A., Schultz, B., and Jacobs, M. (2022). Context mining and graph queries on giant biomedical knowledge graphs. *Knowledge and Information Systems, 64*(5), 1239–1262. https://doi.org/10.1007/s10115-022-01668-7

[13] Yu, T., Li, J., Yu, Q., *et al.* (2017). Knowledge graph for TCM health preservation: design, construction, and applications. *Artificial Intelligence in Medicine, 77*, 48–52. https://doi.org/10.1016/j.artmed.2017.04.001

[14] Gómez-Romero, J., Molina-Solana, M., Oehmichen, A., and Guo, Y. (2018). Visualizing large knowledge graphs: a performance analysis. *Future Generation Computer Systems, 89*, 224–238. https://doi.org/10.1016/j.future.2018.06.015

[15] Meckel, S., Zenkert, J., Weber, C., Obermaisser, R., Fathi, M., and Sadat, R. (2019). Optimized automotive fault-diagnosis based on knowledge extraction from web resources. In *2019 24th IEEE International Conference on Emerging Technologies and Factory Automation (ETFA)*, pp. 1261–1264. https://doi.org/10.1109/ETFA.2019.8869057

[16] Sun, K., Liu, Y., Guo, Z., and Wang, C. (2016). Visualization for knowledge graph based on education data. *International Journal of Software and Informatics, 10*(3), 13.

[17] Li, D. and Madden, A. (2019). Cascade embedding model for knowledge graph inference and retrieval. *Information Processing & Management, 56*(6), 102093. https://doi.org/10.1016/j.ipm.2019.102093

[18] Yan, J., Wang, C., Cheng, W., Gao, M., and Zhou, A. (2018). A retrospective of knowledge graphs. *Frontiers of Computer Science, 12*(1), 55–74. https://doi.org/10.1007/s11704-016-5228-9

[19] Saha, A., Pahuja, V., Khapra, M., Sankaranarayanan, K., and Chandar, S. (2018). Complex sequential question answering: towards learning to converse over linked question answer pairs with a knowledge graph. In *Proceedings of the AAAI Conference on Artificial Intelligence, 32*(1), Article 1. https://doi.org/10.1609/aaai.v32i1.11332

[20]   Diomedi, D. & Hogan, A. (2021). Question answering over knowledge graphs with neural machine translation and entity linking. arXiv preprint arXiv:2107.02865.

[21]   Rohrer, M. W. (2000). Seeing is believing: the importance of visualization in manufacturing simulation. In *2000 Winter Simulation Conference Proceedings (Cat. No.00CH37165)*, *2*, 1211–1216 vol.2. https://doi.org/10.1109/WSC.2000.899087

[22]   Kalaycı, T. E., Bricelj, B., Lah, M., Pichler, F., Scharrer, M. K., and Rubeša-Zrim, J. (2021). A knowledge graph-based data integration framework applied to battery data management. *Sustainability*, *13*(3), 1583. https://doi.org/10.3390/su13031583

[23]   Thorat, P., M. Goudar, R., and Barve, S. (2015). Survey on collaborative filtering, content-based filtering and hybrid recommendation system. *International Journal of Computer Applications*, *110*(4), 31–36. https://doi.org/10.5120/19308-0760

[24]   Ilkou, E. (2022). Personal knowledge graphs: use cases in e-learning platforms (arXiv:2203.08507). arXiv. http://arxiv.org/abs/2203.08507

[25]   Li, X., Tur, G., Hakkani-Tur, D., and Li, Q. (2014). Personal knowledge graph population from user utterances in conversational understanding. In *2014 IEEE Spoken Language Technology Workshop (SLT)*, pp. 224–229. https://doi.org/10.1109/SLT.2014.7078578

[26]   Abu-Salih, B. (2021). Domain-specific knowledge graphs: a survey. *Journal of Network and Computer Applications*, 185, 103076. https://doi.org/10.1016/j.jnca.2021.103076

[27]   Wang, H., Miao, X., and Yang, P. (2018). Design and implementation of personal health record systems based on knowledge graph. In *2018 9th International Conference on Information Technology in Medicine and Education (ITME)*, pp. 133–136. https://doi.org/10.1109/ITME.2018.00039

[28]   Shirai, S., Seneviratne, O., and Mcguinness, D. (2021). Applying personal knowledge graphs to health. CoRR, 2021.

[29]   Cao, L., Zhang, H., and Feng, L. (2020). *Building and Using Personal Knowledge Graph to Improve Suicidal Ideation Detection on Social Media* (arXiv:2012.09123). arXiv. https://doi.org/10.48550/arXiv.2012.09123

[30]   Li, H., Wang, Y., Zhang, S., Song, Y., and Qu, H. (2022). KG4Vis: a knowledge graph-based approach for visualization recommendation. *IEEE Transactions on Visualization and Computer Graphics*, *28*(1), 195–205. https://doi.org/10.1109/TVCG.2021.3114863

[31]   Keim, D. A. (2001). Visual exploration of large data sets. *Communications of the ACM*, *44*(8), 38–44. https://doi.org/10.1145/381641.381656

[32]   Dibia, V. and Demiralp, Ç. (2019). Data2Vis: automatic generation of data visualizations using sequence-to-sequence recurrent neural networks. *IEEE Computer Graphics and Applications*, *39*(5), 33–46. https://doi.org/10.1109/MCG.2019.2924636

[33]   Diomedi, D. & Hogan, A. (2021). Question Answering over Knowledge Graphs with Neural Machine Translation and Entity Linking. arXiv preprint arXiv:2107.02865.

Section 4

Natural language processing

Chapter 8

Query-answering with text and knowledge graph

Aravindarajan Subramanian[a], Sarra Ben Abbes[a] and Rim Hantach[a]

Query-answering (QA) is one of the key areas in Artificial Intelligence, where various researches are performed in recent years. Building query-answering system helps the organization of all sectors. Generating automatic responses saves both time and money. We examine the problem of query-answering over knowledge graphs (KG) where various QA approaches focus on simpler queries and do not work very well for complex queries or vice versa. In addition to that, reasoning over KG is also to be handled properly to predict the proper answer to the corresponding query. Models that use SPARQL are good at domain-related queries, but they are unable to handle out-of-domain queries. Combining contextual text representation and semantic graph representation is a challenge. Our area of research is to combine text and KG for open domain query-answering. Adapting the joint representation ensures that the model can perform well in both simple and complex queries. In this chapter, we explain the various works that have been conducted and the challenges that have come along with it.

8.1 Introduction

Query-answering (QA) is an ongoing research area, where researchers are still trying to achieve perfection. Various rule-based and deep learning approaches adapt reasoning over queries and link them with relevant responses in the answer dataset. These models often end up domain-specific or make it harder to generalize.

Rule-based approaches [1] identify the query pattern and generate a query based on the query. These approaches work with fixed pattern queries, but it is difficult to generalize these approaches to adapt to queries of different types. To avoid problems in structured queries, deep learning models are trained to learn representation. These models can understand the text based on the word position and context. Many applications like recommendation systems [2], query-answering [3], text/document classification, sentiment analysis [4], etc., where the representations

[a]Computer Science and Artificial Intelligence labs Engie, France

become inevitable. By calculating the similarity between the query and answer representations, the solution has arrived.

The knowledge graph (KG) is a way of structuring and storing information in graph form, by representing entities as nodes, and relationships as edges between entities. Entities can be real-world objects and abstract concepts, and relationships represent the connectivity between entities. Generally, statements represent a fact or opinion. For example, Albert Einstein is an expert in Physics is a statement supporting a fact. This fact is represented in KG as **(Albert Einstein, ExpertIn, Physics)** where Albert Einstein and Physics are head and tail entities, and ExpertIn refers relation between these two entities.

Similar to textual representations, KG has to be encoded in such a way that its properties have to be preserved. Generally, head and tail entities represent points in an embedding space and relations between them are an operation or a function between them. The model learns their representations by minimizing a loss function, such that all the relations between single head and tail entities along with their properties have to be preserved. Thus, we can reason new facts from learned embeddings.

Creating a system based on textual representation is feasible and scalable with the recent advancements in language models. The same can apply to the KG models as well. But the dataset is not enough or complete to create a generalized QA, ending up answering either domain-specific or certain types of queries. By combining them, we are enriching the dataset and we can achieve generalization. Even though combining text and KG is not something new, there is no advanced research for a combined generalized QA. In this chapter, we address these problems by combining text and KG for a generalized QA.

8.2   State of the art

Query-answering is a key component in machine learning comprehension. We have analyzed various works that are conducted on query-answering. These approaches use either text or KG as their input. There are some approaches where both KG and text are considered, but those approaches are either for a domain-specific KG or designed for a particular type of queries. Even though recent text-only approaches achieved new benchmarks, when we compare them with our approach, we have outperformed them. The following are the various approaches that we have analyzed during our research.

Zhang *et al.* [5] used reinforcement learning to learn order sub-queries for complex query-answering. Their work is to learn an optimal order of answering sub-queries. Queries are decomposed into multiple simple queries and a reinforcement model with self-attention orders the decomposed queries. There is no guarantee that the answering function is perfect as this model focuses only on ordering rather than the answer accuracy.

Complex factoid query-answering with a free-text knowledge graph [6] uses a free text knowledge graph to resolve the coverage issue. They build a KG directly from a free-text corpus. QA model (which only needs to output an answering entity) figures out the sentence containing the relevant information to answer the query. The general assumption of this approach is that the answer entity from the candidate nodes has more links to the query nodes than the other nodes. A graph neural network is trained to store all the candidate entity nodes. Even though the approach seems convincing, implementing the model in a real-time scenario is complex. In addition to that, this approach struggles to solve queries with a smaller number of entities and works only for trivial queries.

Luo *et al.* [7] encode complex query structure into a uniform vector representation and capture the interactions between individual semantic components within a complex query. First, a candidate query graph is generated using the staged generation method. Finally, the semantic similarities between the query and query graph are measured using deep neural networks. Then an ensemble approach is used for entity-linking enrichment.

Yu *et al.* [8] use a hierarchical recurrent neural network (RNN) enhanced by residual learning which detects KB relations given an input query. The model is trained using hinge loss. The positive relation is paired against all the negative relations that are similar to it. This approach is less efficient when dealing with complex queries and the model failed to predict the relations that are either unseen during training or with a limited set of negative examples.

Apoorvsaxena *et al.* [9] uses a pruning model for relation filter, then an answer selection model scores the answer. The pruning model uses a multi-layer perceptron (MLP) along with a sigmoid function for filtering the relation corresponding to the queries. We have adopted the relation pruning idea by training a BERT [10] encoder which filters the relation based on their relevance with the queries. The answer-scoring model uses the corresponding KG equation, with a sigmoid activation function. This approach is probably suitable for domain-specific KG, but it is impossible to generalize a complete KG like Freebase or Wikidata. Another problem with this approach is scalability, i.e. complexity of this approach increases linearly with the number of entities.

Retrospective reader for machine reading comprehension [11] designed a model with two layers to classify queries based on answerability and to predict the starting and ending spans. Each layer is a transformer-based pre-trained language model (PLM). The first model is a sketchy model which does lazy supervision and the second model is an intensive model with an attention mechanism from the sketchy embeddings. The final score is calculated based on the sum of scores from both models.

Enabling language representation with knowledge graph (K-BERT) [12] merges text sentences with the triples from KG to add domain knowledge to the model. Knowledge noise has been avoided by a visibility matrix with a soft position. Their work proves that this approach works well for domain-specific tasks. But our goal is to build a generalized QA system.

Reasoning with language models and knowledge graphs for query-answering [13] combines queries and KG. PLM is used to encode the query and a subgraph is retrieved for the corresponding query. A scoring mechanism is used to score the subgraph nodes to predict the relevancy. Context and the KG are jointly reasoned using graph neural network (GNN). In this approach, each query has given a choice of answers and the model predicts the answer from the choice. In a generalized approach, the model has to be capable of predicting the answers from the given source.

Dense passage retrieval (DPR) [14] for open-domain query-answering based on a supervised bi-encoder using PLM created a new benchmark. Two BERT encoders are used to encode queries and passages to a dense embedding space. Top K passages are retrieved based on the similarity between the query and the passage embedding. It outperforms the existing benchmarks and also demonstrated that it is scalable. This approach provides us insights to develop a scalable generalized QA.

RocketQAv2 [15] is an advancement of DPR with an additional re-ranking module. Re-ranker is designed with PLM's cross encoder. In addition to that, training has improved through data augmentation. Using dynamic list-wise distillation both passage retriever and re-ranker is jointly trained for mutual improvements. The difference between DPR and this approach is that the encoder is trained with cross-batch negatives rather than in batch negatives.

Though we are trying generalized QA systems, various experiments such as triplet classification and relation extraction have already been performed using joint representation combining both text and KG.

Fan *et al.* [16] use joint embedding for relation extraction. The model can learn the low-dimensional vector representation of the triplet from the knowledge base, as well as the relation from the free text. The joint representation helps to bridge the gap between the structured knowledge base and the unstructured free text.

Wang and Li [17] proposed a text-enhanced knowledge embedding (TEKE) method for knowledge graph representation learning. From an entity-annotated text corpus, a co-occurrence network is constructed between entities and words. Pointwise and pairwise context textual embeddings are learned. Finally, the entity/relation representation model is trained to adapt the textual context information.

Wang *et al.* [18] utilized joint embeddings for predicting facts. A knowledge model based on TransE [19] is used for knowledge graph embedding and a text model similar to skip-gram is used for text embedding. Both the embeddings are aligned into the same space using a Wikipedia anchor model. Results proved that the joint model achieved better accuracy than the individual model in fact prediction.

In our work, we analyzed the pros and cons of all these approaches and designed a generalized QA system combining both text and KG.

8.3   Methodology

We started our work in 2020. Initially, we designed a joint representation approach for a generalized QA. Our initial approach is to predict the answer based on relations from the KG. This approach is better when compared to its benchmark. But it is difficult to generalize it.

We have illustrated the evolution of our work in Figure 8.1.

To overcome the drawbacks of our initial Joint representation approach in 2021, we designed a joint representation with relational graph convolutional network (GCN).

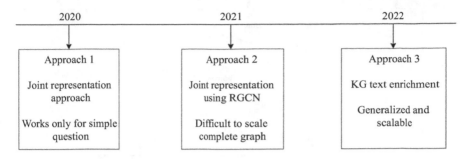

Figure 8.1   Project timeline

For each query, we extract the entities present in the query as query entity nodes and we extract the subgraph based on the query entities. Word embeddings of the relations are combined with their corresponding KG embeddings. We have encountered graph coverage and scalability problems with this approach.

In 2022, we designed a KG text enrichment approach to avoid the drawbacks of our previous two approaches. With this approach, we have achieved generalization along with scalability. We trained our model with complete WikiData and hence it is proved that this approach can scale KG of any size.

The following sections explain our approaches in detail.

8.3.1   Approach 1: joint representation approach

Overview

We present our joint representation approach for QA based on Yu *et al.* [8]. The entities present in the query are considered query entity nodes. A subgraph is prepared for each query based on the query entities. Subgraph are the triplets extracted from KG that have query entity as head. We extract all the triplets that have query entities as head. The relation and tail entity of the subgraph are considered as evidence edge and candidate entity nodes, i.e. (query entity nodes QE are the entities from the queries that match our KG. Evidence is the relations between the entities. Candidate entity nodes are the nodes that contain the answer to our query).

Figure 8.2 illustrates our approach. We identify the query entities. Based on that we prepare our subgraph. Finally, our model calculates the score of all the evidence from the subgraph. We predict the answer by choosing the corresponding candidate entity associated with the evidence that has the maximum score.

Step 1: Query entities identification

The initial step of this approach is to identify the entities to prepare our subgraph. Any entity linking model with good accuracy will help to extract entities from the queries.

Example: What is the capital of France? Query entities: France

As shown in the example above, France is the entity present in the query. Hence, France is considered as a query entity node.

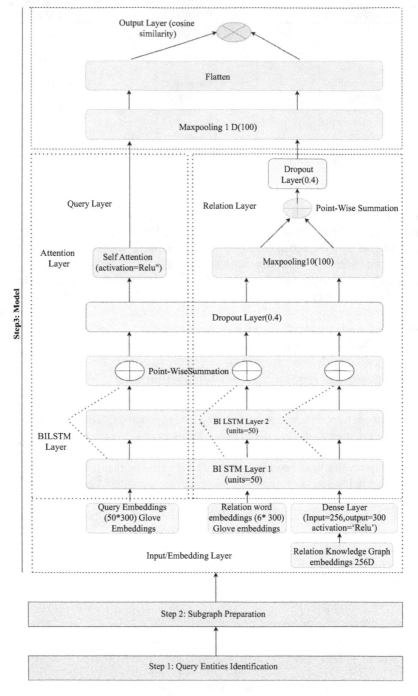

Figure 8.2 Approach 1: joint representation architecture

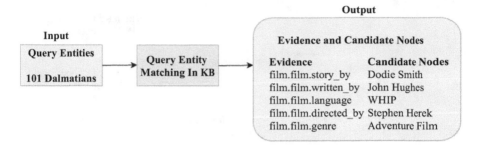

Figure 8.3   Subgraph

Step 2: Subgraph preparation

For each query, we ground the knowledge graph into a query-related subgraph with query tokens as head joined to candidate entity nodes as tail via evidence as relations.

Query entity nodes

The entities that are present in the queries are the query entity nodes. Each query differs by the entities present in it and the answer should be linked to the query entities.

Evidence

Relations between the entities are the evidence. The evidence that has maximum relevance to the query has the answer.

Candidate entity nodes

is the pool of entities that contain the answer to corresponding queries. The system should select the answer based on the evidence matching the query.

We have shown a subgraph in Figure 8.3 for the following example.

Who is the author of the movie '101 Dalmatians'?

Step 3: Answer prediction

Our model uses bidirectional long short-term memory (BiLSTM) and is based on Yu *et al.* [8]. In our approach, we have stacked BiLSTM for both queries and answers along query's self-attention for better abstraction.

Query embedding

The queries are tokenized, and a vocabulary is created from the tokens. We used pre-trained GloVe embeddings [20]. Each word is projected into a size of 300 dimension. The queries are encoded by a size of 50 × 300 dimension. Queries of size lesser than 50 are padded with 0. For better scoring, named entities in the queries are masked while encoding.

Relation embedding

Relations are represented as 256 dimension vectors using complEx KG embedding model [21]. As shown in Figure 8.4, relation representation is a combination of text and knowledge embeddings. Similar to query embeddings, evidence are embedded

Figure 8.4   Relation embedding

using GloVe embeddings by size 6 × 300 dimension and complEx KG embedding by size 256 dimension.

Model

BiLSTM is stacking two independent LSTMs together. This structure allows the networks to have both backward and forward information about the sequence at every time step. It runs your inputs in two ways, one from past to future and one from future to past. It uses two hidden states combined, which can preserve information from both the past and the future at any point in time.

The first layer of BiLSTM works on the word embeddings of query words, relation words, and relation embeddings and gets the hidden representations. The second layer of BiLSTM works on the first layer to get the second set of hidden representations. The second BiLSTM starts with the hidden vectors from the first layer. To align the KG representation and query embedding, we project the 256 dimension of knowledge representation into 300 dimension using a dense layer. For relation word representation, a relation is treated as a sequence of words from the tokenized relation name. It has better generalization. The self-attention mechanism of the query helps to treat each word with importance finding the best word for our evidence matching.

The final dot product gives us the cosine similarity score between the query representation and the evidence representation (relation). We assume that evidence with the candidate nodes gets the maximum score.

Normal QA systems use loss functions based on cosine similarity. Values closer to −1 indicate greater similarity. The values closer to 1 indicate greater dissimilarity. But in this joint representation model, we have adapted the mean square loss function. The advantage of MSE over cosine loss function is that it pushes positive relations towards the −1 and negative more towards the +1.

8.3.2   Approach 2: joint representation with relational graph convolutional network (RGCN)

Overview

We have constructed an RCGN similar to Boyd-Graber *et al.* [6] along with joint representation. Query entities, candidate entities, and evidence edge creation are all similar to our previous approach. Query entities and the candidate entities are treated as nodes of the graph and the relation between them is the edge between the nodes. Finally RGCN model computes the score of all candidate nodes.

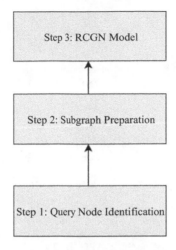

Figure 8.5   Approach 2: Joint Representation using RCGN

The difference between our previous and this approach is that in our previous approach we have not considered the candidate nodes representation, which we have included in this approach. Second, this approach can handle both simple and complex queries. Subgraphs are prepared by extracting the triplets based on all the entities present in the query.

The initial two steps from Figure 8.5 are similar to our previous approach (Approach 1). We used the same technique for entity identification and subgraph extraction. Finally, our RCGN model scores the candidate entities.

Answer scoring

Query embedding

Pretrained GloVe embeddings are used to embed the query. Each word is of 300 dimension. The queries are encoded by a size of 50×300 dimension. As shown in Figure 8.6, query word embeddings are passed through RNN along with attention to get sequence embeddings.

Node embedding

ComplEx KG embedding model is used to embed query and candidate entity nodes. It is projected into a 512 dimension vector.

Edge embedding

The relation between the nodes is an edge and it is a combination of text and KG embeddings. A 6×300 dimension Glove embedding is the text embedding and a 512 dimension complEx embedding is the KG embedding.

As shown in Figure 8.7, edge word embeddings and edge KG embeddings are passed through RNN along with attention to get sequence edge embeddings.

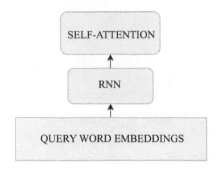

Figure 8.6   Query representation

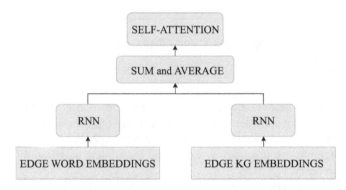

Figure 8.7   Edge representation

Model

The initial representation of the query tokens, nodes, and edges are calculated by RNN. The query tokens use Glove embeddings and nodes (both candidate entity node and query entity node) are represented by complex KG representation. Individual word embeddings of query changes to sequence representation using RNN with self-attention. The final representation is a weighted average of all hidden states.

The node representation of each node is a sum of KG entity representation and query representation. The representation is applied to both query entity nodes and candidate answer nodes. Self-attention is not needed for the nodes, as our approach does not have multiple sentences for a node.

Edge representation is a combination of KG embedding and their corresponding text embedding. Similar to the query, relation word embedding is converted to sequence representation by the RNN layer. KG embedding of the relation which passes through the RNN layer is then added and averaged with its sequence representation.

Query representation is fused with edge tokens using an attention layer. It first weights each evidence token position and then the weight is combined into the query-aware edge score.

Query entity node representations are updated by combining the query representation and the query entity node's representation from the previous layer. We update the query tokens and edge representation by their corresponding previous layer and current layer through a feed-forward network.

The edge score for each edge is calculated by computing the similarity between the edge representation and the updated query representation.

The final layer representation of the candidate entity node is scored using MLP. The model has to score the answer node higher than the other candidate nodes. The GCN is trained using binary cross-entropy loss.

8.3.3 Approach 3: KG text enrichment

Overview

Even though we have achieved better results from our approach 2, it is difficult to scale the approach for a complete KG. Also, the model suffers from graph coverage issues. If there is no link between the query and candidate entity nodes, then the model is unable to predict the answer.

To overcome the limits of our previous two approaches, we have created a generalized approach. We used Wikipedia passages as our source of text and Wikidata for kg. We have added a relation filter model in our subgraph extraction step. Our model proved that it is scalable and outperforms existing benchmarks.

As explained in Figure 8.8, we have used a pre-trained DPR model to extract the relevant Wikipedia passages based on queries. Entities from each passage are extracted

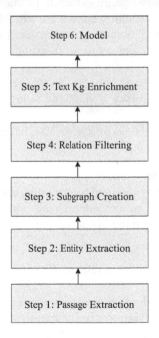

Figure 8.8   Approach 3: KG text enrichment approach

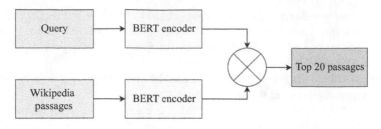

Figure 8.9   Passage extraction

by matching with KG. A relation filtering model helps to filter the irrelevant triplets from the KG. Finally, KG-enriched text is passed to the model to score the passages.

Step 1: Passage extraction
The initial step of our approach is to extract relevant passages based on the queries as mentioned in Figure 8.9. We used the DPR model directly. Two BERT encoders are trained, one for the query and the other for passage to embed them in a low-dimensional space. Passages corresponding to the queries are extracted using the dot product. For each query, we extract the top 20 passages.

Step 2: Entity extraction
Entities from each relevant passage are extracted. Entities from Wikidata have passed through the passage and the matching entities are extracted. Wikidata has around 70 million entities. Matching and extracting the entities is a challenging task. We used fuzzy matches with three different stages of filtering to extract proper entities from the Wikidata.

    Example:

    Passage: The Vought-Sikorsky VS-300 (or S-46) is a single-engine helicopter designed by Igor Sikorsky

    Extracted entities: Vought-Sikorsky, VS-300, helicopter, Igor Sikorsky, single-engine, engine

Step 3: Subgraph creation
A subgraph for each passage is obtained by extracting corresponding triplets from the Wikidata. Entities from step 2 are considered head entities. Triplets corresponding to those entities are extracted from the Wikidata.

Step 4: Relation filtering
As shown in Figure 8.10, we used a relation filtering model to filter the irrelevant triplets.

    We trained a BERT encoder to embed the queries in low-dimensional space. KG is embedded using ToursE [22] approach. The encoder is trained to embed the queries such that a dot product helps to retrieve the top K relation between query and relation embeddings. This helps to purge our subgraph, by eliminating the irrelevant triplets.

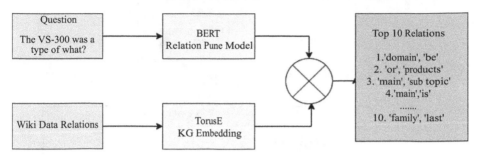

Figure 8.10   Relation filtering

Using our encoder we have achieved a generalized subgraph retrieval approach, by extracting the triplets that have relevance to the queries.

Step 5: Text KG enrichment
We have adopted the K-BERT idea to enrich our text with KG. Extracted packages and triplets are combined by adding the subgraph for each entity in the text. A subgraph for each entity is added to its corresponding location. This step applies to all the entities for each passage. Our relation filtering encoder efficiently filters the relation from the subgraph that is irrelevant. Only triplets containing relations that have relevance to the query are added.

Step 6: Model
KG text enrichment model architecture is shown in Figure 8.11. An encoder model using longformer [23] based on global attention is trained to score the KG-enriched text passages from a pool of the top 20 passages for each query. Given a query Q, relevant passages P and extracted subgraph K. KG enriched text PK is obtained by integrating relevant triplets with the corresponding entities in the text.

Q along with PK is encoded using an encoder where Q is the global attention token. We use a longformer transformer to encode queries along with KG-enriched text. Attention is scaled linearly based on the sequence lengths. The limitation of the BERT transformer is that it can encode up to 512 tokens. This limitation can be avoided by using a longformer to encode the long sequence.

The model is trained to retrieve the top passages from a pool of relevant top 20 passages. Results from the model show that our generalized KG-enriched text approach achieves better results than the text-only approach, which we can develop further for QA.

Experiments and results
In this section, we evaluate the performance of our approaches and compare them with their corresponding benchmarks. In all of our approaches, we have combined both text and KG as our input source. Results demonstrate that our approaches have good performance when comparing them to their corresponding benchmarks.

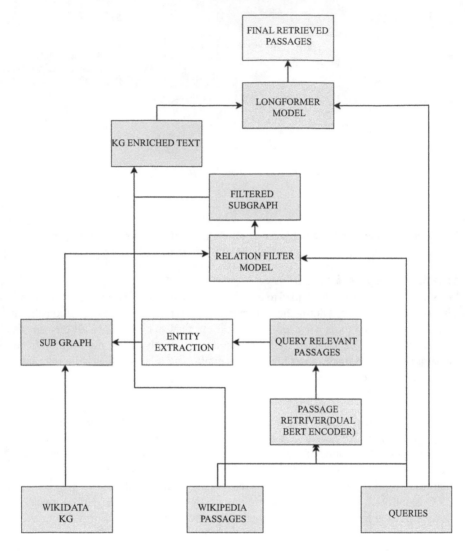

Figure 8.11   KG text enrichment model

8.3.4   Dataset

For the joint representation approach model, we have used FreebaseQA – open-domain factoid query-answering (QA) [24] as query dataset and Freebase as KG. For the joint representation with RGCN, we have used the Trivia factoid dataset as the query dataset and Wikidata 5m as the KG.

We trained our KG text enrichment model on Natural queries. We used the dev data for demonstration purposes. Queries that do not have answers in their extracted passages or KG-enriched text are not considered for our experiments.

Table 8.1   Dataset summary

Dataset	Train	Test	Dev
Freebase QA	3,334	3,334	–
Wiki QA	22,803	2,419	3,202
NQ dataset	5,112	1,706	–

A detailed description of the dataset is shown in Table 8.1.

8.3.5   Results

The results of our first approach are shown in Table 8.2. Results show that our joint representation approach outperforms its benchmark.

The results of our second approach are in Table 8.3. For a fair comparison, we have removed some queries which do not have answers in the candidate nodes. Our approach with RGCN outperforms the existing benchmark. Our model benefits from both KG and text.

We evaluate our KG text enrichment approach by training the model with the same transformer parameters.

Table 8.4 shows the efficiency of our relation filtering model. We have achieved 76% Top 1 accuracy, meaning that given a query, our relation filter model picks the top 10 relations relevant to the query.

Our relation filtering model is very much effective and pruned the subgraph to the maximum. This helps to limit our KG-enriched text tokens. We have chosen the top 10 relations for each query.

Table 8.2   Results of joint representation model

Models	Top 1 accuracy	Top 3 accuracy
Yu *et al.*	28%	47.7%
Ours	**61%**	**87%**

Table 8.3   Result of joint representation with relational GCN model

Models	Top 1 accuracy
Boyd-Graber *et al.*	52%
Ours	**58%**

Table 8.4   Results of KG text enrichment relation filtering model

Relation filtering model	Top 1	Top 5	Top 10	Top 20
Accuracy (in percentage)	76%	83%	85%	88%

Table 8.5   Results of KG text enrichment retrieval model

Models	Top 1 accuracy	Top 5 accuracy
Text only model	70.8%	89.7%
Ours	**76.4%**	**93.3%**

Retrieval model results (Table 8.5) show that our model outperforms the text-only model, which is a replication of the DPR model with a longformer encoder. We have achieved 5.6% better accuracy than the existing approach. The enriched text helps the model to learn better than the text-only approach. In addition to that our KG enrichment approach uses complete Wikipedia passages for text and Wikidata for KG. Thus we have demonstrated the scalability of our approach and overcame the challenges faced by our previous approaches for a generalized QA.

8.4   Conclusion

In this chapter, we explained various research for combining the text and KG for a generalized QA system. QA systems in the real world should answer different types of queries irrespective of the domains. Our experiment results show that we are closer to achieving that goal. Enriching text with KG yields better results than the text-only model. Further, we have omitted some queries because of the coverage issue. Our approach depends on the base encoder in retrieving the top 20 passages. Some queries are not answerable even with enriched text. Increasing the base encoder efficiency also increases the performance of our approach. Our next step is to add modules to our model to predict unanswerable queries and extract answers from the top passages.

References

[1]   Riloff E and Thelen M. A rule-based question answering system for reading comprehension tests. In: *Proceedings of the 2000 ANLP/NAACL Workshop on Reading Comprehension Tests as Evaluation for Computer-Based Language Understanding Sytems* – Volume 6. ANLP/NAACL-ReadingComp '00. USA: Association for Computational Linguistics; 2000. pp. 13–19. Available from:

https://doi.org/10.3115/1117595.1117598.

[2]   Isinkaye FO, Folajimi YO, and Ojokoh BA. Recommendation systems: princi-
      ples, methods and evaluation. *Egyptian Informatics Journal*. 2015;16(3):261–
      273. Available from: https://www.sciencedirect.com/science/article/pii/S111
      0866515000341.

[3]   Bouziane A, Bouchiha D, Doumi N, *et al.* Question answering systems: sur-
      vey and trends. *Procedia Computer Science*. 2015;73:366–375. *International
      Conference on Advanced Wireless Information and Communication Technolo-
      gies (AWICT 2015)*. Available from: https://www.sciencedirect.com/science/
      article/pii/S1877050915034663.

[4]   Mohanty MD and Mohanty MN. Chapter 5 – Verbal sentiment analysis and
      detection using recurrent neural network. In: De S, Dey S, Bhattacharyya S,
      et al., editors. *Advanced Data Mining Tools and Methods for Social Comput-
      ing. Hybrid Computational Intelligence for Pattern Analysis*. Academic Press;
      2022. p. 85–106. Available from: https://www.sciencedirect.com/science/
      article/pii/B9780323857086000126.

[5]   Zhang Y, Cheng X, Zhang Y, *et al.* Learning to order sub-questions for complex
      question answering. ArXiv. 2019;abs/1911.04065.

[6]   Zhao C, Xiong C, Qian X, *et al.* Complex Factoid Question Answering with
      a Free-Text Knowledge Graph. In: *Proceedings of The Web Conference 2020*.
      New York, NY, USA: Association for Computing Machinery; 2020. p. 1205–
      1216. Available from: https://doi.org/10.1145/3366423.3380197.

[7]   Luo K, Lin F, Luo X, *et al.* Knowledge base question answering via encod-
      ing of complex query graphs. In: *Proceedings of the 2018 Conference on
      Empirical Methods in Natural Language Processing*. Brussels, Belgium: Asso-
      ciation for Computational Linguistics; 2018. p. 2185–2194. Available from:
      https://www.aclweb.org/anthology/D18-1242.

[8]   Yu M, Yin W, Hasan KS, *et al.* Improved neural relation detection for knowl-
      edge base question answering. CoRR. 2017;abs/1704.06194. Available from:
      http://arxiv.org/abs/1704.06194.

[9]   Saxena A, Tripathi A, and Talukdar P. Improving Multi-hop Question Answer-
      ing over Knowledge Graphs using Knowledge Base Embeddings. In: *Pro-
      ceedings of the 58th Annual Meeting of the Association for Computational
      Linguistics*. Online: Association for Computational Linguistics; 2020. p.
      4498–4507. Available from: https://aclanthology.org/2020.acl-main.412.

[10] Devlin J, Chang M, Lee K, *et al.* BERT: pre-training of deep bidirectional trans-
      formers for language understanding. CoRR. 2018;abs/1810.04805. Available
      from: http://arxiv.org/abs/1810.04805.

[11] Zhang Z, Yang J, and Zhao H. Retrospective reader for machine reading com-
      prehension. In: *Proceedings of the AAAI Conference on Artificial Intelligence*,
      vol. 35; 2021. p. 14506–14514.

[12] Liu W, Zhou P, Zhao Z, *et al.* K-BERT: enabling language representation with
      knowledge graph. In: *Proceedings of AAAI*; 2020.

[13] Yasunaga M, Ren H, Bosselut A, *et al.* QA-GNN: reasoning with language
      models and knowledge graphs for question answering. In: *North American
      Chapter of the Association for Computational Linguistics (NAACL)*; 2021.

[14] Karpukhin V, Oguz B, Min S, *et al.* Dense passage retrieval for open-domain question answering. In: *Proceedings of the 2020 Conference on Empirical Methods in Natural Language Processing (EMNLP)*. Online: Association for Computational Linguistics; 2020. p. 6769–6781. Available from: https://www.aclweb.org/anthology/2020.emnlp-main.550.

[15] Ren R, Qu Y, Liu J, *et al.* RocketQAv2: a joint training method for dense passage retrieval and passage re-ranking. In: *Proceedings of EMNLP*; 2021.

[16] Fan M, Cao K, He Y, *et al.* Jointly embedding relations and mentions for knowledge population. In: *Proceedings of the International Conference Recent Advances in Natural Language Processing*. Hissar, Bulgaria: INCOMA Ltd. Shoumen, BULGARIA; 2015. p. 186–191. Available from: https://www.aclweb.org/anthology/R15-1026.

[17] Wang Z and Li J. Text-enhanced representation learning for knowledge graph. In: *Proceedings of the Twenty-Fifth International Joint Conference on Artificial Intelligence. IJCAI'16*. AAAI Press; 2016. pp. 1293–1299.

[18] Wang Z, Zhang J, Feng J, *et al.* Knowledge graph and text jointly embedding. In: *Proceedings of the 2014 Conference on Empirical Methods in Natural Language Processing (EMNLP)*. Doha, Qatar: Association for Computational Linguistics; 2014. p. 1591–1601. Available from: https://www.aclweb.org/anthology/D14-1167.

[19] Bordes A, Usunier N, Garcia-Duran A, *et al.* Translating embeddings for modeling multi-relational data. In: *Advances in Neural Information Processing Systems*; 2013. p. 2787–2795.

[20] Pennington J, Socher R, and Manning CD. GloVe: global vectors for word representation. In: *Empirical Methods in Natural Language Processing (EMNLP)*; 2014. p. 1532–1543. Available from: http://www.aclweb.org/anthology/D14-1162.

[21] Trouillon T, Welbl J, Riedel S, *et al.* Complex embeddings for simple link prediction. In: Balcan MF and Weinberger KQ, editors. *Proceedings of the 33rd International Conference on Machine Learning*. vol. 48 of Proceedings of Machine Learning Research. New York, NY: PMLR; 2016. p. 2071–2080. Available from: https://proceedings.mlr.press/v48/trouillon16.html.

[22] Ebisu T and Ichise R. TorusE: knowledge graph embedding on a lie group. CoRR. 2017;abs/1711.05435. Available from: http://arxiv.org/abs/1711.05435.

[23] Beltagy I, Peters ME, and Cohan A. Longformer: The Long-Document Transformer; 2020. arXiv:200405150.

[24] Jiang K, Wu D, and Jiang H. FreebaseQA: a new factoid QA data set matching trivia-style question-answer pairs with freebase. In: *Proceedings of the 2019 Conference of the North American Chapter of the Association for Computational Linguistics: Human Language Technologies*, Vol. 1 (Long and Short Papers). Minneapolis, MN: Association for Computational Linguistics; 2019. p. 318–323. Available from: https://www.aclweb.org/anthology/N19-1028.

Chapter 9

Extracting personal information from conversations

Anna Tigunova[a]

Personal knowledge graph (PKG) is an extremely useful asset, supporting many downstream applications, which facilitate user experiences. However, populating the PKG with the facts about the user is time-consuming and requires continuous revisions for the changeable user attributes. Instead of outsourcing this task to humans, one can leverage the existing machine learning methods to *automatically* populate a PKG. In this setting, personal facts can be extracted from the user's *conversational data*, such as chats and social media submissions. This kind of data exists in abundance for almost every person and contains rich signals of personal attributes.

In this chapter, we provide a comprehensive survey of existing methods for personal knowledge extraction from conversational data, including inferring demographic facts, interests and relationships of the speakers. We discuss the pros and cons of the current approaches and propose directions for future work.

9.1 Introduction

Manually inserting information into a PKG is a cumbersome routine for the users; thus, it is important to investigate the ways to populate a PKG automatically. This task could be approached with traditional information extraction methods applied to the structured knowledge sources containing personal facts (such as Wikipedia entries or biographical articles). Unfortunately, such sources are usually available only for celebrities, providing little chance to find information about an average person.

As opposed to using encyclopedic articles, we propose to leverage conversational data of an individual, such as their chats in text messengers, social media posts and transcribed dialogues (e.g., phone conversations). Conversational data is available in abundance and contains a lot of personal facts disclosed by the speakers. Consider, for instance, the following conversation:

[a]Max Planck Institute for Informatics, Germany

> A: *Hey, sweetheart, I'll be late from the hospital tonight, need to clean and organize the lab.*
>
> B: *Oh, can I please go to the court for a couple of hours in the evening? You know I love basketball so much!*
>
> A: *Well, make sure you do your homework first, your dad will check it I hope.*

From this dialogue, it is possible to infer several personal facts, which could be used to populate PKGs of speakers *A* and *B*. In some cases, personal information is relatively easy to spot; for instance, the *hobby* of speaker *B*, *basketball* can be extracted with a simple pattern-matching approach (using a pattern "*I love* + ⟨*hobby name*⟩").

However, it is uncommon for people to openly disclose their personal information in conversations. Instead, we can infer this knowledge using latent cues: the *profession* of speaker *A*, *nurse*, can be inferred from the fact that they will be "*staying late*" at the *hospital* and will "*clean and organize the lab.*" Note, that while the use of single terms (e.g., *lab*) could already be descriptive, to precisely distinguish the *nurse* occupation from *doctor* or *surgeon*, it is important to use the whole context (i.e. "*clean and organize*").

Finally, the speakers' interactions serve as a unique source to extract interpersonal relationship information. From the warm address term *sweetheart* as well as the order to "*finish the homework*" we can infer that speaker *A* is a *parent* of speaker *B*. Interpersonal relationships mentioned in the user's content (such as "*my mother, Nataly*") are rare and are difficult to map to the precise entities for building a PKG. On the other hand, it is possible to directly indicate a link between two people by analyzing the way they interact.

Extracting users' information from their conversational utterances to populate PKGs, or *user profiling*, is an important topic in NLP [1,2]. Yet, it is a difficult task, because dialogues contain a lot of noise, include colloquial language, the length of the conversational utterances is short [3] and there is a lot of topic drifting and smalltalk. This challenging nature of conversational data, as well as the lack of labeled datasets, resulted in only limited attempts to approach the problem of PKG population from dialogue utterances.

Moreover, many personal attributes are loosely defined, subjective and changeable, making them specifically challenging to infer and process. While construction latent representations of the speakers received significant attention from the researchers [4,5], building a PKG requires extracting crisp personal *attributes* and their *values*.

The challenges of conversational data determine the need to develop specific techniques for automatic extraction and inference of personal information from dialogues. In this chapter, we are going to review and compare the existing approaches and discuss their drawbacks and directions for improvement.

The rest of the chapter is structured as follows. In Section 9.2, we will talk about existing dialogue datasets, labeled with personal facts, including users' demographic attributes, interests and relationships. Such datasets, which contain crisp triplets describing the speakers, are extremely rare, as opposed to unstructured personality descriptions, which are not useful in the context of a PKG.

In Section 9.3, we will describe the methods for extracting personal information about an individual (like their *gender* or *hobbies*) from their conversational content. We will discuss the approaches covering various types of input data, such as dialogue transcripts and social media submissions. We will provide a detailed description of the zero-shot learning method [6] for inferring personal attributes with a long-tailed value distribution.

In Section 9.4, we will provide an overview of the existing methods for predicting relationships of the speakers, ranging from binary classification of the sentiment between the speakers to the more sophisticated fine-grained relationship inference methods. We will give a detailed description of the model PRIDE [7] for predicting directed fine-grained relationships from conversations, using a transformer-based architecture.

Finally, in Section 9.5, we will make a summary of the chapter and discuss potential directions of future work on extracting personal knowledge from conversations for PKG population.

9.2 Conversational datasets

To train the supervised models to infer personal information, one has to obtain a significant amount of labeled dialogue data. Although there is a large number of available dialogue datasets for training conversational systems, the profiles of the participants of these conversations are rarely accessible. There are only a few publicly available datasets of dialogue utterances containing the speakers' information; however, they mostly include only very basic demographic knowledge, like *age* or *gender*.

Dialogue data in textual format comes in different flavors: the transcripts of spoken utterances, e-mails and texts in messenger apps, posts in online forums, etc. In this chapter we overview existing datasets, which include the following kinds of textual dialogue data: (i) transcribed conversations, and (ii) social media submissions.

9.2.1 Transcribed dialogue datasets

Demographic traits: Privacy grounds prevent from publishing conversational datasets with the personal traits of the speakers, given the sensitivity of user information. The few publicly available datasets include transcriptions of the conversations [8,9], artificial dialogues, created for research purposes [10,11], or scripts of screenplays [12].

Cieri *et al.* [8] collected transcribed telephone chats, where the participants were given some predefined general topics to discuss; each speaker specified their age, gender, occupation, education and the dialect they speak. Love *et al.* [9] constructed a dataset of transcribed casual British English conversations, where all participants specified their demographic (*nationality* or *age*) and linguistic attributes (e.g., *mother tongue*).

The study [11] proposed an extension to the goal-oriented conversational dataset bAbI, between users and a chat-bot [13], which includes the information about the users' ages, genders, and food preferences. Zhang *et al.* [10] introduced a corpus of the crowdsourced dialogues, Persona-Chat, where each speaker was given a few sentences' description of some personality they had to use. A disadvantage of the Persona-Chat dataset is that it provides unstructured free-text descriptions of personas, which are different from precise demographic facts for a PKG. In general, the chats, which were created in a controlled environment sound artificial; they are targeted toward communicating a specific predefined goal and, therefore, lacking natural topic variations.

Tigunova *et al.* [14] introduce MovieChAtt dataset, which consists of a subset of characters in the Cornell Movie-Dialogs Corpus [15], including the texts of 617 movie scripts. The characters in selected movies were labeled with *age*, *gender*, and *profession* attributes using crowdsourcing.

Relationship prediction: Two well-known sources of dialogue data, which are used for predicting interpersonal relationships, are literary texts and transcriptions of the screenplays. Several related studies provided the annotations of relationships of fictional novel characters as binary labels [16] (indicating the sentiment as positive or negative) or in a bag-of-words [17] representation. Massey *et al.* [18] created the annotations of the relationships between the literary text characters, including temporal changes in their relationships.

As opposed to literary texts, the transcriptions of movies and series include conversational utterances in a structured form, additionally providing speaker attribution. Chen *et al.* [19] compiled a conversational dataset of Chinese TV series scripts and labeled them with 24 relationships and 7 emotions. The relationship labels in this dataset are hierarchically split by field (*family*, *company*, *school*, *other*) and seniority (*junior*, *elder* or *peer*).

Yu *et al.* [20] also annotated the characters in the TV series. The authors employed two judges to annotate the script of the Friends series, providing ground truth for the relation extraction task among 36 predicates; 14 of the considered predicates were indicative of the relationship between people. Jia *et al.* [21] annotated relationships of the movie script characters with 13 labels, which were additionally classified into several coarse categories (*family*, *intimacy*, *official*, *others*), which resulted in the DDRel corpus.

The dataset FiRe [22] contains both the scripts of movies and TV series, which enables to investigate how the predictive models perform across these genres. Unlike other works, Tigunova *et al.* [22] consider *directed* relationships (e.g., distinguishing the difference between *parent* and *child* labels) and allowing *multiple* relationship labels per speaker pair. The FiRe dataset was annotated through crowdsourcing and each derived label was based on the majority vote among 10 annotators.

9.2.2   Social media datasets

Most of the previous work in identifying users' personal facts from social media utilize Twitter as the source of conversational utterances; several studies also explore Facebook [23,24] or Reddit [25–27] posts.

Data collection from social media sources is usually performed via keyword or hashtag extraction [28,29], utilizing the facts specified in the publicly available user profile [1,30], using self-reports collected as part of an online survey [1,23,26,31–33], or pattern-based search through user profile descriptions and the posts of the users [14,25,34,35].

Identification of the demographic attributes of Reddit users has received less attention, as compared to Twitter users. However, other personal characteristics of the Reddit users have been predicted from their posts, such as *users' personality traits* [27] or *mental health state*. The author of [36] researched how the subreddit topic influences the gender ratio of the users making posts in this subreddit. The gender information used for this study was predicted directly from the usernames, among the users of 100 subreddits grouped by interest.

Tigunova *et al.* [12] created a large-scale publicly available dataset RedDust, which contains over 16M submissions from Reddit users covering five personal attributes: *profession, hobby, family status, age,* and *gender*. RedDust was automatically labeled using a distant supervision technique based on several heuristics, such as pattern matching and search for relevant lexicon. A subset of RedDust was evaluated by humans, showing around 0.9 labeling precision. Reddit datasets of a smaller scale exist for *gender*, *location* and *age* attributes [25,26]; these datasets are unfortunately not publicly available.

9.3   Extracting personal attributes

In this section, we describe existing approaches to extract personal information from conversational data. We classify the methods based on the type of input data they are suited for, namely transcribed conversations (phone calls or movie scripts) and social media submissions, including a line of research on predicting speakers' interests. The described studies cover a broad range of methods to predict personal traits (from explicit pattern matching to neural inference), as well as different forms of prediction outputs (e.g., latent speaker representations or crisp ⟨subject, predicate, objects⟩ triplets).

Additionally, we overview hierarchical models, which can effectively capture the conversational structure and build dialogue representations in a variety of NLP tasks. Finally, in this section we provide a detailed description of the novel CHARM architecture [6], which enables inference of rare personal attribute values without any training data.

9.3.1   Demographic attributes from transcribed dialogues

There has been ample previous work on using dialogues (such as telephone interactions, text messages, posts and comments) to extract the information about the speaker's demographics, varying from age [37,38], gender [37–39], or speaker's ethnicity [38,39] to their biography facts [40].

The latent speakers' representations are mostly created using language models [41], linguistic features [5,38,40] or speaker embeddings [4,42]. These representations are perfectly suited for end-to-end response generation systems; however, they cannot be directly used to populate a PKG. Another disadvantage of creating a latent representation of a personality is the difficulty to directly examine and interpret it, which prevents from verifying its credibility with respect to explicit attributes. A speaker's profile can be presented in a form of a textual description [10], constructed from a pool of several candidate sentences. This representation, however, is unstructured, providing no crisp information, which can be directly inserted into a PKG.

There are several related studies, attempting to extract precise personal facts [37–39], which required capturing an explicit predefined pattern (*"I am a doctor"*) [39]. Unfortunately, the speakers rarely use such assertions in the real conversations, which can cause very low recall of the pattern-based approaches. Classification via linguistic features is used as an alternative method in some related studies [5,38]. To additionally enhance their approach to classify age or gender, Garera and Yarowsky add the information about the partner identity and n-grams from the utterances [38]. One drawback of this study is that the predicted personal facts could only take binary values.

Wu *et al.* [43] predict personal facts as triplets ⟨subject, predicate, object⟩, allowing the object and the subject to be generated as any term in the given vocabulary. This lifts the restriction on the list of possible values to be predicted, compared to the method described in [39], where the predicted values were required to be present in the input text. Nevertheless, the triplets obtained in [43] also require further processing before they can be inserted into a personal knowledge graph: the predictions are generated on a per-utterance basis, ignoring the full user's interaction history. We argue that personal facts in a PKG should be aggregated from all evidence that could be collected from single conversational utterances.

The study [37] looks at the task from a different perspective; the authors single out a particular individual and investigate how this individual's personal traits are related to the traits of their interlocutors (for instance, if the interlocutor is older/younger than the primary speaker). This approach establishes links between the PKGs of different people, allowing to use these links for restoring missing knowledge (e.g., for a given speaker A we can infer the school they went to, if we know the school of their interlocutor, speaker B, and the fact that the speakers are classmates).

The tools used to predict explicit or latent personality commonly include standard machine learning methods, such as conditional random fields [4] or logistic regression [44], which require as input manually defined linguistic features [38]. Some studies enhance the input by including the traits of the dialogue interlocutor, such as their personality features [38], their utterances [37], and identity [44].

More recently, the speakers' representations are built using neural approaches, including recurrent neural networks [10,37], memory networks [10,11,42], attention models [14], and transformer-based methods [6,45].

Wang *et al.* [45] develop a transformer-based approach, which can be used for both extracting and inferring personal facts from conversational utterances; the candidate ⟨attribute, value⟩ pairs are generated using an autoregressive language model and are afterwards reranked to produce high-precision predictions. Although the generative approach to produce attribute values is very promising considering the lack of explicit mentions, in this work the generation was restricted only to the attribute values seen in training data, which in a way reduces the problem to classification. Another limitation of the proposed method is considering the extraction and inference tasks separately, while in real-life settings the model should be able to operate in a hybrid mode.

9.3.2 Social media profiling

In this section, we provide an analysis of the studies covering prediction of personal facts from social media, including work on extracting users' demographic facts and their interests. While the former is a well-established task usually solved through classification into a limited number of values, prediction of interests is a challenging open-ended problem because of its subjectivity and the lack of structure.

Personal attributes: Social media texts are very noisy, colloquial and short [3], which makes them sound close to spoken dialogue utterances. Moreover, the discussion threads in topical forums resemble the flow of a natural conversation. Most existing work on user profiling focuses on Twitter [4,23,28,29,34,46,47]. Other research explores Reddit [27], Facebook [23,48] and other social media [49]; user reviews can also be used to infer demographics [50]. However, texts stemming from social media are quite distinct from natural dialogue utterances in terms of additional nonverbal signals (such as user activity or hashtags), which the related studies often use to enhance predictions [27,29].

The most popular attributes of the social media users explored in related work are gender and age [23,29,34,49–51] and their personality [27,48]. Less attention received such attributes as users' origin [29], occupation [28,52], education [52], political views [29,46], ethnicity [46] or mental health issues [53].

Users' representations are constructed using language models [23] and n-grams [29], linguistic features [27,48], latent embeddings [28], or contextualized neural models [50]. The created features are afterwards used in a wider range of machine learning models, like SVMs [27,29], topical models [46], and neural networks [34,49].

Tigunova *et al.* [14] develop an attention-based method for predicting demographic information (age, gender, occupation, and family status) by hierarchically building a representation of the conversation, so that useless words and utterances are filtered out. Notably, this approach works for both social media submissions as well as transcribed conversations, also showing promising results in transfer learning between these data types.

The limitation of most work mentioned in this section is that it considers only a small number of possible attribute values. As opposed to it, the author of [52] does not use redefined attribute value lists; they predict for education, spouses, and jobs of the users drawing the values from the set of entities mentioned in user's posts. This method utilizes explicit mentions; however, it does not require to have predefined lists of attribute values in advance. Another area that benefited from open-ended predictions is the inference of users' interests.

User interests: Predicting interests of the users (e.g., politics, literature or music) is a well-researched topic because the knowledge of interests is helpful in many downstream domains. The speakers discuss their interests more often than their personal information [54,55], which makes interests prediction from dialogues a feasible task. Still, it is important to keep track of the change in users' interests [56], making necessary adjustments to the past predictions.

To infer speakers' interests the related studies use supervised learning methods [55], which involve training machine learning models to make predictions of the interests from a given restricted set. The disadvantages of such methods include being restricted to predefined lists of interest topics, as well as requiring to have labeled training data, which is rarely available. Alternatively, other related studies use topic modeling methods, which are unsupervised, such as LDA [57], representing predicted topics of interest as a bag of words. However, such approaches do not produce crisp values for the interests predicted, which makes them inapplicable for building a PKG.

Another group of studies uses the sources of external knowledge (such as Wikipedia) to link the utterances of the users to the concepts they are interested in, therefore producing explicit values for the predicted interests. Several studies extract named entities, which are explicitly mentioned in the social media submissions, and map them to the Wikipedia pages for these entities [47,58]. Alternatively, the whole submissions' texts can be linked to a Wikipedia category [54], determining the speaker's interest. A significant drawback of this approach is their relying on an external knowledge source, which requires additional preprocessing, may not be available or may be lacking required concepts.

9.3.3   Hierarchical conversational models

Effectively processing dialogue data involves making use of its unique features, such as conversational structure, utterance order and speaker attribution. In the following, we will describe existing *hierarchical* models, which are tailored specifically to the conversational data.

Serban *et al.* [59] introduced hierarchical models to represent dialogues, utilizing RNNs to create hierarchical representations of the input utterances and the context of the conversation, for the response generation task in conversational assistants. The same task was researched in [60], where the attention mechanism was added to the hierarchical architecture in the encoder. The study [60] used word- and utterance-level RNNs to build the representations for words and utterances as attention-weighted averages of the model's hidden states.

Other conversational tasks also benefit from utilizing hierarchical attention models, including emotion prediction from dialogues [61,62] or dialogue state tracking [63]. Usually word representations are created with BERT and utterance representations with a Transformer encoder [61,63] or an RNN [62].

Hierarchical attention methods are also broadly used to predict the features of the speakers. Lynn *et al.* [64] predicted personality aspects of Facebook users by creating word and utterance representations with an RNN and applying attention mechanisms to them. Li *et al.* [51] proposed to use a hierarchical model to infer gender, location, and age information of the users of Weibo.

Graph representation is another way to encode the conversational structure. Multi-party conversations (involving more than two speakers) are a common domain where such models can be effectively applied. Multi-party conversations have a non-sequential order, for instance, when a single utterance can have multiple addressees and there are multiple responses. In this case, one can construct a dialogue graph, with conversational utterances as vertices and edges connecting each utterance to its parent utterance [65]. Building a fully-connected graph [66] is another approach, which exploits the assumption that all utterances are dependent on each other. Modeling conversations as graphs was shown to be effective on several NLP tasks, such as emotion prediction [66,67].

9.3.4   Long-tailed personal attribute prediction with CHARM

Most of the approaches to extract personal information described previously are based on supervised learning and, therefore, cannot generalize beyond attribute values with a sufficient number of examples, necessary for model training. Such methods are applicable for the personal attributes with a *long-tailed* value distribution, for instance, *hobby*, when there is little hope to get a decent number of labeled training samples for unusual attribute values. For instance, while there is plenty of social media users posting about their interest in *music*, it is unlikely to find a comparable number of people interested in *quilting*.

In the following, we introduce an approach to overcome the limitations of supervised methods. We will describe a **C**onversational **H**idden **A**ttribute **R**etrieval **M**odel (CHARM) [6], which uses keyword extraction and document retrieval for inference of personal attribute values that were not seen by the model during training. CHARM is thus able to operate in a zero-shot setup, alleviating the limitations of the classification models. CHARM can be applied to any open-ended personal attribute (such as *favorite drink* or fine-grained *occupation*) without altering the architecture of the model.

9.3.4.1   Methodology

Figure 9.1 shows the operation of CHARM, used here as a running example. Taking a sequence of utterances as input (e.g., *"I use paddles when I go to the pool to increase speed,"* ...), CHARM has to predict a set of values for some given personal attribute. In the mentioned example, CHARM should identify that the speaker's hobby is *swimming*.

CHARM's operation consists of two steps: (i) *keyword extraction*, where the model extracts attribute-relevant keywords from the speaker's utterances (e.g., *"paddles"*) and (ii) *value ranking*, where these keywords are matched against documents, indicative of the possible values of the given personal attribute (e.g., *swimming*).

The list of attribute values predicted by CHARM must be *known* but CHARM does not require all values to be *seen* during training.

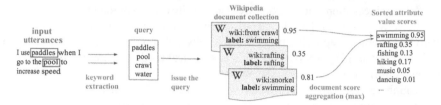

Figure 9.1   CHARM's operation scheme

Keyword extraction: During the first step, CHARM uses a *term scoring model* to evaluate terms in the input utterances. The term scoring model predicts how useful each term is for predicting the correct attribute value. For instance, the words "paddles" and "pool" will get high scores when the model predicts *hobby*, whereas "use" has to be assigned a lower score. The K terms with the greatest scores are selected for the query, which is used in the second stage.

To be able to handle the attribute values without any training examples (which are "unseen" during training), the term scoring model has to assign high scores to the words which are descriptive of the given personal attribute in general, as opposed to focusing on its particular values. Therefore, the model has to effectively grasp attribute-related contexts. In our example, the term "pool" in the context *"After work you can find me in the pool"* should be selected by the model as a relevant term for predicting *hobby*, as opposed to the term's presence in the context *"I picked one candidate from the pool."*

Value ranking: During the second stage, CHARM queries a collection of web documents, prepared so that each document is mapped to a set of known attribute values (for instance, such a collection could be constructed from all pages in the Wikipedia's list of hobbies). The *retrieval model* estimates the relevance scores of the query from the previous step to each document in the external document collection. In the running example, Wikipedia documents *wiki:Snorkel* and *wiki:Front crawl* will be assigned high relevance scores, whereas the document *wiki:Rafting*, will be assigned a lower score, because it is less relevant to the selected query.

Each attribute value might have several documents that are linked to it; therefore, the relevance scores of the documents have to be further aggregated to produce the final scores for each attribute value. In our example, if one applies *max* aggregation of scores, *swimming* will have the same score as that associated with its top scoring document *wiki: Front crawl*. The top scoring attribute values are returned as the model's predictions.

The use of an external document collection, which maps to the attribute values, enables CHARM to adapt to the large and open-ended lists of possible values. Having trained CHARM once, we only need to update the document collection to make CHARM able to predict any added or changed attribute values in a zero-shot setup.

Training: The term scoring model is trained using distant supervision because there are no truth labels for the selected keywords. The query is accumulated by sampling one term at a time and issuing the current query. This way the term scoring model gets an intermediate feedback from the value ranker of how helpful the sampled term was.

9.3.4.2 Experimental results

Data: The performance of CHARM is evaluated on two personal attributes: *profession* and *hobby* [6]; the lists of possible attribute values were collected from Wikipedia lists,[1] which contained 149 and 71 values for *profession* and *hobby*, respectively.

The training and evaluation inputs to CHARM include two types of data:

- the utterances of the users, together with the corresponding pairs of attributes and values (for instance, *hobby:swimming* from the example given in Figure 9.1), and
- an external document collection, where each document was associated with a subset of attribute values (e.g., documents, which describe *swimming* as a hobby, like *wiki: Front crawl*).

CHARM was trained on input utterances from a subset of RedDust dataset [12] labeled with weak supervision, described previously in Section 9.2.2. For experiments, all posts containing explicit personal assertions (for instance, "*I am a teacher*") were removed, to evaluate the ability of CHARM to *infer* attribute values, as opposed to performing pattern-based extraction. This resulted in obtaining 6,000 users for each attribute, with an average of 23 users per attribute value.

Web document collections were formed using *Wikipedia categories* for both *profession* and *hobby* attributes. The automatically labeled pages were collected by picking a Wiki-category relevant for each attribute value and collecting all pages from this category (for instance, all pages under *Wiki category:acting* are labeled with a *profession* value *actor*).

Component instantiation: CHARM has a flexible architecture, allowing to plug in various models as its two components: the term scoring model and the retrieval model. BERT [68] was used as the term scoring component because this model has excellent performance on multiple NLP tasks, effectively learning the words' contexts. The retrieval model was instantiated with KNRM [69], a neural architecture incorporating the embedding similarity of input terms. CHARM was found to produce better results with an embedding-based retrieval model as opposed to a sparse model, such as BM25 [70] model, additionally allowing to fine-tune the neural retrieval model's parameters [6].

Quantitative results: Note that CHARM cannot be directly compared to the supervised classification models, because they are not able to operate in the zero-shot setup. Instead, as baselines, the authors of CHARM use unsupervised keyword extraction methods, TextRank [71] and RAKE [72] paired with a KNRM ranker. Such setup follows the architecture of CHARM; however, in this case, the keyword extraction component is frozen. This does not let the model learn from the distant supervision of the document scoring step, and extract *attribute-related* keywords, based on implicit contexts in the utterances.

---

[1]Wikipedia pages: List_of_hobbies & Lists_of_occupations

Table 9.1   Performance of CHARM vs the baselines on profession and hobby attributes in a zero-shot setup

	Profession		Hobby	
Model	MRR	nDCG	MRR	nDCG
RAKE + KNRM	0.13	0.34	0.12	0.31
TextRank + KNRM	0.18	0.36	0.16	0.36
BERT IR	0.28	0.44	0.18	0.42
CHARM	**0.35**	**0.55**	**0.27**	**0.49**

CHARM is also evaluated against BERT as an end-to-end ranking method, which is trained to produce similarity scores for the pairs of input utterances and each document from the corresponding collection.

Table 9.1 shows the models' zero-shot performance (MRR and nDCG scores), evaluated on the 'unseen' attribute values, not present during training. It can be seen that CHARM significantly outperforms all unsupervised keyword-extraction baselines on both examined personal attributes. This implies that it is essential to train the cue detector to identify contexts and words descriptive of the attribute, as opposed to extracting general keywords, which the unsupervised keyword extractors produce. Additionally, CHARM outperforms BERT, which can be attributed to the lack of signal to fine-tune BERT's parameters so that the model could be extended to the unseen attribute values.

Analysis of selected terms: To perform qualitative analysis of the keywords that CHARM extracts, all query terms for the users with each predicted attribute value were collected and aggregated per attribute value. After that, the top 10 terms by the score from the cue detector were selected to represent the attribute value. Table 9.2 shows the results for several *professions*.

Table 9.2   CHARM's top 10 terms per label for profession *attributes*

	Profession					
	Barista (MRR=0.4, #sample=73)		Screenwriter (MRR=0.65, #sample=52)		Airplane pilot (MRR=0.64, #sample=14)	
CHARM terms	coffee	shop	script	story	pilot	flying
	starbucks	guitar	screenplay	film	flight	teacher
	store	student	screenwriting	films	training	fire
	school	customer	scripts	photo	fly	trading
	manager	college	writing	movie	pilots	military

It can be noted that the small sample size for some attribute values, such as *airplane pilot*, does not prevent CHARM from detecting meaningful words. To predict *barista* profession, CHARM did not even extract the term "barista" itself, but identified other related terms, such as "starbucks" and "coffee." Terms like "scripts," "screenwriting" or "screenplay," helped CHARM distinguish *screenwriter* from the other film-related occupations, for example, *director*.

The detected keywords are more meaningful and distinctive for the attribute values which obtained considerably high MRR scores (for instance, *profession:screenwriter*). On the other hand, although the low-scoring attribute values also have meaningful terms associated with them, they might be easily mixed with other similar attribute values.

9.3.5   Conclusion

In this section, we have reviewed the methods for predicting personal facts from conversational data, including dialogue transcriptions and social media interactions. We described a wide range of approaches to solving this task, from conventional pattern extraction to transformer-based approaches.

From the reviewed studies, we observe that one of the obstacles is the lack of precise definitions of *which* personal facts are critical and feasible to extract and *what form* of prediction is required. The outputs of current methods come in different flavors, such as the speaker's personal attribute values, classified on different granularity levels, textual descriptions, or latent representations of the speaker. It will take additional effort to process such results so that they are ready to be inserted in a PKG in a unified manner.

We described the model CHARM, which is a state-of-the-art model capable of predicting rare personal attribute values in a zero-shot setup. The drawback of this model is that its performance heavily hinges on external document collections, which has to be considerably clean and complete (e.g., to capture the most recent *hobby* trends, the document collection has to be regularly updated).

To conclude this section, we discuss possible future research directions for personal attribute prediction.

Transfer learning between different conversational genres is an important aspect that has to be addressed. Most experiments in the discussed studies rely on the assumption that the input utterances are similar to real daily conversations. Still, this is very often not the case: the dialogues in the movie scripts usually discuss fictional events and their utterances often sound metaphorical; crowdsourced chats are tailored for the given task and thus sound artificial; discussion threads on social media are different from face-to-face real dialogues in structure, length, and time span. Thus, transfer learning abilities of the proposed model are a valuable asset, enabling the model, trained on large-scale annotated artificial datasets, to make proper inference on the dialogues in real life.

Additionally, we find that there has been very limited work on predicting several personal attributes simultaneously. However, most personal traits are dependent on each other (e.g., a 5-year-old person cannot be a boss or have kids). Therefore, the model for predicting multiple personal attributes has to be able to take into account relationships between these attributes to make an end-to-end prediction of all available personal information with a single model. This enables to extend the proposed architecture to any new personal attribute and optimizes the use of computational resources, as opposed to training an isolated model for every attribute.

9.4   Extracting interpersonal relationships

A PKG which contains the knowledge about the users' interpersonal relationships is a valuable resource for various applications. For instance, a personalized chatbot, which has access to the relationship information, is able to better parse the user's commands, such as *"send a text to my father."* Moreover, the information about the user's relationships will enable the personal assistant to make more suitable suggestions (for instance, recommending the user to take their *child* to the amusement park instead of a night club). Finally, speech style of the AI assistant, which could vary from casual and friendly to strict and official, could be modified depending on the relationship between the present conversation participants.

Conversational data is the best source for interpersonal relationship inference: the demographic facts about the users could be inferred from their social media posts and user profile descriptions, while interpersonal relationships can only be predicted from the interactions between the users. For instance, recall the example conversation given in Section 9.1: specific terms (e.g., *sweetheart*) and speech style of the dialogue allowed us to predict that speaker B is a *child* of speaker A.

In this section, we will describe current work on predicting interpersonal relationships from conversations and provide an in-depth overview of the model PRIDE [22] for inferring directed fine-grained relationship labels.

9.4.1   Predicting interpersonal relationships

The body of research on relationship prediction in spoken conversations is pretty limited, while literary texts are more popular in this domain. Interpersonal relationships between book characters are often inferred as coarse categories (whether the sentiment of the interactions is positive or negative) [16], modeled in terms of emotions (fear or love) [73], or represented using topic-modeling techniques [17,74]. Literary texts contain not only dialogues but also narrative texts, the format of which is very different from conversations. The language in the narratives is descriptive, structured, and less colloquial, which helps to extract relationships of the fictional characters.

Meanwhile, scripts of movies, TV series, and theatre plays are closer to the dialogues happening in real life. Nalisnick and Baird [75] analyzed Shakespeare plays and predicted the intensity and polarity of characters' emotions toward each other. Azab *et al.* [44] also used the same data to infer fine-grained relationship labels formulated by Massey *et al.* [18]. To make predictions for a pair of learned *character embeddings*, the study [44] used a logistic regression model. Yet, the proposed approach considers only characters' latent attributes, while the dialogue context is not taken into account.

The study [20] predicted speakers' relationships as a part of a general relation extraction task for a pair of entities mentioned in a conversation (e.g., *place_of_residence* or *spouse*), taken from the TV series Friends; the authors consider 14 predicates descriptive of interpersonal relationships. To predict relations from a conversational snippet the authors used BERT [68], which input was constructed from the text of the dialogue concatenated with two relation arguments.

Chen *et al.* [19] also worked with dialogues from TV series; the authors asked three human workers to annotate the scripts with 7 emotions and 24 relationship labels. The relationship classes were split by field (school, family, company, or other) and seniority of the interlocutors (elder, junior or peer); each dialogue excerpt was labeled with only one relationship class. As input for the relationship prediction models (BERT and CNN), the authors used a single pair of utterances, which can be misleading without the surrounding context.

Jia *et al.* [21] considered 13 relationship labels to annotate a set of movie scripts to create the DDRel dataset; the labels were split into four categories (family, official, intimacy, or others). The authors use BERT to infer the labels, taking as input a dialogue session for a given pair of interlocutors. The limitation of this work is that the predicted set of labels is not directed (e.g., the model does not distinguish between *boss* and *employee* relationships) and the model allows only for one relationship value to be predicted.

An important aspect of relationship prediction is identifying the addressee of each utterance in a multi-speaker context. One possible simplifying assumption is suggested by Nalisnick and Baird [75], proposing to assume that the sentiment in the utterance is always targeted toward the speaker who spoke right before it. Another approach, utilized in the studies working with literary texts, is to use text spans containing mentions of two characters of interest [17]; other works applied a Markov model to find the sentences that discuss the relationship [16].

Finally, there is ample research on constructing *social networks* of characters in books and movies. Although this task is pretty close to relationship prediction, it is mostly concerned with predicting whether two people interact, as opposed to figuring out the nature of their interaction (i.e., their relationship). A social network is usually formed by considering the interactions (conversations) or co-occurrences of characters (for instance, appearing together in screenplay acts [76]). Movie scripts are used in [77] to construct a social network, which is later used for text analysis (characterizing the script by author, date, etc.). A comprehensive survey for character network construction is provided in [78].

A useful cue for both inference and pattern-based approaches is the address terms (such as "sir" in the utterance "*Here you are, sir*"). They are comprehensively studied in [79], where the address terms are inferred jointly with a character social network.

9.4.2   Predicting relationship characteristics

Interactions between people can be characterized by several descriptive features, which represent various aspects of the way people communicate. For instance, interactions could be described in terms of the attachment style (for instance, *avoidance* or *commitment*) [80] or power hierarchy (*superior* or *subordinate*) [81]. There exists a large body of social studies researching these characteristics; however, there is no unified formal ontology that all of these studies utilize [82]. Still, analyzing the relationships with the help of communication-style features can be useful in development of predictive models, because most relationships have a characterizing set of such features. For instance, a *child-parent* relationship is usually *intimate*; a relationship between *enemies* can be characterized as *competitive* as opposed to *cooperative*.

Rashid and Blanco [83] proposed an approach to organize the features of interpersonal communication, defined as *interpersonal dimensions*, which consist of dimensions of relationships and interactions. The authors investigated the inference of nine interpersonal dimensions (e.g., *pleasure-oriented* or *intense*) [84] from the dialogue utterances in the TV series Friends. The authors used SVM classifiers on the bag-of-words features, trained separately for each dimension of relationships, which predicted for each input utterance whether it can be characterized by the given dimension.

Similarly, Qamar *et al.* [80] classified movie dialogues by building vector representations of emotion terms. The authors consider 4 attachment styles (for instance, *family* or *friend* attachment) and 4 association types (for example, *fearful* or *secure* association); their combinations produced 16 relationship labels. However, both described methods mostly focus on relationship characteristics, as opposed to providing explicit and specific facts about the speakers' relationships (such as who is the *child* of whom between the speakers).

9.4.3   PRIDE: predicting directed, fine-grained interpersonal relationships

To be applicable in the downstream services, predicted relationships should draw clear distinction between different interaction types. To achieve that, predictions should be

*   on a fine-granularity (e.g., not only predicting the *business* category of the relationship but also specifying whether the user is talking to a *colleague* or a *boss*);
*   taking into account the direction of the relationship between the speakers in the conversation (i.e., not only stating that the conversation is happening between a *parent* and *child* but also specifying, who of the speakers is a *parent*).

Drawing such distinctions is crucial for the downstream applications to correctly address the requests of the user.

The studies described in this section have only investigated predicting *undirected relationships*. In the following, we are going to describe the model PRIDE for **P**redicting **R**elationships **I**n **D**ialogu**E** [22], which addresses this limitation by building efficient multi-speaker representations of conversations. PRIDE is enhanced with additional information about the conversation style (e.g., *superficial* or *intense*) and the users' personal facts (for instance, *occupation* or *age*). These signals help PRIDE make accurate predictions on the fine-grained scale, performing inference among 12 directed relationships.

9.4.3.1   Methodology

The design of PRIDE, shown in Figure 9.2, is based on dialogue features, for instance the structure of the conversation and the attribution of each utterance to its corresponding speaker. PRIDE hierarchically constructs representations of words and utterances, which are afterwards combined with interpersonal dimensions and the representations of personal attributes, which together create a whole representation of the conversation history. Taking as an input this representation of the conversation, a classification layer predicts a subset of relationship labels in a multi-label classification setup. Next we provide a few details on each component of the model.

Contextual word representations: The representations of the input terms w_i^j in the conversational utterances are created with BERT [68]. BERT's segment embeddings are used as information about the current speaker, so that segment A corresponds to the words produced by speaker A and segment B to the words from speaker B. Further, the information about the boundaries of the utterance is encoded by prepending special tokens to every input utterance: the utterances of speaker A are prepended with [s1] and [s2] is added to the utterances of speaker B.

Utterance representations: After that, the representations of input terms are aggregated for each utterance to construct the utterance representation using an aggregation function (which can be max- or average-pooling).

The representations of the utterances, r_i, are summed with speaker embeddings sp_i and sinusoidal positional encoding p_i. Positional encoding, which is added to

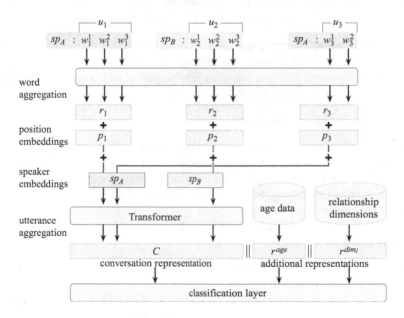

Figure 9.2   PRIDE model

the utterances, is calculated following [85]; the speaker embeddings are learned during model training. After that, to capture the utterance interaction in the unified context, they are passed through a Transformer encoder. The resulting utterance representations are aggregated using max- or average-pooling to produce conversation representation C.

To add external information, which is relevant to relationship prediction, the authors concatenate embeddings of interpersonal dimensions and personal attributes to the representation of the conversation C.

Incorporating personal attributes: Relationship prediction can be facilitated by adding *age* information into the model because many relationships can be characterized by differences between the speakers' ages (e.g., parents are usually much older than their children).

The age information in PRIDE is incorporated via a representation of speakers' age difference r^{age}, which is assigned to one of 6 age bins, the embeddings for which are learned during model training.

Incorporating interpersonal dimensions: As discussed previously, the relationships between people have fine-grained characteristics, which are called *interpersonal dimensions* [84]. For example, a relationship between a *boss* and an employee is hierarchical, whereas *colleague* is an equal relationship. Likewise, *spouse* can be considered an intimate relationship, as opposed to *colleague*.

PRIDE is enhanced with representations of 11 such relationship dimensions. To obtain the representation for each dimension l, the authors use a pre-trained BERT classifier on the concatenation of the input utterances. Each trained classifier produces a representation of the input conversation r^{dim_l} for lth dimension.

Classification layer: The representation of conversation C is then concatenated with age information r^{age} and relationship dimension representations r^{dim_l}. A fully connected layer consumes the concatenated representation and outputs the probability scores for the 12 relationship labels.

9.4.3.2 Experimental results

Setup: PRIDE is trained on data from the FiRe dataset [22], described in Section 9.2. FiRe contains movie character pairs, labeled by crowdsourcing workers with fine-grained directed relationship labels. The age information about the characters in the dataset is obtained by taking the ages of the actors who played them at the time the movie was filmed.

PRIDE was compared to the state-of-the-art models for predicting personal information and relationships:

- **HAM** [14] builds hierarchical representations for dialogues but does not distinguish the speakers.
- **BERT**$_{conv}$ for sequence classification [86] applies BERT on the concatenated sequence of dialogue utterances, cropping the inputs which do not fit into 512-token limit.

Table 9.3   Results of PRIDE and baselines on FiRe dataset.

	F1	precision	recall
BERT$_{ddrel}$	0.20	0.20	0.25
HAM	0.23	0.25	0.22
BERT$_{conv}$	0.27	0.25	0.33
PRIDE	**0.38**	**0.42**	**0.37**

- **BERT$_{ddrel}$** [21] makes relationship predictions for each short snippet, ignoring the context of the whole conversational history.

Quantitative results: Table 9.3 presents the main quantitative results. PRIDE was found to significantly outperform all considered baselines, including BERT-based models. PRIDE internally learns to build a representation of the whole conversation, as opposed to BERT$_{ddrel}$, which makes predictions on separate conversation snippets and aggregates them outside of the model. Moreover, compared to BERT$_{conv}$, PRIDE does not use cropping to limit the input sequence to only 512 tokens, additionally incorporating the hierarchical structure of the input dialogues.

Ablation study: The authors of PRIDE performed an ablation analysis, to check how different components of PRIDE influence its performance. This was done by removing the model's components one at a time, such as eliminating interpersonal dimensions and age representations or removing positional and speaker embeddings from Transformer's input. The ablation on Transformer is done by removing this whole component and creating the representations for words and utterances using only consecutive aggregation operations.

Table 9.4 shows the results of the ablation study. Removing the positional encoding impacts least to the performance drop. Meanwhile, the quality of predictions considerably reduces when Transformer is removed, which in particular causes a very low recall. It can be observed that eliminating other elements reduced precision, which shows that adding interpersonal dimensions and age differences improves performance.

9.4.4   Discussion

In this section, we summarized the existing methods for interpersonal relationship prediction. The information about relationships is a valuable asset in a PKG, which can be used in a wide range of practical applications, such as chat-bot assistants. The studies that we discuss cover various input data sources (literary texts, movie, and TV series scripts), prediction methods (topic modeling, neural classifiers, etc.), and relationship label granularity (binary labels, indicating the sentiment, or fine-grained classes). Finally, we discussed the model PRIDE, showing the impact of

Table 9.4   Ablation of PRIDE model's components

Model	F1	Precision	Recall
PRIDE	**0.38**	0.42	0.37
PRIDE – dimensions	0.36	0.36	0.40
PRIDE – age	0.37	0.38	0.37
PRIDE – speaker	0.35	0.37	0.36
PRIDE – positional	0.37	0.36	**0.41**
PRIDE – transformer	0.35	**0.46**	0.33

incorporating external signals (such as personal information about the speakers and relationship characteristics) into relationship prediction.

Additionally, we note that there is no universally accepted classification of inter-personal relationships and no established benchmarks for relationship prediction, which arguably causes slow progress in this area. It is worth mentioning that identify-ing relationships is a subjective task, challenging not only for the automated methods but also for humans, which is surfaced by the low inter-annotator agreement in the labeled relationship datasets [22].

Finally, we outline several possible future research directions. First, there is a need to collect or annotate diverse *real-life* conversational datasets with relationship labels. Most of the current studies use movie scripts as a proxy for real dialogues, because of the complexity, costs, and privacy issues with manually labeling relation-ship datasets. However, movie plots contain unnatural texts and skewed relationship label distribution. Such artificial data is not the best option for training downstream models operating in real-life settings.

Another important issue is enabling the models to handle conversations with more than two speakers. The studies we have discussed are limited to the dialogues between two interlocutors; in real life people usually interact in a group, therefore, taking into account only speaker pairs can cause a loss of useful cues from other conversation participants. Designing methods for group conversations is specifically challenging because in this setting, the model has to keep track of all conversation participants and distinguish the addressee of each utterance.

9.5   Conclusion

In this chapter, we gave an overview of the current research on predicting personal facts from dialogue data. Personal facts can be utilized to populate a personal knowl-edge graph, which is a useful resource for multiple downstream applications. Dialogue utterances are very ambiguous, which makes it challenging to process them automat-ically; therefore, there is only very limited research on the inference of speakers' personal facts. In the current section, we will summarize the contents of the chapter and provide an outlook on further research.

In Section 9.2, we described existing conversational datasets, labeled with personal attributes. Training supervised models for inferring personal facts heavily relies on these datasets; however, we note that currently there is a very limited amount of them.

Predicting personal features of the speakers is described in Section 9.3, where we looked at the broad range of current methods for this task. Although the related studies managed to develop efficient approaches to inferring personal facts with high accuracy, we still find several open problems to address, such as inter-dataset transfer learning and coverage of predicted attributes and their values.

Finally, in Section 9.4, we discussed the methods for predicting interpersonal relationships. The major disadvantage of most current methods is the coarse granularity of the relationships predicted, whereas few proposed models making fine-grained predictions do not provide sufficient precision to be used in practical applications.

9.5.1 Future research directions

In conclusion, we outline possible research directions to facilitate personal attribute prediction from conversations.

Open-ended attributes: One of the major limitations of the existing models is their inability to predict *open-ended* speakers' attributes, for example, their *favorite song*. It is not possible to compile comprehensive lists of possible attribute values for this kind of attributes, especially in cases when there are new values constantly emerging (e.g., new songs appearing every day). Zero-shot learning methods can be used to address this problem, especially the ones relying on external sources of information, like encyclopedic articles or knowledge bases.

Continuous incremental predictions: The utterances in dialogues are usually spread in time, being produced one by one in a conversation. Each new utterance can contain cues, contradicting the ones from the previous utterances, which reflects how the speaker's preferences (or even demographic information) change. Personal knowledge graph should be kept up-to-date with respect to this kind of changes, which requires updating and weighting the cues extracted from the dialogue utterances and incrementally learning personal information.

Leveraging third-party information: Populating a personal knowledge graph for a particular user can involve digesting what other people say *to* this person or *about* them. The majority of discussed methods do not draw specific distinction between the information that comes from different speakers. The model ideally has to be able to incorporate the cues from both the direct interlocutor of the current subject ("*you must be coming from your shift at the hospital*") and a third party, especially in the cases when the subject does not produce any utterances in the current conversation ("*Brandon is doing a lot of overtime in the hospital recently*").

Using speaker network: In addition to the previous point, we suggest that several personal attributes and relationships can be predicted simultaneously for all dialogue participants as a group, which can be done within a current conversation or incorporating the whole interaction history. For instance, using the dependency of interpersonal relationships, one can increase the accuracy of the relationship classifier (for example, knowing that speakers A and B are the *children* of speaker C one can infer with greater probability that A and B have a *sibling* relationship). Graph methods can be used to perform joint inference for all conversation participants, enabling information sharing between the representations of speakers as graph nodes.

References

[1]   Flekova L, Carpenter J, Giorgi S, *et al*. Analyzing biases in human perception of user age and gender from text. In: *Proceedings of the 54th Annual Meeting of the Association for Computational Linguistics (Volume 1: Long Papers). Berlin, Germany: Association for Computational Linguistics*; 2016. p. 843–854. Available from: https://aclanthology.org/P16-1080.

[2]   Basile A, Dwyer G, Medvedeva M, *et al*. N-GrAM: new Groningen author-profiling model—notebook for PAN at CLEF 2017. In: *Working Notes Papers of the Conference and Labs of the Evaluation Forum, CLEF 2017 Evaluation Labs*; 2017.

[3]   Bontcheva K and Rout D. Making sense of social media streams through semantics: a survey. *Semantic Web*. 2014;5(5):373–403.

[4]   Li J, Galley M, Brockett C, *et al*. A persona-based neural conversation model. In: *Proceedings of the 54th Annual Meeting of the Association for Computational Linguistics* (Volume 1: Long Papers). Berlin, Germany: Association for Computational Linguistics; 2016. p. 994–1003. Available from: https://aclanthology.org/P16-1094.

[5]   Lin G and Walker M. All the world's a stage: Learning character models from film. In: *Proceedings of the AAAI Conference on Artificial Intelligence and Interactive Digital Entertainment*. vol. 6; 2011.

[6]   Tigunova A, Yates A, Mirza P, *et al*. CHARM: inferring personal attributes from conversations. In: *Proceedings of the 2020 Conference on Empirical Methods in Natural Language Processing (EMNLP)*. Online: Association for Computational Linguistics; 2020. p. 5391–5404. Available from: https://aclanthology.org/2020.emnlp-main.434.

[7]   Tigunova A, Mirza P, Yates A, *et al*. Exploring personal knowledge extraction from conversations with CHARM. In: *Proceedings of the 14th ACM International Conference on Web Search and Data Mining*; 2021. p. 1077–1080.

[8]   Cieri C, Miller D, and Walker K. The Fisher Corpus: a resource for the next generations of speech-to-text. In: *Proceedings of the Fourth International Conference on Language Resources and Evaluation (LREC'04)*. Lisbon, Portugal: European Language Resources Association (ELRA); 2004. Available from: http://www.lrec-conf.org/proceedings/lrec2004/pdf/767.pdf.

[9]   Love R, Dembry C, Hardie A, *et al*. The Spoken BNC2014: designing and building a spoken corpus of everyday conversations. *International Journal of Corpus Linguistics*. 2017;22(3):319–344.

[10] Zhang S, Dinan E, Urbanek J, *et al*. Personalizing dialogue agents: I have a dog, do you have pets too? In: *Proceedings of the 56th Annual Meeting of the Association for Computational Linguistics* (Volume 1: Long Papers). Melbourne, Australia: Association for Computational Linguistics; 2018. p. 2204–2213. Available from: https://aclanthology.org/P18-1205.

[11] Joshi CK, Mi F, and Faltings B. Personalization in goal-oriented dialog. In: *Proceedings of Conversational AI Workshop, Neural Information Processing Systems*, NIPS'17; 2017.

[12] Tigunova A, Mirza P, Yates A, *et al*. RedDust: a large reusable dataset of Reddit user traits. In: *Proceedings of the 12th Language Resources and Evaluation Conference*. Marseille, France: European Language Resources Association; 2020. p. 6118–6126. Available from: https://aclanthology.org/2020.lrec-1.751.

[13] Bordes A, Boureau Y, and Weston J. Learning end-to-end goal-oriented dialog. In: *5th International Conference on Learning Representations, ICLR 2017*, Toulon, France, April 24–26, 2017, Conference Track Proceedings. OpenReview.net; 2017. Available from: https://openreview.net/forum?id=S1Bb3D5gg.

[14] Tigunova A, Yates A, Mirza P, *et al*. Listening between the lines: learning personal attributes from conversations. In: Liu L, White RW, Mantrach A, *et al*., editors. *The World Wide Web Conference, WWW 2019*, San Francisco, CA, USA, May 13–17, 2019. ACM; 2019. p. 1818–1828. Available from: https://doi.org/10.1145/3308558.3313498.

[15] Danescu-Niculescu-Mizil C and Lee L. Chameleons in imagined conversations: a new approach to understanding coordination of linguistic style in dialogs. In: *Proceedings of the 2nd Workshop on Cognitive Modeling and Computational Linguistics*. Portland, OR, USA: Association for Computational Linguistics; 2011. p. 76–87. Available from: https://aclanthology.org/W11-0609.

[16] Chaturvedi S, Srivastava S, III HD, *et al*. Modeling evolving relationships between characters in literary novels. In: Schuurmans D and Wellman MP, editors. *Proceedings of the Thirtieth AAAI Conference on Artificial Intelligence*, Phoenix, AZ, USA, February 12–17, 2016. AAAI Press; 2016. p. 2704–2710. Available from: http://www.aaai.org/ocs/index.php/AAAI/AAAI16/paper/view/12408.

[17] Iyyer M, Guha A, Chaturvedi S, *et al*. Feuding families and former friends: unsupervised learning for dynamic fictional relationships. In: *Proceedings of the 2016 Conference of the North American Chapter of the Association for Computational Linguistics: Human Language Technologies*. San Diego, CA: Association for Computational Linguistics; 2016. p. 1534–1544. Available from: https://aclanthology.org/N16-1180.

[18] Massey P, Xia P, Bamman D, *et al*. Annotating character relationships in literary texts. ArXiv preprint. 2015;abs/1512.00728. Available from: https://arxiv.org/abs/1512.00728.

[19] Chen YT, Huang HH, and Chen HH. MPDD: a multi-party dialogue dataset for analysis of emotions and interpersonal relationships. In: *Proceedings of*

the 12th Language Resources and Evaluation Conference. Marseille, France: European Language Resources Association; 2020. p. 610–614. Available from: https://aclanthology.org/2020.lrec-1.76.

[20] Yu D, Sun K, Cardie C, *et al*. Dialogue-based relation extraction. In: *Proceedings of the 58th Annual Meeting of the Association for Computational Linguistics*. Online: Association for Computational Linguistics; 2020. pp. 4927–4940. Available from: https://aclanthology.org/2020.acl-main.444.

[21] Jia Q, Huang H, and Zhu KQ. DDRel: A new dataset for interpersonal relation classification in dyadic dialogues. *AAAI* 2021;35(14):13125–13133.

[22] Tigunova A, Mirza P, Yates A, *et al*. PRIDE: predicting relationships in conversations. In: *Proceedings of the 2021 Conference on Empirical Methods in Natural Language Processing*; 2021. p. 4636–4650.

[23] Sap M, Park G, Eichstaedt J, *et al*. Developing age and gender predictive Lexica over social media. In: *Proceedings of the 2014 Conference on Empirical Methods in Natural Language Processing (EMNLP)*. Doha, Qatar: Association for Computational Linguistics; 2014. p. 1146–1151. Available from: https://aclanthology.org/D14-1121.

[24] Schwartz HA, Eichstaedt JC, Kern ML, *et al*. Personality, gender, and age in the language of social media: the open-vocabulary approach. *PLoS ONE*. 2013;8(9):e73791.

[25] Fabian B, Baumann A, and Keil M. Privacy on Reddit? Towards large-scale user classification. In: *Proceedings of ECIS'15*; 2015.

[26] Finlay SC. Age and gender in Reddit commenting and success. *Journal of Information Science Theory and Practice*. 2014;2(3):18–28.

[27] Gjurković M and Šnajder J. Reddit: a gold mine for personality prediction. In: *Proceedings of the Second Workshop on Computational Modeling of People's Opinions, Personality, and Emotions in Social Media*. New Orleans, LO, USA: Association for Computational Linguistics; 2018. p. 87–97. Available from: https://aclanthology.org/W18-1112.

[28] Preoţiuc-Pietro D, Lampos V, and Aletras N. An analysis of the user occupational class through Twitter content. In: *Proceedings of the 53rd Annual Meeting of the Association for Computational Linguistics and the 7th International Joint Conference on Natural Language Processing* (Vol. 1: Long Papers). Beijing, China: Association for Computational Linguistics; 2015. p. 1754–1764. Available from: https://aclanthology.org/P15-1169.

[29] Rao D, Yarowsky D, Shreevats A, *et al*. Classifying latent user attributes in twitter. In: *Proceedings of the 2nd International Workshop on Search and Mining User-Generated Contents*. ACM; 2010. p. 37–44.

[30] Burger JD, Henderson J, Kim G, *et al*. Discriminating gender on Twitter. In: *Proceedings of the 2011 Conference on Empirical Methods in Natural Language Processing*. Edinburgh, Scotland, UK: Association for Computational Linguistics; 2011. p. 1301–1309. Available from: https://aclanthology.org/D11-1120.

[31] Preoţiuc-Pietro D, Liu Y, Hopkins D, *et al*. Beyond binary labels: political ideology prediction of Twitter users. In: *Proceedings of the 55th Annual Meeting of*

the Association for Computational Linguistics (Volume 1: Long Papers). Vancouver, Canada: Association for Computational Linguistics; 2017. p. 729–740. Available from: https://aclanthology.org/P17-1068.

[32] Preoţiuc-Pietro D, and Ungar L. User-level race and ethnicity predictors from Twitter text. In: *Proceedings of the 27th International Conference on Computational Linguistics*. Santa Fe, NM, USA: Association for Computational Linguistics; 2018. p. 1534–1545. Available from: https://aclanthology.org/C18-1130.

[33] Schwartz HA, Eichstaedt JC, Kern ML, *et al.* Personality, gender, and age in the language of social media: the open-vocabulary approach. *PLoS ONE.* 2013;8(9):e73791.

[34] Kim SM, Xu Q, Qu L, *et al.* Demographic inference on Twitter using recursive neural networks. In: *Proceedings of the 55th Annual Meeting of the Association for Computational Linguistics* (Vol. 2: Short Papers). Vancouver, Canada: Association for Computational Linguistics; 2017. p. 471–477. Available from: https://aclanthology.org/P17-2075.

[35] Sloan L, Morgan J, Burnap P, *et al.* Who tweets? Deriving the demographic characteristics of age, occupation and social class from Twitter user meta-data. *PLoS ONE.* 2015;10(3):e0115545.

[36] Thelwall M and Stuart E. She's Reddit: a source of statistically significant gendered interest information? *Information Processing & Management.* 2019;56(4):1543 – 1558. Available from: http://www.sciencedirect.com/science/article/pii/S0306457318304692.

[37] Welch C, Pérez-Rosas V, Kummerfeld JK, *et al.* Look who's talking: inferring speaker attributes from personal longitudinal dialog. ArXiv preprint. 2019;abs/1904.11610. Available from: https://arxiv.org/abs/1904.11610.

[38] Garera N and Yarowsky D. Modeling latent biographic attributes in conversational genres. In: *Proceedings of the Joint Conference of the 47th Annual Meeting of the ACL and the 4th International Joint Conference on Natural Language Processing of the AFNLP.* Suntec, Singapore: Association for Computational Linguistics; 2009. p. 710–718. Available from: https://aclanthology.org/P09-1080.

[39] Li X, Tür G, Hakkani-Tür DZ, *et al.* Personal knowledge graph population from user utterances in conversational understanding. In: *Proceedings of IEEE Spoken Language Technology Workshop (SLT)*; 2014.

[40] Jing H, Kambhatla N, and Roukos S. Extracting social networks and biographical facts from conversational speech transcripts. In: *Proceedings of the 45th Annual Meeting of the Association of Computational Linguistics.* Prague, Czech Republic: Association for Computational Linguistics; 2007. p. 1040–1047. Available from: https://aclanthology.org/P07-1131.

[41] Song Y, Liu Z, Bi W, *et al.* Learning to Customize Language Model for Generation-based dialog systems. ArXiv preprint. 2019;abs/1910.14326. Available from: https://arxiv.org/abs/1910.14326.

[42] Luo L, Huang W, Zeng Q, *et al.* Learning personalized end-to-end goal-oriented dialog. In: *The Thirty-Third AAAI Conference on Artificial Intelligence,*

AAAI 2019, Honolulu, Hawaii, USA, January 27–February 1, 2019. AAAI Press; 2019. p. 6794–6801. Available from: https://doi.org/10.1609/aaai.v33i01.33016794.

[43]   Wu CS, Madotto A, Lin Z, *et al*. Getting to know you: user attribute extraction from dialogues. In: *Proceedings of the 12th Language Resources and Evaluation Conference*. Marseille, France: European Language Resources Association; 2020. p. 581–589. Available from: https://aclanthology.org/2020.lrec-1.73.

[44]   Azab M, Kojima N, Deng J, *et al*. Representing movie characters in dialogues. In: *Proceedings of the 23rd Conference on Computational Natural Language Learning (CoNLL)*. Hong Kong, China: Association for Computational Linguistics; 2019. p. 99–109. Available from: https://aclanthology.org/K19-1010.

[45]   Wang Z, Zhou X, Koncel-Kedziorski R, *et al*. Extracting and inferring personal attributes from dialogue. In: *Proceedings of the 4th Workshop on NLP for Conversational AI*; 2022. p. 58–69.

[46]   Pennacchiotti M and Popescu AM. A machine learning approach to twitter user classification. In: *Fifth International AAAI Conference on Weblogs and Social Media*; 2011.

[47]   Kapanipathi P, Jain P, Venkataramani C, *et al*. User interests identification on twitter using a hierarchical knowledge base. In: *Proceedings of Extended Semantic Web Conference, ESWC'14*. Springer; 2014. p. 99–113.

[48]   Markovikj D, Gievska S, Kosinski M, *et al*. Mining Facebook data for predictive personality modeling. In: *The International AAAI Conference on Web and Social Media, ICWSM 2013*; 2013.

[49]   Zheng Y, Chen G, Huang M, *et al*. Personalized dialogue generation with diversified traits. ArXiv preprint. 2019;abs/1901.09672. Available from: https://arxiv.org/abs/1901.09672.

[50]   Lai Y, Su Y, Xue C, *et al*. Neural demographic prediction in social media with deep multi-view multi-task learning. In: *International Conference on Database Systems for Advanced Applications*. Springer; 2021. p. 271–279.

[51]   Li Y, Yang L, Xu B, *et al*. Improving user attribute classification with text and social network attention. *Cognitive Computation*. 2019;11(4):459–468.

[52]   Li J, Ritter A, and Hovy E. Weakly supervised user profile extraction from Twitter. In: *Proceedings of the 52nd Annual Meeting of the Association for Computational Linguistics* (Vol. 1: Long Papers). Baltimore, MD: Association for Computational Linguistics; 2014. p. 165–174. Available from: https://aclanthology.org/P14-1016.

[53]   Shen JH and Rudzicz F. Detecting anxiety through Reddit. In: *Proceedings of the Fourth Workshop on Computational Linguistics and Clinical Psychology—From Linguistic Signal to Clinical Reality*. Vancouver, BC: Association for Computational Linguistics; 2017. p. 58–65. Available from: https://aclanthology.org/W17-3107.

[54]   Seghouani NB, Jipmo CN, and Quercini G. Determining the interests of social media users: two approaches. *Information Retrieval Journal*. 2019;22(1–2):129–158.

[55] Raghuram MA, Akshay K, and Chandrasekaran K. Efficient user profiling in twitter social network using traditional classifiers. In: *Intelligent Systems Technologies and Applications*. Springer; 2016. p. 399–411.

[56] Piao G and Breslin JG. Inferring user interests in microblogging social networks: a survey. *User Modeling and User-Adapted Interaction*. 2018;28(3): 277–329.

[57] Weng J, Lim E, Jiang J, *et al*. TwitterRank: finding topic-sensitive influential twitterers. In: Davison BD, Suel T, Craswell N, *et al*., editors. *Proceedings of the Third International Conference on Web Search and Web Data Mining, WSDM 2010*, New York, NY, USA, February 4–6, 2010. ACM; 2010. p. 261–270. Available from: https://doi.org/10.1145/1718487.1718520.

[58] Michelson M and Macskassy SA. Discovering users' topics of interest on twitter: a first look. In: *Proceedings of the Fourth Workshop on Analytics for Noisy Unstructured Text Data*; 2010. p. 73–80.

[59] Serban IV, Sordoni A, Bengio Y, *et al*. Building end-to-end dialogue systems using generative hierarchical neural network models. In: Schuurmans D and Wellman MP, editors. *Proceedings of the Thirtieth AAAI Conference on Artificial Intelligence*, Phoenix, AZ, USA, February 12–17, 2016. AAAI Press; 2016. p. 3776–3784. Available from: http://www.aaai.org/ocs/index.php/AAAI/AAAI16/paper/view/11957.

[60] Xing C, Wu Y, Wu W, *et al*. Hierarchical Recurrent Attention Network for Response Generation. In: McIlraith SA and Weinberger KQ, editors. *Proceedings of the Thirty-Second AAAI Conference on Artificial Intelligence, (AAAI-18)*, New Orleans, LO, USA, February 2–7, 2018. AAAI Press; 2018. p. 5610–5617. Available from: https://www.aaai.org/ocs/index.php/AAAI/AAAI18/paper/view/16510.

[61] Li Q, Wu C, Wang Z, *et al*. Hierarchical transformer network for utterance-level emotion recognition. *Applied Sciences*. 2020;10(13). Available from: https://www.mdpi.com/2076-3417/10/13/4447.

[62] Ma H, Wang J, Qian L, *et al*. HAN-ReGRU: Hierarchical attention network with residual gated recurrent unit for emotion recognition in conversation. *Neural Computing and Applications*. 2020;33:2685–2703. Available from: https://link.springer.com/article/10.1007%2Fs00521-020-05063-7.

[63] Shan Y, Li Z, Zhang J, *et al*. A contextual hierarchical attention network with adaptive objective for dialogue state tracking. In: *Proceedings of the 58th Annual Meeting of the Association for Computational Linguistics*. Online: Association for Computational Linguistics; 2020. p. 6322–6333. Available from: https://aclanthology.org/2020.acl-main.563.

[64] Lynn V, Balasubramanian N, and Schwartz HA. Hierarchical modeling for user personality prediction: the role of message-level attention. In: *Proceedings of the 58th Annual Meeting of the Association for Computational Linguistics*. Online: Association for Computational Linguistics; 2020. p. 5306–5316. Available from: https://aclanthology.org/2020.acl-main.472.

[65] Hu W, Chan Z, Liu B, *et al.* GSN: a graph-structured network for multi-party dialogues. In: Kraus S, editor. *Proceedings of the Twenty-Eighth International Joint Conference on Artificial Intelligence, IJCAI 2019*, Macao, China, August 10–16, 2019. ijcai.org; 2019. p. 5010–5016. Available from: https://doi.org/10.24963/ijcai.2019/696.

[66] Ghosal D, Majumder N, Poria S, *et al.* DialogueGCN: a graph convolutional neural network for emotion recognition in conversation. In: *Proceedings of the 2019 Conference on Empirical Methods in Natural Language Processing and the 9th International Joint Conference on Natural Language Processing (EMNLP-IJCNLP)*. Hong Kong, China: Association for Computational Linguistics; 2019. p. 154–164. Available from: https://aclanthology.org/D19-1015.

[67] Zhang D, Wu L, Sun C, *et al.* Modeling both context- and speaker-sensitive dependence for emotion detection in multi-speaker conversations. In: Kraus S, editor. *Proceedings of the Twenty-Eighth International Joint Conference on Artificial Intelligence, IJCAI 2019*, Macao, China, August 10–16, 2019. ijcai.org; 2019. p. 5415–5421. Available from: https://doi.org/10.24963/ijcai.2019/752.

[68] Devlin J, Chang MW, Lee K, *et al.* BERT: pre-training of deep bidirectional transformers for language understanding. In: *Proceedings of the 2019 Conference of the North American Chapter of the Association for Computational Linguistics: Human Language Technologies*, Vol. 1 (Long and Short Papers). Minneapolis, MN: Association for Computational Linguistics; 2019. p. 4171–4186. Available from: https://aclanthology.org/N19-1423.

[69] Xiong C, Dai Z, Callan J, *et al.* End-to-end neural ad-hoc ranking with kernel pooling. In: Kando N, Sakai T, Joho H, *et al.*, editors. *Proceedings of the 40th International ACM SIGIR Conference on Research and Development in Information Retrieval*, Shinjuku, Tokyo, Japan, August 7–11, 2017. ACM; 2017. p. 55–64. Available from: https://doi.org/10.1145/3077136.3080809.

[70] Robertson SE, Walker S, Jones S, *et al. Okapi at TREC-3*. Nist Special Publication Sp. 1995. p. 109.

[71] Mihalcea R and Tarau P. TextRank: bringing order into text. In: *Proceedings of the 2004 Conference on Empirical Methods in Natural Language Processing*. Barcelona, Spain: Association for Computational Linguistics; 2004. p. 404–411. Available from: https://aclanthology.org/W04-3252.

[72] Rose S, Engel D, Cramer N, *et al.* Automatic keyword extraction from individual documents. *Text Mining: Applications and Theory*. 2010;1:1–20.

[73] Kim E and Klinger R. Frowning Frodo, Wincing Leia, and a seriously great friendship: learning to classify emotional relationships of fictional characters. In: *Proceedings of the 2019 Conference of the North American Chapter of the Association for Computational Linguistics: Human Language Technologies*, Vol. 1 (Long and Short Papers). Minneapolis, MN: Association for Computational Linguistics; 2019. p. 647–653. Available from: https://aclanthology.org/N19-1067.

[74] Chaturvedi S, Iyyer M, and III HD. Unsupervised learning of evolving relationships between literary characters. In: Singh SP and Markovitch S, editors. *Proceedings of the Thirty-First AAAI Conference on Artificial Intelligence*, February 4–9, 2017, San Francisco, CA, USA. AAAI Press; 2017. p. 3159–3165. Available from: http://aaai.org/ocs/index.php/AAAI/AAAI17/paper/view/14564.

[75] Nalisnick ET and Baird HS. Character-to-character sentiment analysis in Shakespeare's plays. In: *Proceedings of the 51st Annual Meeting of the Association for Computational Linguistics* (Vol. 2: Short Papers). Sofia, Bulgaria: Association for Computational Linguistics; 2013. p. 479–483. Available from: https://aclanthology.org/P13-2085.

[76] Makris C and Vikatos P. Community detection of screenplay characters. In: *Ifip International Conference on Artificial Intelligence Applications and Innovations*. Springer; 2016. p. 463–470.

[77] Gil S, Kuenzel L, and Caroline S. Extraction and analysis of character interaction networks from plays and movies. *CS 224W Final Project Report Sunday*. Retrieved June. 2011;15:2016.

[78] Labatut V and Bost X. Extraction and analysis of fictional character networks: a survey. *ACM Computing Surveys (CSUR)*. 2019;52(5):89.

[79] Krishnan V and Eisenstein J. "You're Mr. Lebowski, I'm the Dude": Inducing Address Term Formality in Signed Social Networks. arXiv preprint arXiv:14114351. 2014.

[80] Qamar S, Mujtaba H, Majeed H, *et al.* Relationship identification between conversational agents using emotion analysis. *Cognitive Computation*. 2021;13:673–687. Available from: https://link.springer.com/article/10.1007/s12559-020-09806-5.

[81] Prabhakaran V and Rambow O. Predicting power relations between participants in written dialog from a single thread. In: *Proceedings of the 52nd Annual Meeting of the Association for Computational Linguistics* (Vol. 2: Short Papers). Baltimore, MD: Association for Computational Linguistics; 2014. p. 339–344. Available from: https://aclanthology.org/P14-2056.

[82] Rashid F and Blanco E. Characterizing Interactions and Relationships between People. In: *Proceedings of the 2018 Conference on Empirical Methods in Natural Language Processing*. Brussels, Belgium: Association for Computational Linguistics; 2018. p. 4395–4404. Available from: https://aclanthology.org/D18-1470.

[83] Rashid F and Blanco E. Dimensions of interpersonal relationships: corpus and experiments. In: *Proceedings of the 2017 Conference on Empirical Methods in Natural Language Processing*. Copenhagen, Denmark: Association for Computational Linguistics; 2017. p. 2307–2316. Available from: https://aclanthology.org/D17-1244.

[84] Wish M, Deutsch M, and Kaplan SJ. Perceived dimensions of interpersonal relations. *Journal of Personality and Social Psychology*. 1976;33(4):409–420. Available from: https://www.sciencedirect.com/science/article/pii/B9780080237190500176.

[85]   Vaswani A, Shazeer N, Parmar N, *et al.* Attention is all you need. In: Guyon I, von Luxburg U, Bengio S, *et al.*, editors. *Advances in Neural Information Processing Systems 30: Annual Conference on Neural Information Processing Systems 2017*, December 4–9, 2017, Long Beach, CA, USA; 2017. p. 5998–6008. Available from: https://proceedings.neurips.cc/paper/2017/hash/3f5ee243547dee91fbd053c1c4a845aa-Abstract.html.

[86]   Lu J, Ren X, Ren Y, *et al.* Improving contextual language models for response retrieval in multi-turn conversation. In: Huang J, Chang Y, Cheng X, *et al.*, editors. *Proceedings of the 43rd International ACM SIGIR Conference on Research and Development in Information Retrieval, SIGIR 2020*, Virtual Event, China, July 25–30, 2020. ACM; 2020. p. 1805–1808. Available from: https://doi.org/10.1145/3397271.3401255.

Chapter 10

Fact summarization for personalized knowledge graphs

Danai Koutra^a, Davide Mottin^b, and Jing Zhu^a

Knowledge graphs (KGs) can be leveraged to effectively answer complex questions involving relationships among entities. Such question answering has important applications in various scientific areas such as biology, medicine, and engineering. Often the graphs occurring in these domains are massive consisting of many millions or billions of facts, which poses challenges for the methods that are used for question answering. In this chapter, we focus on one promising approach for handling the massive-size challenge, namely fact summarization for personalized knowledge graphs, which is a variant of graph summarization [1].

We refer to two different types of personalized KGs. The first type is a **compact "personal KG summary" that is constructed from encyclopedic KGs** such that it contains only the facts that are most relevant to an individuals' interests. These compact representations (that are typically orders of magnitude smaller than the original KG) can support faster query answering, and can also be stored and utilized on-device, allowing individuals private, anytime access to the information that interests them most [2]. The second type is **KGs that contain only personal, sensitive information about an individual** (i.e., non-encyclopedic facts about the world) and their activities (e.g., calendar events, friends/colleagues and how they relate, health-related information). Summaries of these KGs can support more efficient and higher-quality search and recommendations [3] for each individual user.

Summarization for personalized KGs has several key challenges that need to be addressed when designing new computational approaches:

- *Data volume*: As mentioned above, KGs tend to be massive as they contain facts about the world. Though summarization aims to reduce the size of the data, summarization approaches need to be carefully designed in order to be scalable and process these graphs efficiently.

^{a}University of Michigan, USA
^{b}Aarhus University, Denmark

Table 10.1   Common knowledge graph statistics

	# entities |E|	# relations |R|	# triples |T|
DBPedia	2,026,781	1,043	10,964,261
YAGO	5,155,416	72	19,635,755
Freebase	115,765,760	269,984	1,000,000,000

- *Data complexity*: KGs encode heterogeneous semantic information and contain a large number of entity and relationship types e.g. the widely used encyclopedic knowledge graphs such as DBPedia[1], YAGO[2], and Freebase[3] contain over ten million triples, spanning topics like music, movies, sports, etc. The detailed statistics of these KGs are shown in Table 10.1.

  Moreover, due to the automatic way that KGs are constructed [4], they tend to contain various types of errors or miss information [5], which can affect the summarization process, the quality of the summary, and subsequently the performance in the downstream task of interest.
- *Data evolution*: Some facts in KGs are static (e.g., the Eiffel Tower is in Paris), but many facts change over time at different rates (e.g., the score of a sports game changes over the span of a couple of hours, while the president of a country usually changes every 4 years). The summarization methods should account for these changes, which should be reflected in the resultant summaries in order to reduce errors in the downstream tasks.
- *Evaluation*: Depending on the downstream task, different evaluation metrics may be appropriate for each KG summarization method. This makes the comparison of different methods challenging. Moreover, due to privacy concerns, there is lack of publicly available personalized KGs or historical queries per individual, which hinders the evaluation of proposed methods in real settings.

Chapter organization: In the following sections, we review the most important work in this area, starting from general KG summarization methods for encyclopedic knowledge graphs and then moving towards personal KG construction and summarization. We conclude the chapter with promising future directions and open problems in this space.

10.1   Knowledge graph summarization

One way to obtain personalized KG summaries is to apply general-purpose KG summarization methods on personal KGs that contain user-specific information. For this

---

[1] https://wiki.dbpedia.org/services-resources/datasets/data-set-35/data-set-351
[2] https://old.datahub.io/dataset/yago
[3] https://developers.google.com/freebase – latest available version

reason, in this section, we review four representative works on fact summarization for knowledge graphs.

Keyword-induced graph summarization: Initially, knowledge graph summarization aimed to effectively summarize the input KG with representative structures and content for a specific query [6]. Specifically, given a query Q that contains a set of keywords $\{k_1, k_2, ..., k_n\}$, the goal is to find a summary graph $G_s = (V_s, E_s, L_s)$, where (1) each node v_s represents a node set $[v_s]$ from G, such that (a) $[v_s]$ is either a keyword node set corresponding to a set of keyword queries or an intermediate node set on a path between keyword nodes. Given the fact that finding the smallest summary graph of a specific coverage ratio α (i.e., the number of the keyword pairs covered by G_s vs. the total number of keyword pairs) is NP-complete, the authors propose two alternative problems: finding the smallest summary graph that can cover all keyword pairs and finding a minimum summary graph set such that it forms a k-partition of G. The first problem can be easily solved by figuring out the dominance relations of nodes between G and G_s, while the latter one can be approximated by iteratively refining a k-center clustering process. The proposed algorithm achieves not only a higher compression ratio (smaller graphs) compared with traditional graph summarization algorithms [7] but is also able to capture keyword relationships in the query-induced graphs, as illustrated in a small case study.

KG summarization via pattern recognition: Instead of generating a separate answer for each keyword query and then summarizing the induced graphs together, Song *et al.* [8] propose to generate a summary for a *single* KG itself, no matter what is the input query. The KG summarization problem is reformulated as a bi-criteria pattern mining problem that tries to find k diversified d-summaries that maximize the informativeness measure for a knowledge graph. The class of the proposed graph patterns, namely d-summaries, is a lossy representation that summarizes similar entities and their neighbors up to d hops away using d-similarity relations. This lossy representation makes it possible to verify if a graph is a summary in polynomial time, instead of doing an NP-hard graph isomorphism check.

Formally, given a knowledge graph $G = (V, E, L)$, a summary P is a d-summary, if for every summary node u and every node $v \in [u]([u] \neq \emptyset), (u, v)$ forms a d-similarity relation R_d. Intuitively, a d-summary P guarantees that for any incoming (resp. outgoing) path of a summary node u with a bounded length d in P, there must exist an incoming (resp. outgoing) path of each entity summarized in $[u]$ with the same label. Then, the summarization for a knowledge graph G is defined as a set of the d-summaries S_G. The authors introduce a bi-criteria function $F = (1 - \alpha) \sum_{P_i \in S_G} I(P_i) + \frac{\alpha}{card(S_G)-1} \sum_{P_i \neq P_j \in S_G} \text{diff}(P_i, P_j)$ to measure the informativeness and diversity of a summary. Since finding optimal summarization by mining and verifying all k subsets of summaries is not practical for large G, the anytime 2-approximate algorithm is introduced to solve this problem based on a-priori pattern mining called **streamDis**. Results show that the d-summaries are not only able to provide high-quality summaries but are also orders of magnitude faster than summarization based on mining frequent subgraph patterns.

KG summarization through soft, inductive rules: Compared with previous pattern-based approaches [8], KGist [5] seeks more interpretable KG summarization by finding a set of inductive, soft rules. Formally, given a knowledge graph G, the goal is to find a concise model M^* of inductive rules that summarize what is normal (facts that correctly exist in G), what is erroneous (facts that erroneously exist in G), and what is missing (facts that are missing, but should exist in $\hat{G}$). This inductive summarization problem is solved by leveraging the minimum description length since it is closely related to the idea of using compression to find patterns (and, by extension outliers):

$$M^* = \operatorname{argmin}_{M \in \mathcal{M}} L(G, M) = \operatorname{argmin}_{M \in \mathcal{M}} L(M) + L(G|M), \tag{10.1}$$

where $\mathcal{M}$ denotes the model space. Each rule is iteratively selected as a candidate according to its explanatory power – i.e., how much reduction in error it could lead to. The candidate rules are further refined by rule merging and rule nesting in order to obtain more complex and expressive rules. Experiments show that (1) KGist provides more interpretable and smaller rule-based KG summaries than the baselines, thanks to the Minimum Description Length (MDL) principle. (2) KGist is more effective than the baselines at identifying anomalous edges, demonstrating its generality. (3) KGist can find missing information from a KG effectively. (4) KGist is also scalable; it mines summaries in only a few minutes on standard benchmarks.

Knowledge base summarization based on first-order logic rules: While most of the previous work focuses on summarizing knowledge graphs according to their graph patterns, the extracted patterns fail to include general patterns with arbitrary variables and limit the knowledge coverage of the resultant summaries. An alternative approach [9] aims to summarize the input KG based on first-order logic rules.

For first-order logic rules of the form: $Q \leftarrow \wedge_i P_i$ where Q, P_i are predicates, Q is entailed by P_i if P_i are all True, $(\wedge_i P_i) \wedge (Q \leftarrow \wedge_i P_i) \models Q$. Let $\mathscr{S}, \mathscr{T}$ be sets of grounded predicates, $\mathscr{H}$ be the set of first-order horn rules, $\mathscr{S} \models_{\mathscr{H}} \mathscr{T}$ if $\forall T \in \mathscr{T}, \exists S' \in \mathscr{S}, r \in \mathscr{H}$, such that $S' \models_r T$. The KG summarization problem based on first-order Horn rules is defined as follows. Let $\mathscr{D}$ be an RDF KB. The summarization on $\mathscr{D}$ is a triple $(\mathscr{H}, \mathscr{N}, \mathscr{C})$ with minimal size, where $\mathscr{H}$ (for "hypothesis") is a set of inference rules, both $\mathscr{N}$ (for "necessaries") and $\mathscr{C}$ (for "counterexamples") are sets of predicates. $\mathscr{D}, \mathscr{H}, \mathscr{N}, \mathscr{C}$ satisfies: (1) $\mathscr{N} \subseteq \mathscr{D}$; (2) $\mathscr{N} \models_{\mathscr{H}} (\mathscr{D} \backslash \mathscr{N}) \cup \mathscr{C}$; (3) $\forall e \notin \mathscr{D} \cup \mathscr{C}; \nexists r \in \mathscr{H}, \mathscr{N} \models_r e$. The rules are summarized using top-down rule mining techniques.

Experiments show that the first-order logic rule-based approaches are able to achieve a smaller compression ratio as well as much better knowledge coverage than alternative summarization approaches.

10.2 Personalized knowledge graph summarization

As we discussed in the previous section, KG summarization yields user-agnostic summaries with the purpose of preserving some information, such as topology and relationship distributions. Yet, such approaches disregard user-specific preferences. Here, we fill this gap and survey the main works that take a *personalized* approach. Although personalization for KGs is a growing research area as evidenced by recent works [10–13], the research is still sporadic and focused on a few domains. Another encouraging signal is the recent emergence of specialized forums and workshops in which researchers can discuss KG personalization [14,15].

In Section 10.2.1, we review *personalized KG construction* approaches that aggregate information from users and common KGs to offer each user an individual view of the data. Then, in Section 10.2.2, we provide a detailed view of the most prominent methods for personalized KG summarization.

10.2.1   Personalized KG construction and applications

In a position paper [16], researchers from Google define a *Personal KG (PKG)* as a *"resource of structured information about entities personally related to its user, their attributes and the relations between them."* Personalized KGs have emerged in a variety of domains spanning from conversational systems [13], to health and medicine [17,18], to user profiling [10,19], to e-learning [12], and to fact-checking [20]. Below we describe the main KGs that belong to each of these domains, and summarize key information about them in Table 10.2.

Conversational systems: In conversational systems, the goal is to extract facts as triples from user conversations, such as e-mails, messages, and dialogues with a bot. The extracted triples are then used to train predictors to improve the quality of the

Table 10.2   *Representative examples of personalized KGs. Per KG, we provide its domain and the link to the corresponding resources.*

KG	Year	Domain	Link
DialogRE [13]	2020	Conversational	https://dataset.org/dialogre/
CHARM [11, 21]	2020	Conversational	https://github.com/Anna146/CHARM
PHR [22]	2007	Health	–
PHO [23]	2021	Health	https://semantics-for-personal-health.github.io/
HeLiS [18]	2018	Health	http://perkapp.fbk.eu/
PHKG [24]	2018	Health	–
kHealth [25]	2014	Health	–
Thymeflow [10]	2016	User profiling	https://github.com/thymeflow/thymeflow
Personal web [3]	2020	User profiling	–
EduCor [12]	2022	E-learning	https://tibonto.github.io/educor/
FACE-KEG [20]	2021	Fact-checking	–

conversation or build user profiles. While conversational systems do not explicitly construct knowledge graphs, they provide triples to enrich an existing KG.

A representative dataset is **DialogRE** [13], which consists of entities and relationships extracted from dialogues in TV series. Specifically, the authors annotate 36 relation types in 1,788 dialogues on transcripts from the *Friends* TV series. The goal of this work is to provide an evaluation of dialogue-based systems and an opportunity to build personalized KG graphs. Beyond TV series, **CHARM** [11] automatically extracts implicit attributes from speech using a zero-shot learning approach. For instance, CHARM can infer the hobby of a person from a description of activities, e.g., *swimming* from "*going to the pool every Monday.*" CHARM is a building block for extracting intentions from dialogue systems [26].

Health and medicine: Personalized systems in health can significantly improve processes such as patient handling in the hospital. Unfortunately, the development of personalized approaches in this domain is hindered by privacy concerns and lack of data. One solution to this impasse is to extract a KG from synthetic data and infer triples using a classifier, such as Naïve Bayes [27]. Yet, personal information, which is critical in this domain, is not included in such KGs. There have been some attempts in the community towards personalized data in health- and medicine-related KGs. At a high level, a personalized health knowledge graph (PHKG) includes information about a person, including their medical history, demographics, social information, and preferences [24]. It can be seen as a subgraph of a larger KG that aggregates knowledge from heterogeneous sources, including medical datasets and IoT devices containing only information relevant to one person.

For example, **PHR** [17] is the first methodological attempt to integrate personal health records with KGs. The method relies on some existing medical ontologies and KGs, such as medical terms, and patient records. PHR provides extraction methods for personalized patient information, but the paper only describes the methodology without providing any data. Similarly, the **Personal Health Ontology** (PHO) [23] defines entity types and relationships to organize daily habits, dietary preferences, social determinants, and patient information. The authors propose a system to generate a dietary recommendation for patients from an available food KG and personal patient data. The authors use observations from interviews and synthetic food logs to demonstrate the system's capabilities. Another ontology, **HeLiS** [18] aims at integrating food (e.g., fruit) and user activities (e.g., running) for personalized monitoring. HeLiS provides a rich ontology that integrates vocabularies from different available sources. The dictionaries are harvested automatically from sources provided by the Italian Minister of Agriculture and the Italian Epidemiological department as well as ingredients from recipes and terms from the Compendium of Physical Activities[4]. The PerKApp system[5] integrates and uses the ontology to provide personalized recommendations for healthy lifestyles. Gyrard *et al.* [24] construct personalized health knowledge graphs based on patients by aggregating information from a variety of

---

[4]https://sites.google.com/site/compendiumofphysicalactivities/home?pli=1
[5]http://perkapp.fbk.eu/

resources such as medical datasets and IoT devices, and adding them to existing knowledge bases. Sheth *et al.* [25] aggregate patients' information of asthma, obesity and Parkinson's disease to help clinicians make recommendations.

User profiling: User profiling assembles user data to provide targeted recommendations. PKGs can easily integrate data from different sources, such as user devices, social networks, and e-mails, and provide a unified view of user preferences.

A representative example is **Thymeflow** [10,19], which is a system and an open source KG that integrates personal data and data from general purpose KGs in a spatio-temporal fashion. The system supports personal questions, such as time-related queries on past events. ThymeFlow models events, places, messages, and personal data into a single KG that can easily accommodate multiple formats. Besides the data storage, Thymeflow provides disambiguation algorithms for entities. Another related example is the so-called "**personal web**" [3], which is used for activity discovery and can power e-mail clients and productivity tools to enable people better manage their data and time. A computer logging tool was designed to collect information about e-mails, calendar appointments, and other personal information items, user interactions with those (e.g., click on a meeting, time spent on a webpage), as well as textual attributes (e.d., noun phrases from email subject lines, document titles). Each personal web consists of `Email`, `Calendar Appointment`, `Web Document`, `File`, and `Contact` entities, and multi-relational link between them (e.g., e-mail replies, e-mail connected to the sender and receivers). The personal web was used to efficiently learn representations for personal information items (accounting for structural and textual changes in the graph over time) in order to support a variety of recommendation tasks (e.g., recommend items that are related to a specific activity/project, or e-mail recipients).

E-learning: E-learning platforms, such as Coursera and Udemy, can also benefit from both KGs and personalization. On the one hand, a learning system requires the flexibility of the knowledge graph to accommodate the different learning methodologies and teaching demands. On the other hand, personalization could induce improved content and easier learning.

EduCor [12,28] is an ontology for digital learning resources. The ontology optimizes for different learning paths, material, goals, psychological parameters, and skills, as well as user data. A recent prototype [12] shows the possibility to integrate collaborative search and e-learning data into a PKG for personalized recommendations. Since EduCor is simply an ontology, the possibility of creating a PKG using EduCor depends on the availability of data.

Fact-checking: Fact-checking, the process of verifying factual information, has attracted significant interest recently. Though a variety of approaches have been proposed in the literature, here we discuss two approaches that are based on "personalized" versions of KGs.

FACE-KEG [20] aims not only to investigate the veracity of a fact but also to generate a human comprehensible explanation clarifying its truthfulness by leveraging

KGs. FACE-KEG comprises three steps: (1) construction of a KG personalized to the input claim and retrieval of the relevant text contexts; (2) application of a bidirectional RNN to encode text and a graph transformer to encode the summarized KG; and (3) joint training of a classifier that predicts whether the input fact is true and a decoder that learns to generate a natural language explanation, as shown in Figure 10.1. In depth, given a textual claim and a large knowledge graph (e.g., DBPedia) to verify a fact, FACE-KEG first constructs a small KG summary that is specific to an input claim. Given the claim, FACE-KEG extracts all associated DBPedia entities $\mathcal{E}$ using entity linking. To avoid restricting the context to the direct or 1-hop interactions of the entities of interest, three additional types of entities are retrieved: (1) all entities $\mathcal{E}_1$ occurring in the respective fact's textual context, (2) all entities $\mathcal{E}_2$ that are linked to each entity in $\mathcal{E}_1$, and (3) all entities $\mathcal{E}_3$ linked to each entity in $\mathcal{E}_2$. Then, the node set V of the KG summary consists of k_1% randomly sampled entities from $\mathcal{E}_1$, k_2% randomly sampled entities from $\mathcal{E}_2$ and k_3% randomly sampled entities from $\mathcal{E}_3$. Each edge in the personalized KG summary, $G = (V, E)$, referring to the input claim connects the entities to ontology concepts in DBPedia. If the constructed KG is disconnected, a global node is added and connected to a randomly chosen node in each connected component of G in order to sustain flow of information in the graph. In the second step, FACE-KEG applies a graph transformer to the constructed personalized KG in order to learn the global context patterns of the graph structure. The graph transformer mainly uses self-attention to compute the hidden representations by attending to each node's first-order neighbors. For encoding the relevant textual context, an ELMo embedding module is used along with a bi-LSTM. We denote the output of the text encoder as $\mathbf{o}_T$ and the output of the graph encoder as $\mathbf{o}_G$; then, in the third step, $\mathbf{o}_T$ and $\mathbf{o}_G$ are first passed through an attention layer to learn the final output $\mathbf{o}$. A classifier consisting of dense ReLU layers and a softmax layer predicts the veracity based on $\mathbf{o}$. A sequential LSTM decoder with attention generates the output sequence of words as the natural language explanation for the input claims.

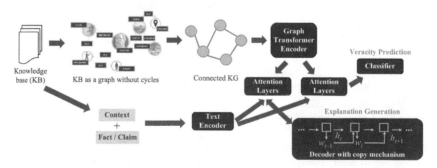

Figure 10.1   Pipeline of FACE-KEG [20], which constructs a summarized KG based on the input claims via entity linking and use the summarized KG to investigate the veracity of the fact and generate an explanation. Figure adapted from [20].

Table 10.3   *Qualitative summary of personalized graph summarization work. All of the methods included here leverage node grouping and output supergraphs.*

Method	KG	Static	Temporal	Objective	Supported queries
GLIMPSE [2]	✔	✔	✔	Utility	Question answering (subgraph queries)
UDS [30]	✗	✔	✗	Size, utility	PageRank, Link Prediction
T-BUDS [31]	✗	✔	✗	Utility	Triangle counting, PageRank, shortest-path
PeGaSus [32]	✗	✔	✗	Reconstruction	RWR, shortest-path, hitting probability

Another fact-checking approach [29] relies on summarizing the graph fact-checking rules (GFCs) in the KG. The authors first introduce a supervised pattern discovery algorithm to compute GFCs over a set of training facts by solving a submodular optimization problem with provable optimization guarantees. The GFCs are then used to enhance the existing rule-based and learning-based models for fact-checking. Results show that finding GFCs is not only feasible for large KGs but also achieves high accuracy and interpretability.

10.2.2   Personalized graph summarization

In this section, we discuss approaches for summarizing personalized KGs, as well as related personalized approaches for summarizing unlabeled graphs, i.e., graphs with no node and edge labels.

10.2.2.1   Personalized KG summarization

Personalized KG summarization (PKGS) can be performed with two distinct approaches. The first approach is a *two-step* approach where: (a) a personalized KG is constructed; and then (b) any of the KG summarization algorithms in Section 10.1 can be used to compress it. In this case, the personalized KG contains personal information, while the summarization method is agnostic to the user data and preferences. The second approach is *end-to-end*, and the summarization process explicitly captures the user preferences. The promise and importance of this direction was highlighted in a communications of the ACM article on industry-scale KGs [33].

The first approach is an application of KG construction and KG summarization techniques discussed in Sections 10.2.1 and 10.1, respectively. Thus, here we discuss the end-to-end approach that takes into account the user preferences.

Personal encyclopedic KGs: submodularity-based summaries: Motivated by the disparity between individuals' limited information needs and the massive scale of encyclopedic KGs, recent work proposed the problem of constructing a personalized, user-specific knowledge graph summary for settings that are resource-constrained [2, 34], going beyond the traditional approach of querying a KG that resides on the cloud (Figure 10.2). The resultant personal summary contains only facts in which the

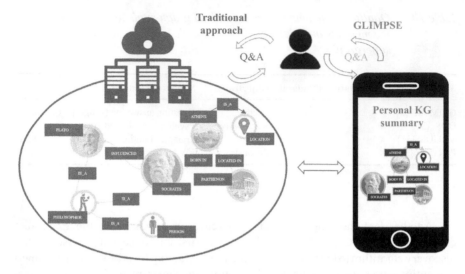

Figure 10.2   Personalized KG summarization problem: an on-device personal summary of the KG with facts that are of interest to the user allows private, anytime querying. Figure adapted from [2].

individual is most interested. The resource-constrained setting allows the summary to be stored and accessed locally (e.g., on a device such as a mobile phone or a conversational assistant), and support private, anytime access.

At a high level, the goal is to construct a sparse graph (personal summary) that maximizes a user's inferred "utility" over a given KG (i.e., coverage of inferred preferences for facts based on their historical queries), subject to a resource constraint (e.g., available device storage space). More formally, given (1) a knowledge graph G, (2) a user u and her query history Q_u to G (in the form of query subgraphs), and (3) a resource constraint of K triples, the goal is to find the personal summary $S_u \subseteq G$ that consists of K triples and maximizes the log likelihood of $\Pr(S_u|Q_u)$, which is an estimate of how well the summary covers the user's inferred preferences for facts:

$$\text{argmax}_{S_u \subseteq G} \log \Pr(S_u|Q_u) \text{ s.t. } |T_u| \leq K. \tag{10.2}$$

As shown in Figure 10.3, the solution, **GLIMPSE**, consists of two steps: (1) inference of user preferences for entities and relations in the KG via a random walk-based approach, and (2) KG summary construction via submodular optimization. Since exactly optimizing (10.2) requires a computation complexity of $O\binom{|T|}{K}$, exact optimization is infeasible. Instead, the authors reformulate it as a utility maximization problem, where the utility function to be optimized is non-negative. The non-negative utility function is proven to be submodular, and choosing the triple with the highest marginal utility $\Delta_\theta(x_{ijk}|S_u, Q_u)$, up to K triples is a near-optimal solution with guarantees (it has a $(1 - \frac{1}{e})$ approximation). However, this naive solution is too

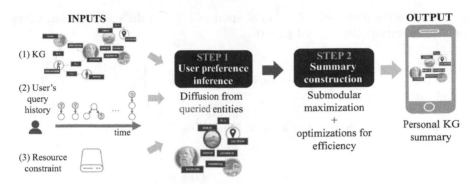

Figure 10.3   Overview of GLIMPSE [2], which summarizes facts into a personal knowledge graph summary in a two-step process

slow for KGs with $|T|$ on the order of millions or billions. To solve this, GLIMPSE provides three optimizations (including updating only a subset of marginal utilities, and leveraging sampling) to do fast summary construction. GLIMPSE provides theoretical guarantees on the summaries utility and is linear in the number of edges in the KG. Experiment results show that it efficiently creates summaries that outperform strong baselines by up to 19% in query-answering tasks. GLIMPSE is also shown to handle massive KGs with up to 1 billion triples.

Experiments show that FACE-KEG is able to significantly outperform the existing baselines in terms of both the veracity of input claims and the quality of explanations. Human evaluations also demonstrate that the explanations learned by FACE-KEG are more coherent, concise and grammatical compared to competitive baselines. FACE-KEG is also able to do fact-checking in specific domains like COVID-19 pandemic.

10.2.2.2   Personalized summarization of unlabeled graphs

Here, we present the three main techniques for personalized summarization of unlabeled graphs (i.e., graphs without node and edge labels, which are typically key components of KGs). Even for unlabeled graphs, the literature is quite limited, showing potential for future research.

Utility-driven graph summarization (UDS) [30] aims to summarize the graph $G = (V, E)$ with a summary supergraph $G_S = (V_S, E_S)$ where V_S are supernodes and E_S superedges, and the supernodes do not overlap (i.e., $\bigcup_{v \in V_S} v = V, v_i \cap v_j = \emptyset$). For the summarization process, UDS defines a utility function $U(G_S)$ that preserves edge and node weights, graph connectivity, and the impact of an edge/node removal. It ensures that the utility never drops below a user-specified value Γ. Although UDS does not have an explicit notion of personalization, changes in the edge weights and the utility threshold Γ reflect in the summary. The utility of a summary G_S reflects the importance $C(u, v)$ of edges (u, v) in the summary for edges that exist in the original graph minus the importance $C_s(u, v)$ of spurious edges in the summary (i.e., edges that do not exist in the original graph):

$$U(G_S) = \sum_{(v_i,v_j)\in E_S} \left(\sum_{\substack{(u,v)\in E \\ u\in v_i, v\in v_j}} C(u, v) - \sum_{\substack{(u,v)\notin E \\ u\in v_i, v\in v_j}} C_s(u, v) \right). \tag{10.3}$$

The overall UDS objective aims at minimizing the size of the summary while preserving the utility

$$\min \ (|V_S|)$$
$$\text{subject to} \ \ U(G_S) \geq \Gamma. \tag{10.4}$$

Since the problem in (10.4) is **NP**-hard and unapproximable, a greedy heuristic is proposed to find the summaries. The summary can be used to answer PageRank and link prediction queries.

T-BUDS [31] builds on UDS and studies lossless utility-driven summarization. T-BUDS shows that, as opposed to the lossy version, lossless utility-driven summarization admits polynomial algorithms. Moreover, the authors propose a faster version of UDS that uses spanning trees. The results show up to 80% relative time improvement over UDS.

PeGaSus [32] finds a *node-centric personalization* of a graph that preserves the relevant connections to a set of target nodes T. Similar to UDS and T-BUDS, a summary graph $G_S = (V_S, E_S)$ is a graph with supernodes V_S and superedges E_S. PeGaSus aims to find a summary of size k that minimizes the personalized error $RE^{(T)}$ of a set of target nodes T. The personalized error is a weighted version of the utility in (10.3).

$$RE^{(T)}(G_S) := \sum_{u,v\in V} W_{uv}^{(T)} |C(u, v) - C_s(u, v)|, \tag{10.5}$$

where $W_{uv}^{(T)}$ is a weight that decreases exponentially with the distance from the closest nodes in T of the nodes u, v. Since the minimization of the personalized error is hard to compute and approximate, PeGaSus is a greedy heuristic.

10.3   Conclusion, future directions and opportunities

This chapter examined the status of research on summarization for personalized KGs. We reviewed key lines of work on general KG summarization methods for encyclopedic knowledge graphs, as well as approaches and applications of personalized KG construction and summarization.

Next, in order to enable future research in this area and forward progress, we describe the most pressing challenges that the community faces. A recent vision paper [33] advocates an increasing need for personal summaries for KGs. Yet, while personalized data summarization [35] both in text and multi-dimensional data is well-established, the research on PKG summaries is still in its infancy. One viable possibility is to capitalize on previous work on data summarization and adapt the techniques for KGs. Yet, this direction remains unexplored. Moreover, the research on personalized KG summaries typically experiences one or more of the following challenges.

Challenge 1: lack of real workloads: The lack of publicly available real workloads and user query logs hinders the research in this area. As pointed out in [2], the research on personalized summaries revolves around user logs. Recent directions have proposed the possibility to generate high-quality synthetic datasets via large pre-trained machine learning models [36] and "realistic" user simulations [2] that reflect real search behaviors detailed in the information retrieval literature [8,37,38]. However, a synthetic generator might introduce biases due to the implicit assumptions over the data distribution. GLIMPSE [2], for instance, proposes a synthetic workload generator for subgraph queries that assumes the user likes one or more topics. Besides synthetic generators, there are a few query workloads for SPARQL, such as LSQ [39] and Wikidata queries [40]. However, in most cases, these query logs contain simple queries [41] due to the limitation of the query interface or duplicate queries caused by bots or automatic systems.

Challenge 2: privacy: Personalization requires detailed user habits and preferences that can disclose the identity of a user. As a consequence, the research on personalized summaries should also consider anonymity as an additional objective. Preserving data utility and, at the same time, user privacy is therefore one of the challenges for the community. The research in general-purpose data summarization and differential privacy has considered the balance of data utility and privacy [42].

Challenge 3: dynamic updates in KGs: Updates occur on a regular basis in a KG.

At the same time, summaries should readily adapt to the changes even on low-resource devices, such as mobile phones. Traditional graph summaries consider two main models of data dynamicity, the snapshot and the streaming model. In the *snapshot model*, such as TimeCrunch [43], the algorithm receives a number of graph updates in a certain timeframe. The snapshot model assumes a known history and compresses temporal patterns or data dynamics during a specific timeframe into a static snapshot. In the *steaming model* [44,45] the data updates occur continuously and the algorithm typically maintains a lossy summary in a hashing data structure. Recently, MoSSo [46] proposed a lossless incremental graph summarization that bridges the snapshot and the streaming model.

Challenge 4: preference evolution: Besides dynamic updates, user preferences also change over time. So far, GLIMPSE [2] proposed a model that constructs a summary from a query workload that predicts also future queries. However, besides the streaming model [44], current methods do not take into account the evolution of user preferences. A promising direction is to take into account the preferences on adaptive data structures, such as adaptive indexes and database cracking for relational databases [47]. An alternative direction is to consider the summary of a machine learning model of the user preferences and apply few-shot learning strategies [48].

References

[1]   Liu Y, Safavi T, Dighe A, *et al*. Graph summarization methods and applications: a survey. *ACM Computing Surveys*. 2018;51(3):62.

[2]   Safavi T, Belth C, Faber L, *et al*. Personalized knowledge graph summarization: from the cloud to your pocket. In: *2019 IEEE International Conference on Data Mining (ICDM)*. IEEE; 2019. p. 528–537.

[3]   Safavi T, Fourney A, Sim R, *et al*. Toward activity discovery in the personal web. In: *Proceedings of the 13th International Conference on Web Search and Data Mining*; 2020. p. 492–500.

[4]   Nickel M, Murphy K, Tresp V, *et al*. A review of relational machine learning for knowledge graphs. *Proceedings of the IEEE*. 2016;104(1):11–33.

[5]   Belth C, Zheng X, Vreeken J, *et al*. What is normal, what is strange, and what is missing in a knowledge graph: unified characterization via inductive summarization. In: *Proceedings of the Web Conference 2020*; 2020. p. 1115–1126.

[6]   Wu Y, Yang S, Srivatsa M, *et al*. Summarizing answer graphs induced by keyword queries.   *Proceedings of the VLDB Endowment*. 2013;6(14): 1774–1785.

[7]   Tian Y, Hankins RA, and Patel JM. Efficient aggregation for graph summarization. In: *Proceedings of the 2008 ACM SIGMOD International Conference on Management of Data*; 2008. p. 567–580.

[8]   Song Q, Wu Y, Lin P, *et al*. Mining summaries for knowledge graph search. *IEEE Transactions on Knowledge and Data Engineering*. 2018;30(10):1887–1900.

[9]   Wang R, Sun D, and Wong R. RDF knowledge base summarization by inducing first-order Horn rules. In: *ECML-PKDD*; 2022.

[10]   Montoya D, Pellissier Tanon T, *et al*. Thymeflow, a personal knowledge base with spatio-temporal data. In: *CIKM*; 2016. p. 2477–2480.

[11]   Tigunova A, Yates A, Mirza P, *et al*. CHARM: Inferring personal attributes from conversations. In: *EMNLP*; 2020. p. 5391–5404.

[12]   Ilkou E. Personal Knowledge Graphs: Use Cases in e-learning Platforms; 2022. arXiv preprint arXiv:220308507.

[13]   Yu D, Sun K, Cardie C, *et al*. Dialogue-based relation extraction. In: textitACL. Association for Computational Linguistics; 2020. p. 4927–4940.

[14]   Workshop on Personal Knowledge Graphs. Accessed: 2022-11-14. https://pkgs.ws/.

[15]   The Personal Health Knowledge Graph Workshop. Accessed: 2022-11-14. https://phkg.github.io/.

[16]   Balog K and Kenter T. Personal knowledge graphs: a research agenda. In: *ICTIR*; 2019. p. 217–220.

[17]   Wang C, Xiong M, Zhou Q, *et al*. Panto: a portable natural language interface to ontologies. In: *European Semantic Web Conference*. Springer; 2007. p. 473–487.

[18] Dragoni M, Bailoni T, Maimone R, *et al.* HeLiS: an ontology for supporting healthy lifestyles. In: *ISWC*; 2018. p. 53–69.

[19] Montoya D, Tanon TP, Abiteboul S, *et al.* A knowledge base for personal information management. In: LDOW@ WWW; 2018.

[20] Vedula N and Parthasarathy S. Face-keg: fact checking explained using knowledge graphs. In: *Proceedings of the 14th ACM International Conference on Web Search and Data Mining*; 2021. p. 526–534.

[21] Tigunova A. Extracting personal information from conversations. In: *Companion Proceedings of the Web Conference 2020*; 2020. p. 284–288.

[22] Wang H, Miao X, and Yang P. Design and implementation of personal health record systems based on knowledge graph. In: *ITME*; 2018. p. 133–136.

[23] Seneviratne O, Harris J, Chen CH, *et al.* Personal health knowledge graph for clinically relevant diet recommendations; 2021. arXiv preprint arXiv:211010131.

[24] Gyrard A, Gaur M, Shekarpour S, *et al.* Personalized health knowledge graph. In: *CEUR Workshop Proceedings*. vol. 2317; 2018.

[25] Sheth A, Anantharam P, and Thirunarayan K. Khealth: proactive personalized actionable information for better healthcare. In: *Workshop Personal Data Analytics in the Internet of Things*; 2014.

[26] Tigunova A, Mirza P, Yates A, *et al.* Exploring personal knowledge extraction from conversations with charm. In: *WSDM*; 2021. p. 1077–1080.

[27] Rotmensch M, Halpern Y, Tlimat A, *et al.* Learning a health knowledge graph from electronic medical records. *Scientific Reports*. 2017;7(1):1–11.

[28] Ilkou E, Abu-Rasheed H, Tavakoli M, *et al.* EduCOR: an educational and career-oriented recommendation ontology. In: *ISWC*. Springer; 2021. p. 546–562.

[29] Lin P, Song Q, Shen J, *et al.* Discovering graph patterns for fact checking in knowledge graphs. In: *International Conference on Database Systems for Advanced Applications*. Springer; 2018. p. 783–801.

[30] Kumar KA and Efstathopoulos P. Utility-driven graph summarization. *Proceedings of the VLDB Endowment*. 2018;12(4):335–347.

[31] Hajiabadi M, Singh J, Srinivasan V, *et al.* Graph summarization with controlled utility loss. In: *KDD*; 2021. p. 536–546.

[32] Kang S, Lee K, and Shin K. Personalized graph summarization: formulation, scalable algorithms, and applications. In: *ICDE*; 2022. p. 2319–2332.

[33] Noy N, Gao Y, Jain A, *et al.* Industry-scale knowledge graphs: lessons and challenges. *Communications of the ACM*. 2019;62(8):36–43.

[34] Faber L, Safavi T, Mottin D, *et al.* Adaptive personalized knowledge graph summarization. In: *MLG Workshop (with KDD)*; 2018.

[35] Mirzasoleiman B, Badanidiyuru A, and Karbasi A. Fast constrained submodular maximization: personalized data summarization. In: *ICML*; 2016. p. 1358–1367.

[36] Bassani E and Pasi G. Evaluating the use of synthetic queries for pre-training a semantic query tagger. In: *ECIR*; 2022. p. 39–46.

[37]   Radlinski F, Kleinberg R, and Joachims T. *Learning Diverse Rankings with Multi-Armed Bandits*. ACM; 2008. p. 784–791.

[38]   Fan W, Li J, Wang X, *et al*. *Query Preserving Graph Compression*. ACM; 2012. p. 157–168.

[39]   Saleem M, Ali MI, Hogan A, *et al*. LSQ: the linked SPARQL queries dataset. In: *ISWC*. vol. 9367 of LNCS. Springer; 2015. p. 261–269.

[40]   Bielefeldt A, Gonsior J, and Krötzsch M. Practical linked data access via SPARQL: the case of wikidata. In: LDOW@ WWW; 2018.

[41]   Bonifati A, Martens W, and Timm T. An analytical study of large SPARQL query logs. *PVLDB*. 2017;11(2):149–161.

[42]   Cormode G, Procopiuc C, Srivastava D, *et al*. Differentially private summaries for sparse data. In: *Proceedings of the 15th International Conference on Database Theory*; 2012. p. 299–311.

[43]   Shah N, Koutra D, Zou T, *et al*. Timecrunch: interpretable dynamic graph summarization. In: *Proceedings of the 21th ACM SIGKDD International Conference on Knowledge Discovery and Data Mining*. ACM; 2015. p. 1055–1064.

[44]   Tang N, Chen Q, and Mitra P. *Graph Stream Summarization: From Big Bang to Big Crunch*. ACM; 2016. p. 1481–1496.

[45]   Gou X, Zou L, Zhao C, *et al*. Fast and accurate graph stream summarization. In: *ICDE*. IEEE; 2019. p. 1118–1129.

[46]   Ko J, Kook Y, and Shin K. Incremental lossless graph summarization. In: *KDD*; 2020. p. 317–327.

[47]   Idreos S, Kersten ML, Manegold S, *et al*. Database cracking. In: CIDR. vol. 7; 2007. p. 68–78.

[48]   Wang Y, Yao Q, Kwok JT, *et al*. Generalizing from a few examples: a survey on few-shot learning. *ACM Computing Surveys*. 2020;53(3):1–34.

Chapter 11

Personalized recommender systems based on knowledge graphs

Ronald O. Ojino[a,b] and Fatima N. AL-Aswadi[c,d]

The importance of personalized knowledge graphs (PKGs) cannot be understated as they are applied across various spheres of our lives where they continuously had a positive impact. PKGs are a form of knowledge graphs that have completely changed the way item recommendations are made by introducing explainable recommendations, and alleviating the cold-start and data sparsity issues which are common in the traditional recommender systems. These heterogeneous graphs contain connectivity patterns and semantic relations which can be exploited for quality recommendations. This chapter focuses on explaining how PKGs can be used to recommend items to users when faced with a large variety of items to select from. Methods can be used for the implementation of accurate and explainable recommendations via PKGs such as embeddings and structure-based methods and are presented as well as the challenges and limitations entailed in applications development using this technology. The application of PKG recommendations in commerce and finance, Internet of Things (IoT), and healthcare are used to demonstrate its utility and competitive performance. In order to appreciate the importance of PKG recommendation systems, an example application of PKG recommendation in the field of personalized badminton training is also presented.

11.1 Introduction

In recent years, the explosion of data and information has posed significant challenges for organizations and individuals in terms of storing, managing, and accessing relevant knowledge [1,2]. Traditional databases and knowledge management systems are no longer sufficient to handle the vast amount of data generated by modern digital systems, including the Internet of Things (IoT), social media, and sensors. To overcome these challenges, researchers and developers have proposed

[a]Department of Computer Science and Engineering, College of Information and Communication Technologies (CoICT), University of Dar es Salaam, United Republic of Tanzania
[b]School of Computing and Mathematics, The Co-operative University of Kenya, Kenya
[c]School of Computer Sciences, Universiti Sains Malaysia, Malaysia
[d]Faculty of Computer Science and Engineering, Hodeidah University, Yemen

various approaches, such as semantic web technologies, ontologies, and knowledge graphs [3].

A knowledge graph is a representation of a set of interconnected facts and concepts within a domain. It provides a way to organize and understand large amounts of data and information by linking concepts together in a way that reflects the relationships between them [4,5] and this can be exploited by recommendation systems. Knowledge graphs can be used to represent a wide range of information, including general knowledge, expert knowledge, and specialized knowledge. They are often used to create personalized experiences for users by providing relevant information and recommendations based on their interests and past interactions. In the context of personalization, a knowledge graph can be used to create a more personalized user experience by recommending content and resources that are specific to the user's needs and interests.

Since the modern incarnation of knowledge graphs in 2012 and its uptake by technology giants, the development of personalized recommendation systems based on knowledge graphs has gained popularity due to their ability to effectively classify domain knowledge and solve traditional recommender issues in turn achieving better personalization results. The concept of personalized knowledge graphs has been proposed by several researchers in recent years. It can be defined as a large-scale heterogeneous graph that represents the knowledge of a user in a personalized way [6]. PKG recommendation systems can provide users with more personalized and relevant information on the web, as they are constructed based on the user's interests, preferences, and context. They use known information about an entity from a range of sources such as social media and location, and pivot through multiple levels of relationships to suggest relevant content in different domains.

The purpose of this chapter is to provide an overview of PKG recommendation systems and discuss their potential applications in various sectors. We look at how PKG recommendation systems can be used in conjunction with IoT to provide personalized experiences to users, for provision of personalized recommendations in commerce and explore their use in the healthcare industry. We also discuss some of the challenges and limitations of PKG recommendation systems. Finally, we provide a sample PKG recommendation application that illustrates how this technology can be used in personalized badminton training.

The outline of this chapter is as follows: Section 11.2 presents the background information on PKG recommendation systems. In Sections 11.3 and 11.4, the methods of constructing PKG recommendation systems and the challenges involved in using them are discussed, respectively. Section 11.5 explains various application domains of this kind of recommendation system, while a sample PKG application in badminton training is presented in Section 11.6. Section 11.7 concludes the chapter.

11.2   Background information

Different users have varying information and service needs due to their personal characteristics, interests, perceptions, learning abilities, living environment and other myriad of factors. Personalization is about understanding the users and their needs in detail. It is the ability to provide contents and services tailored to individuals based on knowledge about their needs, expectations, preferences, constraints, and behaviors [7]. This definition emphasizes the need for the provision of services and contents while taking into account the personal needs and circumstances of individuals. In some instances, personalization also involves monitoring the user's interactions in real-time or near real-time and then responding with content, products or information, etc. that align with the user's needs.

Personalization is basically a recommendation of what a user needs based on what is known about him or users who have similar characteristics to him. In personalization, we try to make a prediction based on what is known about a user or similar people. Personalization can only occur if users and their needs are understood at greater detail, the digital body language of the user is monitored if possible in real-time, and response is given to the user needs with appropriate content, information or services that align with the user's mental model. Recommender systems intend to address information explosion by finding a small set of items for users and also discover items that might be interesting to meet their personalized interests. It involves retrieving a list of nodes related to some query nodes, by taking a node and assigning it a proximity score based on the node's position relative to the query. However, it is hard to compute node similarity if the knowledge graph is too large and expensive since the computation requires to traverse the graph multiple times.

Recommendation systems are considered personalized services as they have an independent profile for each user, taking into account the peculiarities of each of them [8]. They often provide users with a sorted personalized item recommendation list based on the user's historical preferences and constraints [9]. Popular traditional recommendation systems used across different sectors include: (a) collaborative filtering recommenders in which a comparison of the information about one user is done against those of other users with similar interests to form a systemic prediction. (b) Content-based recommenders that entail unobtrusively recommending new items similar to user's favorable items by extracting the content features of the recommended objects to match the users' preferences, and the items with higher relevance score will be recommended to users [10]. (c) Demographic recommenders which recommend items based on the demographic profile of the user such as his age, gender, and nationality [11], and (d) hybrid recommendation algorithms which combine different algorithms into composite systems to avoid the limitations of either approach while enhancing their merits. However, they are complex and expensive to implement.

It is worth noting however that traditional recommender-based systems act as black boxes, not presenting the user with insights into the system logic or reasons for recommendations [12]. When applied to recommender systems, PKGs have attracted considerable interest due to their ability to alleviate the cold-start and data sparsity issue, improving performance in making more accurate recommendations and provision of explanations for recommended items [13]. Knowledge graphs address the cold-start and data sparsity issues by inculcating additional information such as contextual data, social network data, or multimedia information. Therefore, they can help us make reasonable inference of user interests and can reasonably extend a user's history which help explore a user's interest. In PKG recommendation systems, there is a semantic layer and framework based on user's needs and preferences that present users with explanations for recommendations given. The PKGs recommender systems semantic layer contains rich semantics, connections and relations between items and real word entities, and considers capturing the semantics of different paths and the distinctive saliency of those paths in order to understand user's preferences towards items. They accept data as parameters and use query results to detect personalized resource suggestions. Furthermore, certain nodes and prerequisite links among them are hierarchically organized and customized for a specific user, which means that a PKG recommendation system is essentially a user-centric knowledge graph application that can enable the management of user data and building knowledge about them devoid of vendor lock-in.

As noted, in PKG recommendation applications, every user's knowledge graph is different and unique to them. The PKG just like conventional knowledge graph has increased the ability to integrate disparate structured data sources and enabled the amalgamation of both structured and unstructured data. They formalize and standardize knowledge definition based on ontology thereby enabling information access from multiple perspectives within given domains. However, even though knowledge graphs cover important domain concepts, personal concepts of users in these domains are not sufficiently covered, leading to the need of developing PKGs [14]. PKGs are a buzz as many are becoming aware of their potential which includes fostering autonomy and directing a user's interaction by pointing them to relevant concepts thereby easing retrieval of data, reducing cognitive overload, and providing full data control. They take intelligent content to many applications including search engines, research repositories, and personal assistants among others. The PKG takes into account personal data about a user which could be enriched with other contextualized knowledge about a situation or context. They offer summaries about the facts that are mostly relevant to individual's queries and interests that can be accessed privately at any time from one's device.

11.3   Methods of constructing PKG recommendation systems

The task of creating PKG recommendation systems is non-trivial as it requires one to have knowledge engineering skills and be able to address the PKG complexity. PKG recommendation systems can be constructed using two main methods:

1. **Embedding-based methods**: Knowledge graph embeddings are low-level low-dimensional representations of the entities and relations in a knowledge graph that can be used to infer relations. They are supervised learning models that capture nodes, types, and relationships and involve fitting concepts in a vector space by essentially converting sparse vectors into dense vectors. They tend to keep similar nodes together (preserve similarity) and keep neighbors close together (preserve topology) in the vector space. By this, they simplify the PKG's high

dimensionality while preserving semantics, structure and entity relative similarities. Generally, embeddings learn what is important in a generalizable way. It is important to note that sparse vectors make it hard for any algorithm to pick up important patterns. Embedding-based methods are thus task and dataset independent, preserve information which is in the original graph, are computation efficient as they compress information to manageable bits for ML algorithms, and are compatible with traditional data mining algorithms and tools as it creates one vector for each entity. Entity and relation embeddings in knowledge graphs are used to extract information which is applied by recommender systems to produce embeddings for users and items. For instance, knowledge graph embeddings could cluster behavior of students in e-learning networks. Popular KGE models are used for learning meaningful set of embeddings (positioned in such a way that enables prediction of missing links) which can be projected and deployed into a platform to build a recommendation system. The assumption here is that entities which are similar are close by in the vector space and this can be exploited for recommendation. PKG recommendation systems are also able to capture hierarchies and different types of properties such as transitive, symmetry, and asymmetry in a compact way. Popular KGE models include and are not limited to those which are based on translation scoring functions such as:

- **Translation-based embedding model (TransE):** This is a classic embedding model for handling data with multiple relations by regarding the relation as a translation between head and tail entities. It tries to put as close as possible the tail vector with the sum of the head and relation vector. It models relationships by interpreting them as translations operating on the low-dimensional embeddings of the entities [15]. It is a simple and powerful embedding method that performs quite well in link prediction. It is appropriate in representing one-to-one relations.
- **Translation on hyperplanes (TransH):** In this embedding model, an entity possesses different representations under different relations by employing relation-specific hyper-planes. Its goal is to deal with different types of relations while decreasing model complexity. Basically, it interprets a relation as a translating operation on a hyper-plane. Each relation has two vectors, the norm vector (Wr) of the hyperplane, and the translation vector (dr) on the hyperplane. It overcomes the flaws of TransE concerning the reflexive/one-to-many/many-to-one/many-to-many relations while inheriting its efficiency [16], thereby achieving much better performance.
- **Translation on relation spaces (TransR):** Is an extension of TransH that models entities as vectors in the entity space and models each relation vector in the relation space as the projection matrix. It basically models entities and relations in two distinct spaces, i.e. entity space and multiple relation spaces (relation-specific entity spaces), and performs the translation in the corresponding relation space. This covers an issue that was previously not covered in TransH and TransE which assume that entity and relation are

vectors in the semantic space and similar entities are close to each other in the semantic space.

Apart from translation-based KG embeddings, other notable KG embedding methods that are used in recommendation systems are based on **tensor factorization scoring functions** such as RESCAL which carries out a low rank factorization with tensor product, DistMult which is based on a bilinear diagonal model using a three-way dot product between embeddings of relations, subjects and objects; and ComplEx (Complex Embeddings) which is an extension of DistMult that operates in the complex space.

Other categories are **Holographic embeddings** and **Deeper scoring functions** are another category of KG embeddings and include models like ConvE (Convolutional Embeddings) which use reshaping and convolution to score a triple. The embedding-based methods can be combined with machine learning algorithms in order to improve recommendation accuracy.

2. **Structured based methods:** They focus more on the graph structure information of the user–item interaction and use KGs to structure the information. Some of the methods that can be used here include:

- **Construction of PKGs from text:** This entails Named Entity Recognition (NER) from text (i.e. automatic process of finding entities from text). It involves the identification of key information in the text and classification in a set of pre-defined categories [17]. Deep learning NER is much more accurate at it can assemble words due to the fact that it uses word embedding that is capable of understanding the semantic and syntactic relationship between various words. It is also able to analyze topic-specific and high-level words automatically, and this can be used in the construction of PKG recommendation systems in given domains. For instance, a student in a given domain such as nutrition can use deep learning NER PKG recommendation system to extract nutrition named entities from the considerable body of nutrition literature in a digital library and have content recommendations of other similar mentioned articles. This technology would also aid in automatic discovery of newly added content in the digital library.

- **Ontology:** Ontologies being a semantic schema made up of subject, predicates, and objects are the foundational layers of building PKGs [4]. They give a representation structure of items and reasoning in a domain that makes reasoning explicit [18] and allows for graph traversal and custom application building. PKG recommendation systems based on ontologies are basically interlinked real-world entities described in a formal structure and populated with real-world data that is relevant to a user. Connections between objects that were not explicitly represented can be inferred to further enrich the PKG recommendations. Additionally, new knowledge can be generated in the PKG recommendation systems by reasoning with rules. Once the ontology is defined, it can be populated with instances and their inter-relations, which are later queried to provide recommendations of items in a given domain.

The PKG recommendation methods can be integrated with machine learning and deep learning model is then tested for the generation of more accurate recommendations.

11.4 PKG challenges in recommendation systems

There are many challenges and limitations of PKGs that highlight the need for continued research and development in this area in order to improve the scalability, performance, quality, and their usability [19–23] in the domain of recommender systems. The following list presents the key challenges of building and developing PKGs:

1. *Scalability and performance*: PKGs need to be able to handle large-scale data and provide fast and efficient access to knowledge. This requires robust algorithms and data structures for storing and querying the knowledge, as well as efficient methods for updating and maintaining the PKG.
2. *Quality and reliability*: PKGs need to ensure that the knowledge they represent is accurate, consistent, and up-to-date. This requires robust methods for data integration, ontology alignment, and knowledge validation, as well as mechanisms for detecting and resolving conflicts and inconsistencies in the knowledge.
3. *User participation and involvement*: The personalized aspect of PKGs relies on users providing their preferences, characteristics, and feedback. This can be a challenge in some contexts, where users may be unwilling or unable to provide the required information. For example, users may be concerned about privacy or may not have the time or expertise to provide input to the PKG.
4. *Domain expertise and domain-specific knowledge*: PKGs need to be able to represent domain-specific concepts and relationships in order to provide accurate and relevant knowledge. This requires domain experts to develop and maintain the PKG, as well as domain-specific ontologies and knowledge bases.
5. *Knowledge representation*: Knowledge representation seeks to facilitate the making of deductions from knowledge in the PKGs which should be fast and accurate. In many applications and domains, knowledge is dispersed across disparate locations in heterogeneous formats which often lead to difficulty in managing and structuring it for efficient representation. If knowledge is not represented in an efficient manner, it can result in cognitive overload to the users (since not all nodes would be important to a user). In the case of a large PKG, it is usually challenging to select a knowledge representation technique from which an initial structure for describing a given situation is based, and even more difficult to determine how to find a better structure for knowledge representation if the initial one is found not to be appropriate.
6. *Privacy and security*: PKGs need to ensure that the personal information they store and manage is protected from unauthorized access and misuse. Due to privacy and security concerns, many users tend to limit the amount of information they share with members of the public. Ensuring the privacy and security of information while sharing records is important but challenging to implement in

the diverse and heterogeneous data found across most PKGs. Storage of personal information in most PKGs is treated like a liability due to the difficulty in ensuring that privacy concerns are adequately addressed. There are some instances where developers of PKGs do not separate users' data from the applications that use the data in their product architecture thereby leading to cases of unauthorized access. This calls for robust security and privacy mechanisms, such as encryption, authentication, and access control in the development of PKGs.

7. *Ethical and legal issues*: PKGs need to comply with ethical and legal standards and regulations, such as data protection laws and medical ethics. This requires careful consideration of the implications of PKG use and development, as well as mechanisms for addressing any ethical or legal concerns that may arise.

8. *Integration with existing systems*: PKGs should integrate with existing knowledge management and data systems, such as databases, ontologies, and semantic web technologies. This requires robust interoperability and integration mechanisms, as well as methods for mapping and aligning different data and knowledge representations.

9. *User interface and usability*: It is necessary for PKGs to provide user-friendly and intuitive interfaces that allow users to easily access and use the knowledge represented in the PKG. This requires designing and implementing user interfaces that are tailored to the specific needs and goals of the users, as well as methods for evaluating and improving the usability of the PKG.

10. *Maintenance and updates*: PKGs need to be able to adapt and evolve over time, in order to keep up with changing data and knowledge. This requires mechanisms for maintaining and updating the PKG, as well as methods for detecting and responding to changes in the data and knowledge.

11. *Evaluation and assessment*: PKGs should be evaluated and assessed in order to determine their effectiveness and usefulness. This requires developing and implementing evaluation and assessment methods, such as user studies, experiments, and metrics, as well as mechanisms for feedback and improvement.

11.5   Application domains of PKGs recommendation systems

PKG recommendations have a wide range of potential applications depending on the domain and the user's needs. They are used in various domains such as social media, education, healthcare, Internet of Things (IoT), tourism and entertainment, and commerce and financial services [24].

In the commerce and financial services domain, PKG recommendations can be used to recommend personalized products, investment options, and advertisements to customers, based on their browsing and purchase history, demographic information, and interests. These systems can also analyze reviews and ratings of products, as well as the customer's financial goals and investment profiles to make more accurate recommendations.

In the healthcare domain, PKG recommenders can be used to track and monitor patients' health data, such as vital signs and medication adherence. For example, the authors of [25] proposed to capture the rich semantic information and monitor patients' health data for providing personalized recommendations and feedback that help physicians to understand and explain the patient's symptoms, disease progression, and potential treatment options. In the education domain, PKG recommendations can be used to analyze students' learning progress and provide personalized learning recommendations for courses as described in [26].

In the tourism and entertainment domain, PKG recommendations can be used to analyze the user's history data, options, and preferences, to make more accurate personalized recommendations such as in [27]. For example, it can recommend travel options that are similar to what the user has shown an interest in. These recommendations can include similar travel options, complementary travel options, or travel options that other users who traveled to similar destinations have also traveled to. Another example is in the hotel service industry where PKG recommendations can be used to personalize the hotel room environment prior to lodging and for post-stay guest engagement [28].

In the retail domain, PKGs can be used to track and monitor customers' purchasing habits and preferences and provide personalized product recommendations and discounts; while in personal devices, they are used to provide personalized conversation systems.

In addition, PKG recommendation systems can be used in entertainment to recommend personalized movies, TV shows, and games to users. By analyzing the user's viewing and playing history, the system can recommend entertainment options that are similar to what the user has shown an interest in [29]. These recommendations can include similar movies, TV shows, or games, complementary movies, TV shows, or games, or entertainment options that other users who viewed or played similar entertainment options have also viewed or played.

Moreover, PKG recommendation systems are widely used in social media to recommend friends, groups, and pages to users. The system can analyze the user's social media activity, including their interactions with friends, groups, and pages, to recommend similar connections. These recommendations could include friends, groups, or pages that have similar interests, similar demographics, or that are connected to the user's existing friends, groups, or pages. In the section below, we delve deeper in discussing the application of PKG recommendation systems in three different domains.

11.5.1 Personalized commerce and financial recommendation systems

Personalizing commerce and financial knowledge graph (PCFKG) recommendation systems help businesses and organizations to provide personalized products, services, and investment options to their customers. It can use various types of data, including transactional, demographic, and behavioral data [30]. Transactional data includes information about the customer's purchases, browsing history, and reviews. Demographic data includes the customer's age, gender, location, and income information. While behavioral data includes information about the customer's usage patterns and preferences. PCFKG can also use data from external sources, such as social media, to provide more accurate recommendations.

11.5.1.1 Applications of PCFKG

PCFKG can be applied in various commercial fields, it is used for various purposes and can be divided into three main sorts based on the application used such as the following:

1. *Applications of PCFKG in E-commerce*: PCFKGs have a significant impact on the e-commerce industry; they analyze the customer's browsing, purchase history, search history and preferences to recommend personalized products and services, to personalize the search results and to personalize the shopping experience [31]. For example, a customer who has previously purchased sports equipment will be recommended sports-related products when browsing. Another example is if a customer has searched for a specific product in the past, PCFKG can recommend similar products when the customer performs a search in the future.
2. *Applications of PCFKG in financial services*: PCFKGs play a crucial role in the financial services industry; they are used to recommend personalized investment options, predict creditworthiness, and provide personalized financial planning and advice. For example, by analyzing the customer's investment history, financial goals, and risk tolerance [32], a customer with a high-risk tolerance will be recommended more aggressive investment options, while a customer with a low-risk tolerance will be recommended for more conservative options. Another example is if a customer wants to save for retirement, the PCFKG will recommend investment options and plans that align with the customer's retirement savings goals.
3. *Applications of PCFKG in advertising*: PCFKGs have a significant role in the advertising industry; they are used to target personalized advertisements, retarget users, and segment audiences. A PCFKG can also analyze the user's browsing history and demographic information to personalize recommendations, leading to higher conversion rates and increased business revenue. For instance, a user who is a young parent will be recommended advertisements for products and services that align with the needs of young parents. Another instance is if a user has added a product to their shopping cart but has not completed the purchase, the PCFKG can recommend an advertisement for the product to encourage the user to complete the purchase.

11.5.2 PKG recommendation in the Internet of Things

One of the key applications of PKGs is in the area of Internet of Things (IoT), where they can enable personalized and dynamic access to large-scale structured and unstructured data generated by various connected devices and sensors. PKGs can represent the complex relationships and interdependencies between different data sources and provide a unified view of the data, allowing users to quickly and easily find the information they need. They make human–machine interaction much more natural and enable machines to solve problems by combining reasoning with machine learning to analyze and understand very large datasets in real-time, making it possible to gain new insights from complex systems at scale.

PKGs can be used to integrate and manage data from different IoT devices and sensors, such as smart phones, wearable devices, home appliances, and environmental sensors. For example, a PKG-based IoT system could integrate data from a smart watch, a fitness tracker, and a smart thermostat to provide a comprehensive view of the user's health and activity levels. The PKG could store information about the devices, sensors, and user preferences, and use this knowledge to generate personalized recommendations and actions. The author of [33] recommends the personalization of IoT via the Semantic Web of Things (SWoT) which focuses on ensuring a common understanding among heterogeneous objects, to provide personalized experiences.

Most IoT data is machine based and for this reason, it is quite difficult to gain insights from it. One of the benefits of PKGs in the IoT context is their ability to provide context-aware and personalized knowledge because they work in the same way that our brains think. A PKG-based IoT system could use location-aware sensors and user preferences to provide personalized recommendations and services. Take for instance a worker in an office who tells an intelligent system that there is low humidity in the office. The PKG-based system would analyze the text for low humidity and understand that it is an environmental concept. It would therefore access the PKG system to search all assets in the office that determine this environmental variable, and use artificial intelligence to determine if indeed it is low. If it finds for instance the humidifier switched off, it would then turn it on.

In addition, PKGs in the IoT context are beneficial in enabling the development of intelligent and adaptive IoT systems. A PKG-based IoT system could use machine learning and artificial intelligence techniques to enhance data with layers of semantic abstraction; thereby learning from the user's data and preferences, and adapt its recommendations and actions accordingly while also gaining new insights. For instance, a PKG-based smart home system could learn the user's habits and preferences, and automatically adjust the temperature, lighting, and other environmental factors to provide a more comfortable and personalized living environment.

11.5.3 *Personalized healthcare knowledge graphs*

Personalized healthcare knowledge graph (PHKG) is a promising application of PKGs. PHKGs can represent the complex relationships between medical concepts, such as diseases, symptoms, treatments, and genes, and provide a personalized view of the knowledge based on the individual patient's characteristics, such as age, gender, medical history, and genetic profile.

PHKGs can be used to integrate and manage data from different sources, such as electronic medical records, clinical trials, and genomic databases. For example, a PHKG-based system could integrate data from a patient's electronic medical record, genetic profile, and clinical trial data to provide a comprehensive view of the patient's health and treatment options. The PHKG could store information about the patient's characteristics, medical history, and treatment preferences, and use this knowledge to generate personalized recommendations and actions.

One of the key benefits of PHKGs is their ability to provide personalized medical recommendations to patients. For example, a PHKG-based system could use the patient's medical history and genetic profile to identify the most likely diagnoses and treatments for the patient's symptoms, as well as potential risks and side effects. The system could then use the patient's preferences and characteristics to generate a personalized treatment plan, taking into account the patient's specific needs and preferences.

Another potential benefit of PHKGs is their ability to enable the development of personalized medicine [34]. Personalized medicine is a new approach to healthcare that focuses on providing tailored and individualized treatment plans to patients, based on their specific characteristics and medical history. PHKGs can support this approach by providing accurate and relevant knowledge about the patient's health and treatment options.

Based on many studies such as [19,25,35,36], we can summarize the practices and processes to develop PHKG systems as follows: (a) modeling a knowledge graph for healthcare or chronic disease management; (b) incorporating personalization and context-awareness to understand patient symptoms and derive actionable insights; (c) analyzing heterogeneous datasets generated by different devices to extract meaningful information; (d) promoting reproducible experiments and sharing of datasets, data models, and reasoning mechanisms; (e) customizing and instantiating relevant knowledge from existing health knowledge bases to gain insights from health-related social media text; and (f) insuring the privacy provision of the personal data.

Nevertheless there are many challenges for developing PHKG systems, one of the key challenges is the need for robust and reliable data sources. PHKGs need to be able to integrate data from multiple sources, such as electronic medical records, clinical trials, and genomic databases. However, these data sources can be complex, heterogeneous, and often have missing or incomplete information. Therefore, PHKGs need to be able to handle missing and uncertain data, and use advanced algorithms and machine learning techniques to infer and predict missing information.

Another main challenge of PHKGs is the need for user participation and involvement. The personalized aspect of PHKGs relies on the users providing their preferences, characteristics, and feedback. This can be a challenge in some contexts, where users may be unwilling or unable to provide the required information. For example, patients may be reluctant to share their personal medical information, or may not have the time or expertise to provide input to the PHKG.

11.5.3.1   PHKG techniques

There is no standard classification for PHKG approaches and techniques. PHKGs are a relatively new area of research, and different researchers and organizations may have different ways of categorizing the various methods and techniques used in this field. Some possible ways of classifying PHKG methods and techniques could include the types of data used, the methods for building and maintaining the knowledge graph, and the applications of the PHKG in healthcare.

PHKG based on the types of data used: The PHKG systems could be classified based on the types of data used in these systems. It is worth mentioning that some

PHKGs may fall under more than one category due to the fact that they used and analyzed different types of data. The PHKG based on used data can be classified into the following types:

1. *Clinical data*: This includes medical records, lab results, imaging reports, and other information related to patient care.
2. *Genomic data*: DNA sequences, gene expression profiles, and other molecular data related to individual health fall in this category.
3. *Environmental data*: This includes air quality, water quality, and other environmental factors that may impact health.
4. *Behavioral data*: This type of data includes lifestyle choices, dietary habits, physical activity levels, and other behaviors that may affect health.
5. *Social data*: This includes demographic information, social networks, and other social factors that may influence health.
6. *Economic data*: This type of data includes economic indicators, financial information, and other economic factors that may impact health.

PHKG methods for building and maintaining KGs: There are several different methods for building and maintaining knowledge in PHKGs, which can be broadly classified into the following categories:

1. *Data integration and alignment*: This includes techniques for data cleaning, transformation, and matching, as well as methods for detecting and resolving conflicts and inconsistencies in the data that integrate and align data from different sources, such as electronic medical records, clinical trials, and genomic databases.
2. *Ontology development and alignment*: This consists of techniques for ontology engineering, such as class and property modeling, as well as methods for aligning and merging different ontologies, that aims at developing and maintaining domain-specific ontologies and knowledge bases, which are used to represent the concepts and relationships in the PHKG.
3. *Machine learning and artificial intelligence*: This involves methods for classification, clustering, and prediction, as well as techniques for natural language processing (NLP) and information extraction. These methods seek to learn from the data and knowledge in the PHKG, and to generate personalized recommendations and predictions.
4. *User participation and feedback*: This involves methods for involving users in the development and maintenance of the PHKG, such as providing preferences, characteristics, and feedback. It involves methods for curating and validating the knowledge represented in the PHKG, in order to ensure its accuracy, consistency, and relevance.
5. *Knowledge curation and validation*: This can include techniques for manual and automatic fact checking, as well as methods for detecting and resolving errors and inconsistencies in the knowledge.
6. *Data privacy and security*: This includes techniques for encryption, authentication, and access control, as well as methods for detecting and preventing data breaches and other security threats. These techniques aim at protecting the

personal and sensitive data stored in the PHKG from unauthorized access and misuse.

7. *User interface and usability*: This involves techniques for user-centered design, as well as methods for evaluating and improving the usability of the PHKG. It includes the methods for designing and implementing user interfaces that allow users to easily access and use the knowledge in the PHKG

8. *Maintenance and updates*: This consists of techniques for detecting and responding to changes in the data and knowledge, as well as methods for evolving and adapting the PHKG over time, that aim at maintaining and updating the PHKG, in order to keep up with changing data and knowledge.

9. *Data visualization and exploration*: This could include techniques for creating interactive graphs, maps, and charts, as well as methods for supporting data exploration and discovery, and it involves methods for visualizing the data and knowledge in the PHKG, in order to allow users to easily explore and understand the information.

10. *Knowledge representation and reasoning*: This involves techniques for representing and reasoning with concepts, relationships, and rules, as well as methods for supporting probabilistic and uncertain reasoning for representing the knowledge in the PHKG in a formal, logical, and semantically rich way to support reasoning and inference.

11. *Collaborative and social knowledge*: This could include techniques for supporting community-based knowledge creation, as well as methods for fostering collaboration and communication among users. These methods seek to enable collaboration and social interaction among users of the PHKG for supporting knowledge sharing, feedback, and discussion.

PHKG by applications: The PHKGs have been used for various purposes and can be classified into categories based on the application used for as follows:

1. *Clinical decision support*: Clinical decision support systems (CDSSs) utilize PHKG to provide clinicians with evidence-based information to support clinical decisions.

2. *Disease management*: PHKG can be used to help monitor and manage chronic conditions, such as diabetes, by providing timely and accurate data.

3. *Population health management*: PHKG can be used to identify population health trends and analyze patient data for disease prevention and management.

4. *Risk stratification*: PHKG can be used to identify and stratify patients based on their risk factors, allowing providers to better target interventions.

5. *Drug discovery and development:* PHKG can be used to identify potential drug targets and analyze drug safety and efficacy.

6. *Diagnostics and prognostics*: PHKG can be used to develop diagnostics and prognostics that identify diseases earlier and more accurately.

7. *Precision medicine*: PHKG can be used to develop personalized treatments and therapies based on a patient's individual characteristics.

11.6 Sample PKG recommendation application

Badminton is one of the five major racket sports and it can be played by singles or doubles. It is a purely volley sport in which the shuttlecock is not allowed to fall on the floor before the opponent hits it. The equipment used in badminton is very similar to tennis and includes a racket and a shuttlecock (projectile that is struck with the racket). Formal badminton games are played on a rectangular indoor court where points are scored by hitting the shuttlecock and landing it inside the rival's side portion of the court. The indoor court must have proper lighting, a minimum height of 14 m and suitable flooring. In order to play the game, one must wear appropriate gear which includes indoor sport shoes, socks, comfortable shorts, wrist band, towel, and a dry-fit t-shirt. The scoring in badminton is up to 21 points per game or per set. In order to emerge victorious in a match, one has to win 2 out of 3 sets in a game.

The badminton training PKG recommendation system represents how trainers can have a personalized view of badminton trainees served by a view of the graph that is specific to them. It can be used in scalable applications where various trainees with different levels of skills are trained for instance at a club. In building the badminton PKG, data was collected from domain experts, i.e. (badminton trainers) who provided the rules of the game and the kind of training expected at each level of training. A simple badminton training ontology was created that included key classes like *trainee, trainer, facility, equipment, sports gear and training*, object and data properties and some instances.

The badminton training PKG is able to manage large amounts of information about badminton trainees, training, equipment, facility, sports gear, and trainers while at the same time generating the relationships among the involved classes and outputting relevant recommendation knowledge. Through the web-based application implemented in Python and Django framework, one can enter various details of trainees, trainers, and trainings as shown in Figures 11.1–11.4.

Figure 14.1 shows the form through which trainer details are entered. Based on the level of trainer entered, e.g. beginner trainer, the application only allows him to

Figure 11.1   Trainer form

Figure 11.2　Trainee form

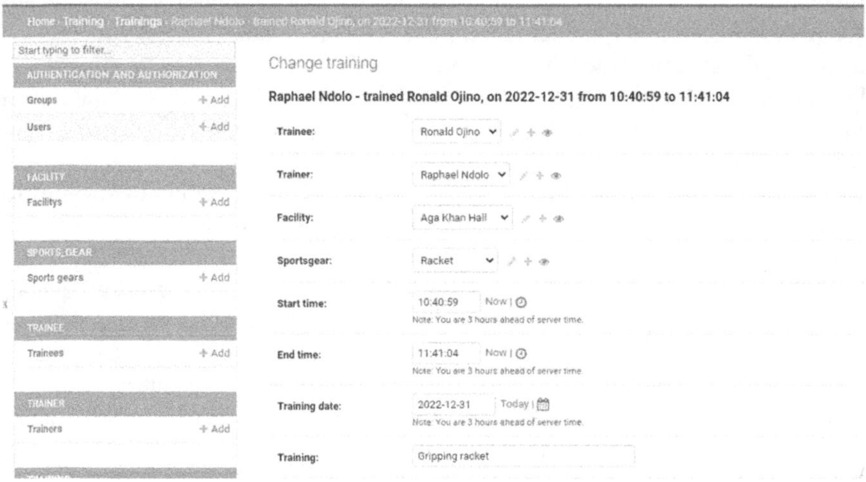

Figure 11.3　Training form

train beginner trainees. Figure 14.2 shows the form through which trainee details are entered or edited. Figure 14.3 shows the form through which training details are entered including date and time of training as well as the training activities carried out. Figure 14.4 lists all the training entered in the application. One can filter the kind of trainings that he wants to view based on the menu presented. Figure 11.5 is a visual of the nodes and relations in the badminton training PKG when the view graph button is clicked. It is important to note that the PKG has output details that are of interest to a particular training level. This can also be narrowed down to a particular trainer as shown in Figure 14.5.

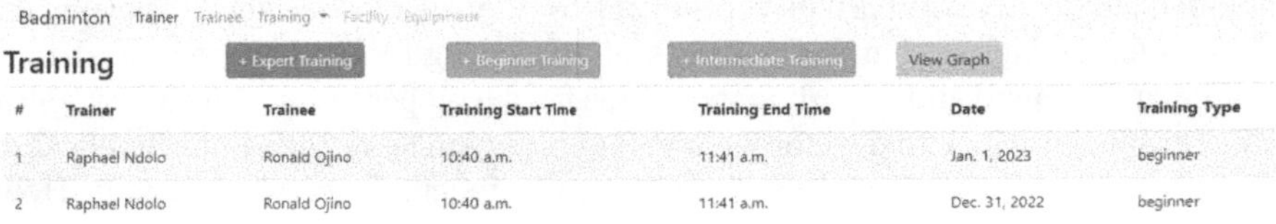

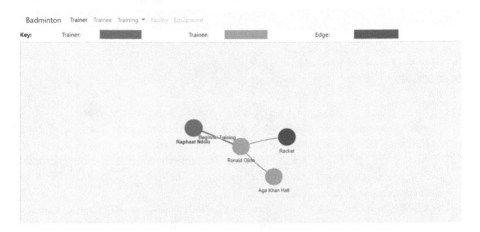

Figure 11.4   *Trainings list*

Figure 11.5   Visual nodes of interest to the beginner trainee

In the above web application, a view of the PKG in Figure 1.5 is able to show that trainer 'Raphael Ndolo' who specializes in beginner training trains 'Ronald Ojino', a beginner trainee at Aga Khan Hall. The trainee has brought with him a racket. Details like the relationship are shown when hovers over the edges while the type of node is also shown when one hovers over a node. Given that in the above case Raphael is a beginner trainer, the training that he offers is focused on beginner activities that include gripping the racket, serving, footwork, clears and dropping. Such details can be displayed on the PKG based on the user's needs.

11.7   Conclusion

PKG recommendations are novel technologies that are already being adopted in some of the day-to-day services we use and it is likely that their usage is going to be widespread in the near future. In this chapter, we have illustrated the ways in which PKG recommendation systems exploit the expressive power of KGs to revolutionize personalized services and products provision by offering more accuracy and explainable recommendations. Various methods of developing PKGs for recommendations have been presented and it is ultimately upon the developer to select the most appropriate technique to use in developing a PKG for a given task. The sample application has demonstrated how PKGs can be leveraged to generate recommendations. However, in developing PKG for recommendation applications, there is need for devising more innovative methods to address the challenges encountered so as to encourage uptake. In future, we hope to build PKGs for other domains such as climate change research and agriculture where we will run the recommendation methods based on the PKGs integrated with deep learning or other novel machine learning algorithms, and compare the recommendation performance.

References

[1]   Al-Aswadi FN, Chan HY, and Gan KH. Automatic ontology construction from text: a review from shallow to deep learning trend. *Artificial Intelligence Review*. 2020;53(6):3901–3928.

[2]   Al-shalabi H, Tiun S, Omar N, *et al.* The effectiveness of Arabic Stemmers using Arabized word removal. *International Journal of Information Science & Management*. 2022;20(4):87–102.

[3]   AL-Aswadi FN, Chan HY, Gan KH, *et al.* Enhancing relevant concepts extraction for ontology learning using domain time relevance. *Information Processing & Management*. 2023;60(1):103140.

[4]   AL-Aswadi FN, Chan HY, and Gan KH. From ontology to knowledge graph trend: ontology as foundation layer for knowledge graph. In: *IberoAmerican Knowledge Graphs and Semantic Web Conference*. Springer; 2022. p. 330–340.

[5]   Zou X. A survey on application of knowledge graph. In: *Journal of Physics: Conference Series*. 2020;1487:012016.

[6]   Liu J, Shi C, Yang C, *et al.* A survey on heterogeneous information network based recommender systems: concepts, methods, applications and resources. *AI Open*. 2022;3:40–57.

[7]   Berkovsky S and Freyne J. Web personalization and recommender systems. In: *Proceedings of the 21th ACM SIGKDD International Conference on Knowledge Discovery and Data Mining*; 2015. p. 2307–2308.

[8]   Porcel C, Martinez-Cruz C, Bernabé-Moreno J, *et al.* Integrating ontologies and fuzzy logic to represent user-trustworthiness in recommender systems. *Procedia Computer Science*. 2015;55:603–612.

[9]   Aljunid MF and Huchaiah MD. An efficient hybrid recommendation model based on collaborative filtering recommender systems. *CAAI Transactions on Intelligence Technology*. 2021;6(4):480–492.

[10] Lian Z and Hui C. Research on recommendation algorithms in web of things system. In: *2014 7th International Conference on Intelligent Computation Technology and Automation*. IEEE; 2014. p. 569–572.

[11]   Bobadilla J, Ortega F, Hernando A, *et al.* Improving collaborative filtering recommender system results and performance using genetic algorithms. *Knowledge-Based Systems.* 2011;24(8):1310–1316.

[12]   Doh RF, Zhou C, Arthur JK, *et al.* A systematic review of deep knowledge graph-based recommender systems, with focus on explainable embeddings. *Data.* 2022;7(7):94.

[13]   Guo Q, Zhuang F, Qin C, *et al.* A survey on knowledge graph-based recommender systems. *IEEE Transactions on Knowledge and Data Engineering.* 2020.

[14]   Schröder M, Jilek C, and Dengel A. A human-in-the-loop approach for personal knowledge graph construction from file names. In: *Third International Workshop on Knowledge Graph Construction*; 2022.

[15]   Bordes A, Usunier N, Garcia-Duran A, *et al.* Translating embeddings for modeling multi-relational data. *Advances in Neural Information Processing Systems.* 2013;26.

[16]   Wang Z, Zhang J, Feng J, *et al.* Knowledge graph embedding by translating on hyperplanes. In: *Proceedings of the AAAI Conference on Artificial Intelligence.* vol. 28; 2014.

[17]   Al-Aswadi FN, Chan HY, and Gan KH. Extracting semantic concepts and relations from scientific publications by using deep learning. In: *International Conference of Reliable Information and Communication Technology.* Springer; 2021. p. 374–383.

[18]   Ojino RO. Towards an ontology for personalized hotel room recommendation: student research abstract. In: *Proceedings of the 35th Annual ACM Symposium on Applied Computing*; 2020. p. 2060–2063.

[19]   Ahmed IA, AL-Aswadi FN, Noaman KM, *et al.* Arabic knowledge graph construction: a close look in the present and into the future. *Journal of King Saud University—Computer and Information Sciences.* 2022;34: 6505–6523.

[20]   Chen X, Jia S, and Xiang Y. A review: knowledge reasoning over knowledge graph. *Expert Systems with Applications.* 2020;141:112948.

[21]   Dong XL. Challenges and innovations in building a product knowledge graph. In: *Proceedings of the 24th ACM SIGKDD International Conference on Knowledge Discovery & Data Mining*; 2018. p. 2869–2869.

[22]   Faber L, Safavi T, Mottin D, *et al.* Adaptive personalized knowledge graph summarization. In: *MLG Workshop (with KDD)*; 2018.

[23]   Xie K, Jia Q, Jing M, *et al.* Data analysis based on knowledge graph. In: *International Conference on Broadband and Wireless Computing, Communication and Applications.* Springer; 2020. p. 376–385.

[24]   Chicaiza J and Valdiviezo-Diaz P. A comprehensive survey of knowledge graph-based recommender systems: technologies, development, and contributions. *Information.* 2021;12(6):232.

[25]   Gyrard A, Gaur M, Shekarpour S, *et al.* Personalized health knowledge graph. In: *CEUR Workshop Proceedings*; 2018.

[26]   Xu G, Jia G, Shi L, *et al.* Personalized course recommendation system fusing with knowledge graph and collaborative filtering. *Computational Intelligence and Neuroscience*. 2021;2021.

[27]   Nilashi M, bin Ibrahim O, Ithnin N, *et al.* A multi-criteria collaborative filtering recommender system for the tourism domain using expectation maximization (EM) and PCA–ANFIS. *Electronic Commerce Research and Applications*. 2015;14(6):542–562.

[28]   Ojino R, Mich L, and Mvungi N. Hotel room personalization via ontology and rule-based reasoning. *International Journal of Web Information Systems*. 2022; ahead-of-print.

[29]   Catherine R, Mazaitis K, Eskenazi M, *et al.* Explainable entity-based recommendations with knowledge graphs; 2017. arXiv preprint arXiv:170705254.

[30]   Wang H, Wang Z, Hu S, *et al.* DUSKG: a fine-grained knowledge graph for effective personalized service recommendation. *Future Generation Computer Systems*. 2019;100:600–617.

[31]   Singh MK and Rishi OP. Event driven recommendation system for E-commerce using knowledge based collaborative filtering technique. *Scalable Computing: Practice and Experience*. 2020;21(3):369–378.

[32]   Wu J, Lécué F, Gueret C, *et al.* Personalizing actions in context for risk management using semantic web technologies. In: *International Semantic Web Conference*. Springer; 2017. p. 367–383.

[33]   Ojino R. User's profile ontology-based semantic model for personalized hotel room recommendation in the web of things: student research abstract. In: *Proceedings of the 34th ACM/SIGAPP Symposium on Applied Computing*; 2019. p. 2314–2316.

[34]   Silva MC, Faria D, and Pesquita C. Matching multiple ontologies to build a knowledge graph for personalized medicine. In: *European Semantic Web Conference*. Springer; 2022. p. 461–477.

[35]   Seneviratne O, Harris J, Chen CH, *et al.* Personal health knowledge graph for clinically relevant diet recommendations; 2021. arXiv preprint arXiv:211010131.

[36]   Tiwari S, Al-Aswadi FN, and Gaurav D. Recent trends in knowledge graphs: theory and practice. *Soft Computing*. 2021;25(13):8337–8355.

Section 5

Evaluation and other applications

Chapter 12

Evaluation approaches of personal knowledge graphs

Hanieh Khorashadizadeh[a], Frederic Ieng[b],
Morteza Ezzabady[c], Soror Sahri[b], Sven Groppe[a] and
Farah Benamara[c]

Knowledge graphs (KGs) provide structured data for users' applications such as recommendation systems, personal assistants, and question-answering systems. The quality of the underlying applications relies deeply on the quality of the knowledge graph. However, KGs inevitably have inconsistencies, such as duplicates, wrong assertions, and missing values. The presence of such issues may compromise the outcome of business intelligence applications. Hence, it is crucial and necessary to explore efficient and effective methods for tackling the evaluation of KGs. These techniques get much tougher when the KG deals with personal data, which is referred to as Personal Knowledge Graph (PKG). This chapter covers PKG's creation, population, and more importantly their evaluation from a data quality perspective.

12.1 Introduction

Knowledge graphs (KGs) are a graph representation of knowledge in entities, edges, and attributes, where the entity represents the real world, the edge represents a relationship, and the attribute defines an entity. It allows for potentially interrelating arbitrary entities with each other and covers various topical domains [1]. It is getting more attention recently for building more intelligent systems such as building knowledge-based information retrieval systems, conversation systems, question and answer (Q&A) systems, topic recommendation systems, and many others [1,2]. However, the quality of the knowledge graph can impact the performance of knowledge-based systems built on it. In this context, the KG evaluation is a critical task to provide reliable, correct, and complete knowledge [1,3,4].

[a]Institute of Information Systems (IFIS), Universität zu Lübeck, Germany
[b]Université Paris Cité, France
[c]IRIT, Université de Toulouse, CNRS, Toulouse INP, UT3, France

The evaluation of KGs, considered as a curation/refinement task, is typically a shared responsibility of a group of people volunteers (public KGs) or knowledge editors (proprietary KGs), who must abide by a strict set of guidelines [5]. However, when knowledge graphs deal with the personal data of people, what is commonly referred to as PKGs, this task becomes more difficult. Indeed, PKGs differ from general KGs in several aspects, particularly with their high time dependency and user privacy concerns.

The goal of this work is PKGs' evaluation from a data quality perspective. Although a significant amount of work has been conducted for the evaluation of KGs, this remains an open challenge for PKGs. For KGs, several frameworks and approaches have been proposed to evaluate KGs' quality [1–4]. The quality of KG mainly concerns the fitness of purposes to an application that is built on the graph. KGs are more often evaluated to check whether a KG meets basic quality standards and to ensure it fits the purpose. It is multi-dimensional, and the main evaluation dimensions for KG quality are accuracy, completeness, consistency, timeliness, trustworthiness, and availability [4].

In this paper, we review existing work about PKGs in their various processes, from creating/populating PKGs to their utilization. Then, we focus on the evaluation approaches proposed in each existing work and throughout its corresponding process, with also considering its evaluation measures. We propose a classification of existing evaluation approaches according to these criteria: their application domain, the approach, the process type, and the evaluation measures. Specifically, this paper makes the following contributions:

- We present an extensive review of the existing work about PKGs according to their application domain and analyze their various processes (creation, population, and utilization).
- We summarize the main evaluation approaches for KGs and their evaluation measures, to provide guidance for PKG evaluation. We focus on quality aspects such as completion and error detection.
- We present PKGs evaluation approaches in the literature, based on the categorization presented for KGs. We classify them according to their processes, application domain, and evaluation measures.

The remainder of this paper is organized as follows. In Section 12.2, we present PKGs, their main processes and their main challenges. Then, in Section 12.3, we overview existing evaluation approaches for KGs. In Section 12.4, we focus on the evaluation approaches for PKGs. Finally, we conclude and discuss some open problems in Section 12.5.

12.2   Personal knowledge graphs

These days the benefits of using knowledge graphs have become apparent as they have many different use cases. They range from chatbots [7], knowledge management [8], recommendation systems [9] to fraud detection [10]. PKGs are those knowledge

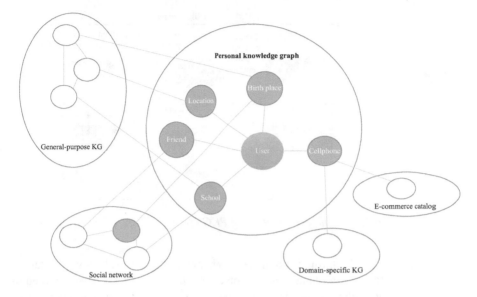

Figure 12.1   Personal knowledge graph. Inspired by [5].

graphs that deal with the personal data of people [11]. PKGs differ from general KGs in several aspects. First, the entities belong to a specified person and might not interest others. Second, the user is at the center of the KG and all other nodes are connected to a central node, as it has the spiderweb schema model as shown in Figure 12.1. Third, entities can be connected to external sources like domain-specific KGs, general-purpose KGs, or even social networks [5]. For example, if that person is a scientist who would like to know about the papers she has already read and the topics she has covered so far, she can maintain a personal knowledge graph to get the answers to her questions [11]. This PKG contains all data related to her lab tools, co-workers, ongoing projects, the employees working on the projects, and the resources they are utilizing at the moment. Below, we present the different PKGs processes in the literature.

12.2.1   PKG's creation

In recent years, the size of produced data has grown tremendously due to the principles of Findability, Accessibility, Interoperability, and Reuse of digital assets (FAIR) [12]. An even much higher growth rate is anticipated in the coming years [13]. This heterogeneous data in various formats can be integrated into a knowledge graph. Data might be available in unstructured format or plain text, semi-structured, and structured formats or tabular. If data resides in natural language text, natural language processing (NLP) tools and techniques must be applied to the text to get the triples and build the knowledge graph. And if data is in a structured format, RDF mapping tools convert the tables to RDF knowledge graphs. There has been a need to represent

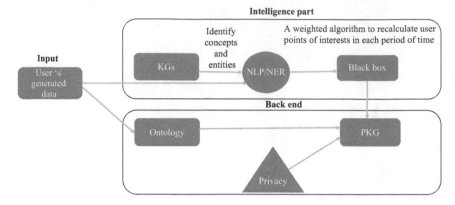

Figure 12.2   The architecture of PKG creation. Inspired by [6].

user personal data which might not interest others and there must be a way to tackle the personal information management problem [14]. Hence, PKGs have emerged to represent patients' relevant data [15], e-learning platforms user and learners [6], and personalized recommendation systems like diet recommendation systems [16]. As Figure 12.2 depicts, the data along with ontology is processed by NLP techniques to extract entities and relations. As users might consider various things through time, there remains a weighted algorithm to recalculate users' central attention at different points in time. The black box deals with the weights and filters the entities from the KGs. These entities are then fed to the PKG and the PKG is created regarding the user privacy concerns [6].

12.2.2   PKG's population

A typical pipeline to populate a knowledge graph comprises Entity Recognition, Entity Classification, Entity Resolution, Relation Extraction, and Link Prediction. There is active research in the area of extraction of entities and relationships from natural language text. Joint entity and relation extraction frameworks have successfully used long short-term memories (LSTMs), dynamic span graphs, and pre-trained transformers [4].

Since entities relevant to a PKG are often present in personal conversations, researchers have proposed methods to extract such entities from conversations. In KG terminology, entity linking refers to the process of identifying entity mentions and linking them with KG entities. KG entity mentions are commonly mapped to unique identifiers representing KG entities. Currently, state-of-the-art entity linking solutions are also limited in performance, making this a challenging task.

Entity linking usually involves three subtasks, i.e., detection, entity disambiguation, and NIL detection, all of which typically rely on an existing KG as a source of information. This immediately brings out a key difference between the generic and the PKG case: a PKG can contain little information about entities to be used by linking algorithms [5].

12.2.3 PKG's utilization

The PKG evaluation should be linked to specific requirements of knowledge-based applications that are built on the PKG. From a data quality perspective, evaluating a PKG is about checking whether it meets basic quality standards and ensuring it fits the purpose. Hence, an overview of the different applications of PKGs and their utilization is essential to explore the PKG evaluation approaches in the next sections. Below, we review existing work about PKGs according to their application domain.

12.2.3.1 Healthcare applications

Healthcare applications can benefit the most from PKGs, as mostly healthcare systems like patients' diet recommendations are very focused on each individual person. In [16], the patient's health records and food logs are represented in a Personal Health Knowledge Graph (PHKG), modeled according to the Personal Health Ontology. The PHKG is used to capture personal dietary behaviors such as carbohydrate intake with the extended time series summarizing technique. It can also use semantic reasoners to recommend clinically relevant dietary recommendations. PKGs can delineate the patient's evolving preference and information and are well aware of the patient's evolving health status and nutritional demands of the patient [17]. PKGs also include some information in general-purpose knowledge graphs. This information is relevant to all patients. Then PHKGs contain knowledge that is specific only to a set of patients or an individual patient. So, a health recommendation system would be able to respond well to queries having access to user's preferences, health history, cultural background, and preferences that are maintained in PHKGs [17].

12.2.3.2 Intelligent personal systems

A conversational agent (CA) is a system that can communicate intelligently with humans. This technology has become increasingly popular in e-commerce, information retrieval, personal assistants, and a variety of other applications. There are challenges for CAs in providing meaningful responses to users, that is, providing a meaningful response to a user while also taking into consideration user preferences or information [18]. A plausible reason for the CAs lack of ability in providing personalized responses is that the models used in the CAs do not effectively capture the user-specific information from the conversations before responding to the user as the personal information tends to be implicitly represented [19]. In order to mitigate this problem, it would be helpful to represent the personal information explicitly and then use this representation to provide personalized responses. The graph structure of PKGs makes them an ideal method of storing information for CAs [20]. Additionally, PKGs are used in the modeling of personal information, where textual triples are extracted [21]. There are surface-form words as subject and object within the textual triples, i.e., phrases from the conversation. This means that entities can be represented multiple times. As a result, entity linking is required so that phrases can be mapped to entities. This problem is addressed by a pipelined architecture consisting mainly of the Personal Entity Classifier (PEC) and the Personal Entity Disambiguator (PED).

While PEC determines whether an entity is mentioned in the PKG, PED associates the entity mentioned with a specific entity.

In [22], spoken dialog queries to a dialog system were classified as informational, transactional, and navigational in a similar way to the taxonomy for web search. In virtual personal assistant (VPA) systems such as Microsoft Cortana, in addition to these three main categories, more and more personal assertion utterances are conveyed from the users, where users are talking about themselves (e.g., *I am vegetarian* or *My daughter is getting married*). As such utterances may vary greatly, a novel spoken language understanding approach was proposed in [22], aiming to construct personal knowledge graphs in spoken utterances. This approach contains three main language understanding components: personal assertion classification, relation detection, and slot filling.

12.2.3.3   Personal information systems

In [23], the authors hypothesize that file names could be a promising source for constructing PKGs. File names are usually short ungrammatical (sometimes noisy) text snippets and contain differently ordered and concatenated keywords. These circumstances make it difficult to discover and extract relevant named entities from them. Besides labeling, users can also assemble files in hierarchically structured folders, without any definition of how named entities relate to each other. To cope with this semantic gap, the authors include knowledge workers as humans-in-the-loop to guide the building process with their feedback. This semi-automatic PKG creation approach consists of four major stages: domain term extraction, ontology population, and taxonomic and non-taxonomic relation learning.

12.2.3.4   Social applications

In [24], the authors developed a framework to build a PKG about life logging using social media (e.g. Twitter, Facebook) data. The main focus is on general life events such as dining, visiting a local place, or buying a new phone. First, a ground-truth is manually built by an annotator based on the life event in the FrameNet ontology. The annotator started by detecting if the tweet describes a personal life event. Then, for tweets describing personal life events, the annotator specifies the subject, predicate, object, and time of each life event, and whether the event is implicit or explicit. Finally, the annotator selects a suitable frame name for each predicate and label semantic roles. The framework is then built to extract life logging that can be separated into five components: (i) life event detection to filter out a tweet that does not contain a life event. This subtask is regarded as a problem of binary classification; (ii) explicit life event detection to extract predicates that trigger explicit life events; (iii) implicit life event detection; (iv) life event quadruples extraction to extract subject, object, and time for each predicate; and (v) frame semantics parsing to label predicates using Chinese FrameNet.

12.2.3.5   Recommendation applications

In [25], the PKG is built on mobile data from different services like e-mails, messages, contact lists, music, calendars, location histories, etc. Using many sources makes it hard and difficult to organize, manage, and utilize. The personal knowledge graph is created locally on the users' devices to avoid any privacy issues. First, information is processed, and the first estimation of users' intents is made. Two types of data are collected: (i) structured, i.e. information about clicking, adding, or deleting operations from contacts lists, calendars, e-mails, etc. The intention behind these operations is clear, thus intention, classes, entities, and relations are created by hand-made rules; and (ii) unstructured, i.e. data are mainly natural language that is harder to exploit and needs more complex methods. Such data are processed using a neural network to extract intentions, entities, and relations. At the same time, symbolic rules based on common sense knowledge are used to validate the results of the neural network. The second step is to build the PKG, with the following subtasks:

- **Defining the ontology of PKG:** Every PKG is defined by a set of classes and by a set of relations between classes. Classes usually include central users, intentions, events, time, etc. Relations between different classes can be couples between people or if a location is a workplace for some person.
- **Building a common knowledge graph:** Users' information is interacting with the same outside world. Therefore, creating a common knowledge graph is probably a more efficient way to treat common knowledge.
- **Analyzing intention:** Finding the right intention leads to extracting more relevant information. For example, "Taylor Swift is awesome", the information is that the user expresses positive interest in "Taylor Swift".
- **Generating triple:** Once the information is processed, the next step is to generate triples that link two entities with a relation.
- **Linking entity to common knowledge graph:** Once the triples are generated, they are connected to the common knowledge graph to make recommendations more accurate. The entities are linked using Elasticsearch to match the right entities in the common knowledge graph.

Finally, the last part is the recommendation module, separated into two parts: (i) path-based recommendation, where the information is processed and analyzed, a recommendation is made based on pre-defined grammatical habit rules, then the closest entities are given under the restrictions of recommendation item type, time information, interests, and entity weights; and (ii) inference-based recommendation, where inference is made over common knowledge graph, e.g., if the user follows "Christopher Nolan" and "Creed", then the inference module will predict that the user prefers "science fiction movie" and "action movie".

12.2.3.6   Educational and learning applications

A PKG for researchers can be useful in designing personalized forms of knowledge-aware applications like scholarly search engines, and also conversational AI agents and recommendation systems, that can greatly assist a researcher in her everyday chores. In [11], the authors present a personal research knowledge graph (PRKG). They particularly explore what entities and relations could be potentially included in a PRKG, how to extract them from various sources, and how to share a PRKG within a research group. To extract entities and relations, these mechanisms were discussed: (i) conversations between the researcher and chat-bot to mine personal information about a researcher by analyzing her conversions with it; (ii) tracking activities of the researchers as the downloaded papers or the entered queries in scholarly search engines; and (iii) extraction from papers by leveraging manuscripts that allow the identification of more fine-grained entities like performance scores, future work, etc. To extract relations, symbolic and neural algorithms were discussed.

In [6], PKGs were used to better semantically enhance personalized features for e-learning platforms. Indeed, there is an increased need for systems with highly personalized capabilities, personalized collaborative search, and more productive and impactful platforms that can support collaborative learning, particularly since the COVID-19 pandemic. The authors proposed a novel PKG development that relies on ontology and interlinks to Linked Open Data. That is to use PKGs to connect individuals' and group's search with the semantic web and offer a better collaborative and personalized experience. For the creation of such PKG, the user's generated, considered as input data, are combined, and processed with the named entity recognition and natural language processing software to identify the concepts and entities from the KGs. To cope with the user's actions changing through time, a weighted algorithm is used to recalculate the main points of interest for the user in each period of time. A black box calculates those weights and offers a filter in the recognized entities from the KGs, which will be passed to the PKG. Then, the PKG is created with respect to user's and user group privacy.

12.2.4   PKG's challenges

Given the aforementioned about the creation, population, and utilization of PKGs, some issues can be confronted while constructing and using the PKGs [5].

1. Connection with central node: Unlike general knowledge graphs, all entities must be connected to the central node which is the user, as it has the spiderweb schema model as shown in Figure 12.1.
2. Temporal relations: As data varies at different times, PKGs highly depend on time. Relations might be temporary in a PKG because of its nature [5]. An example might be the people I met yesterday. As some predicates and entities are temporal in a PKG, their representation in the KG and their manipulation can be a problem. This might also impact the application which is based on the PKGs backend [6].
3. Link prediction: Link prediction is usually based on knowledge graph embedding methods. Such methods require a huge amount of data, which is not the case for PKGs.
4. Privacy concerns: This is about to ensure that user's personal data is safe.
5. PKG curation: The KG curation is the process of assessing and improving the quality of KGs. In [3], KG curation involves (i) assessing the status of KGs based on quality dimensions and metrics, (ii) detecting and correcting wrong assertions, and (iii) enriching the KGs by adding new statements. For PKGs, the curation task becomes more difficult, because of consideration for users' control over and verification of information stored in their PKG, is important to take into

account. One important question that a rises is: how can PKGs be automatically populated and reliably maintained [5].

Our work focuses on the PKG curation for evaluating their quality. In any case, all the above challenges could impact the PKG curation. Following, we particularly review existing work about PKGs and the various processes (creation, population, and utilization) they take into account. For each process, we focus on its influence on the PKG quality and the evaluation approach to deal with the eventual quality issues. To do so, we first present the KGs evaluation approaches, to provide guidance for PKG evaluation.

12.3 Evaluation methods of KGs

KGs provide structured data for users' applications such as search engines, personal assistants, and question-answering systems. However, KGs can have quality issues such as inconsistencies (duplicates, wrong assertions, missing values, etc.). The presence of such issues may compromise the results of business intelligence applications. Hence, it is important to explore efficient and effective methods and tools for tackling the evaluation of KGs [3].

Many frameworks were proposed for the evaluation of knowledge graphs. Zaveri *et al.* explored the existing data quality assessment methodologies to evaluate the quality of linked datasets [26]. Different quality dimensions were identified to assess the quality of linked datasets and then KGs. They are classified into four categories: accessibility, representation, contextual, and intrinsic. The accessibility category includes dimensions related to data access as availability, licensing, interlinking, security, and performance. For example, the dimension availability measures the functioning of every access method and the readiness to use the data; and dimension licensing is related to the consumer permission to re-using a dataset under conditions. The intrinsic category includes context-free dimensions: syntactic validity, semantic accuracy, consistency, conciseness, and completeness. For example, dimension syntactic validity evaluates if the data respects the used norm; and semantic accuracy evaluates their representation of real facts. The contextual category includes highly context-dependent dimensions: relevancy, trustworthiness, understandability, and timeliness. For example, dimension relevancy measures the relevance of information for a given task; and dimension trustworthiness measures the credibility of data sources. The representational category includes dimensions related to the design and the easiness to use of data: representational conciseness, interoperability, interpretability, and versatility. For example, dimension interoperability measures the re-use of existing vocabularies by a dataset. Each quality dimension is evaluated by several quality evaluation metrics, such as the metrics for dimension availability include "accessibility of the RDF dumps", "dereferenceability of the URI", and others.

In [2], the authors proposed a quality framework for a knowledge graph that can well balance between ensuring fit for the purpose of knowledge graph and being practical for evaluation. To do so, they first identified the quality requirements of knowledge graphs based on a systematic investigation of representative published applications and performed a mapping between knowledge graph applications and the essential quality requirements. To do so, they proposed a mapping between knowledge graph applications and their quality requirements. The KG applications were identified from an investigation of existing applications in the KG literature. A set of quality dimensions and their corresponding metrics are then selected based on these quality requirements. From existing KGs evaluation approaches and tools, the authors proposed a framework for evaluating each metric considering its feasibility and scalability. The framework can be used for checking the essential quality requirements of knowledge graphs for serving the purpose of knowledge discovery.

In [1], Paulheim provided a survey of knowledge graph refinement approaches, particularly existing methods and their evaluation methodologies. He compared each method according to many criteria such as its type, its refinement target, the evaluation method, the applied knowledge graph (the whole or part of KG), etc. Hereafter, we recall these approaches with a focus on their evaluation methods as presented in [1]. Knowledge graph refinement approaches can differ along different dimensions [27]: (i) the method's overall goal, (ii) the refinement target, and (iii) the data used by the approach. There are two main goals of knowledge graph refinement: (a) completion which consists of adding missing knowledge to the graph and (b) error detection which consists of identifying wrong information in the graph. From a data quality perspective, those goals relate to the data quality dimensions of free-of-error and completeness [28].

In completion, internal methods use only the knowledge contained in the knowledge graph itself to predict missing information. External methods use sources that are not part of the knowledge graph. In error detection, internal methods use only the information given in a knowledge graph to find out whether an axiom in the knowledge graph is plausible or not. For external methods, semi-automatic approaches, which exploit human knowledge, have been proposed.

To evaluate those refinement approaches, Paulheim [1] differentiates possible ways between methodologies that rely strictly on the knowledge graph and methodologies that use external data, such as human annotations. These evaluation methods are:

- **Partial gold standard**: This method allows a manual selection and labeling of subset of graph entities or relations. Other evaluations use external knowledge graphs or databases as partial gold standards. As part of completion tasks, all axioms that should be present in the knowledge graph are collected, while as part of correction tasks, an axiom is manually labeled as correct or incorrect. The recall, precision, and F-measure are used to measure the quality of completion approaches. Whereas, accuracy and/or area under the ROC curve (AUC) are often used alternatively to measure the quality of correction methods. In the case of knowledge graphs and ontologies that are not excessively complex, partially sourcing gold standards from humans can produce high-quality data, but at a high cost, making them infrequent and commonly small.

- **Knowledge graph as silver standard**: This method consists of using the given knowledge graph itself as a test dataset. This method is commonly used to evaluate how well knowledge graph completion methods can replicate relations in a knowledge graph. As for gold standard evaluations, the recall, precision, and F-measure allow to measure the resulting quality. Large-scale evaluations can easily be used, with no human annotations. The silver standard method is only suitable for evaluating knowledge graph completion, not for error detection, since it assumes the knowledge graph to be correct.
- **Retrospective evaluation**: This method involves human judges marking suggested completions or identifying errors as correct or incorrect based on the output of a given approach. Accuracy or precision is the quality metric used, as well as the total number of completions or errors found with the approach, and also a statement about the agreement of the human judges. It is common for automatic refinement methods to produce an enormous number of results, e.g., lists of tens of thousands of axioms that may be wrong. Consequently, retrospective evaluations are often limited to samples. An alternative approach to evaluating the actually affected axioms is the evaluation of the intermediate artifacts generated by some approaches, e.g., error patterns or completion rules.
- **Computational performance**: This method becomes more important accordingly with the growth of KG's size, and the correctness and/or completeness of results. Typical performance measures for this aspect are runtime measurements, as well as memory consumption.

In [3], the authors proposed a practical knowledge curation framework that tackles the assessment, correctness, and completeness of KGs, and the user perspective that allows to determine the KGs' utility in specific application scenarios. To do so, the proposed approach involves (i) assessing the status of KGs based on quality dimensions and metrics, (ii) detecting and correcting wrong assertions, and (iii) enriching the KGs by adding new statements. For assessing the status of KGs, 20 quality dimensions were summarized and considered, such as accessibility, accuracy, completeness, and relevancy. For the correctness and completeness step, the authors distinguish between the verification and the validation of KGs. The verification of KGs aims to evaluate the schema conformance and integrity constraints of KGs. The verification of KGs checks whether KGs accurately describe or represent the *real* world. For enriching KGs and improving their completeness, two tasks were identified: (i) duplicates identification and resolution where duplicates; and (ii) resolution of conflicting property value assertions, also called data fusion, to handle situations such as the pair of duplicated entities have a different value for the same property.

In [4], Wang *et al.* proposed a universal evaluation framework based on quality dimensions that cover most of the evaluation perspectives of a KG, such as accuracy, completeness, consistency, timeliness, trustworthiness, and availability. For KG creation, the authors proposed a number of methods for various processes of KG creation that influence KG quality. Accordingly, KG quality control was divided into different corresponding periods. For example, the process of knowledge source selection determines the quality of knowledge (e.g., its credibility and accuracy). The processes of knowledge extraction and knowledge fusion determine the accuracy and the recall of the extracted knowledge elements, which affect accuracy and completeness dimensions. Quality enhancement methods were also discussed for KG creation, to correct, update, and complete KGs and then enhance their quality. Quality enhancement methods are related to (i) some errors that can occur during KG creation (e.g., missing entity or relation and wrong types of entities or relations); (ii) the timeliness of some KGs that gradually decrease over time, especially for KGs regarding quickly changing domains, such as user interest prediction and dynamic social networks; and (iii) new quality requirements that may arise in KG applications, and then may result in the KG expansion.

12.4   PKG's evaluation approaches

From our review of existing work around PKGs, we now focus on the evaluation approaches proposed in each work and towards its corresponding process (creation, population, and utilization), while considering its evaluation measures. We rely on the categorization of evaluation methods presented in [1] (cf. Section 1.3), including partial goal standards, using the knowledge graph itself as a silver standard, retrospective evaluation, and performance evaluation.

Table 12.1 presents a classification of existing evaluation approaches according to these criteria: their application domain, the approach, the process type, and the evaluation measures.

Table 12.1   Classification of PKGs evaluation approaches

Source	Application domain	Evaluation approach	PKG's process	Evaluation measures
[16]	Recommendation	Question-based methodology	Utilization	User's performance
[25]	Recommendation	Volunteers evaluation	Utilization	Accuracy
[29]	Social media	Performance evaluation	Construction	Precision
[24]	Social media	Ground truth evaluation	Construction	Precision, accuracy, and recall
[11]	Scholarly search applications	Expert-based feedback methodology	Construction, population and utilization	Privacy and security
[6]	eLearning platforms	Question-based methodology	Construction and utilization	Privacy and time constraint
[23]	Personal information system	Expert-based feedback methodology	Construction	Accuracy

12.4.1 Retrospective evaluation

Retrospective evaluation seems to be the more suitable for PKGs. Indeed, even if a PKG can be created from large-scale and open resources (such as Wikidata and DBpedia), its domain lacks such properties.

Scalability and open availability are essential for quantitative and qualitative evaluations: scale enables effective utilization by supervised algorithms; and open availability facilitates the development of task-specific test collections based on them. Generating large open datasets from real data would then require the interaction of users with an existing PKG and for these interactions [5]. From our analysis of existing PKG work, we come up with the following methods related to a retrospective evaluation.

12.4.1.1 Question-based methodology

In [16], the generated PHKGs were evaluated using a competency question-based methodology, to test the PHKG answering to questions like: "Have I been following a Mediterranean diet?" and "What should I eat for breakfast?" Three types of questions were described and how to PHKG generates the answers. The types of questions related to the user's performance are: (i) progress: "How have I been doing (improving, getting worse, maintaining over the past day/week?)"; (ii) consistency: "Have I been consistent in my carbohydrate intake?"; and (iii) compliance: "Have I been following a Mediterranean diet?" To answer these types of questions, the matching between how well their dietary intake and the guidelines within a certain period, is considered. The types of questions related to behavioral recommendations are: (i) improve diet: "How can I improve my diet strategy (considering personal preferences and context)?"; (ii) improve performance: "Will my current diet strategy improve my performance?"; and (iii) satisfying preferences: "Does my current diet strategy meet my preferences?". To answer these questions, the user's personal preferences and context were included in the PHKG. For example, if the user cannot eat breakfast due to their demanding daily schedule, the system has to come up with alternatives to alleviate this problem by recommending different carbohydrate amounts for lunch and dinner or recommending mid-morning snacks. The type of questions related to food recommendations has the form: (i) use implicit knowledge: "What should I eat for breakfast?"; (ii) allergies: "What foods can I eat if I have a dairy allergy?"; and (iii) dislikes: "What can I substitute for almonds?". To answer these questions, an augmentation with some implicit knowledge available in the PHKG is performed and expand it with some constraints (e.g., diabetic, prefers spicy food) using a semantic reasoner to evaluate the PHKG against the guidelines and then generate the user's dietary needs and preferences. These will be in the form of personalized guideline constraints that provide input to downstream machine learning tasks such as recipe recommendations.

In [6], the evaluation was performed on two learning applications and involved human participants in a well-established user experience questionnaire. First, people who have technical background and have their own experiences of the applications, collect and process their data based on some experiments. Then, they create interviews and questionnaires. Some evaluation questions are based on accessibility parameters, such as content access rights and privacy. Finally, they perform qualitative analysis to measure users' experience and satisfaction with the implemented features. Experts can also give their feedback in the evaluation process. Different metrics have been proposed, as the effects on users' short- and long-term memories and gained knowledge, the time it takes to find information online and others.

12.4.1.2   Volunteers-based feedback methodology

In [25], the PKG is used in the environment of users' daily behavior data. Its evaluation was performed by 50 volunteers who used the simulation system and analyzed their feedback. From the initial state of the PKG, they were asked to report recommendation accuracy scores (from 1 to 5) for different applications (social, a news feed, and voice assistant) and satisfaction with the system. The results show that the feedback accuracy of all PKG users (including news feed, voice assistant, and social applications PKGs) is more than 50%, which indicates the effectiveness of PKGs. The recommendation of the news feed is considered as the most accurate because it contains the content mentioned by users before and inferred and can accurately capture users' needs. Then voice assistant that requires further analysis technology. For social applications, they have the lowest recommendation accuracy because unstructured texts have higher requirements for the terms given. Notice that recommendations can be made by inference, through the PKG full life cycle system, when the initial data is small in the early stage, alleviating the problem of a cold start. After a period of time, the recommendation effect will be continuously improved with the accumulation of data.

12.4.1.3   Expert-based feedback methodology

In [23], an interview setting an expert can describe her personal view on their files to a knowledge engineer (KE) who translates the explanations into suitable knowledge graph statements using GUI. The KE is assisted by an artificial intelligence system that proactively makes statements on its own. In addition, machine learning models were used to reduce the manual effort for the KE, and then learn from feedback and predict new statements during usage. To measure the efficiency of the PKG creation, the accuracy measure is considered. It corresponds to the AI's accuracy and is calculated by counting how often the expert agreed to suggestions stated by the AI system. In [11], the evaluation for populating a PRKG consists of either a manual curation by the researcher of the entities and the relations, or their automatic extraction using NLP techniques from structured or unstructured sources through a software agent. Manual curation requires more human intervention, as it can have less errors, but is then less scalable. Information regarding her professional work including her affiliation, research interests, and publications may be primarily extracted from her curriculum vitae.

12.4.2   Performance evaluation

To evaluate the performance of the three subtasks of the proposed multimodal joint learning model in [29], the authors compared the multitask learning model with single task learning model. To do so, they used stratified random sampling to split the videos from three YouTubers for the experiment. The sizes of the training, validation, and test sets are 1,108, 276, and 354 videos, respectively. The evaluation measures on the triple identification were the metrics of precision, recall, and macro F1-score (macro-F1). The results indicate that the model with both visual and textual features achieves the highest F1-score on the subtask of lifelog activity recognition. Thus, leveraging useful information from both textual and visual features is crucial for recognizing lifelong activities and objects in videos.

12.4.3 Ground truth evaluation

In [24], each component is evaluated individually. The result of every tested method is compared to the ground truth and then accuracy, precision, recall, and F1-score are computed to evaluate and find the best method for each component. Since the Chinese language is very complex, most of the time, the extracted event is very close but does not perfectly match the ground truth. Therefore, only the headword is compared to the ground truth to compute the F1-score.

12.5 Conclusion

PKGs and of course PKG evaluation are relatively new research areas but PKG is attracting the attention of researchers. There is a broad range of application scenarios that would benefit from access to PKG, including but not limited to search and recommender systems, education and learning, electronic health records, and digital personal assistants. More broadly, access to structured personal data would give rise to new tasks, architectures, and workflows/protocols [30].

Through our review of the evaluation approaches for PKGs, we observed that PKG evaluation particularly requires an environment where human participants interact with the PKG through question-based methods or feedbacks. Accuracy and precision are the most used measures. Some evaluation methods are developed based on content access rights or privacy concerns. We conclude that involving human participants and considering privacy concerns make the evaluation a non-trivial effort.

Benchmarks are often suggested in the evaluation area. For KGs, benchmarks are used to serve both for comparison in the qualitative as well as computational performance evaluations. For a PKG, since it stores personal data, security and privacy must be given utmost priority when implementing, deploying and sharing it which makes PKGs highly time-dependent. Also, sharing data is difficult but there are few benchmarks to keep this matter going forward, even if datasets comprise only a few individuals. It remains an open question of how rich personal data should be used and how to do so in a privacy-aware manner [30].

Acknowledgments

This work is jointly funded by the French National Agency QualityOnt ANR-21-CE23-0036-01, and the Deutsche Forschungsgemeinschaft (DFG, German Research Foundation) – Project-ID 490998901.

References

[1] Paulheim H. Knowledge graph refinement: a survey of approaches and evaluation methods. *Semantic Web*. 2017;8(3):489–508.

[2] Chen H, Cao G, Chen J, *et al*. A practical framework for evaluating the quality of knowledge graph. In: *CCKS*. vol. 1134 of Communications in Computer and Information Science. Springer; 2019. p. 111–122.

[3] Huaman E and Fensel D. Knowledge graph curation: a practical framework. In: *The 10th International Joint Conference on Knowledge Graphs*. ACM; 2021. Available from: https://doi.org/10.1145%2F3502223.3502247.

[4] Wang X, Chen L, Ban T, *et al*. Knowledge graph quality control: a survey. In: *Fundamental Research*, 2021.

[5] Balog K and Kenter T. Personal knowledge graphs: a research agenda. In: *Proceedings of the 2019 ACM SIGIR International Conference on Theory of Information Retrieval*; 2019. p. 217–220.

[6] Ilkou E. Personal Knowledge Graphs: Use Cases in e-Learning Platforms, 2022. arXiv preprint arXiv:220308507.

[7] Ait-Mlouk A and Jiang L. KBot: a knowledge graph based chat Bot for natural language understanding over linked data. *IEEE Access*. 2020;8:149220–149230.

[8] Rizun M. Knowledge graph application in education: a literature review. *Acta Universitatis Lodziensis Folia Oeconomica*. 2019;3(342):7–19.

[9] Xu W, Gao X, Sheng Y, *et al*. Recommendation system with reasoning path based on DQN and knowledge graph. In: *2021 15th International Conference on Ubiquitous Information Management and Communication (IMCOM)*; 2021. p. 1–8.

[10] Zhan Q and Yin H. A loan application fraud detection method based on knowledge graph and neural network. In: *Proceedings of the 2nd International Conference on Innovation in Artificial Intelligence*; 2018. p. 111–115.

[11] Chakraborty P, Dutta S, and Sanyal DK. Personal Research Knowledge Graphs, 2022. arXiv preprint arXiv:220411428.

[12] Wilkinson MD, Dumontier M, Aalbersberg IJ, *et al*. The FAIR guiding principles for scientific data management and stewardship. *Scientific Data*. 2016;3(1):1–9.

[13] Chaves-Fraga D, Endris KM, Iglesias E, *et al*. What are the parameters that affect the construction of a knowledge graph? In: *OTM Confederated International Conferences "On the Move to Meaningful Internet Systems"*. Springer, 2019. p. 695–713.

[14] Jones WP and Teevan J. *Personal Information Management*. vol. 14. University of Washington Press Seattle, 2007.

[15] Shirai S, Seneviratne O, and McGuinness DL. Applying personal knowledge graphs to health Fensel 2020 knowledge, 2021. arXiv preprint arXiv:210407587.

[16] Seneviratne O, Harris J, Chen CH, *et al*. Personal health knowledge graph for clinically relevant diet recommendations, 2021. arXiv preprint arXiv:211010131.

[17]   Rastogi N and Zaki MJ. Personal health knowledge graphs for patients. *CoRR*. 2020;abs/2004.00071. Available from: https://arxiv.org/abs/2004.00071.

[18]   Al-Rfou R, Pickett M, Snaider J, *et al.* Conversational contextual cues: the case of personalization and history for response ranking, 2016. arXiv. ArXiv:1606.00372 [cs]. Available from: http://arxiv.org/abs/1606.00372.

[19]   Banchs RE and Li H. IRIS: a chat-oriented dialogue system based on the vector space model. In: *Proceedings of the ACL 2012 System Demonstrations*. Jeju Island, Korea: Association for Computational Linguistics, 2012. p. 37–42. Available from: https://aclanthology.org/P12-3007.

[20]   Yoo S and Jeong O. Automating the expansion of a knowledge graph. *Expert Systems with Applications*. 2020;141:112965. Available from: https://www.sciencedirect.com/science/article/pii/S0957417419306839.

[21]   Li X, Tur G, Hakkani-Tur D, *et al.* Personal knowledge graph population from user utterances in conversational understanding. In: *2014 IEEE Spoken Language Technology Workshop (SLT)*. South Lake Tahoe, NV: IEEE; 2014. p. 224–229. Available from: http://ieeexplore.ieee.org/document/7078578/.

[22]   Li X, Tür G, Hakkani-Tür D, *et al.* Personal knowledge graph population from user utterances in conversational understanding. In: *SLT*. IEEE; 2014. p. 224–229.

[23]   Schröder M, Jilek C, and Dengel A. A human-in-the-loop approach for personal knowledge graph construction from file names. In: *Third International Workshop on Knowledge Graph Construction*, 2022. Available from: https://openreview.net/forum?id=HgbGN3MHLZc.

[24]   Yen A, Huang H, and Chen H. Personal knowledge base construction from text-based lifelogs. In: *SIGIR*. ACM; 2019. p. 185–194.

[25]   Yang Y, Lin J, Zhang X, *et al.* PKG: a personal knowledge graph for recommendation. In: *SIGIR*. ACM; 2022. p. 3334–3338.

[26]   Zaveri A, Rula A, Maurino A, *et al.* Quality assessment for linked data: a survey. *Semantic Web Journal*. 2015;7(1):63–93. Available from: http://www.semantic-web-journal.net/content/quality-assessment-linked-data-survey.

[27]   Cimiano P and Paulheim H. Knowledge graph refinement: a survey of approaches and evaluation methods. *Semantic Web*. 2017;8(3):489–508. Available from: https://doi.org/10.3233/SW-160218.

[28]   Polleres A, Hogan A, Harth A, *et al.* Can we ever catch up with the Web? *Semantic Web*. 2010;1(1–2):45–52.

[29]   Yen A, Chang C, Huang H, *et al.* Personal knowledge base construction from multimodal data. In: Cheng W, Kankanhalli MS, Wang M, *et al.*, editors. *ICMR '21: International Conference on Multimedia Retrieval*, Taipei, Taiwan, August 21–24, 2021. ACM; 2021. p. 496–500. Available from: https://doi.org/10.1145/3460426.3463589.

[30]   Balog K, Mirza P, Wang Z, *et al.* Report on the workshop on personal knowledge graphs (PKG 2021) at AKBC 202. *ACM SIGIR Forum*. 2022;56(1):11.

Chapter 13

Personal health knowledge graph construction using Internet of Medical Things

Oshani Seneviratne and Manan Shukla[a]

13.1 Introduction

The advent and the rise of the Internet of Medical Things (IoMT) has led to the proliferation of wearable devices that collect a vast amount of personal health data. This data can create personal health knowledge graphs to help individuals better understand their health, manage chronic conditions, and improve overall well-being. This chapter will explore the process of collecting data from wearable devices, creating personal health knowledge graphs, and utilizing them in various health applications. Such personal health knowledge graphs are useful for healthcare providers in assessing health outcomes of patients that are not evident to them during the clinical visits. However, not all the data will be useful to healthcare providers, and further analysis is needed to make sense of the data, for which semantic technologies would help. We will outline how to extract data from personal health devices, transform the data into an appropriate modality, and load it to relevant systems for consumption by healthcare providers.

13.1.1 The challenge of data integration in IoMT health applications

The rise of IoMT has brought about an abundance of data in various domains, including healthcare. It has emerged as a transformative paradigm in the healthcare landscape, revolutionizing the way healthcare is delivered, monitored, and managed. IoMT health applications encompass a vast array of interconnected medical devices and systems to enhance patient care and streamline healthcare processes. These applications encompass a wide spectrum of use cases, ranging from remote patient monitoring and telemedicine to smart wearable devices and AI-driven diagnostic tools. IoMT facilitates real-time data collection, analysis, and transmission, enabling healthcare professionals to make informed decisions and provide timely interventions. Moreover, it empowers patients to actively participate in their own care, promoting proactive health management. As IoMT continues to evolve and integrate with cutting-edge technologies, it holds immense promise for improving healthcare

[a]Rensselaer Polytechnic Institute

quality, accessibility, and efficiency, paving the way for a more interconnected and patient-centric healthcare ecosystem.

Personal health devices, such as wearables, sensors, and medical devices, can collect data on a person's health status, behavior, and environment. However, the data collected from these devices are often fragmented and lacks context, making it challenging to gain insights and derive meaningful recommendations. To address this challenge, a personal health knowledge graph can be created, which integrates and connects health-related data from various sources to generate personalized recommendations. However, care must be taken to ensure the sensitive patient data are not exposed in the resulting graph. At the same time, IoMT devices often come from different manufacturers and may use different communication protocols. Ensuring seamless data interoperability and integration across devices and platforms can be complex, requiring standardized interfaces and protocols. Furthermore, as the data collected by IoMT devices will be crucial for clinical decision-making, the reliability and accuracy of data collected will also be of paramount importance, while ensuring the large volume of data collected does not overburden the clinicians.

13.1.2   Personal health data integration

Data integration among various stakeholders in the healthcare space remains a challenge, despite the impressive advances in Health AI in the past decade. There is a lot of "messy" non-standard but structured data that are continually being collected from personal health devices. While efforts such as the Fast Healthcare Interoperability of Resources (FHIR)[1] are underway in standardizing the data representation formats, there is currently a gap in the standard in addressing the health data ecosystem's decentralized nature. Personal health devices are manufactured by various device makers, and they may not follow standards or integrate with existing electronic health record (EHR) systems. It is also imperative that any data sharing that happens will occur in a secure and trustworthy environment, without being too restrictive, i.e., tied to a particular EHR vendor.   As a solution to this problem, we developed a system called "*BlockIoT*" [1] that uses FHIR compliant semantic web-based data templates in conjunction with smart contracts on the blockchain to provide healthcare providers with insights on their patients' daily activity that cannot be readily determined solely through patient encounters at the clinic.

Health information is increasingly available through EHRs, with a growing number of EHR systems connected through health information exchange networks currently dominated by commercial vendors. One of the barriers to health record exchange is the lack of shared data standards to enable systems to exchange documents and correctly interpret them. Fortunately, there is a transition toward shared interface standards to enable exchange. This design methodology increases usability by defining the document structure returned from a query without dictating the

[1] https://www.hl7.org/fhir

underlying system design. Shared Application Programming Interfaces (APIs) enable data retrieval regardless of participating systems' design. At the forefront of this change is FHIR, a Health Level-7 (HL7) project defining a set of data resources and APIs for accessing them [2]. FHIR improves flexibility over previous exchange protocols by introducing a higher level of abstraction, allowing data to be represented in a unified format independent of the underlying data architecture used by the health system implementing the API [3]. FHIR also supports representation formats that are friendly to semantic web applications [4,5].

13.1.3   Applications of integrated personal health data

One of the main advantages of IoMT-based personal health devices is that they can facilitate innovative AI, machine learning, mathematical and statistical approaches to build predictive patient physiological learning models, which improve health outcomes. An example for applying such learning algorithms can be found in our work on utilizing personal health data gleaned from IoMT devices for predicting mental health disorders using privacy-preserving machine-learning technologies [6].

Integrative technology can liberate healthcare providers from the growing burden of clerical work and synthesize patient data, including behavioral, genomic, microbiomic, and so on, into genuinely personalized healthcare. On the patient's end, healthcare devices such as insulin pumps can be wirelessly connected to glucose meters to automatically inject insulin into diabetic patients to improve their quality of life without the burden of manually checking the readings and administering the medication themselves. Most importantly, the healthcare provider can use this information to provide better health outcomes for their patients because the only quantifiable, reliable, and accurate data they currently have are lab results and measurements taken in the office. Medical device data have the potential to provide more granular and relevant day-to-day information to the healthcare provider, which can lead to better patient outcomes.

However, this ideal future is hindered by a lack of integration between medical devices and other electronic medical record systems. We have not found any personal medical devices currently integrated with EHR systems during our search for possible integration solutions present in the market. This is true not only for smaller device manufacturers, but also is similarly true for larger companies such as Medtronic and Epic systems [7]. This lack of integration prevents vital patient information from reaching the healthcare provider, preventing the provider from making the best health decision possible. Therefore, we believe that there is unrealized potential for personal medical devices to be adopted throughout the healthcare industry through personal health knowledge graphs.

Furthermore, as we have witnessed from the COVID-19 pandemic, there is an increasing need to have reliable at-home monitoring because coming to a clinic may pose a grave risk to specific at-risk populations. Therefore, there is a significant need to have reliable data streams from various devices integrated to provide a cohesive picture of the patients. As was mentioned before, to solve this problem, we have developed a prototype system called *BlockIoT* [1] that can merge these various health data

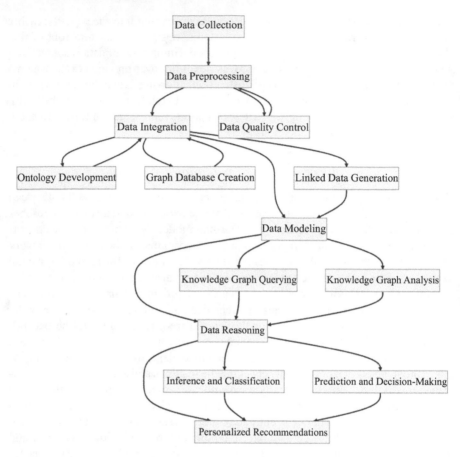

Figure 13.1   Process for personal health knowledge graph creation and application

streams, store patient data securely on a decentralized storage system, and represent patient analytics in an EHR system through the use of smart contracts. BlockIoT can serve as a bridge between the data produced by medical devices, and the healthcare providers who view this data through FHIR-compliant EHR systems. The process for the canonical representation of a personal health knowledge graph creation and application is shown in Figure 13.1.

13.2   Automated personal health knowledge graph construction

Automated knowledge graph construction techniques have gained increasing attention in recent years as a powerful tool for generating knowledge graphs from various data sources. These techniques rely on natural language processing, machine learning, and semantic technologies to extract, transform, and load data into a knowledge graph.

Structured data, such as relational databases, can be directly transformed into a knowledge graph using schema mapping techniques. Schema mapping involves mapping the attributes and relationships in the structured data to the entities and relationships in the knowledge graph schema. This approach is useful in cases where the structured data are well-defined and has a clear schema.

Unstructured data, on the other hand, present a greater challenge for automated knowledge graph construction. Techniques such as entity recognition, relation extraction, entity disambiguation, and ontology mapping are employed to extract knowledge from unstructured text data. Entity recognition involves identifying entities in the text, such as named entities, concepts, and events. Relation extraction involves identifying the relationships between entities in the text, such as cause-effect, part-whole, and temporal relationships. Entity disambiguation involves resolving ambiguities in entity references, such as determining whether "Apple" refers to the fruit or the company. Ontology mapping involves aligning the extracted entities and relations with existing ontologies, taxonomies, and vocabularies to ensure consistency and interoperability.

Automated knowledge graph construction techniques have broad applications in many domains, including healthcare, finance, and e-commerce. In healthcare, these techniques can be used to generate personalized health knowledge graphs that leverage data from wearable devices, electronic health records, and other health-related sources. Automated knowledge graph construction techniques are a powerful tool for especially generating knowledge graphs from various health data sources, including structured and unstructured data IoMT devices. These techniques rely on a combination of natural language processing, machine learning, and semantic technologies to extract, transform, and load data into a knowledge graph. The resulting knowledge graph can be used to develop intelligent applications that analyze, reason, and make decisions based on the rich knowledge represented in the graph.

13.3 Extract transform load

Extract transform load (ETL) [8] is a widely used process for integrating data from multiple sources into a single destination system. The ETL process involves three main stages: extraction, transformation, and loading. In the extraction stage, data are collected from various sources, including databases, files, web services, and in the case of personal health, from IoMT devices. The transformation stage involves cleaning and standardizing the extracted data, so that it conforms to the structure of the destination system. The loading stage involves inserting the transformed data into the destination system, typically a data warehouse or a data lake.

The ETL process is a critical component of data integration, enabling us to consolidate data from multiple sources into a single, reliable, and consistent source of truth. The ETL process is particularly useful for analytics applications, where data are extracted from multiple systems, transformed into a common format, and loaded into a data warehouse for analysis. In addition to business intelligence, the ETL process is also used for data migration, data consolidation, and data synchronization across multiple systems. We believe that such a system is needed for automatically constructing knowledge graphs in the personal health space.

With respect to knowledge graphs, a well-defined ETL process can play a crucial role in generating high-quality knowledge graphs from various data sources. Knowledge graphs are typically constructed using a variety of data types, including structured, semi-structured, and unstructured data, which are stored in various data sources. The ETL process enables the extraction of data from these sources, transforming it into a standardized format, and loading it into a knowledge graph. The transformation process involves standardizing the data by applying ontologies, taxonomies, and other semantic models to ensure consistency and coherence in the knowledge graph.

The ETL process is particularly important in generating personalized health knowledge graphs that leverage IoMT data collected from wearable devices. The process involves extracting raw data from various sources, such as sensors, wearables, and electronic health records, and transforming it into a standardized format that can be loaded into a personal health knowledge graph. The knowledge graph can then be used to provide a comprehensive representation of an individual's health status, enabling personalized health management and disease prevention.

13.3.1   *Extraction of data*

The first stage of creating a personal health knowledge graph involves collecting data from various IoMT devices. The data collected may include physiological data, such as heart rate, blood pressure, and blood glucose levels, as well as behavioral data, such as physical activity, sleep, and nutrition. Other data sources, such as electronic health records, medical literature, and public health data, may also be included to provide a comprehensive view of a person's health status and history. The data are often collected in a raw format and need to be preprocessed before it can be used to create a knowledge graph. Preprocessing involves activities such as cleaning, normalization, and feature extraction. The extraction of the data can also be facilitated using smart contracts that are deployed on a blockchain, as demonstrated in the BlockIoT system [1].

13.3.2   *Transformation of data to knowledge graph*

After collecting the data, the next stage is to integrate and harmonize the data from various sources. This involves transforming the data into a common format, such as the Resource Description Framework (RDF), and reconciling differences in terminology, units, and semantics. Semantic technologies, such as ontologies, can be used to represent the data and establish relationships between entities, such as symptoms, diseases, medications, and treatments.

A knowledge graph is a data model that represents entities as nodes and relationships as edges in a graph structure, and it can be enriched with attributes, such as properties, values, and metadata, to provide additional context and semantics. The knowledge graph can also be populated with external knowledge sources, such as biomedical ontologies, drug databases, and clinical guidelines, to enhance the knowledge representation and inference capabilities.

Although data from various IoMT devices can be extracted by smart contracts, this data tend to be raw signals. While it is possible to send over raw medical device data to an EHR system, the data sent to the EHR system are not useful to the physician as is. It is better to facilitate the physician by providing them with vital statistics or charts. These summarized outputs enabled through smart contracts can quickly allow a physician to review the patient's health metrics and decide further treatment as necessary. To facilitate the process of transforming medical device data into an insightful patient summary, we have used "templates" in BlockIoT [1].

Templates are methods that are used to identify incoming data. Because each medical device sends values with different keys that identify the specific device, templates are essential in determining what type of data is transmitted from the device.

Each type of device will have its own template. For example, a heart rate sensor will have a template that will contain all types of information transmitted by the heart rate monitor (such as beats per minute and SpO2). The upper limit and lower limit values are also present to recognize whether a specific incoming value is within or outside a normal limit, leading to alerting the physician if the patient's condition is life threatening. At the same time, alerts can also be driven from external ontologies. Ontologies such as Diabetes Mellitus Treatment Ontology (DMTO) [9] allow for an even deeper understanding of patient health with respect to diseases such as diabetes. By inputting various patient characteristics (such as age, prior health conditions, etc.) along with the specific physiological data point, an ontology can be leveraged to indicate whether a data point is truly considered normal, or requires an alert. Templates are essential because not only are they used as a template for data storage, but also they can also serve as labeled anonymous data that can serve as training data for AI/ML algorithms for that specific physiology. For instance, based on templates created for each type of data, physician-accessible graphs are generated and exported to the EHR system. AI/ML algorithms are used to further determine trend lines and pinpoint metrics of interest. These algorithms can be trained to generate greater insight with real-time data, which may be further useful for a physician.

13.3.3   Loading knowledge graph to patient-specific applications

The final stage involves loading the generated knowledge graph into a target application and reasoning over it to generate personalized recommendations. This involves applying various reasoning techniques, such as inference, classification, and prediction, to derive insights and actionable recommendations. For example, the knowledge graph can be queried to identify patterns and correlations between symptoms and diseases, predict the likelihood of developing a certain condition based on risk factors, or suggest personalized treatments based on the person's health profile and preferences.

13.4   Applications of IoMT-based personal health knowledge graphs

Personal health knowledge graphs can be used in various health applications such as chronic care, post-operative management, and disease prevention. In chronic care, knowledge graphs can be used to monitor an individual's health status, identify potential health risks, and provide personalized recommendations for treatment and lifestyle changes. In post-operative management, knowledge graphs can be used to track an individual's recovery progress and identify potential complications. In disease prevention, knowledge graphs can be used to identify individuals at risk of developing a particular disease and provide personalized recommendations for prevention. In this section, we outline some exemplar applications of personal health knowledge graphs from the literature in chronic disease care, acute illness treatment, and disease screening.

13.4.1   Chronic disease care

Zheng *et al*. [10] offer a comprehensive review of the latest advancements in wearable medical devices for personalized medicine and e-health. They highlight the increasing burden on healthcare systems due to the aging population and the prevalence of chronic diseases. The authors emphasize the importance of technology innovation in IT and biomedical engineering in the development of advanced wearable medical technologies and products that are increasingly being utilized by the public. The authors contend that wearable medical devices have been identified as one of the most promising approaches for healthcare monitoring, early diagnosis, and personalized treatment, and that they will contribute to the development of more cost-effective and sustainable healthcare systems. Furthermore, they provide a thorough review of wearable medical devices, including wearable multi-parameter physiological devices, wearable patch physiological monitoring devices, fitness training devices, wearable biofeedback training devices, and mobile phone-based healthcare applications. The authors discuss the potential benefits and challenges associated with each type of device, including the need for accurate and reliable data collection, data privacy concerns, and regulatory compliance.

Seneviratne *et al*. [11] discuss the use of knowledge graph techniques in chronic diseases such as diabetes and breast cancer. For such diseases, it is necessary to collect the patient data over a long period of time to ascertain if the interventions are effective, and the authors' work portrays personal health knowledge graphs as a viable option. Additionally, the case for using knowledge graph techniques for clinically relevant personal health applications has been illustrated in [12].

13.4.2   Acute illness treatment

IoMT devices can be equally effective in improving outcomes in emergency situations as well. Over the last few years, various IoMT devices have gained the ability to recognize acute situations, whether it be a traumatic incident such as a motor vehicle accident or a medical issue such as a stroke. Based on these recognized situations, IoMT devices now have the potential to alert emergency care providers immediately (instead of the standard approach where the patient or a bystander has to call for an ambulance). Combined with personal health knowledge graphs, this ability can be further enhanced from recognition to potentially personalized treatment as well. Rotmensch *et al.* [13] present a methodology to create personal health knowledge graphs based on 270,000 emergency department patient visits. Such a graph can be combined with data from IoMT devices in order to provide offline medical direction to Emergency Medical Technicians (EMTs) or paramedics without the assistance of an emergency physician, leading to improved care quality in the field.

13.4.3　Disease screening

While we have discussed ways to treat patients with the help of IoMT devices and personal health knowledge graphs, a combination of both technologies can also be used to prevent illnesses from arising. Meraj *et al.* [14] discuss the use of IoMT devices to track aspects of disease spread and verify whether prevention mechanisms such as hand washing are routinely done in specific areas. Such systems can be put in place in order to detect and prevent infection spread in patient populations. When combined with personal health knowledge graphs, such a system can lead to interventions as well , for example, for indicating where enforcement is necessary in order to improve efficiency , and contain the spread of the disease.

13.5　Future directions

As the field of personal health knowledge graphs continues to grow, there are several future directions that can be explored to improve the validity, reliability, privacy, and security of the data collected and the knowledge graph generated after the ETL process, as mentioned in this chapter. One important area of research is the improvement of the accuracy and reliability of measuring devices under free-living conditions. Wearable devices show large variations in accuracy between different devices, which can lead to inaccuracies in the data collected. Therefore, future research should focus on developing more accurate and reliable measuring devices that can provide more accurate data for personal health knowledge graphs. Another important issue that needs to be addressed is the privacy and security of personal health data. As the amount of data collected through personal health knowledge graphs increases, there is a growing concern about who owns the data and how it is being used. Therefore, future research should focus on developing better privacy and security measures to protect personal health data from being shared or sold to third-parties. Additionally, there is a need to address the growing risks from sensor data due to rapid advances in AI for wearables. This includes improving the compensation of noise sources due to quantization or arising from improper on-body unstable placement or misplacement and misalignment of sensors. It also involves characterizing missing data, creating thresholds for inclusion, and defining approaches for handling missing data. Battery life is another technical challenge encountered when using commercial devices for research studies. Many of these devices require frequent charging, which may limit the amount of data that can be collected over a certain period of time. Future research should focus on developing more efficient battery technologies that can enable longer periods of data collection.

In summary, future research on personal health knowledge graphs should focus on improving the accuracy and reliability of measuring devices, developing better privacy and security measures, addressing the growing risks from sensor data, and improving battery life. By addressing these issues, we can improve the quality and utility of personal health knowledge graphs and pave the way for more effective and personalized healthcare.

13.6 Conclusion

A personal health knowledge graph is a graph-based representation of an individual's health-related data. The graph consists of nodes that represent health-related concepts such as symptoms, diagnoses, treatments, and medications and edges that represent relationships between the concepts. The data modeling step involves identifying the data sources, selecting the appropriate data model, and mapping the data to the model. The ontology development step involves defining the health-related concepts and relationships that will be represented in the graph. The graph construction step involves creating the graph structure and populating it with the data.

In conclusion, personal health knowledge graphs that leverage IoMT-based wearable device data have the potential to revolutionize the way we manage our health. The creation of personal health knowledge graphs involves several technical steps such as data modeling, ontology development, and graph construction. Utilizing personal health knowledge graphs can lead to better health outcomes, improved quality of life, and reduced healthcare costs. As wearable devices continue to evolve, and data collection becomes more seamless, personal health knowledge graphs will become increasingly important in the field of healthcare.

Creating a personal health knowledge graph is a complex process that involves collecting, integrating, modeling, and reasoning over health-related data from various IoMT devices and sources. The personal health knowledge graph can provide a comprehensive view of a person's health status and history, as well as generate personalized recommendations to improve their health and well-being. The knowledge graph approach can also facilitate data sharing, interoperability, and collaboration among healthcare providers, researchers, and patients.

References

[1]   Shukla M, Lin J and Seneviratne O. BlockIoT: blockchain-based health data integration using IoT devices. In: *AMIA Annual Symposium Proceedings*. vol. 2021. American Medical Informatics Association; 2021. p. 1119.

[2]   Bender D and Sartipi K. HL7 FHIR: an Agile and RESTful approach to health-care information exchange. In: *Proceedings of the 26th IEEE international symposium on computer-based medical systems*. IEEE; 2013. p. 326–331.

[3]   Ayaz M, Pasha MF, Alzahrani MY, Budiarto R and Stiawan D. The Fast Health Interoperability Resources (FHIR) standard: systematic literature review of implementations, applications, challenges and opportunities. *JMIR medical informatics*. 2021;9(7):e21929.

[4]   Saripalle R, Runyan C and Russell, M. Using HL7 FHIR to achieve inter-operability in patient health record. *Journal of Biomedical Informatics*. 2019;94:103188.

[5]   Luz MP, de Matos Nogueira JR, Cavalini LT and Cook TW. Providing full semantic interoperability for the fast healthcare interoperability resources schemas with resource description framework. In: *2015 International Conference on Healthcare Informatics*. IEEE; 2015. p. 463–466.

[6]   Shukla M and Seneviratne O. MentalHealthAI: Utilizing Personal Health Device Data to Optimize Psychiatry Treatment. arXiv preprint arXiv:230704777. 2023.

[7]   Arundhati P. Masimo CEO: Medtronic, Epic Refuse to Share Data; 2017. Available from: https://www.mddionline.com/business/masimo-ceo-medtronic-epic-refuse-share-data.

[8]   Vassiliadis P. A survey of extract–transform–load technology. *International Journal of Data Warehousing and Mining (IJDWM)*. 2009;5(3):1–27.

[9]   El-Sappagh S, Kwak D, Ali F and Kwak K-S. DMTO: a realistic ontology for standard diabetes mellitus treatment. *Journal of Biomedical Semantics*. 2018;9:1–30.

[10]   Zheng J, Shen Y, Zhang Z, *et al.* Emerging wearable medical devices towards personalized healthcare. In: *Proceedings of the 8th International Conference on Body Area Networks*; 2013. p. 427–431.

[11]   Seneviratne O, Das A K, Chari S, *et al.* Semantically enabling clinical decision support recommendations. *Journal of Biomedical Semantics*. 2023;14(1):8.

[12]   Chen, C-H, Gruen D, Harris J, *et al.* Semantic technologies for clinically relevant personal health applications. In: *Personal Health Informatics: Patient Participation in Precision Health*. Springer; 2022. p. 199–220.

[13]   Rotmensch M, Halpern Y, Tlimat A, *et al.* Learning a health knowledge graph from electronic medical records. *Scientific Reports*. 2017;7(1):1–11.

[14]   Meraj M, Singh SP, Johri P, *et al.* Detection and prediction of infectious diseases using IoT sensors: a review. *Smart Computing*. 2021:56–61.

Chapter 14

Integrating personal knowledge graphs into the enterprise

Dan McCreary[a]

This chapter covers the topic of integrating personal knowledge graphs (PKGs) into a large enterprise. When the term refers to a personal knowledge graph (PKG) that is integrated into the enterprise, it is used as integrated personal knowledge graph (IPKG). The proposed chapter consists of four parts: **Background** on PKGs to explore about the fundamentals of PKGs; **IPKG challenges** to explore the challenges of integrating PKGs into an enterprise knowledge graph and the role that machine learning can play in the future; **IPKG steps** to show the flow of steps in performing the integration; **Security** to find grain access control – using role and authorization.

14.1 Introduction of PKGs

A new generation of note-taking tools helps us quickly organize thoughts as knowledge graphs. The concept of a PKG goes back to 2019[1], the term has recently become popular because of a new generation of note-taking software that uses knowledge graph representations. This chapter will introduce you to PKGs and then discuss how PKGs might impact overall corporate knowledge management strategy and how they might eventually work with enterprise knowledge graphs[2].

What is a PKG? A PKG is a new class of software that allows you to efficiently take notes in the form of flexible non-linear knowledge graphs. PKGs have evolved from older linear note-taking and outlining software as presented in Figure 14.1. PKGs are quickly gaining popularity among students, researchers, software developers, bloggers, and creative content authors.

A brief history of note-taking using linked notecards. Back in the 1500s, researchers in Germany developed a knowledge capture system called Zettelkasten[3]. It was essentially a way of putting ideas on index cards that showed how ideas

[a]Kelly-McCreary and Associates LLC, USA
[1]https://krisztianbalog.com/files/ictir2019-pkg.pdf
[2]https://dmccreary.medium.com/a-definition-of-enterprise-in-ekgs-561283d37deb
[3]https://en.wikipedia.org/wiki/Zettelkasten

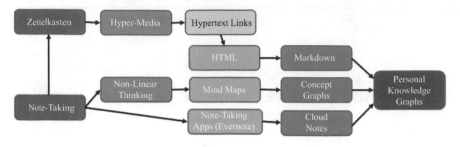

Figure 14.1   The evolution of PKGs

or concepts were related to other concepts. The ideas around One-Concept-Per-Card and Concept-Linking developed in Zettlekasten were then transferred to electronic form in the 1960s through the concept of HyperMedia[4], where any part of a document could be linked to any other part of that document or any other document. HyperMedia evolved into hypertext which became the basis of the Hypertext Markup Language (HTML). In 2001, the authors of the worldwide web (Tim Berners-Lee) also attempted adding relationship types to these links, which became the basis for the Semantic Web[5]. The semantic web was an attempt to make it easier to store distributed but still connected information on web pages.

In parallel to the evolution of concept linking, we saw the growth of the personal note-taking[6] software industry. These electronic tools, such as outlining tools, mind-mapping tools, and cross-platform tools such as Evernote[7], allowed individuals to create and retain their notes on many different devices such as their cell phones and tablets. These disparate devices were all tied to a cloud-connected storage system so all your notes on all your devices could stay in sync.

The rise of Markdown for knowledge capture and knowledge interchange: Although note-taking tools were handy, they lacked a simple way to capture and inter-change linked knowledge between systems. Markup syntax such as HTML is portable, yet most users did not want to capture their notes in hypertext because it required too much work to format things such as links to other concepts. What was needed was a "lightweight" version of HTML that was easier to type in. In 2004, the Markdown[8] format was created to be just that as discussed in Figure 14.2. A lightweight way for users to quickly enter knowledge without requiring them to create highly structured markup. Any text editor such as Notepad can be used to create markup, and a few hundred lines of Python code are all that is needed to convert Markdown into HTML.

---

[4] https://en.wikipedia.org/wiki/Hypermedia
[5] https://en.wikipedia.org/wiki/Semantic_Web
[6] https://en.wikipedia.org/wiki/Note-taking
[7] https://en.wikipedia.org/wiki/Evernote
[8] https://en.wikipedia.org/wiki/Markdown

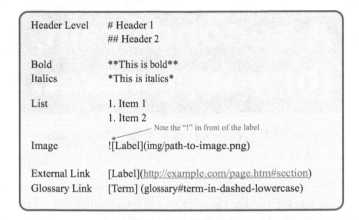

Header Level	# Header 1 ## Header 2
Bold	**This is bold**
Italics	*This is italics*
List	1. Item 1 1. Item 2
Image	![Label](img/path-to-image.png)
External Link	[Label](http://example.com/page.htm#section)
Glossary Link	[Term] (glossary#term-in-dashed-lowercase)

Note the "!" in front of the label

Figure 14.2   Sample cheat sheet showing common markdown syntax

Since 2004, Markdown has steadily grown to be the number one way software engineers and data scientists, create documentation about their code. It is now the default way to capture documentation on GitHub[9], in Data Science with Jupyter Notebooks[10], and create project documentation with Microsites[11]. Even traditional products such as Google Docs[12] are adding Markdown features. Adding "smart auto-complete" into IDEs such as VisualStudio makes it easier to create and edit markup. Want to point to an image in your repo? Just type a '![]("and VisualStudio will start to suggest path image files!

Combining hyperlinks, Markdown, and graphs

Another generation of personal note-taking tools has been explored to combine concept linking, Markdown, and knowledge graphs. These new tools are quickly evolving, and existing note-taking tools are beginning to add more graph-aware features. This new process and software category is called the personal knowledge graph (PKG) space. It started with innovative projects such as Roam Research[13] and the open-source Obsidian[14] product.

Why are PKGs so popular?

The amount of new information about almost any field of study grows exponentially. Doing a simple Google search on a topic is like drinking out of a firehose – it is hard to figure out what is essential in this continual stream of incoming information. PKG

---

[9]https://docs.github.com/en/get-started/writing-on-github/getting-started-with-writing-and-formatting-on-github/basic-writing-and-formatting-syntax
[10]https://jupyter-notebook.readthedocs.io/en/stable/examples/Notebook/Working With Markdown Cells.html
[11]https://dmccreary.medium.com/auto-generating-ekg-documents-2c85f1e45f44
[12]https://support.google.com/docs/answer/12014036?hl=en
[13]https://roamresearch.com/
[14]https://obsidian.md/

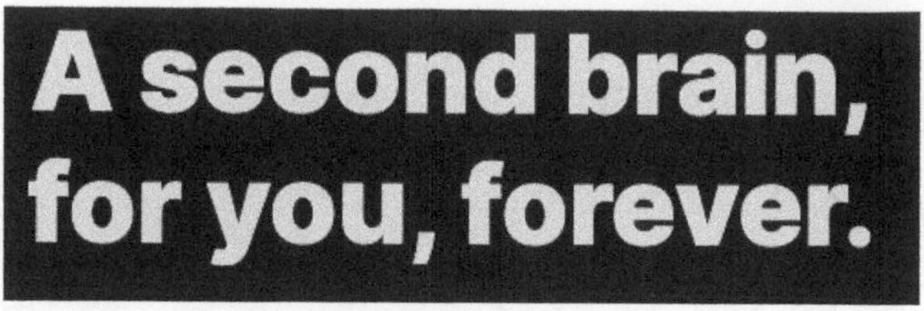

Figure 14.3   "A second brain" in the PKG community

community often repeated a word "second brain" as presented in Figure 14.3. The idea of retaining this knowledge over time is a popular selling point[15].

This section covers a few common reasons people tell why people love their PKGs.

Advantage 1: Quickly organize thoughts

PKGs allow you to quickly organize the information coming out of these streams to figure out what is important, make new connections between existing topics, and create your insights. You can import any text, and just by highlighting a word or phrase and typing "[[" it magically turns into a vertex in the concept graph! As anyone type, the "autocomplete" can tell if they already have it in their PKG, and you can thus quickly link items together.

Advantage 2: Lowers your cognitive load

Before using PKGs, it was possible to frequently get stressed during and after constant back-to-back meeting schedules. In this situation, rarely had time between meetings to write down thoughts and try to re-prioritize tasks as user learned new content. Now user can both take notes during meetings and link the notes to my existing knowledge base. User stress levels have come way down! The problem is that our brain's short-term memory can only hold a fixed number of things. If we do not get them committed to documents, they disappear. User recall user neglected to write down these new ideas only days or weeks later. Many of these are related to the "offloading" of the task of remembering concepts and their relationships to another system. These are often referred to as the "Second Brain" arguments on why PKGs are useful. The PKG becomes a "persistent shadow" of real brain – it stores the key concepts and their relationships in a non-linear structure – a graph – similar to how our brain works.

Advantage 3: Promotes non-linear thinking

The third thing, noticed often is that PKGs help us break away from the "Tyranny of Linear Thinking." The order of traversal is usually fixed. This contrasts with traditional note-taking using documents that contain a fixed order of items lists. Document order requires us to have a series of sections and subsections. But the inherent order you encounter information while taking notes might not be the real way that you have insights into the world. Outlining tools can allow you to rearrange the order of topics

---

[15]https://obsidian.md

and pop down and pop up the order of sections. Still, it is nowhere near as flexible and powerful as connecting each topic to an existing knowledge graph!

Advantage 4: Long-term persistence

It seems like companies change the way they store knowledge every few months. It might be MS Word stored in file folders one year, a wiki the following year, then perhaps Microsoft SharePoint™, and now we are seeing a shift to microsites on GitHub. Every time an organization changes its tools, the knowledge is lost. Because they are built around standards like easy-to-edit Markdown, we now have hope that this data can persist for a long time. Although things like concept links, tags, and aliases are not yet standardized across platforms, our hope is that lightweight PKI inoperability standards without the need to implement a complete DocBook[16] compatibility checklist.

Advantage 5: Breaks writers' block

One of our goals is to try to write a blog every other week. Sometimes we have an idea, write the first paragraph, and we get blocked. We cannot figure out how to organize our thoughts in any way that will be somewhat coherent to our readers. If we keep lots of little graphs around for ideas, we can see them grow over time. The metaphor is to plant your "Digital Garden of Ideas" and let them grow naturally. When we have about a dozen good ideas in a subgraph it might be time to make it an actual blog.

These advantages are their own personal view on how we use PKGs. If anyone searches on Google, it can be found that students, researchers, creative writers, and bloggers are all using PKGs in different ways.

Challenges with PKG tools

Although the PKG tools such as Roam Research[17] and Obsidian[18] are relatively new, they are adding new features (both free and for fee) quickly. My biggest challenge has been trying to share sub-sections of my PKG with others and publishing subgraph layouts on microsites. Right now, we need to do crude import/export operations to combine our knowledge graphs to a place where we can collaborate. However, it is suspected that these new features are coming quickly.

Our biggest challenge with the current generation of tools is the limited ways, we can generate visualizations of subgraphs. Like using the powerful GraphViz[19] libraries, we are able to try multiple constrained layout algorithms and play with top-down and left-to-right layouts. These layout rules are specified in a dot[20]-like language. Figure 14.4 shows that this rendering is "flat" and does not show how the concepts on the bottom are interrelated. It is planned to "pin" the arrangement of various nodes in the layout so they do not randomly change as we add new items. Definitely all these features will come with time. For now, we can write Python scripts

---

[16] https://en.wikipedia.org/wiki/DocBook
[17] https://roamresearch.com/
[18] https://obsidian.md/
[19] https://graphviz.org/docs/layouts/
[20] https://graphviz.org/doc/info/lang.html

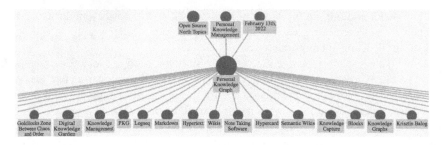

Figure 14.4   A screen image of an early graph on PKGs

that take the Markdown and convert them into Mermaid[21] structures for automatic layouts in our published microsites. These tools also do not allow us to add types or attributes to our relationships. That might also come in a future release. Remember that a little bit of semantics goes a long way!

Impact on the enterprise knowledge graph market

Vertex-level Role-based Access Control (RBAC) is a hallmark of enterprise-grade knowledge sharing systems like TigerGraph or Smartlogic's Ontology Editing tools. Right now, these PKG systems are all cloud-backed desktop tools or websites.They do not have fine-grain role-based access control rules so we can grant our teams read or write access to a subset of my PKG. However, it cannot be believed that the quickly growing PKG market will not find customers who want to combine note-taking's free-flowing nature and formal curated and approved knowledge graph systems. As APIs evolve, it could easily see functions such as "Publish this subgraph to the corporate ontology server for review."

Legal question: Who owns your PKG?

It cannot help but think how the complexity of people building their super-high-quality PKGs will overlap with the concerns of the intellectual property of organizations. During AT&T Bell Labs in the 1980s, all our written engineering notes were required to be done using the standardized AT&T Bell Laboratories blue-lined notebooks with individual page numbers. We were required to date each entry so that we could defend our intellectual property and patents carefully using these formal note-taking systems. We were told that adding a date, a few lines of text, and simple diagrams could save the company millions of dollars. Yet the word "Personal" implies that you own your own second brain. This will run against the concerns of corporate legal staff protecting their intellectual property.

Section summary

We have found it may take teams a while to get used to these new tools. They are a bit rough around the edges and do not yet have the same presentation and flexibility as more mature note-taking tools. My suggestion is to be patient and give yourself a few days/weeks to adjust the tool to meet your style of notetaking and publishing. Try out different ways of organizing concepts and see if you can find a pattern that works.

---

[21] https://squidfunk.github.io/mkdocs-material/reference/diagrams/#usage

14.2 The challenges of integrating PKGs into the enterprise

This section will focus on the challenges of integrating PKGs into larger knowledge ecosystems such as your company's enterprise knowledge graph (EKG) or your college and universities knowledge management system.

How AI is driving PKG technology
The intended perspective of this section is a solution architect that has been asked to understand the trade-offs between many isolated PKG silos and more integrated company knowledge graphs that share knowledge and avoids knowledge duplication and inconsistency. We look at the limited integration options available today and forecast large return-on-investments as PKG products integrate the latest recommendations of large machine learning models. Figure 14.5 shows that adding a new concept to a small PKG is much simpler than adding a new concept to a large complex EKG. If you are new to the area of PKGs, we strongly recommend reading the prior articles on PKGs, EKGs, and knowledge management to fully understand these concepts.

The personal vs. organizational reuse tension
Before we dive into terminology, let us remember that there are always two opposing forces driving PKGs in an organization. The first force is the need for each person to quickly capture notes that are consistent with their personal knowledge base. As you type, auto suggest lists allow you to quickly connect to your own personal concepts in your own PKG. When you type "[[" in the text editor, a list of existing concepts is presented. As you type, the list is automatically narrowed to match the prefix you have already started. The second force is the desire of many companies to capture this knowledge in a way that can be used by others in the company. This means that big organizations will often put in additional rules that prevent quick knowledge capture. Do you want to issue a ticket in the helpdesk system? You must tell us about your computer, what you are trying to do, what application you are using, and some information about how to reproduce the error. Without these required fields filled in, the Save button is disabled. Figure 14.6 shows a gap between free form of knowledge

Figure 14.5   Integration of concept

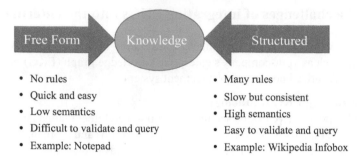

- No rules
- Quick and easy
- Low semantics
- Difficult to validate and query
- Example: Notepad

- Many rules
- Slow but consistent
- High semantics
- Easy to validate and query
- Example: Wikipedia Infobox

Figure 14.6   The inherent tension between free-form personal notetaking and the need for consistent structure across similarly typed knowledge

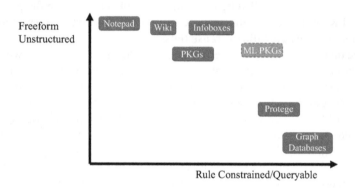

Figure 14.7   This chart shows a spectrum of tools for taking notes and collecting linked knowledge

and structured knowledge. Our experiences are that we will always see trade-offs. Who pays for the software, how the knowledge is captured, and how knowledge-sharing MBOs are written is often driving concern. There is no one-size-fits-all solution here, and the use of large machine-learning Natural Language Processing (NLP) tools is only making the decisions more complex. We will discuss this topic more later in the blog.

To begin our discussion, consider two desktop tools. The first is a standalone editing tool such as Microsoft Notepad™, which comes with your Windows™ desktop applications. Think of this as adding a new leaf of knowledge to a small new sapling of a tree. This tool allows you to type in any text from your keyboard and save it to your local file system. A Notepad is ideal for capturing new information that is disconnected from the rest of the world. You do not even need to be connected to your corporate network to use it. Figure 14.7 presents a spectrum of tools for taking notes and acquiring knowledge. Wikis also allow you to enter freeform text, but always within a page that has a unique name. Your text may contain references to other named pages. Some Wiki pages can contain structured key-value pairs often called Infoboxes. The key difference between Notepad and Wiki is that Wiki pages are stored on a server and converted to web pages with links.

Now let us consider a PKG editor such as Roam or Obsidian. They are always connected to an existing knowledge base, and the focus is creating quick links to your internal personal graph. Here is a metaphor we want to understand clearly from Figure 14.1. PKGs are useful when we also want to capture new information that is an extension of the existing knowledge structure. For example, when you enter a simple concept name, the system checks to verify that it is a new concept and not a duplicate of an existing concept or an alias for an existing concept.

On the lower right corner of the chart are formal ontology editing tools such as Protege and graph databases such as Neo4j or TigerGraph. These graph databases have many constraints, such as formal types for every vertex and edge and strict rules about what types of vertices can connect to each other. Edges also must have a type.

The last box in Figure 14.7 is the Machine-Learning assisted PKG (ML-PKG), where NLP tools are used to automatically suggest text within your PKG editor. These tools do not exist yet, but with the fast evolution of large-language models such as BERT and GPT-3, we expect them to be available soon.

In summary, there are going to be lots of rules in an integrated Enterprise PKG. Many of these rules can be helpful. They can accelerate your work by adding knowledge using intelligent contextual autocomplete. Some of these rules will get in the way and slow down your knowledge capture rate.

Basic terminology
Let us start our discussion with some basic terms and concepts. In a PKG, the goal is to efficiently allow a typed stream of characters to efficiently capture knowledge concepts and make connections to prior concepts. In a PKG, we use a data structure called a knowledge graph. A graph stores not just a flat list of concepts but also the relationship between these concepts. The technical term we use for concept storage is a vertex, and the term for relationships is called an edge.

Untyped vs. typed systems
Many of us are familiar with the concept of a Wiki. The word "wiki" is a Hawaiian term for "quick." These were created so that the user could minimize the number of keystrokes that connect wiki "pages" to each other. In the Wiki data model, all concepts are stored on a wiki page, and the design goal is to follow the one-page-per-concept rule so that the concepts can be easily linked together. If you put two or more concepts on a page, a link to that page would not clearly show a single-concept-to-single-concept pattern.

Wiki's were a wonderful step forward in notetaking because the concept pages or concept cards were shared in a web server. As your peers added new concepts, you could create links to these concepts. As you added new concepts, your peers could also link to them. It was a huge breakthrough in shared knowledge management, and it is the basis for systems such as Wikipedia.

However, most people do not think of a Wiki as true "knowledge graphs" because they really are just collections of linked untyped documents, just like the world wide web. The designers of wiki wanted to extend the concept of "hyperlinks" and make the links easier to type than remembering the complex syntax of HTML anchor references. The fundamental difference between a wiki and a true knowledge graph is the fact that wiki pages are all of the same "type" (a document/card/concept type), and the relationships also all have a single type (is-related-to).

True knowledge graphs allow each vertex and edge to have a specific type. The list of possible types is often configured by a centralized department. For example, some vertices might represent an employee, some might represent products you sell, and some might describe business events such as a call made to your company helpdesk. The key thing about types is that we can associate rules with types, and these rules force consistency that makes knowledge graphs easy to query, just like we query a traditional database using SQL.

If you are adding a new city to a PKG, you can tell the system the vertex is of type "city" and also add a "located-in" relationship to a "state" vertex. Both vertices and relationships have types.

In the field of enterprise knowledge graph strategy, we use the Jim Hendler hypothesis "A little semantics goes a long way.[22]" Adding a few simple types to both vertices and edges is the principal way to add meaning (semantics) to PKGs to supercharge their quearability and reuse. Many organizations have found that shared wikis are an ideal system for storing and linking knowledge. However, most organizations do not query the wikis because they put a priority on free-form editing over strict rules. You can always try to impose structure on a wiki page, but these structures are often optional, and few wiki systems prevent you from saving a wiki page if the required fields are missing. Wikipedia's Infoboxes[23] are an example of how wikis can be retrofitted to add structured data that can be queried.

Forcing name uniqueness
Although most wikis do not allow you to assign types to new pages at creation time, they do have some other rules that knowledge graphs do not have. When you create a new page, you need to give it a name. This name serves as the page identifier with a wiki. Now two pages can have the same name. In most PKGs, we have a similar rule. If you try to enter a new page with the same name, the software will tell you the page already exists. If you rename a page to be the same name as an existing concept, the system will ask you if you want to merge the names. Adding aliases (one or more labels for the same concept) is another challenge many PKGs do not do well.

Applying typed systems to notetaking event loops
Now that we have an idea of the critical difference between wikis and knowledge graphs, let us ask the question, how can we accelerate the ability to make connections as we enter text into a PKG page? We will start with some simple examples and then do a deeper dive into some more complex topics.

---

[22] https://www.cs.rpi.edu/ hendler/LittleSemanticsWeb.html
[23] https://en.wikipedia.org/wiki/Help:Infobox

The general pattern we use is to visualize characters typed on a keyboard. As the user types each new character, we apply a set of rules to assist the user in making the decision if there is an opportunity to add an edge to an existing concept. If there is, the users will use a character, such as a tab key, to confirm the relationships and auto-complete the remaining characters for the edge. If they do not want to accept the suggestion, they can just keep typing.

The key is that when the user is typing, they often want to signal that a link to a specific typed concept is needed. You might already be familiar with this process if you use social media and want to reference a person or a concept using "" to reference a person or a Twitter account. You might add hashtags using a "#" character at the end of your blog post to let recommender systems tie your blog post to people interested in a specific concept. Once you signal to the authoring system you want to reference an existing node with a type, it confirms this as you type or suggest a list of auto-completions.

The key is that organizations have many types of data that you want to include in your edge recommendation. Our focus is finding ways to integrate these organization-specific types into the as-you-type loop in the text editors for our PKG tools. If you want to reference employees in your company, the "@" might pull a list from your list of company employee names. Clicking on the link for that employee will allow the user to go to the PKG page for that employee.

Another common integration point is linking to a standard company glossary of terms and acronyms. Instead of using a special keyboard symbol, we can add a colon-separated prefix to a vertex name. For example, if we have a company glossary of terms, we can have your users use "g:" as a prefix, and the autocomplete will match those terms. If you are using an industry-specific glossary, we can reference those terminology standards in the prefix. For example, in healthcare, we use the "Just Plain Clear" glossary so that the prefix "jpc:" will auto-fill terms from that system.

Adding custom types

My suggestion when we are creating a PKG integration strategy, start small and build on your successes based on the value each integration adds to our user community. Start with simple employee lists and company glossary terms that are commonly referenced. Try experiments with things such as "g:" for a company glossary or "w:" for a Wikipedia term and see how frequently they are referenced. If there is low adoption of these suggestions, then they should be removed. Remember, people can always add external links to Wikipedia.

Acceptance rate monitoring

There have now been extensive studies about how large-language NLP models such as BERT and GPT-3 can be used to aid software developers by suggesting code. When a system makes recommendations to a user about a suggested autocompletion, if the user accepts the suggestion, this is logged in an event log. The parent of suggestions that a user accepts, called the acceptance rate, is critical for their adoption of these tools. In general, if your users do not accept around one-third of the autocomplete suggestions, the tools will become more annoying than helpful. Users will disable the tools, and you will not get the feedback you need to be successful. So it is critical to aim for a 30% or higher acceptance rate before you roll these tools out into production.

Permalinks and PURLs

Adding full URL links from your notes to any internal corporate resources is also something to be wary of. Many internal document management systems, such as Sharepoint (TM), depend on the links to specific files within a hierarchical file system. When the permissions to these folders change, or the documents are moved, these links will no longer work. A better choice is to only make links in your PKGs to locations that your organization has made commitments to not changing – ever. We call these links Permalinks or PURLs. This can be done by careful management of your internal domain-name system so that a link to http://glossary.mycompany.com/#term will always work, even if the servers the glossary is hosted on changes.

The next step is to ensure that your PKG integration team has tools that can monitor broken links and work proactively to prevent links from being broken as content moves around your organization's servers. Consider creating a "value" of one dollar for a working link and help people under the knowledge value that is lost as links break and the time it takes to update broken links.

Most knowledge graphs support bidirectional links. If you change the name of a concept page, all the links to that page will automatically be updated. This is a HUGE win and amounts to super-consistent and low-cost relationship management.

As a general rule of thumb, 60% of the value of a knowledge graph is the nodes, and 40% of the value is the relationships. Broken links discourage authors from making future links, and users are more reluctant to trust systems with many broken links.

Integration with NLP frameworks

One of the key developments is the rise of low-cost real-time tools that can analyze incoming text and look for keywords and phrases that are relevant to an organization. These processes include automatic classification, named entity extraction, and fact extraction. For example, if we typed in the term "yesterday," a system could detect the current date and insert a link to yesterday's date in your timeline so that you could see what notes referenced that date.

When the NLP integration occurs in the editing workflow is also relevant. Real-time inferences over large NLP models can be very expensive. As-you-type checks need to execute quickly. Adding keywords to a document at the end of the day is a much lower cost. In general, real-time autosuggest services need to run in the 1/10th of a second range. These are 100 ms response times, and organizations that provide service-level agreements might have onerous charge-back fees that your user does not want to pay for.

Other integration points Integration with the in-charter-stream autosuggest and integration with real-time NLP analytics are the two areas that will dominate your PKG integration architectures and drive your PKG product decision points. However, there are a few other areas to consider.

Converting Markdown extensions Almost all PKGs today center on extending standard Markdown formats. Unfortunately, different vendors have picked different formats for these extensions. When you import or export Markdown between systems, you may need to add converters between these formats. For example, converting from

Obsidian to Roam or vice versa will require you to load converter extensions to do this work. Fortunately, the conversion scripts are pretty simple syntax changes and are well documented. Many small Python programs are already available to do these conversions. Things to check for include external links, image links, metadata tags, text highlighting, and aliases.

Section summary There will always be a natural tension between quick free-form notetaking unencumbered by rules and the desire for the organization to reuse knowledge and make it consistent. PKGs, wikis, and enterprise knowledge graphs are all evolving in conjunction with the explosion of NLP tools and the growth of large-language models that suggest text within the context of a text editor.

14.3 Steps in building an integrating personal knowledge graphs into the enterprise

In Section 14.3, the key concepts and challenges used in an integrated personal knowledge graph (IPKG), this section will explore the steps to build the integrated system into a large organization. Let us examine how these concepts impact your PKG roll-out plan.

The IPKG hypothesis The basis for much of the logic around these IPKGs efforts is the following hypothesis:

IPKGs will allow users of PKGs to create more valuable and helpful knowledge than if note-taking is done with siloed tools.

The key to this hypothesis is to quantify what valuable and helpful means in metrics that even a finance person with no background in formal knowledge management can understand.

Align your IPKG benefits with organization strategy

There will undoubtedly be many individuals that will be ultra-enthusiastic about finally having an excellent note-taking tool. And integrating PKG with company entity type systems is a huge bonus. However, companies rarely spend millions of dollars to make their employee happy. Employee happiness is a pleasant side effect but should never be considered a primary driver for corporate PKG initiatives.

Here are just a few of the benefits IPKGs can bring to an organization:

1. sharing knowledge
2. avoiding duplication of knowledge
3. making knowledge consistent
4. improving collaboration between teams within a department
5. improving collaboration between departments or business units
6. streamlining communication
7. increasing knowledge worker productivity
8. improving search results and search ranking

The key is not just to state these benefits but to specifically tie these objectives to your organization's annual business strategy.

Find and executive sponsor

My experience is that most successful IPKG projects are driven by empowered staff with formal training in enterprise knowledge management strategies. Not all organizations have these teams, or if they do have them, they do not have the enterprise mandate or sponsorship of an influential executive. But to be successful, you will need this long-term sponsorship and funding. Integration takes time and money. You will need to find staff with the right skills and the ability to get access to essential data services. Your business alignment document will help you convince executives that your Integrated PKG project will help them achieve their strategic objectives.

Define metrics for success

One of the critical challenges of integrating organization knowledge with any text editor is to agree on standard measures of productivity improvement. Let us take a simple example: adding a list of industry-specific terms or company product names to an individual spell checker.

We all know how annoying it is to "train" every new text editor you use to recognize company-specific terms for the correct spelling. The methods for modifying the dictionaries are often hidden or unavailable to the user. For example, the chat feature on your Zoom or Teams program might not allow you to add custom terms. Some people with dyslexia or where English is not their native language depend on good spelling checks. They might be reluctant to engage in any chat when they are not confident the tools will help them look professional.

For example, you open the "compose" window in your e-mail editor. You start writing and using terms specific to your industry and organization are all marked as misspellings. These words can be the names of products you use or products you sell. For each word, you need to find a way to add this term to your dictionary. But what if the text editor could automatically be updated with words that your peers have already confirmed are correct spellings or valid acronyms for systems you work with daily?

Example: customize spell checking

The key is to capture the small productivity gains if your word processor is smart enough to gather terms from the IPKGs of your peers. It takes only a few seconds to add a word to the dictionary of a local word processor. But if you have thousands of terms and each of your 10,000 employees needs to add these words, then lost productivity is measured. You will need to estimate the cost/hour of your knowledge workers and use the best estimates of the increased productivity without the distractions of your text editor constantly telling you there are terms that it needs to understand. These are the types of metrics that can help you build a business case for IPKGs.

We can also extend this checking to include the correct use of the case in an official term. For example, we use "Facebook" but not "FaceBook" and "LinkedIn," not "Linkedin."

Automatic hyperlinking

Let us take this one step further. What if the first time we created a document, and a highly technical term was used, the word processor would automatically add a link to your company business glossary? Then your new employees could quickly jump to the right place to find that term and understand the definition of that term and related terms.

An excellent example is an ability to reference individuals directly on social media sites such as Facebook, Twitter, and LinkedIn. A confirmation list is presented by referencing a person starting with an "@" character. After you click on that item on the list, a link to that person's home page is automatically inserted into the text.

The key to making these features useful is to limit the scope of these selection lists. You might only refer to people in your social network and rank-order the list based on criteria such as if they are on the current discussion or how often you have mentioned them in the past. The scope and sorting rules can be contextual and complex. The scope and sorting rules illustrate the effort required to build scalable IPKG autosuggest algorithms.

Integrating simple productivity features into any note-taking tool and tracking the measurable productivity gains is often the first step in your IPKG journey. Once you have done this alignment and got a sign-off from an executive sponsor, you are ready to create a formal PKG integration plan.

Create an inventory of current knowledge repositories One of the critical challenges of building good IPKGs is understanding where related information and knowledge exist within your organization today. Once we have an inventory of these knowledge stores, we can ask what autosuggest-related services could be designed using existing APIs. You will also need to estimate how frequently a note-taker will want to reference these concepts in their documents and prioritize the most commonly used terms. Here is an example of some of the knowledge sources within a large organization:

1. Approved business terms from a centralized glossary of terms.
2. List of industry-specific words or phrases from medical or legal dictionaries.
3. Names of wiki pages that are the most frequently referenced in other wiki pages or tagged with a specific label.
4. List of products and product attributes in a product catalog.
5. List of the approved desktop applications or tools that employees are using.
6. List of computer systems or databases.
7. List of employee names (both first and last names), including familiar person names from other countries and languages used in your organization.

In summary, anytime your users add new terms to their local spell checkers, you can monitor them and look for trends. Keeping quality levels high is key to building trust in your IPKG initiatives. Add a human-centric quality-checking process whenever you see quality issues enter a system. Sometimes common misspellings can creep into a list of approved terms. A subject–matter expert should review new terms. Ideally, any incorrect business terms are removed before other teams use them. Make sure that users can quickly provide feedback to the team if they dispute the correctness of a word or phrase.

Building a reference architecture diagram After your IPKG team starts to inventory knowledge sources, you should create a single-page "map" showing how knowledge flows into your IPKG system and its new services. These data flow diagrams start

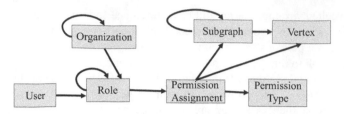

Figure 14.8   A high-level model of how roles are associated with permission assignments with a graph or vertex of a PKG

with a list of input sources on the left, your IPKG in the center, and consumers of this data on the right side.

14.4   Controlling access to IPKGs

Granting the proper access to knowledge to the right roles. Access control in a single person's PKG is simple. We have full rights to everything in our PKG; by default, no one else can see anything. This strategy makes the security design of most PKGs simple. Our PKG can easily link to external public knowledge and will be internally consistent. Figure 14.8 shows a high-level model of roles with permission assignment. The audience for your PKG is just yourself. You may not care about formatting rules, spelling checks, or consistency with organization standards. As you begin to share your knowledge with others, you may be more concerned with the spelling, formatting, and consistency with other knowledge. Before we dive into the security architecture, we need to define a few terms.

Basic graph security terminology

Let us start out with some basic terms and then progress to the more complex concepts.

- Each individual person creates one or more PKGs. Users always have full access to their own PKGs.
- PKGs consist of a set of named concepts represented as documents with distinct names and, optionally, a type. Each concept is called a vertex.
- PKGs may not have two concepts with exactly the same name. If you enter a duplicate concept, they can be renamed or merged together.
- The entirety of all the personal knowledge graphs is called the enterprise graph.
- Any part of the enterprise graph is called a subgraph.
- The public graph is a portion of the enterprise graph that all users can read. All users can always link to concepts in the public graph.
- Each user in an organization will be associated with one or more access roles in your organization.
- Access roles have access types such as read, rename, move, update, and delete.

- Users may also be granted access to subsections of the enterprise graph based on their role. This access is called role-based access control[24] or RBAC.
- Granting access to any resources for a role is called authorization.
- Verifying that a user is whom they say they are is called authentication. Most PKGs use either single-factor (password) or multi-factor authentication.
- The default access is the permissions that are applied when a user creates a new vertex in a graph. The default access may be different based on the location of a vertex in a subgraph or business rules.

User authentication

An enterprise will store a user's login credentials and policy in a centralized database. Most graph products use a protocol called LDAP to verify the user's credentials and, upon validation, send a list of the roles that users have to the application that logs them in. Because authentication processes are common to most databases, we do not spend much time on this topic here. Our focus is on granting access to the correct part of an enterprise group to a person.

Creation of shared subgraphs: Users may create a separate graph in their personal space and then grant access rights to individuals or roles within the organization. For example, you might create a subgraph for a specific project or team that works together. You can then grant full read and write permissions to other team members. This feature is easy to implement and available in most PKG products today, such as Roam Research.

The challenge is, what if some of your knowledge is in your personal space, and you want to share a read-only copy with a group of peers? You want them to be able to add relationships to your knowledge base but keep your foundational graph the same.

The ontology management problem: The ontology management problem requires many users to be able to change low-level ontologies but restricts change control on the upper levels of the ontology to those that understand the impact that these changes have on consumers of the ontology as shown in Figure 14.9. This type of problem comes up frequently in linked ontology design. Ontologies have multiple levels, such as upper ontology, middle ontology, and lower ontology. The higher up we go, the more lower-level components our changes might impact. Many small changes are frequently made to the lowest levels of ontology because a mistake can have a limited scope. Adding a new term, renaming a term, or fixing a typo in a name are examples of small changes. Changes to higher levels may ripple through many business processes that depend on consistent structures. To get around change-control concerns, enterprise-scale ontology management tools must allow you to make changes in a controlled environment and then run consistent regression tests that simulate the graph queries that downstream consumers will also run. Significant changes in upper levels of ontologies require an entirely new version of the ontology and allow downstream consumers to hold off updating their systems until they have modified their business logic to accommodate these changes. We introduced this example to demonstrate that personal notetaking is far from formal ontology management. The same knowledge

[24] https://en.wikipedia.org/wiki/Role-based_access_control

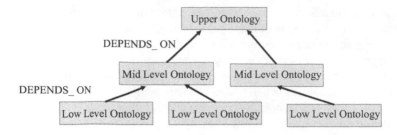

Figure 14.9   The ontology management problem

graph infrastructure can support both processes but having robust role-based access control is essential for high-stakes knowledge graph management.

Leveraging named groups

A better way to handle access to a subgraph is to grant access to a named group name such as "Team47". Then as individuals join or leave that team, we will not need to change our subgraph access permissions constantly. Because being able to modify the names in the group could impact access to the data, an approval process is often associated with adding new members to the group. Until now, the authorization problem has been similar to other database systems. What gets more complicated is when there are high-stakes vertices that need careful version control and testing.

Merging challenges

A typical scenario in PKG to EKG workflows is when informal note-talking evolves into formal knowledge bases designed to be used by a larger audience. A series of "Merge Conflicts" will naturally arise when this happens. If an author simply copies and pastes their page content into a shared graph, the links that used to work within your PKG may stop working. Although the links were consistent in your original PKG, a shared graph may not have access to the private concepts in your PKG.

After a user does the copy/paste, the editing tools might underline the broken links and suggest related links. If no matches are found, the user then has two options:

1. Remove the link
2. Copy the link destination page in your own personal graph
3. The latter option results in another problem. What if the new page you copied also has a set of broken links?

Moving knowledge from a private store to a shared subgraph is not trivial. It may be best to create the original document in the context of the shared group. Creating the new concept in a public subgraph avoids the broken links problem, but it adds a new challenge. What if your personal way of organizing knowledge diverges from how the group wants to organize knowledge?

Security summary

The bottom line is that there are no easy answers to the private-to-public merge problems. Migration of knowledge between subgraphs with different access rules must always deal with the link consistency problems. Role-based access control is a mature design pattern that scales well over a large enterprise. The key is to avoid assigning permissions to individual users. Tying users directly to any resource results in much higher maintenance costs as users move around the organization.

14.5   Conclusion

Although current PKG software is designed for individual notetaking, the potential for leveraging the collective knowledge of all your organization's personal notes is immense. As these tools evolve with better APIs and robust role-based access control, the tools will be easier to integration into an enterprise knowledge management system.

Conclusion

Personal knowledge graphs (PKGs) are important for individuals, organizations, and industries to manage and utilize their knowledge effectively. With the increasing volume and complexity of information available today, PKGs can help individuals and organizations make sense of this information and extract meaningful insights.

Section 1 serves as an important foundation for the rest of the book by introducing readers to the concept of PKGs and their potential applications. It is essential to provide readers with a clear understanding of what PKGs are and how they differ from traditional knowledge management systems. By highlighting the benefits of PKGs, such as improved knowledge discovery, organization, and sharing, readers can appreciate their potential value and consider how they might use them in their own work or personal lives.

Exploring the practical uses of PKGs in different industries can help readers see the broader picture of how PKGs can be applied in various domains. For example, in social media, PKGs can help users better organize and manage their social media activities, connections, and content. In healthcare, PKGs can support personalized health management by integrating data from various sources such as wearables, medical records, and genomic data. In banking, PKGs can help financial advisors provide more personalized investment recommendations based on a client's financial goals, risk tolerance, and investment history. And in education, PKGs can support personalized learning by helping learners discover and organize knowledge resources based on their interests and learning objectives.

By providing concrete examples of how PKGs can be used in different industries, Section 1 can help readers understand the potential value of PKGs and inspire them to explore further.

Section 2 of the book is critical for understanding the core components of PKGs, as it covers knowledge representation and reasoning. Knowledge representation involves defining the formal structure of a PKG and identifying the types of entities, attributes, and relationships that should be included. There are various techniques for knowledge representation, including ontologies, taxonomies, and semantic networks. These techniques help in organizing and categorizing information and can be used to improve the searchability and retrieval of information in a PKG.

Reasoning with PKGs is also an important topic covered in this section. Reasoning with PKGs involves using logic-based reasoning, inference engines, and machine learning to extract insights from a PKG. Reasoning can help users discover implicit relationships between entities, identify patterns, and derive new knowledge from existing data. Machine learning algorithms can be used to make recommendations based on users' preferences and behavior, while inference engines can be used to identify relationships between entities that are not explicitly stated in the PKG.

Section 3 of the book is focused on data management and visualization in PKGs, which is an essential aspect of PKGs. Data management involves pre-processing, cleaning, integrating, and organizing data to be used in a PKG effectively. Pre-processing techniques like entity resolution and relation extraction are used to extract structured information from unstructured data sources such as text and images. Entity cleaning techniques are used to standardize and normalize entity data, ensuring consistency across the PKG. Data integration techniques are used to combine data from multiple sources, enabling users to gain a holistic view of their knowledge resources.

Visualization, on the other hand, involves representing the data in a way that is easy to understand and interact with. There are several visualization techniques that can be used to represent PKGs, such as graph embeddings, matrix visualizations, and node-link diagrams. Graph embeddings enable high-dimensional data to be represented in lower-dimensional spaces, allowing users to explore large PKGs with ease. Matrix visualizations provide a compact representation of a PKG's entities and relationships, making it easy to identify patterns and relationships. Node-link diagrams provide an intuitive and interactive way to explore a PKG's entities and relationships, allowing users to navigate and discover new insights quickly.

Section 4 of the book focuses on natural language processing (NLP) and its application in PKGs. NLP is an important tool for extracting knowledge from unstructured text input and incorporating it into PKGs. This section covers a range of NLP techniques that can be used in PKGs, including named entity recognition, entity linkage, semantic role labeling, sentiment analysis, and summarization.

Named entity recognition involves identifying and categorizing named entities in text, such as people, places, and organizations. Entity linkage involves linking these named entities to their corresponding entities in a PKG, enabling users to identify and explore relationships between them. Semantic role labeling involves identifying the semantic roles played by each entity in a sentence, such as subject, object, and predicate.

Sentiment analysis involves determining the sentiment or emotional tone of a piece of text, which can be useful for understanding how people feel about a particular topic or entity. Summarization involves automatically generating a summary of a larger piece of text, enabling users to quickly gain an overview of a large amount of information. Furthermore, Section 4 of the book also discusses how to create NLP-based tools like chatbots, voice assistants, and question-answering platforms that can communicate with PKGs. These tools can be used to answer user queries, provide personalized recommendations, and assist with decision-making.

Section 5 of the book focuses on evaluating the merits and utility of PKGs, as well as exploring other applications. This section covers a range of topics, including evaluation approaches for PKGs, automated personal health knowledge graph construction using the Internet of Medical Things, and integrating PKGs into the enterprise. This section also discusses various applications of PKGs in personalized marketing, personalized healthcare, and personalized education. For example, PKGs can be used to provide personalized recommendations to customers based on their past purchases and preferences in personalized marketing. In personalized healthcare, PKGs can be used to create a personalized health profile for each patient, enabling healthcare professionals to provide more personalized treatment and care. In personalized education, PKGs can be used to create a personalized learning profile for each student, enabling educators to provide more personalized instruction and support.

Index

abstract syntax 56–8
acceptance rate monitoring 317–18
Access Control Lists (ACL) 43
acute illness treatment 302–3
analogical reasoning tests 93
Apple Siri 6, 176
application programming interfaces (APIs) 297
area under the ROC curve (AUC) 286
Artificial General Intelligence (AGI) 135
artificial intelligence (AI) 3
artificial neural network (ANN) 26
  complementary role of 108–10
assertional box (ABox) statements 25
attention models 214
augmented transition networks (ATNs) 105
authentication 323
authorization 323
automated personal health knowledge graph construction 298–9
automatic speech recognition (ASR) 176

Badminton 269
baseline method 129
Bayesian inference 84
Bayesian networks 169
Bayesian statistics 90
behavioral data 267
bidirectional encoder representations from transformers (BERT) 43, 45, 226
bidirectional long-short term memory (Bi-LSTM) 43, 197–8

binary classification 211
blocking key values (BKVs) 121
blocking method 120
BlockIoT 297–8, 300–1
BLOOM 105
Bluetooth 71
bottom-up approach 32

canopies algorithm 123
chatbots 5, 278
Chinese FrameNet 44
Christopher Nolan 283
chronic disease care 302
chunk rules 101–3
classic Sorted Neighborhood algorithm 133
classification layer 226
classification schema (CS) 31–2
clinical data 267
clinical decision support systems (CDSSs) 268
Closed World Assumption 61
clustering methods 123
cognitive agents 108
cognitive architecture for artificial minds 98–100
collaborative and social knowledge 268
collaborative filtering (CF) algorithm 38
common knowledge graph (CKG) 15, 44, 283
competencies 5
ComplEx (Complex Embeddings) 260
complEx KG embedding model 197
ConceptNet 5, 16
conceptualization 61

concrete syntaxes 58–60
conditional random field (CRF) 43
constraint modeling (CM) 39
contexts 97, 152
continuous learning 107
conversational agent (CA) 281
conversational data 209
Conversational Hidden Attribute
　　　Retrieval Model (CHARM)
　　long-tailed personal attribute
　　　　prediction with 217
　　　　analysis of selected terms 220–1
　　　　component instantiation 219
　　　　data 219
　　　　keyword extraction 218
　　　　quantitative results 219
　　　　training 218–19
　　　　value ranking 218
co-occurrence network 194
cortico-basal ganglia circuit 100–1
COVID-19 pandemic 297
Creed 283

Dalai Lama 153
data economy 77
data fabric 171
data fusion 287
Data Governance Act 73
data integration techniques 267, 328
data pre-processing 14
data privacy and security 267–8
dataset 204–5
dataset FiRe 212
data sharing 76–7
data visualization and exploration 268
DBPedia 5, 16, 18, 38, 45, 133, 150,
　　240
decentralized web (DW) 40–3
　　social linked data SOLID-based PKG
　　　　application 41–3
　　SOLID background 40–1
Deeper scoring functions 260
deep learning models 108, 191
deep neural networks 193
demographic recommenders 257

Dendron 168, 179–81
dense passage retrieval (DPR) 194
Diabetes Mellitus Treatment Ontology
　　(DMTO) 301
diagnostics 268
DialogRE 244
Digital Personal Assistants systems 6,
　　15
directed graphical models 168–9
disease management 268
disease screening 302–3
DistMult 260
Django framework 269
domain-specific feature functions
　　127
domain-specific KG (DKG) 16
drug discovery and development
　　268

e-commerce 281, 299
economic data 267
edge 315
　　embedding 199
　　representation 200
eDoer platform 17
EduCor 245
e-learning 17, 32–3, 168, 176, 245
electronic health records (EHRs) 17,
　　41, 296, 301
electronic medical records (EMRs) 4,
　　8, 34
embedding-based methods 258–60
Emergency Medical Technicians
　　(EMTs) 303
enterprise graph 322
enterprise knowledge graph (EKG) 25,
　　307, 313, 319
entity 277
　　cleaning techniques 328
　　extraction 202
　　linking 16
entity resolution (ER) 16–17, 117, 328
EntitySim 40
environmental data 267
European Commission 73

evaluating named entity resolution 128
  blocking 128–30
  similarity 130–1
Evernote 308
extract transform load (ETL) 299
  extraction of data 300
  loading knowledge graph to
      patient-specific applications
      301
  transformation of data to knowledge
      graph 300–1

FACE-KEG 245–6, 249
Fast Healthcare Interoperability of
      Resources (FHIR) 296
feature-based blocking method 124
feed-forward network 201
few-shot learning techniques 136
Flemish Community 73
Foam 168, 182
FrameNet ontology 282
Freebase 18, 38, 45, 240
Friend of a Friend vocabulary (FOAF)
      9, 29
Fusion Knowledge Graph Collaborative
      Filtering (FKGCF) algorithm
      39
fuzzy logic 91
fuzzy quantifiers 92–3

General Data Protection Regulation
      (GDPR) 74
genomic data 267
GitHub 178, 309
GLIMPSE 7, 38, 248, 251
Gnowsis project 70
Google's Minerva 112
GPT-3 105, 315, 317
graph construction module 36
graph convolutional network (GCN)
      194
graph factchecking rules (GFCs) 247
Graph Latent Factorization (GraphLF)
      40

graph neural networks (GNNs) 44–5,
      193–4
graph representation 217
graphs 168–9
GraphViz 311
ground truth evaluation 291

HAM 226–7
hardened link specification functions
      126
healthcare 176, 281, 299
health information 296
Health Level-7 (HL7) project 297
HeLiS 243–4
hierarchical attention methods 217
hierarchical conversational models
      216–17
hive minds 108
Holographic embeddings 260
human-in-the-loop (HITL) 26, 31, 36
human/machine conversational systems
      176
human–machine interaction 264
HyperMedia 308
Hypertext Markup Language (HTML)
      308
hypertext transfer protocol (HTTP)
      101–2

identity 152
Individualized KG (IKG) 23
Individualized Knowledge Base (IKB)
      23
industry 4.0 150
inference engines 327
Infoboxes 315
Information Extraction dataset 15
integrated personal knowledge graph
      (IPKG) 307
  benefits with organization strategy
      319
    automatic hyperlinking 320–1
    building a reference architecture
        diagram 321–2
    customize spell checking 320

integrated personal knowledge graph
(IPKG) (*continued*)
define metrics for success 320
find and executive sponsor 320
inventory of current knowledge
repositories 321
challenges of 313
acceptance rate monitoring
317–18
adding custom types 317
applying typed systems to
notetaking event loops 316–17
basic terminology 315
converting Markdown extensions
318–19
forcing name uniqueness 316
integration with NLP frameworks
318
permalinks and PURLs 318
personal *vs.* organizational reuse
tension 313–15
untyped *vs.* typed systems 315–16
controlling access to 322
basic graph security terminology
322–3
creation of shared subgraphs 323
leveraging named groups 324
merging challenges 324
ontology management problem
323
security summary 324–5
user authentication 323
hypothesis 319
Integrate. Relate. Infer. Share (IRIS) 70
intelligent personal systems 281–2
International Resource Identifiers
(IRIs) 57
Internet of Medical Things (IoMT)
295, 328
applications of integrated personal
health data 297–8
applications of IoMT-based personal
health knowledge graphs 302
acute illness treatment 302–3
chronic disease care 302

disease screening 303
automated personal health knowledge
graph construction 298–9
challenge of data integration in IoMT
health applications 295–6
extract transform load 299
extraction of data 300
loading knowledge graph to
patient-specific applications
301
transformation of data to
knowledge graph 300–1
personal health data integration
296–7
Internet of Things (IoT) 4, 34, 255,
262, 264
interpersonal dimensions 224

Jaccard function 124
JavaScript 90
joint representation approach 195
answer prediction 197–8
query entities identification 195–7
subgraph preparation 197
JSON-LD 59–60, 95, 97

KGist 242
KG text enrichment approach 201–4
KHealth project 35
knowledge acquisition 17
Knowledge Base Question Answering
(KBQA) system 39
knowledge caching 108
knowledge curation and validation 267
knowledge engineers (KEs) 31, 290
Knowledge Graph Embeddings 16
knowledge graphs (KGs) 4, 33, 150,
167, 169, 192, 239, 256, 277,
299, 315–16
applications of 171
knowledge retrieval 171
provides recommendations 171–2
question–answering systems 171
unified data access 171
data complexity 240

data evolution 240
data volume 239
dynamic updates in 251
evaluation methods of 285
importance of visualizing knowledge
    graphs 169–70
lack of real workloads 251
personalized knowledge graph
    summarization 242
    personalized graph summarization
        247–50
    personalized KG construction and
        applications 243–7
versus PKG 173
    advantages of 175
    knowledge recommendation
        174–5
    representation of knowledge 173
preference evolution 251
privacy 251
summarization 240
    keyword-induced graph
        summarization 241
    knowledge base summarization
        based on first-order logic rules
        242
    through soft, inductive rules 242
    via pattern recognition 241
knowledge management 278
knowledge representation 55, 261, 268,
    327
knowledge representation and reasoning
    (KRR) 6, 268, 327

labeled property graphs (LPG) 46, 96
Latent Dirichlet Allocation (LDA) 36
LearnWeb 17
LegalRuleML 74
Levenshtein distance coefficient 32
lifelogging 71
linear-time distance-based search 123
Linked Data Platform (LDP) 41
linked open data (LOD) 32–4, 41, 131,
    284
Linked Open Vocabulary (LOV) 35

link specification function 120, 125
Lionel Messi 170
Locality Sensitive Hashing (LSH) 124
logic-based reasoning 327
logistic regression 214
Logseq 168, 181–2
long short-term memory (LSTM) 45
LSQ 251

machine learning (ML) 267, 298, 327
    algorithms 155, 327
    approaches 131
    classifier 127
    models 8
    techniques 36
Machine-Learning assisted PKG
        (ML-PKG) 315
Markov networks 169
mean square loss function 198
Mediterranean diet 289
memory networks 214
metacognition 95
meta-learning 107
Microsoft Cortana 37, 176
Microsoft Notepad 314
Microsoft SharePoint 311
mid-course correction 72
MinHash function 124
Minimum Description Length (MDL)
        principle 242
Mobile Personal Health Knowledge
        Graphs (mPHKG) 17
MovieChAtt dataset 212
multi-layer perceptron (MLP) 193
multi-party conversations 217

Naïve Bayes 244
named contexts 104–5
named entity extraction 154
named entity recognition (NER) module
        32, 44, 47, 260, 328
named entity resolution 135
    challenges and opportunities for
        132–5

named entity extraction (*continued*)
    evaluating named entity resolution
        128
        evaluating blocking 128–30
        evaluating similarity 130–1
    evolution of research in 131–2
    two-step framework for 120
        blocking step 121–5
        similarity/matching step 125–8
natural language (NL) 44, 105
    and common sense 106–7
    large language models 105–6
    metaphors in everyday language 107
natural language processing (NLP) 32,
        36, 44, 119, 154, 267, 284, 298,
        314, 328
Natural Language Toolkit (NLTK) 15
Neo4j 26, 46
Nepomuk 70–1
neural networks 127
neural + symbolic method 8
neural-symbolic strategy 43
neuro-symbolic PKGs 43–5
node embedding 199
non-deductive reasoning and imagined
        contexts 95
normal QA systems 198
Notation 3 (N3) 66–7
novel CHARM architecture 213
N-Triples 59–60

object-oriented programming (OOP)
        languages 61
Obsidian 16, 168, 178
OntoLife ontology 9
ontology 46, 151, 260–1
    development 267
    mapping 299
Open AI's ChatGPT 112
Open Digital Rights Language (ODRL)
        75
open knowledge graphs (OKGs) 25,
        32, 38, 46, 47
Open Research Knowledge Graph
        (ORKG) 46

open world assumption (OWA) 61
OWL 2DL 66
OWL 2 EL 66
OWL 2 QL 66
OWL 2 RL 66

Pairs Completeness (PC) metric 129
Pairs Quality (PQ) 130
Paris Saint-Germain (PSG) 170
part-of-speech (POS) tagger 47
passage extraction 202
path-based recommendations 44
pattern-based approaches 214
PeGaSus 250
performance evaluation 290
Persona-Chat dataset 212
personal digital assistants (PDAs) 27,
        35–7, 36
Personal Entity Classifier (PEC) 281
Personal Entity Disambiguator (PED)
        281
personal health data integration 296–7
personal health devices 296
personal health knowledge (PHK) 33
personal health knowledge graphs
        (PHKGs) 27, 33–5, 41, 176,
        281
personal health libraries (PHL) 5, 41
personal health ontology (PHO) 33,
        244, 281
Personal Information Management
        Systems (PIMSs) 3
personal information managers (PIMs)
        24, 27, 29–32
personal information systems 282
personalization 257
personalized education 329
personalized healthcare 329
personalized healthcare knowledge
        graph (PHKG) 5, 8, 17, 34,
        244, 265, 266–8
personalized KG summarization
        (PKGS) 247–9
personalized marketing 328–9
Personalized Page Rank (PPR) 38

personalized/summarized KGs (PKG)
37–40
personalizing commerce and financial
knowledge graph (PCFKG) 263
personal knowledge base (PKB) 4, 23,
29
personal knowledge extraction
conversational datasets 211
social media datasets 212
transcribed dialogue datasets
211–12
extracting interpersonal relationships
222
discussion 227–8
predicting interpersonal
relationships 222–3
predicting relationship
characteristics 223–4
PRIDE 224–7
extracting personal attributes 213
demographic attributes from
transcribed dialogues 213–15
hierarchical conversational models
216–17
long-tailed personal attribute
prediction with CHARM
217–21
social media profiling 215–16
future research directions 229
continuous incremental predictions
229
leveraging third-party information
229
open-ended attributes 229
using speaker network 229–30
personal knowledge graphs (PKGs) 4,
55, 117, 150, 172, 177, 209,
278, 307, 327
application domains of 262
personalized commerce and
financial recommendation
systems 263–4
personalized healthcare knowledge
graphs 265–8

recommendation in the Internet of
Things 264–5
applications of 176
e-learning 176
healthcare 176
human/machine conversational
systems 176
research 176
social media analytics 177
application to privacy-centered
personal assistants 111
background information 256–8
based on RDF 70
from desktop to devices 71–2
re-decentralizing the web 72–3
semantic desktop 70–1
breaks writers' block 311
challenges 284
computational performance 287
knowledge graph as silver standard
287
partial gold standard 286
retrospective evaluation 287
challenges and issues in 17–18
challenges in recommendation
systems 261
domain expertise and
domain-specific knowledge 261
ethical and legal issues 262
evaluation and assessment 262
integration with existing systems
262
knowledge representation 261
maintenance and updates 262
privacy and security 261–2
quality and reliability 261
scalability and performance 261
user interface and usability 262
user participation and involvement
261
challenges with PKG tools 311–12
chunks and rules 101–3
classification according to
application type 27

personal knowledge graphs (PKGs)
(*continued*)
  construction from local/remote
    resources 29
  decentralized web 40–3
  e-learning systems 32–3
  neuro-symbolic PKGs 43–5
  personal digital assistants 35–7
  personal health knowledge graphs
    33–5
  personal information managers
    29–32
  personalized/summarized KGs
    37–40
  personal research knowledge
    graphs 45–6
cognitive architecture for artificial
  minds 98–100
common reference architecture for
  semantic web-based 46–8
complementary role of artificial
  neural networks 108–10
computing certainty 90–1
construction 11–15
continuous learning 107
contributions 27
cortico-basal ganglia circuit 100–1
creation 279–80
current status and future research 48
data management and visualization in
  328
data sharing and compliance 73
  data annotations to connect
    policies 75–6
  data sharing 76–7
  policies 74–5
definition 307
definition/terminology/synonyms
  23–4
Dendron 179–81
different from general KGs 16
evaluation approaches 288
Foam 182
future scope 18
ground truth evaluation 291

healthcare applications 281
hive minds, knowledge caching and
  swarm intelligence 108
impact on enterprise knowledge
  graph market 312
inferences vs model construction 94
intelligent personal systems 281–2
introduction 83–5
iteration over properties 103
  more complex queries 105
  named contexts 104–5
  operations on comma-separated
    lists 104
knowledge capture and knowledge
  interchange 308
knowledge graph *versus* PKG 173–5
knowledge representation in 8–10
Logseq 181–2
long-term persistence 311
lowers your cognitive load 310
metacognition 95
methods of constructing PKG
  recommendation systems 258
  embedding-based methods
    258–60
  structured based methods 260–1
motivation 83
natural language 105
  and common sense 106–7
  large language models 105–6
  metaphors in everyday language
    107
non-deductive reasoning and
  imagined contexts 95
note-taking using linked notecards
  307–8
Obsidian 178
performance evaluation 290
PKN in relation to RDF and LPG
  95–7
plausible knowledge 85
  plausible inferences 88–90
  plausible knowledge notation
    85–7
  statement metadata 87–8

popularity 10–11
population 280
promotes non-linear thinking 310–11
quickly organize thoughts 310
reasoning by analogy 93–4
related/overlapping/convergent fields
    24
relationship to fuzzy logic 91–2
RemNote 178–9
richer queries and fuzzy quantifiers
    92–3
Roam Research 182–5
sample PKG recommendation
    application 269
scalable knowledge engineering
    110–11
scaling and graphs of overlapping
    graphs 97–8
second brain in 310
semantic web stack 56–70
Tiddlyroam 179
tools and techniques 15–16
use-cases 17
utilization 281
    educational and learning
        applications 283–4
    healthcare applications 281
    intelligent personal systems 281–2
    personal information systems 282
    recommendation applications
        282–3
    social applications 282
personal knowledge networks (PKNs)
    134
Personal Online Data Stores (PODs)
    40–1, 73
personal research knowledge graphs
    (PRKGs) 27, 45–6, 283
personal web 245
Person entity 9
PersonLink ontology 9
PHR 244
plausible inferences 88–90
plausible knowledge 85
    plausible inferences 88–90

plausible knowledge notation 85–7
    statement metadata 87–8
plausible knowledge notation (PKN)
    85–7, 106
    eBNF grammar for 113–14
plausible reasoning 84, 111
policies 74–5
population health management 268
precision medicine 268
prediction quality metrics 120
pre-trained language model (PLM) 193
PRIDE
    experimental results 226
        ablation study 227
        BERT 226, 227
        HAM 226
        quantitative results 227
    methodology 225
        classification layer 226
        contextual word representations
            225
        incorporating interpersonal
            dimensions 226
        incorporating personal attributes
            226
        utterance representations 225–6
prognostics 268
Python code 308
Python framework 269
Python programming language 47

query-answering (QA) 191
    methodology 194
        dataset 204–5
        joint representation approach
            195–8
        joint representation with relational
            graph convolutional network
            198–201
        KG text enrichment 201–4
        results 205–6
    state of the art 192–4
query embedding 197, 199
query expansion (QE) 39
querying 67–8

query representation 200
query response module 36
question and answer (Q&A) systems
    277

RDF-izers 47
RDF schema (RDFS) 26, 119
reasoning 61–7, 327
receiver operating characteristic (ROC)
    130–1
recurrent neural network (RNN) 193,
    214
Reddit 178, 213
RedDust 213
reduction ratio (RR) 129
relational databases (RDB) model 84,
    118
relation embedding 197–8
relation extraction techniques
    for knowledge graphs 153
        ABox common techniques 155–6
        overview of 154–5
        TBox common techniques 155
    from knowledge graphs to personal
        knowledge graphs 151
        diversity aspects in 152
        of personal nature 152–3
relation filtering 202–3
RemNote 168, 178–9
residual neural network (ResNet) 45
resource description framework (RDF)
    26, 56, 58, 95, 118, 150, 300
    abstract syntax 56–8
    concrete syntaxes 58–60
    data validation 48
    Notation 3 66–7
    OWL 63–4
    schema 61–3
Résumé2RDF ontology 10
retrieval model 218
retrospective evaluation
    expert-based feedback methodology
        290
    question-based methodology 289

volunteers-based feedback
    methodology 290
richer queries 92–3
risk stratification 268
Roam Research 16, 168, 182–5
RocketQAv2 194
role-based access control (RBAC) 46,
    312, 323–4
rule-based approaches 191
rule-based/pattern-based system 44
RuleML 74

scalable knowledge engineering
    110–11
schema 152
schema-free approaches 132–3
schema mapping 299
seed entity 123
self-attention 200
semantic desktop (SD) 24, 70–1
semantic language module 36
Semantic Middleware 71
semantic parser module 36
semantic web community 131
Semantic Web of Things (SWoT) 265
semantic web stack 56
    querying 67–8
    reasoning 61–7
    representing knowledge 56–60
    validating 68–70
SemNodes 71
sentiment analysis 191, 328
Shape Constraint Language (SHACL)
    69–70
ShEx 70
sigmoid function 193
simple knowledge organization system
    (SKOS) 26, 31, 46
singular value decomposition (SVD) 36
skip-gram 194
smart contracts 300
Smartlogic's Ontology Editing tools
    312
SnowBall 15
social data 267

Social Determinants Of Health (SDoH) 41

Social Linked Data (SOLID) 49

social media analytics 177

social media datasets 212

social media profiling 215
   personal attributes 215–16
   user interests 216

solid PODs 73

Sorted Neighborhood blocking method 122

space-complexity reduction 129

Span-based Entity and Relation Transformer (SpERT) 46

SPARQL 8, 34, 67–8, 152, 251

SPECIAL project 76

spider web layout 26

spider-web topology 37

statement metadata 87–8

steaming model 251

Story telling 95

streamDis 241

string-matching algorithm 120

structural homogeneity 126

structured based methods 260–1

structured data 299

structured/semi-structured data 47

subgraph 322

subgraph creation 202

supervised learning methods 216

support vector machine (SVM) 11, 37, 127

swarm intelligence 108

Swoosh family of algorithms 134

Systematized Nomenclature of Medicine Clinical Terms (SNOMED-CT) 35

TACRED dataset 44

taxonomy creation 14

T-BUDS 250

Team47 324

Teams program 320

template methods 301

tensor factorization scoring functions 260

terminological box (TBox) 24

text-enhanced knowledge embedding (TEKE) 194

text KG enrichment 203

Thymeflow system 29, 245

Tiddlyroam 168, 179

TigerGraph 312

TimeCrunch 251

time series summarization (TSS) 33

Top K passages 194

traditional blocking 123

transcribed dialogue datasets 211
   demographic traits 211–12
   relationship prediction 212

TransE 194

transfer learning 134, 221

transformer-based methods 214

translation-based embedding model (TransE) 259

translation on hyperplanes (TransH) 259

translation on relation spaces (TransR) 259–60

triples 56

triplestore/graph database 47

Trivia factoid dataset 204

Turtle 59

type 2 diabetes (T2D) 34

TypeSim method 40

undirected graphical model 168–9

Unified Medical Language System (UMLS) 16, 34–5

Uniform Resource Identifiers (URIs) 119

unique name assumption (UNA) 61

universal resource locators (URLs) 57, 96

unstructured data 47, 299

utility-driven graph summarization (UDS) 249–50

Utterance-based Knowledge Tool 36

vertex 322
virtual personal assistant (VPA) systems
    6, 176, 282
virtual PKG 47
visualization techniques 328
visualization tools 168
  graphs 168–9
  importance of 177
  knowledge graphs 169
    applications of 171–2
    importance of visualizing
      knowledge graphs 169–70
  used in PKGs 177
    Dendron 179–81
    Foam 182
    Logseq 181–2
    Obsidian 178
    RemNote 178–9
    Roam Research 182–5
    Tiddlyroam 179
vocabularies 46
Vought-Sikorsky VS-300 202

wearable devices 303
Web Access Control (WAC) 43
web ontology language (OWL) 26, 63,
    119, 152
  inferences with 64–5
  profiles 65–6
WebVOWL 15
WiFi 71
Wikidata 16, 18, 150, 195
WordNet 155
World Three Consortium (W3C)
    standards 24
World Wide Web (WWW) 40

Yago 5, 38, 150, 240

zero-shot learning techniques 136, 211
Zettelkasten 307–8
Zoom program 320